NESTING BIRDS OF A TROPICAL FRONTIER

Perspectives on South Texas
Sponsored by Texas A&M University–Kingsville

TIMOTHY BRUSH

NESTING BIRDS OF A TROPICAL FRONTIER

The Lower Rio Grande Valley of Texas

TEXAS A&M UNIVERSITY PRESS   COLLEGE STATION

LIBRARY OF CONGRESS CATALOGING-IN-PUBLICATION DATA

Brush, Timothy.
Nesting birds of a tropical frontier : the Lower Rio Grande Valley
of Texas / Timothy Brush.
p. cm. — (Perspectives on South Texas)
Includes bibliographical references and index.
ISBN 1-58544-436-7 (cloth : alk. paper) —
ISBN 1-58544-490-1 (pbk. : alk. paper)
1. Birds—Habitat—Texas—Lower Rio Grande Valley.   2. Birds—
Texas—Lower Rio Grande Valley.   I. Title.   II. Series.

QL684.T4B78 2005
598'.09764'4—dc22

2005006216

The birds of the air nest by the waters;
they sing among the branches.

PSALM 104:12

CONTENTS

PREFACE

Extending across the southernmost tip of Texas, the Lower Rio Grande Valley is often considered one of the top ten birding areas in the United States. Many visitors are surprised by the temperate and tropical mixture of breeding, wintering, and transient migratory bird species found in "the Valley." Here, halfway between Dallas and Mexico City, is where the temperate zone meets the tropics. For example, beavers (*Castor canadensis*) build bank lodges along the lower Rio Grande, while a few ocelots (*Leopardus pardalis*) still roam unseen in thorny thickets. Likewise, Bank Swallows (*Riparia riparia*) nest in riverbanks while from remote riparian forests small numbers of Red-billed Pigeons (*Patagioenas flavirostris*) raise their "jungle voices" (Oberholser 1974).

Since arriving in the Valley to work at the University of Texas–Pan American in Edinburg in August, 1991, I too have regularly been surprised by the diversity of this subtropical corner of the United States. Around 300 miles (480 km) to the south are the true tropics, the land of strangler figs (*Ficus cotinifolia*) and mild winters, where birds like Northern Potoos (*Nyctibius jamaicensis*) and Masked Tityras (*Tityra semifasciata*) exemplify a tropical bird community (Howell and Webb 1995, Shanahan et al. 2001). An equal distance north is the true temperate zone, with regular winter freezes and occasional snow, where Carolina Chickadees (*Poecile carolinensis*), American Crows (*Corvus brachyrhynchos*), and other typical North American birds reside (Oberholser 1974). In the transition zone in between, I have found it necessary to throw out most of my preconceived notions about the birds and their habitats and to be open to what I see and hear.

I began my Valley fieldwork with a simple survey of shorebirds along the Laguna Madre in the early 1990s as well as field trips in Hidalgo County for ornithology classes. Eventually I progressed to studies of particular breeding species of which little was known, and I gradually became interested in the broader spectacle of the Valley's changing bird life. As I spent time in the field, both while doing fieldwork on particular species and while leading field trips for classes or bird festivals, I soon found myself collecting notes, making scattered field observations, and collecting articles and books on a variety of species and habitats.

Of obvious interest were the Valley or South Texas "specialties," those species with extremely limited U.S. ranges. It was also interesting to observe the behavior, ecology, and population trends of species better known in other parts of North America or Latin America. Some species that were supposed to be common here were not, while others thought to be absent were in fact present. Some species that were supposed to need trees for foraging or nesting were able to use thorn scrub or open fields; others that were supposed to be common breeders turned out merely to be migrants through the area. Although the weather varies greatly in its suitability for fieldwork, the birds always seemed to be doing something interesting.

Recognizing that there was too much information about Valley birds to try to summarize in a single book, I decided to focus on the breeding birds. With some notable exceptions, the breeding birds have largely been ignored because of the general lack of observers in the long, hot summers. Often I would read the same misleading or incorrect statement repeated in various sources. Despite the danger of spreading my net too widely and missing important details, I decided to try my hand at a summary of the breeding bird life of the Valley.

SCOPE AND PURPOSE

It is my goal in this book to give an overview of the past and present diversity and ecology of Valley breeding bird communities and their habitats. I emphasize the history, natural history, and ecology of breeding birds, mainly the subtropical specialties that make the area famous among visiting birders but also the temperate, desert, and coastal species that share the Valley's diverse habitats. When possible, I compare the ecology and behavior of birds in the Valley and in other parts of their range, especially for species widespread in the tropics or the temperate zone. This is not an exhaustive treatment of all Valley breeding birds. As explained at the beginning of the species accounts, I present varying amounts of information on the breeding bird species, depending on the amount of data available and other factors. I hope that the detail included may be of value to the general public and also to professional ornithologists interested in particular birds or habitats.

Another goal in writing this book has been to share some of the experiences I have had in and near the Valley, to help convey the excitement and fascination created by such a special place. Thus the presentation has some similarities to the work of Alexander F. Skutch and George M. Sutton, whose writings have expanded our knowledge and appreciation of tropical and Mexican birds, respectively. I hope that such appreciation, plus greater knowledge of what is here now and what has been, will encourage continued efforts to maintain and restore the riparian, wetland, upland, and coastal habitats in the Valley.

I must admit to a riparian and freshwater bias. This reflects my research emphasis in tall riparian forest, thorn forest, and on the river itself for most of the last ten years, particularly in major protected areas of the central Valley such as Santa Ana National Wildlife Refuge, Bentsen–Rio Grande Valley State Park, and Anzalduas County Park (Anzalduas is pronounced with emphasis on the *u*). I have done some fieldwork in most other areas of the Valley, such as the Rio Grande between Falcon Dam and Roma, the Laguna Atascosa National Wildlife Refuge, and South Padre Island (the latter two areas mainly during shorebird surveys from 1992 to 1994). I have visited several tracts of Lower Rio Grande Valley National Wildlife Refuge, particularly those near Bentsen, Santa Ana, and Anzalduas.

My visits to the Brownsville–San Benito–Harlingen area, southwestern and central Hidalgo County, and the mouth of the river have been quite limited. I have not spent as much time as I would like at the National Audubon Society's Sabal Palm Grove Sanctuary or at the nearby Southmost Preserve of the Nature Conservancy, both on the southeastern fringes of Brownsville. I have done almost no fieldwork in Willacy County, northern Hidalgo County, or northern and central Starr County.

To make up for these gaps, I have searched the literature and collected field reports from visiting and resident ornithologists and birders. More research is definitely needed, especially on breeding birds of inland thorn scrub and grasslands, the salt lakes area, the northeastern coastal zone, and in remnant riparian forests between Brownsville and Santa Ana. John W. Tunnell, Jr., and Frank W. Judd (2002) ably summarize what is known and unknown about the Laguna Madre of Texas and Tamaulipas and present much useful information about coastal bird life and habitats.

Thus in addition to drawing on my own research and that of my students, I have also relied quite heavily on the published literature and unpublished observations. The rapid development of email and listserves (such as Texbirds) in the mid-1990s was a great benefit, although I had to use some judgment in deciding what would be valid evidence of breeding for various species. I cannot claim that the resulting compilation is equally strong for all species, habitats, and periods, but I hope it proves a useful summary of the breeding avifauna and stimulates further study.

❧

There are so many people I need to thank that I greatly fear omitting some or not remembering all that they did. I thank the many observers whose names are listed throughout the book, mainly in the species accounts, for their willingness to take the time to report what they saw. I am grateful for the information they have provided.

I must especially thank John C. Arvin, currently of Mission, Texas. Raised in the Valley and getting to know birds there at a time when few were interested, he combines strong identification abilities with a great interest in the history of the avifauna of the area and northeastern Mexico. Countless times he has responded generously to my questions by providing useful information on what he has seen, and the book would not have been the same without him.

Others who have provided me directly with a large amount of information on Valley and regional bird life are Steve Bentsen, Ray Bieber, Oscar Carmona, Mark Conway, Mel Cooksey, Michael Delesantro, Jack C. Eitniear, Mike Farmer, Brush Freeman, Charles (Red) and Louise Gambill, Martin Hagne, Petra Hockey, Jimmy Jackson, Jane B. Kittleman, Tom Langschied, Greg W. Lasley, Mark Lockwood, Brad McKinney, Laura Moore, Brent Ortego, Paul C. Palmer, Father Tom Pincelli, Charles W. (Chuck) Sexton, and Roland H. Wauer. Ernesto Enkerlin-Hoeflich, Allan R. Phillips, Andres M. Sada, and many of those named earlier helped me learn much about the range and abundance of many Valley birds in northeastern Mexico, part of the same ecosystem. Glenn A. Proudfoot designed the nest-checking device that Chris Hathcock and I used to check Altamira Oriole (*Icterus gularis*) nests.

The national wildlife refuge and state park employees of the Valley have contributed in several ways, providing access, logistical assistance, and often their own field observations. Of these people, Martin L. (Marty) Bray especially stands out for his long hours of showing me around when I was new to the Valley and for his love of canoeing, which first got me out onto our international river. Other state and federal employees who have provided data or permission to do fieldwork include Steve Benn, David Blankinship, Harold Burgess (retired), Mike Carlo, Marie Fernandez, Eric Hopson, Steve Labuda, Rey Ortiz, Jeff Rupert, Steve Phillips, Mitchell Sternberg, Dorie Stolley, Steve Thompson, and Gary Waggerman.

Those who came before have provided information indirectly but of great value. I especially thank the late L. Irby Davis of Harlingen, whose early checklists, breeding bird studies, sightings reports to national journals, and distributional knowledge about Valley and Mexican birds have been incredibly useful to me. Others include former national wildlife refuge managers Luther C. Goldman, Wayne Shifflett, and Raymond J. Fleetwood, who took the trouble to record their observations at a time when Valley bird life was considerably different than it is today.

Among the researchers and writers who have published on particular species or on Valley, regional, or international bird life, I especially thank Frederick R. (Fred) Gehlbach of Baylor University for his pioneering field studies along the Rio Grande and Rio Corona in the 1970s. George M. Sutton's extensive studies contributed greatly to our knowledge base, and his graceful nature writing and beautiful artwork in *At a Bend in a Mexican River* have been inspirational as well (my working title might have been "At a Bend in an International River"). Although many of the bird species Alexander Skutch writes about are different than the ones in the Valley, I have nonetheless gleaned much useful information from his large body of work. I have also been inspired by his dedication and patience in observing elusive tropical birds (although an hour watching a nest entrance was usually enough for me). Edwin Way Teale's informative, readable nature travel books provided another model for me. Michael D. Carter's (1986) pioneering studies of Bronzed Cowbird (*Molothrus aeneus*) brood parasitism in the Valley provided a baseline for more recent work.

Cited as Oberholser (1974), *The Bird Life of Texas* is a magnificent resource for historical breeding bird distributions, with information originally gathered by Harry C. Oberholser and edited by Edgar B. Kincaid, Jr. More recent data from the Texas Breeding Bird Atlas program was freely shared by Karen Benson and Keith Arnold. This is not yet published in paper form but is cited as a web site (Benson and Arnold 2001). I thank Fred S. Webster and later editors for their regular "South Texas" or "Texas" reports in *Audubon Field Notes* and its successors, plus all those who contributed their observations. The monumental Birds of North America series, edited by Alan Poole and Frank Gill, has been of great use in providing thorough summaries of what is known (and not known) about our birds, and I thank the editors and all the contributors.

My seemingly endless literature searching has been aided greatly by the Interlibrary Loan Office of the University of Texas–Pan American (UTPA) and at key moments by Jack C. Eitniear and James V. (Van) Remsen. I thank the staff and faculty of Earlham College in Richmond, Indiana, for teaching me how to use a library and write a term paper.

The many publications of Robert I. (Bob) Lonard and Frank W. Judd have been essential in providing me with an ecological and botanical framework. I also thank Bob Lonard for his patience in identifying for me numerous plants I did not know. My predecessor at UTPA, the late Pauline James, whom I knew briefly, provided books of historic value and also stimulated much fieldwork in the Valley. She was one of the pillars of the early

Valley conservation community, along with the late Cyndi Chapman of Weslaco and the late Joe Ideker of Edinburg. Their extensive contributions will never be fully known.

I thank my M.S. students whose studies of particular species or habitats I have drawn on freely: Alberto Cantu, Charles Castillo, Tina L. Gallegos, Christopher M. Gamel, Roberto (Bobb) Gorena, Christopher R. Hathcock, Steven G. Monk, Corinna E. Rupert, Jeffery R. Rupert, and Patrick L. Wright. Among undergraduates, I must especially thank Delinda S. White and Grady Carlile, who helped in early studies of Altamira Orioles, and Ruby Lopez, who found several breeding waterbirds in an unexpected location in Pharr.

Several public and private agencies have funded my research on Valley birds, namely UTPA (Faculty Research Council), the American Birding Association, the U.S. Fish and Wildlife Service, and the U.S. Geological Survey (Species-at-Risk Program). Summer funding during 2000 and 2001 from the Office of the Provost (Rodolfo Arevalo) of UTPA allowed me to computerize my field notes and to get an excellent start on writing this book.

I thank the early influences on my birding and ornithological career, especially Bertin W. Anderson, William H. (Bill) Buskirk, Charles F. Leck, Don Mullison, Dan Walton, Alan Simon, Robert D. Ohmart, Kenneth V. Rosenberg, Edmund W. (Ted) Stiles, and Bret Whitney. I especially appreciate the warmth, encouragement, and example provided by the late James B. (Jim) Cope of Earlham College.

I thank Shannon Davies for her continuing interest in the project and in my work in general. John C. Arvin and an anonymous reviewer provided many useful comments, which corrected some errors and greatly improved the book. Any errors remaining are, of course, my responsibility.

My parents, Miriam K. Brush and John E. Brush, currently of Medford, New Jersey, contributed in many ways to my development as a person and as a birder and ornithologist—not least by taking me on trips. How can I thank you enough? My in-laws, John R. Craun and Margaret R. Craun of Lakeside-Marblehead, Ohio, have supported my research and interest in birds for many years. My wife, Catherine C. Brush, has stood with me and encouraged and shared my interest in birds for more than two decades now, supporting me in so many ways that words fail me. My children, Elizabeth, John, and Laura, have each encouraged me and helped in some way with fieldwork and have tolerated my preoccupation with birds. Finally but foremost, I thank Him "who is before all things and in whom all things hold together" (Colossians 1:17).

NESTING BIRDS OF A TROPICAL FRONTIER

INTRODUCTION

Ideally, one who grew up in the North Temperate Zone should enter the tropics by easy stages, working southward in one's own hemisphere at a leisurely pace, observing how, as the latitude decreases, certain northern plants and animals drop out of the landscape, to be replaced by southern or tropical forms.

ALEXANDER F. SKUTCH, TROPICAL ORNITHOLOGIST

The Lower Rio Grande Valley of Texas, neither temperate nor tropical, neither dry nor wet, presents the observer with unusual opportunities and challenges. The Valley's climate provides a long growing season for plants, since frosts are infrequent and generally light, but whether plants do grow and flower depends largely on the amount of moisture available (Vora 1990a). Many Valley birds have long breeding seasons, but their success may depend on the weather.

A longer breeding season means that local birds may be nesting while a few winter residents are still present and long-distance (neotropical) migrants are passing through. For example, I remember watching Northern Beardless-Tyrannulets (*Camptostoma imberbe*) building nests and incubating early clutches in April while northbound Indigo Buntings (*Passerina cyanea*), Yellow Warblers (*Dendroica petechia*), Orchard Orioles (*Icterus spurius*), and other migrants were stranded in the Valley due to rainy weather. Similarly, resident Common Yellowthroats (*Geothlypis trichas*) establish territories and nest while wintering Common Yellowthroats are still present. Southbound Orchard Orioles may look into active Altamira Oriole (*Icterus gularis*) nests, sometimes provoking a chase by the nesting pair. The challenge here is for the observer to stay focused on what one is studying; the fun is to see unusual combinations of birds and their activities.

Some breeding species can be difficult to find, not only because they may be uncommon or rare but also because of differences in the intensity of

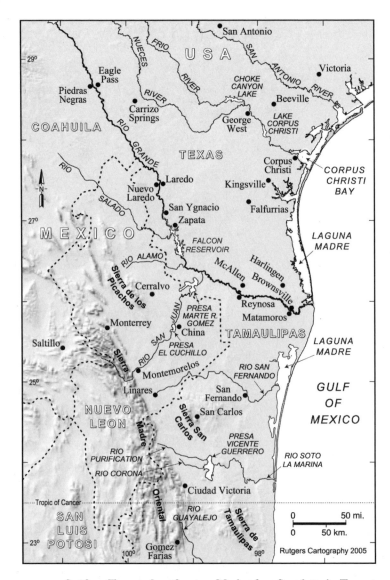

MAP 1. *Southern Texas and northeastern Mexico, from San Antonio, Texas, to Tampico, Tamaulipas. The Lower Rio Grande Valley is partially isolated from other riparian areas by dry thorn scrub and grasslands, but there are no major ecological or geographical barriers preventing bird movement through this area. Note that the Río Sabinas (mentioned in the text but not shown here) flows into the Río Salado, west of Nuevo Laredo.*

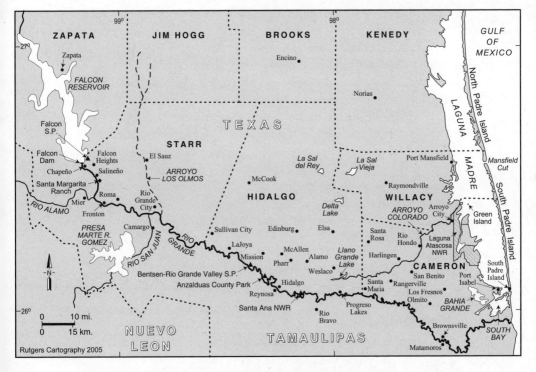

MAP 2. *The Lower Rio Grande Valley of Texas. The only regularly flowing tributaries to the lower Rio Grande are the Río San Juan and the Río Alamo, on the Mexican side. The Arroyo Los Olmos and others not shown flow only after major storm events. The Arroyo Colorado, an old distributary, carries much urban and agricultural runoff into the Laguna Madre. Several resacas (old river channels) in the Brownsville area are not shown. Most major bird observation spots are shown. However, the Sabal Palm Grove and Southmost Preserve, in the southernmost bends of the Rio Grande southeast of Brownsville, are not shown. The Salt Lakes region of La Sal del Rey and La Sal Vieja provide a saline, coastal type environment well inland.*

territorial and mating behavior. Most tropical forest birds have long breeding seasons and maintain year-round territories. Singing and territorial defense may occur throughout the year, usually at a fairly low level. A tropical bird may sing only ten times per hour during its breeding season, whereas a temperate-zone bird may sing four to five times per minute (Stutchbury and Morton 2001). Likewise, territorial intrusion occurs less often in tropical birds due to lower bird densities. Finally, males in low-density populations generally sing less frequently than those in denser populations (McShea and Rappole 1997). All these factors make it harder to detect and see many Valley birds, especially in dense foliage.

The Valley is intermediate ecologically between the temperate zone and the tropics (map 1). Some species sing infrequently and seldom get involved in territorial conflicts. I have seen only two cases of territorial intrusion by Altamira Orioles. Once a pair briefly tried to take over the nest tree of another pair, but the intruders were quickly chased off. In the other instance, two pairs postured and called at an apparent territory boundary. I have never seen Northern Beardless-Tyrannulets defend their territory against another pair, probably because territories are far apart from each other (Brush 1999a).

Other bird species, like Long-billed Thrasher (*Toxostoma longirostre*) and Olive Sparrow (*Arremonops rufivirgatus*), show the temperate-zone pattern of frequent singing during the nesting season. During the breeding season, it is easy to hear singing males, and with some effort one can see the singing bird. I have regularly observed countersinging by males (of both species) that had adjacent territories, and territory intrusions and chasing are fairly common. The density of a species does affect how vigorously it marks and defends its territory: Tropical Parulas (*Parula pitiayumi*) may sing very frequently if there are neighboring males within earshot, as at the Santa Ana National Wildlife Refuge (map 2; hereafter Santa Ana) in 1996. But they are usually fairly quiet if there is only one male in a given area, as at Bentsen–Rio Grande Valley State Park (hereafter Bentsen) in the mid- to late 1990s.

For the short-term visitor to the Valley, the ease with which one finds birds can be influenced by longer-term patterns of rainfall. The erratic rainfall makes tremendous differences in the breeding seasonality and productivity of at least some local birds and how easy they are to find. In a five-year study of breeding bird productivity and survival at Santa Ana, the only year with really high productivity (number of young birds hatched and raised) was 1997; this was also the only year with heavy spring rainfall (Gallegos 2001). The number of adult birds—those more than one year old and capable of breeding—was highest in the following year, 1998. For the birder, rainfall can eventually affect the density of birds, the amount of singing, and how easy it is to find a particular species. On a short-term basis, a heavy rain after several months of drought can stimulate singing and nesting; for example, I heard fifteen to twenty Olive Sparrows singing while I was driving part of the Santa Ana tour road in the early morning of August 29, 1996. That late in the year, the species would generally not be singing much.

The weather during one's visit can be important, as is well known, but not always in the way one might think. Cold, rainy, windy weather is obviously not conducive to seeing birds in most woodlands or forests, and winter-weary visitors may prefer "the soft perfumed air of a tropical December" (Viele 1858). For example, a Long-billed Thrasher that is skulking in a dense thicket during a norther may be singing in a treetop on a mild, calm winter morning.

However, cold weather can also help the observer in that it concentrates birds at feeding stations, especially those in parks and refuges. This is well known to winter birders, who learned to walk the former recreational vehicle campground at Bentsen, checking the feeders, and to people visiting the blinds such as those at Santa Ana, Laguna Atascosa National Wildlife Refuge (hereafter Laguna Atascosa), or the visitor center at Sabal Palm Grove Sanctuary (hereafter Sabal Palm Grove). Also, forest birds are more likely to flock in bad weather, meaning that once the flock is found, many species and individuals can be seen (Gehlbach 1987). Warm weather in winter or early spring may actually make it harder to find birds by allowing them to spread out into the forest and scrub (or to migrate north early). In contrast, northers that occur during spring migration concentrate birds in patches of remaining native habitat and well-vegetated residential areas.

Truly hot weather generally lasts from sometime in May into October, with abundant sunshine on most days. The heat and humidity are offset somewhat by the strong prevailing southeast breeze, so that it may be more comfortable than in areas considerably farther north or west. Many times in summer, low clouds form overnight and persist for several hours the next morning. Heavy dew often forms, making it look as if rain has fallen. Heavy rains fall infrequently, usually in August–October, occasionally in May–June.

Arthropod pests can be abundant at times and quite scarce at others. Chiggers (larval mites in the family Trombiculidae) and mosquitoes (Culicidae) are the main annoyances in my experience. Dense, lush grass is the usually the main habitat for chiggers, while mosquitoes are most often a problem near wetland areas or after recent rains. Ticks may be a problem in heavily grazed areas, but in typical Valley parks and refuges it is rare to encounter one. Western diamondback rattlesnakes (*Crotalus atrox*) may be encountered, mainly on the western, northern, and eastern fringes of the Valley, where larger tracts of thorn scrub and mesquite (*Prosopis glandulosa*) savanna remain. In general, it is too hot for snake boots or leggings, but folks staying on trails seldom encounter a rattlesnake. The much smaller Texas Coral Snake (*Micrurus fulvius*) poses little danger, despite its potent venom, and in my opinion it is a treat to see one.

Although some species are "60 mile-per-hour birds"—those capable of being seen or heard from a speeding car, like Dickcissels (*Spiza americana*)—in general the best way to see Valley birds is on foot, by canoe, or under cover of a blind. I have seldom made use of a blind in my work, mainly because I was always covering lots of ground or because observations could be made in simpler ways. However, sometimes my house and truck have functioned as blinds, much as Alexander Skutch found.

Most of my observations have been on foot in places like Santa Ana, Bentsen, Anzalduas, and various other Valley spots. Special memories of birds I have encountered while walking or while standing partly concealed behind a tree include seeing a Hook-billed Kite (*Chondrohierax uncinatus*) with a full crop sitting in a quiet corner of Santa Ana; seeing the newly laid, peach-tinted egg of a Red-billed Pigeon in a nest near Bentsen; and watching fledgling Altamira Orioles being fed by their vigilant, beautiful parents, less than 20 feet (6 m) from me at eye level.

I have been thrilled to find the hidden, domed nest of a Northern Beardless-Tyrannulet after several hours or days of searching and to see my first fledgling Green Jays (*Cyanocorax yncas*) after watching several pairs feeding fledgling Bronzed Cowbirds. A "mystery hummingbird" that I watched displaying in the dim light of early morning at Santa Ana turned out to be a Buff-bellied Hummingbird (*Amazilia yucatanensis*).

Other special moments when I have been birding on foot include hearing the territorial call of a Gray Hawk's (*Asturina nitida*) at Anzalduas and then seeing the pair attend an active nest; finding three nesting kingbird (*Tyrannus*) species, plus two other flycatchers and one oriole within earshot at the Rangerville substation on Cannon Road in Cameron County; and showing a molting immature Northern Jacana (*Jacana spinosa*) to ornithology students at Santa Ana.

One summer I found two different Short-tailed Hawks (*Buteo brachyurus*) at Santa Ana. The spring of 1997 yielded a bumper crop of Olive Sparrow fledglings, and later I heard a few "whisper songs." I enjoyed the summer of 1999, when Rose-throated Becard (*Pachyramphus aglaiae*), Altamira Oriole, Northern Beardless-Tyrannulet, Tropical Parula, Black Phoebe (*Sayornis nigricans*), Clay-colored Robin (*Turdus grayi*), Gray Hawk, plus many "regular" Valley specialties all nested at Anzalduas.

By canoe, mainly with Marty Bray, I have especially enjoyed finding my first Red-billed Pigeon nest, on the late date of August 7, and seeing hundreds of Neotropic Cormorants (*Phalacrocorax brasilianus*) pounding the water with their wings in a cooperative foraging flock. We encountered a family group of Muscovy Ducks (*Cairina moschata*) along a quiet side channel near the historic Paso de Azúcar and El Cántaro fords near Fronton, Texas, and Mier, Tamaulipas; and we saw *cuatro patos,* four ducks, in one day below Falcon Dam, all possibly nesting in the only area where their ranges overlap—Mottled Duck (*Anas fulvigula*), "Mexican Mallard" (*Anas platyrhynchos diazi*), Muscovy Duck, and Wood Duck (*Aix sponsa*). More broadly,

I treasure seeing the reaction of first-time paddlers to the unique perspective and beauty of experiencing the lower Rio Grande by canoe—the sights, sounds, and smells of our subtropical river. Despite all our assaults upon it, the river still somehow retains a portion of its former splendor.

Negative impressions include seeing land cleared all the way to the water's edge, inevitably leading to soil erosion and siltation; seeing large trees cleared from land to be planted with trees that will take years to become large; and smelling the burning of brush on recently cleared land. It hurts to see large old cedar elms (*Ulmus crassifolia*), Texas ebonies (*Chloroleucon ebano*), and sugar hackberries (*Celtis laevigata*) dying due to drought and lack of flooding; to see and smell a polluted Rio Grande after a heavy rain; and to drive through poorly vegetated sections dominated by Great-tailed Grackles (*Quiscalus mexicanus*) and House Sparrows (*Passer domesticus*).

As in so much of the world, humanity has had a great impact. There is much left to see, however, including some new species not formerly nesting here. Observers are encouraged to search actively, taking needed caution as proper for the season and specific locale. Although there is an understandable tendency to go where interesting birds have already been reported, I encourage exploration (as permitted) of a variety of areas at a variety of seasons. Such exploration, with an open mind, has greatly increased our knowledge and appreciation of Valley birds and will doubtless continue to do so.

The Lower Rio Grande
Valley of Texas

We left New Orleans on the 11th of July [1847] and arrived here on the 18th. . . . People in the States misrepresent the climate of Mexico, or perhaps know nothing about it. It is the impression there that the heat of the sun here is almost fatal, which is a very great mistake. . . . We have the benefit of the Gulf breeze here constantly, which is only 30 miles distant, which counter-acts, in a great measure, the heat produced upon a salt plain without trees or any sign of vegetation.

ANONYMOUS SOLDIER IN MATAMOROS
DURING THE MEXICAN WAR, 1847

There was ice this morning about half an inch thick. The wind is still from the north and very cold and chilling.

SAMUEL R. CURTIS, STATIONED IN MATAMOROS, JANUARY 7, 1846

The Lower Rio Grande Valley of Texas is a politically and geographically defined area of more than 1.2 million hectares and about one million people. It includes the southernmost four counties of the Lone Star State: Cameron and Willacy along the coast, Hidalgo in the middle, and Starr farthest west and upstream (map 2). Subtle variation in geology, topography, and soil type affect plant and animal communities and the human uses of the Valley, one of the most bird-rich and intensively cultivated regions of the United States.

TOPOGRAPHY, WEATHER, AND CLIMATE

Most of the Valley is quite flat, with an average elevational rise of only about 5 feet per mile (0.4 meters per km). South Padre Island, in easternmost Cameron and Willacy counties, is a long, narrow barrier island that protects the southern half of the shallow Laguna Madre from the Gulf of Mexico. Prevailing southeast winds form sand dunes on South Padre Island and Bra-

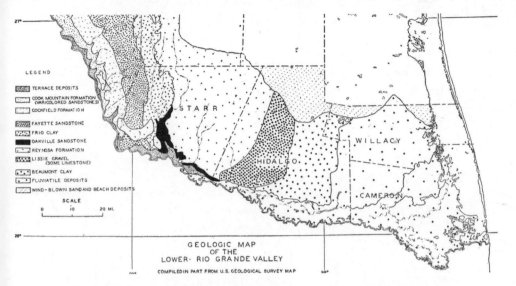

LEGEND

TERRACE DEPOSITS
COOK MOUNTAIN FORMATION (VARICOLORED SANDSTONES)
COCKFIELD FORMATION
FAYETTE SANDSTONE
FRIO CLAY
OAKVILLE SANDSTONE
REYNOSA FORMATION
LISSIE GRAVEL (SOME LIMESTONE)
BEAUMONT CLAY
FLUVIATILE DEPOSITS
WIND-BLOWN SAND AND BEACH DEPOSITS

SCALE
0   10   20 MI.

STARR

WILLACY

HIDALGO

CAMERON

GEOLOGIC MAP
OF THE
LOWER· RIO GRANDE VALLEY

COMPILED IN PART FROM U.S. GEOLOGICAL SURVEY MAP

MAP 3. *Geology of the Lower Rio Grande Valley. The fluviatile (stream-borne) deposits covering nearly all of Cameron and Willacy counties were laid down by the Rio Grande and are sometimes called the Rio Grande Delta. A roughly equal delta area exists, south of the Rio Grande and east of Reynosa. The Oakville Sandstone forms small bluffs along the Rio Grande and part of the Bordas Scarp in Starr County. Part of an extensive South Texas sand sheet covers northernmost Hidalgo and Willacy counties. From Clover 1937*

zos Island and clay dunes (*lomas*) near the mouth of the Rio Grande and west of the Laguna Madre. Most of Cameron and Willacy counties and southernmost Hidalgo County are part of the recent delta of the Rio Grande, with broad areas of low, clayey soils separated by narrow levees of sandy loam. Central Hidalgo County is dominated by older delta deposits rich in clay and gravel, often with a noticeable hardpan (*caliche*) layer due to high evaporation rates.

The northern third of Willacy and Hidalgo counties is on the South Texas Sand Sheet, covered by sandy loam and stabilized sand dunes (map 3). Starr County consists mainly of flat to gently rolling uplands on older deposits of sandstone and clay, but there are some modest bluffs and arroyos along the Rio Grande and the Bordas Scarp (Wynd 1944). Valley terrain is generally similar to that immediately across the Rio Grande in Tamaulipas, Mexico, and one can drive south from Reynosa and Matamoros for more than two hours in flat land (now farmland). West and southwest of Reynosa, however, there is rolling upland terrain broken by arroyos.

The Valley's climate is subtropical and semiarid, with long, hot summers and short, generally mild winters. The prevailing onshore (southeast) winds keep the Valley cloudier and more humid than areas farther inland (Shelton

2001). This in turn keeps daytime temperatures lower and nighttime temperatures higher from east to west across the Valley and compared to areas farther inland. Although rain showers sometimes develop along the regular daily sea breeze, the general lack of adequate trigger mechanisms and consistent upper-level subtropical high pressure usually prevent the development of the thunderstorms and showers that might otherwise be expected in such a humid climate. Rainfall is higher closer to the coast, with an average of 27 inches (68 cm) at Brownsville and 20 inches (51 cm) at Falcon Dam. September is the rainiest month on average, generally getting 4−5 inches (10−13 cm) due to tropical low-pressure systems.

Rainfall is notably erratic and unpredictable. During 1961−96, annual precipitation at Brownsville ranged from 16 to 42 inches (41−107 cm). During the last 150 years, precipitation at Brownsville ranged from a low of only 12 inches (30 cm) in 1953 to 59 inches (150 cm) in 1896. Significant droughts may last two to five years. The lower Rio Grande dried up in 1953, the same year that Falcon Dam was closed. For at least a few months, the Rio Grande no longer reached the Gulf of Mexico (Smith 1961). This event was repeated in the early 2000s due to another severe drought. Although flooding has been greatly reduced due to upstream dams, there have been at least two major floods in the region since the mid-1960s that have caused extensive and prolonged inundation along the lower Rio Grande. During Hurricane Beulah in September, 1967, Pharr (Hidalgo County) reported 21.5 inches (55 cm) of rain (Webster 1968a). Such climatic variation affects plant and animal communities in various ways (Webster 2001).

As one would expect, the eastern part of the Valley, closer to the Gulf of Mexico, is cooler in summer than the western section. In the summer (May−September), Brownsville daily highs average 90−95°F (32−35°C), while at Falcon Dam and Rio Grande City daily highs of 95−100°F (35−38°C) are common. Daily temperatures vary the least on the beach, with overnight lows in the low 80s (around 28°C) and daytime highs in the upper 80s (around 31°C).

In winter, overcast skies, which usually follow strong cold fronts, reduce the chances of frosts, especially in Cameron and Willacy counties. As a result, killing frosts are infrequent, and the ranges of many tropical plants and animals extend into the Valley from eastern Mexico. The occasionally severe, killing frosts (1912, 1951, 1983, and 1989, for example) prevent the area from being truly tropical and may have both short-term and long-lasting effects on plants and animals (James 1963, Lonard and Judd 1991). Snow is a historic event, the 1880 storm that dropped one to two feet of snow in Matamoros being the apparent all-time record (Robertson 1985; Goldman 1951). Likewise, ice storms are extremely rare (Webster 1973). A series of mild winters in Texas in the late 1990s to early 2000s has perhaps suggested climatic warming, but there is no clear trend in the twentieth-century climatic record of the U.S.-Mexico border region (Shelton 2001).

LANDSCAPE AND LAND USE

As of the 2000 U.S. national census, the Valley had 978,369 people, with about 92 percent of the population in Hidalgo and Cameron counties combined. Brownsville and McAllen are the only cities that exceed 100,000 people, but many smaller cities and towns along U.S. Highways 83 and 77 are now merging together into one urban/suburban strip between La Joya and Brownsville. Large ranches, with varying amounts of grass and thorn scrub and some agricultural fields, cover the northern and western sections of the Valley. On the Mexican side of the Rio Grande is a population of 1,045,593 million, the large urban municipalities of Reynosa and Matamoros accounting for 80 percent of the total, with the rest in smaller cities, towns, and rural areas between Falcon Dam and the Gulf (2000 Mexican census). Large agricultural fields supplied by irrigation water dominate on both sides of the river between the Starr-Hidalgo county line and Brownsville. The total population of more than 2 million people on both sides of the lower Rio Grande is quite an increase from the early days when Jose de Escandón first established the small Mexican towns of Camargo, Mier, and old Reynosa about 250 years ago.

THE VALLEY'S BIOLOGICAL DIVERSITY

Biogeographically, the Valley is the Matamoran District of the larger Tamaulipan Biotic Province, which covers much of southern Texas and northern and central Tamaulipas (Blair 1950). Ecologically, most of the Valley is in the brushy, grassy South Texas Plains, but the eastern halves of Cameron and Willacy counties are in the Gulf Prairies and Marshes (Schmidly 2002). Both the flora and fauna are mixtures of species typical of temperate, tropical, desert, and coastal habitats. For example, 46 percent of the Valley's woody plants are widespread in Mexico and have ranges terminating either in the Valley or in the Edwards Plateau of Central Texas, while 37 percent have affinities with the southwestern deserts. The remainder are made up of 11 percent that are widespread in North America and Mexico, about 5 percent that are widespread in coastal areas, and 1 percent that are found on every continent (Lonard and Judd 1993). Different sensitivities to cold and lack of moisture produce a gradient of tropical, temperate, and desert plant species in the broader region. The Valley's higher but still varying soil moisture and its thicker alluvial soils have allowed development of extensive but poorly defined riparian forests, marshes, and fringing thorn scrub (chaparral).

This area is confusing to biologists from other places even today. For example, the statement that pecan (*Carya illinoiensis*), shagbark hickory (*C. ovata*), and black hickory (*C. texana*) are common in forests of the central and eastern Valley (Webster 2001) is likely based on confusion between the Valley (southernmost Texas) and South Texas as a whole (from Austin or San Antonio south). Similarly, despite statements to the contrary elsewhere, cottonwoods (*Populus* spp.) do not occur naturally in the Valley (Lonard et al. 1991; Everitt et al. 2002) although they do extend downstream to Webb County (Oring 1964) and they occur along some rivers in northeastern Mexico.

Much more understandable confusion is the lack of agreement on what constitutes riparian forest: David D. Diamond (1998) called forests dominated by Texas ebony (*Chloroleucon ebano*) "subtropical upland forests," while Frederick R. Gehlbach (1981, 1987) referred to the same forests, with anacua (*Ehretia anacua*) and tepeguaje (*Leucaena pulverulenta*) being subdominants, as "riparian evergreen forests." Robin Vora (1990b) includes Texas ebony stands in a drier floodplain-chaparral habitat, with anacua, western soapberry (*Sapindus drummondii*), and tepehuaje in moister, floodplain-bottomland habitat. The problem here is a matter of definition, since all authors recognize the same dominant trees and the long-term significance of flooding to the habitat.

If one is coming from the south, up the Gulf Coast of Mexico, or from the oak (*Quercus*) and pine (*Pinus*) forests of the eastern United States, Valley trees seem quite small by comparison. Many of our woody plants are smaller than their temperate or tropical relatives and are adapted to a semi-arid climate with undependable moisture. For example, anacahuita (Mexican olive; *Cordia boissieri*) and fiddlewood (*Citharexylum berlandieri*) are usually shrubs, while their tropical relatives are trees (Mason and Mason 1995). Likewise, cedar elm is a smaller elm than the American elm (*Ulmus americana*) found in the eastern and central United States. In the Valley, any woody plant with a single stem (trunk) more than 3–5 feet (1–1.5 meters) above the ground may be considered a tree.

On the other hand, if one is coming from the western deserts and scrubland or the coastal beaches and tidal flats, the Valley's trees seem quite large. Mesquite (also known as honey mesquite) is a small to medium-sized tree in riparian habitats in the Valley, while only reaching shrub stature over drier areas of Texas and northern Mexico (Clover 1937). Black mangrove (*Avicennia germinans*) is the only "tree" in the Valley's coastal salt flats, but it is sel-

dom 3 feet (1 meter) in height and has a shrubby growth form due to occasional freezes (Lonard and Judd 1991).

Although the Valley contains relatively few tall forests, trees can grow tall
in moist bottomland soils. Black willow (*Salix nigra*), cedar elm, sugar hackberry, Mexican ash (*Fraxinus berlandieriana*), and the rare Montezuma
bald-cypress (*Taxodium mucronatum*) may reach 65 feet (20 m) in height.
Sabal palm (*Sabal mexicana*), Texas ebony, anacua, tepehuaje, and western
soapberry may reach 50 feet (15 m) in height in moist soils. Live oak (*Quercus virginiana*, locally called *encino*), native only on the northern fringes of
Willacy and Hidalgo counties but planted widely in Valley towns, may also
reach 50 feet (15 m) in height in sandy or irrigated soils. Mesquite, coma
(*Sideroxylon celastrinum*), and brasil (*Condalia hookeri*) may reach 30 feet
(9 m) in height. Growth of any of these species may be stunted by dry, shallow, or saline soils, fires, or freezes. The tallest trees are not always along the
riverbank itself but often in old river channels several hundred feet back
from the river, because of the buildup of natural levees along the river. Sandbar willow (*Salix exigua*) and black willow are common in disturbed, wet
soils at the water's edge, but common reed (*Phragmites australis*) reaches
small-tree stature also. Grasses and dry-land willow (*Baccharis neglecta*)
quickly take over abandoned agricultural fields.

Several introduced woody plants, such as giant reed (*Arundo donax*), fan
palms (*Washingtonia filifera* and *W. robusta*), castor bean (*Ricinus communis*),
and popinac (*Leucaena leucocephala*) have become common in the Valley's
landscape. Many more—Chinaberry (*Melia azedarach*), athel tamarisk
(*Tamarix aphylla*), Brazilian pepper (*Schinus terebinthifolius*), and others—
sometimes spread from plantings. In addition, several introduced herbaceous plants have become established, the most prevalent being guineagrass
(*Panicum maximum*) in moister soils and buffelgrass (*Pennisetum ciliare*) in
drier soils. Hydrilla (*Hydrilla verticillata*) became a widespread problem in
the river and irrigation canals, especially during the late 1990s. Water hyacinth (*Eichhornia crassipes*) chokes the river and other aquatic habitats,
mainly in Cameron County. Shrubby salt cedar (*Tamarix ramosissima*) has
invaded alkaline soils in the western Valley but thus far is not the problem
that it has become in arid lands from western Texas to eastern California.

The hot, semiarid climate with erratic rainfall creates environments suitable for grasslands, saline coastal prairies, mesquite savanna, thorn scrub,
and hypersaline algal flats, while the modifying presence of the Rio Grande
and associated watercourses creates riparian forest, thorn forest, freshwater
ponds, and disturbed river-edge habitats. People have created grassy pastures, intensively cultivated agricultural fields, orchards of grapefruit (*Citrus
paradisi*) and other citrus fruits, and residential and commercial areas of var-

ious sizes. Some of these habitats support a diversity of birds; others sustain very few species but often at high densities.

REGIONAL LANDSCAPES AND DISPERSAL CORRIDORS

Interestingly, Falcon Dam, at the western end of the Valley, is closer to Monterrey, Nuevo León, than it is to Brownsville, Texas. On a clear day, one can see the Sierra de los Picachos mountain range from the Roma–Falcon Dam area. These mountains, near historic Cerralvo, Nuevo León, reach over 5,000 feet (1,500 m) in elevation and are only 40 miles (64 km) from the Rio Grande at the closest point. The montane pine and oak forests and lower Tamaulipan thorn forest may be a source for several rare or uncommon Valley bird species, such as Yellow-green Vireo (*Vireo flavoviridis*), Tropical Parula, and Northern Beardless-Tyrannulet.

The Rio Grande itself provides a corridor from west-central Texas to the Valley, since there is still a nearly continuous strip of woody vegetation along its shores. The Bordas Scarp (or Escarpment) may provide dispersal routes to the north and south, since it is a fairly continuous band of low thorn scrub running from central Tamaulipas across the Rio Grande near Rio Grande City into southern Texas (Prieto 1873; Johnston 1963; see map 5 in the present volume). In the twentieth century, spreading oak forests of the Wild Horse Desert (roughly today's Kenedy and Brooks counties; Johnston 1963) have provided alternative habitat for several declining forest birds of the Valley (Brush 1999a; Hilbun and Koltermann 2002) and possibly a north-south dispersal corridor as well.

Mexican tributaries of the Rio Grande may also have provided corridors of suitable habitat for some birds, like Muscovy Duck, Brown Jay (*Cyanocorax morio*), and Clay-colored Robin, and possibly parrots, all species that have spread into the Valley during historical times. The short Río Alamo connects the foothills of the Sierra de los Picachos to the Rio Grande a short distance above Roma (maps 1 and 2). The longer Río San Juan, with its headwaters in the Sierra Madre Oriental around Monterrey and Montemorelos in central Nuevo León, empties into the Rio Grande just above Rio Grande City. Today one may see a limited amount of riparian habitat along the Río San Juan, although the flow has been greatly reduced below the reservoirs Presa El Cuchillo (near China, Nuevo León) and Presa Marte R. Gomez (also known as Sugar Lake, upstream of Camargo, Tamaulipas; map 1), and the reservoirs themselves flooded some good riparian habitat. Just west of the Valley, the poorly known Rio Salado–Sabinas watershed (see map 1) provides a western corridor of riparian habitat to the Sierra Madre Oriental in Coahuila.

ECOLOGICAL DIVERSITY
AND HISTORY

The Rio Grande Valley is of much interest botanically because plants repre-senting western desert, northern, coastal, and tropical floras all are found in a relatively small area.

ELZADA U. CLOVER, BOTANIST LIVING
IN THE VALLEY IN 1932–34

It is estimated that 98% of the lush, subtropical region of the delta has been cleared in the United States and a large percentage of similar habitat has been cleared in Mexico.

SONJA E. JAHRSDOERFER AND DAVID M. LESLIE, JR.,
ARGUING FOR A WILDLIFE CORRIDOR REFUGE, 1988

Originally inhabited by hunting and gathering tribes, the Valley was even-tually settled by Spanish immigrants moving north from colonial Mexico. The famed Cabeza de Vaca probably passed through the area in 1535, likely crossing the Rio Grande and Río San Juan on his way to the Mexican high-lands. His report of the discovery of silver in northeastern Mexico may have led to the establishment of the first settlement in the region in the late 1570s: modern-day Cerralvo, only 31 miles (49 km) southwest of the nearest bend of the lower Rio Grande (Jones 1996).

PIONEERS (1570S–1730S)

Livestock—first sheep, then cattle and horses—were brought northward in large numbers into central and northern Nuevo León in the 1630s. Some an-imals wandered north from the frontier of New Spain at Cerralvo and Mon-terrey toward the Rio Grande (Simmons 1992). Agualeguas, only 21 miles (34 km) from the Rio Grande, was established in 1675 (Gerhard 1982), and a

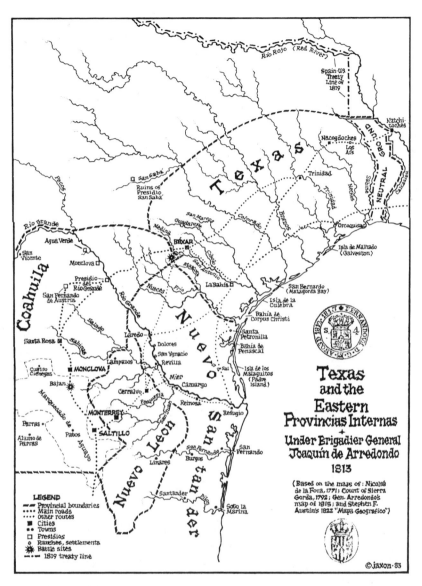

MAP 4. *Historical map of southern Texas and northeastern Mexico. The Lower Rio Grande Valley was a lightly settled part of New Spain and then was part of the Mexican province Nuevo Santander. After the Texas War of Independence, 1836, this area became part of the new state of Texas. However, the Rio Grande still flooded regularly, discouraging extensive agriculture. Courtesy of Jack Jackson*

Wilson's Plovers are summer residents in the Valley, living mainly along the Laguna Madre but also breeding inland in the Salt Lakes region (La Sal del Rey and La Sal Vieja). Photo by Greg W. Lasley

Muscovy Ducks expanded their range into the Valley in the 1980s, probably from a population found by Starker Leopold in Nuevo León in the 1940s. These shy, agile birds are very different from the tame, overweight city park birds. Photo by Timothy Brush

The international bridge between Roma, Texas, and Ciudad Miguel Alemán, Tamaulipas, spans the riparian habitat corridor. Photo by Timothy Brush

Coastal prairie and wetlands habitats abut Port Isabel. Photo by Timothy Brush

The city of South Padre Island lies between the Gulf of Mexico and Laguna Madre (foreground).
Photo by Timothy Brush

Santa Ana National Wildlife Refuge from the air, photographed between 1934 and 1953. Note that the Rio Grande was wider than it is today and had sandbars—the river flooded regularly before the closing of Falcon Dam in 1953. Photo courtesy Pauline James

Santa Ana from the air, photographed in 1981. By 1981, thirty years of flood control had allowed silt deposits to become stabilized and vegetation to encroach on the river. Some additional land clearing had occurred since the 1950s, especially on the Mexican side (bottom of photo). Photo courtesy U.S. Fish and Wildlife Service, Lower Rio Grande Valley National Wildlife Refuge

Vast amounts of sand flats and algal flats are exposed frequently on the bay side of South Padre Island. Similar habitats, on a clay substrate, occur along the mainland shore of Laguna Madre. Snowy Plovers and Least Terns are common nesters.
Photo by Timothy Brush

Narrow strips of trees line the Rio Grande in a few areas, but usually steeper banks allow only shrubs or small trees to grow at the water's edge.
Photo by Timothy Brush

Inland, small patches of woodland dominated by sugar hackberry remain in soils with adequate moisture. A Clay-colored Robin was singing here during one of my visits to this tract near La Joya.
Photo by Timothy Brush

One of the rarest forest types is tall ash forest, since this species requires above-average soil moisture. A Gray Hawk nest is hidden in this view (slightly above center). It contained one nestling, which was alert but still downy. Photo by Timothy Brush

Ferruginous Pygmy-Owls were common residents of Valley forests until about the 1960s or 1970s, when they vanished from the highly fragmented Valley. Photo by Steve Bentsen

White-tipped Doves are among the species that have done well in the modified landscape of the late twentieth century and new millennium, faring fine as long as some woodland remains. Photo by Russell C. Hansen

In some areas, a few emergent trees tower over low thorn scrub or thorn forest, providing nest sites for species that can forage in or over lower vegetation, like the Altamira Oriole and Couch's Kingbird, respectively. Photo by Timothy Brush

An Altamira Oriole's hanging nest is unmistakable. This one, at the Southmost Preserve, was in a willow tree. Photo by Timothy Brush

Cattails provide crucial nesting habitat for marsh birds such as Least Bitterns, Common Yellowthroats, Common Moorhens, and occasionally King Rails. Photo by Timothy Brush

Small freshwater wetlands and ponds are common refuges for Black-bellied Whistling-Ducks. Broods hatch inside a cavity nest in a dry forest or residential area, and the young are accompanied by their parents to water. Photo by Steve Bentsen

An urban forest of sorts develops in well-watered residential areas more than thirty years old, where property owners have taken an interest. Purple Martin nest boxes are favorites of many year-round Valley residents. Photo by Timothy Brush

The Common Moorhen is a colorful and prolific marsh breeder. Photo by Alan Murphy

Agricultural land, much of it irrigated, covers large sections of the Valley between the coastal prairies to the east and the drier ranch country to the north and west. Some crops, such as cotton and winter vegetables, provide little for nesting birds, but sorghum fields and citrus groves provide nesting and foraging sites for Barn Owls and some other species. Photo by Frank W. Judd

The western Valley, especially western Starr County, includes one of the most scenic stretches of the lower Rio Grande. Growing at the foot of sandstone bluffs, well-developed riparian forest supports nesting Red-billed Pigeons and Audubon's Orioles. In the country at the top of the bluffs Scaled Quail, Ash-throated Flycatcher, and Black-tailed Gnatcatcher are found. Photo by Timothy Brush

Most Groove-billed Anis head south for the winter, returning in April to nest in dense foliage near water. Photo by Steve Bentsen

The impressive voice of Plain Chachalacas is one of the quintessential sounds of the lower Rio Grande riparian forest. Painting by Gerald Sneed

OPPOSITE PAGE, TOP: *Crested Caracaras are increasingly common nesters in open thorn-scrub and mesquite savanna, where they capture live prey as well as consuming carrion. Painting by Gerald Sneed*

OPPOSITE PAGE, MIDDLE: *Green Kingfishers are year-round Valley residents, while American White Pelicans are winter residents and migrants. Both are seen regularly along the Rio Grande and old river channels called resacas. Painting by Gerald Sneed*

OPPOSITE PAGE, BOTTOM: *Hook-billed Kites often search for their land snail prey in quite dry habitats, such as this cactus patch. Painting by Gerald Sneed*

The Great Kiskadee is a flycatcher with a diverse diet, including fruit, terrestrial and aquatic insects, fish, amphibians, and sometimes small mammals. A characteristic bird of tropical rivers, it has become increasingly common in the Lower Rio Grande Valley. Painting by Gerald Sneed

Green Jays are conspicuous birds in the open, but their bright colors blend into the foliage, where they can be hard to see. Painting by Gerald Sneed

OPPOSITE PAGE, TOP: *Clay-colored Robins, once extremely rare in the Valley, have become an increasingly regular part of the breeding bird community of forests, both natural and suburban. Painting by Gerald Sneed*

OPPOSITE PAGE, BOTTOM: *The Tropical Parula spends much of its life in forests with abundant Spanish moss, where it nests. Painting by Gerald Sneed*

Anacua berries are eaten eagerly by many birds, including the Altamira Oriole. Painting by Gerald Sneed

Cane (carrizo) *provides dense cover for a number of bird species. Audubon's Orioles sometimes descend from the trees to seek insects in the cane. Painting by Gerald Sneed*

Common Pauraques are easily heard at night in Valley forests, scrub, and sometimes residential areas. However, finding a roosting or nesting bird is a rare event. Photo by Steve Bentsen

Red-crowned Parrots have established a breeding population in the Valley in recent decades, consuming a variety of seeds, fruits, and even flowers. Photo by Laura Elaine Moore

Green Parakeets were first reported in the United States in 1960. Breeding flocks occur today in Brownsville, McAllen, San Benito, and other towns where they have a year-round supply of seeds and fruits. Photo by Steve Bentsen

A characteristic species of mesquite savanna and open thorn scrub is the elegant Scissor-tailed Flycatcher, a summer resident. Flocks of fifty to a hundred or more can be seen during spring and fall migration. Photo by Alan Murphy

Species that were historically present and then declined include the Gray Hawk, an uncommon but increasingly regular breeder in the most extensive tracts of riparian forest and thorn forest.
Photo by Alan Murphy

The Northern Jacana is among several species that first bred in the Valley more than twenty years ago but are still irregular or rare breeders today.
Photo by Alan Murphy

Masked Ducks are irregular in coastal Texas, occurring in greater numbers during wet periods such as the early 1990s. Photo by Alan Murphy

The Brown Jay is a tropical bird reaching its northern limits in South Texas and first reported in the United States in 1969. Photo by Alan Murphy

Effective flood control practices and withdrawals of water for a rapidly increasing population have taken their toll. Photo by Timothy Brush

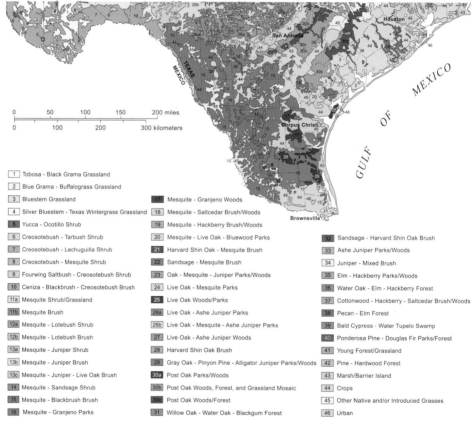

1	Tobosa - Black Grama Grassland
2	Blue Grama - Buffalograss Grassland
3	Bluestem Grassland
4	Silver Bluestem - Texas Wintergrass Grassland
5	Yucca - Ocotillo Shrub
6	Creosotebush - Tarbush Shrub
7	Creosotebush - Lechuguilla Shrub
8	Creosotebush - Mesquite Shrub
9	Fourwing Saltbush - Creosotebush Shrub
10	Ceniza - Blackbrush - Creosotebush Brush
11a	Mesquite Shrub/Grassland
11b	Mesquite Brush
12a	Mesquite - Lotebush Shrub
12b	Mesquite - Lotebush Brush
13a	Mesquite - Juniper Shrub
13b	Mesquite - Juniper Brush
13c	Mesquite - Juniper - Live Oak Brush
14	Mesquite - Sandsage Shrub
15	Mesquite - Blackbrush Brush
16	Mesquite - Granjeno Parks

17	Mesquite - Granjeno Woods
18	Mesquite - Saltcedar Brush/Woods
19	Mesquite - Hackberry Brush/Woods
20	Mesquite - Live Oak - Bluewood Parks
21	Harvard Shin Oak - Mesquite Brush
22	Sandsage - Mesquite Brush
23	Oak - Mesquite - Juniper Parks/Woods
24	Live Oak - Mesquite Parks
25	Live Oak Woods/Parks
26a	Live Oak - Ashe Juniper Parks
26b	Live Oak - Mesquite - Ashe Juniper Parks
27	Live Oak - Ashe Juniper Woods
28	Harvard Shin Oak Brush
29	Gray Oak - Pinyon Pine - Alligator Juniper Parks/Woods
30a	Post Oak Parks/Woods
30b	Post Oak Woods, Forest, and Grassland Mosaic
30c	Post Oak Woods/Forest
31	Willow Oak - Water Oak - Blackgum Forest

32	Sandsage - Harvard Shin Oak Brush
33	Ashe Juniper Parks/Woods
34	Juniper - Mixed Brush
35	Elm - Hackberry Parks/Woods
36	Water Oak - Elm - Hackberry Forest
37	Cottonwood - Hackberry - Saltcedar Brush/Woods
38	Pecan - Elm Forest
39	Bald Cypress - Water Tupelo Swamp
40	Ponderosa Pine - Douglas Fir Parks/Forest
41	Young Forest/Grassland
42	Pine - Hardwood Forest
43	Marsh/Barrier Island
44	Crops
45	Other Native and/or Introduced Grasses
46	Urban

MAP 6. *Current South Texas vegetation. Urban areas and croplands cover much of the Valley, especially central and eastern sections. Relatively natural habitats (grasslands, savannas, and thorn scrub) occur mainly in western, northern, and the immediate coastal setions. Small tracts of thorn forest and riparian forest, as well as freshwater wetlands, occur mainly within a few miles of the river but cannot be shown at this scale. Other sections of South Texas contain more extensive areas of thorn scrub and savanna with some thorn forest and grasslands. Extensive agricultural areas other than the Valley are centered around Corpus Christi, San Antonio, and a few other areas. Courtesy Texas Bureau of Economic Geology*

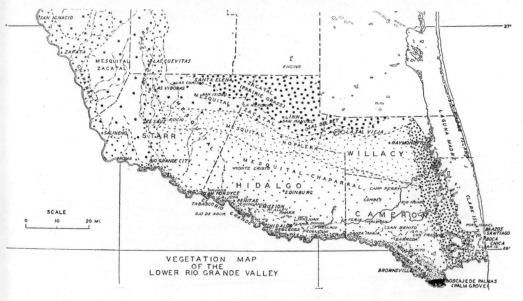

MAP 5. *Vegetation of the Lower Rio Grande Valley during the 1930s, based on Elzada U. Clover's extensive field research. Note that monte del rio, a narrow riverside strip that widens near Brownsville, was a dense forest of deciduous trees like cedar elm and Mexican ash and evergreen species such as Texas ebony and anacua. Vegetation height decreased from south to north in much of the Valley. Seasonal wetlands occurred in much of the Valley, especially near the coast and the Rio Grande. Sacahuistal was Clover's term for the coastal prairie–saltwater wetland complex. Zacatal was inland prairie established on the sandy soils on the northern fringes of the Valley. From Clover 1937*

ranch was established at modern-day Mier by at least 1734 (Guerra 1953). However, no towns were established along the lower Rio Grande until 1749. With relatively small numbers of livestock and no agriculture, the Valley must have remained relatively untouched ecologically in the 1600s and early 1700s.

Most rivers in what is now southern Texas and northeastern Mexico were originally clear and fast-flowing, with narrow riparian forests of Montezuma bald-cypress, black willow, cottonwood, mesquite, Texas ebony, and other trees along their banks, in a grassland-dominated landscape. Smaller rivers, such as the Río San Juan, flooded mainly during August–October, when tropical storms often dump significant rainfall on the Sierra Madre Oriental watershed (Berlandier 1826–34; Schmidly 2002). Flooding along these tributaries was probably limited to the narrow floodplains of the smaller rivers, where it helped maintain the tall riparian forests.

The Rio Grande, in contrast, was described as a muddy river, subject to flooding for up to half the year, depending on snowmelt and rainfall amounts in the sprawling watershed. High water was most predictable in the warmer months, with winter generally being a time of low water. Erratic flooding probably helped produce the complex vegetation patterns and bird communities along the lower Rio Grande, as it does elsewhere (Molles et al. 1998). Alonso de León, in his explorations of the Valley and areas immediately to the north in 1686, took ten days to travel through thick woods, brush, and swamps along the lower Rio Grande between modern-day Mier and the coast (Cavazos 1985; Foster 1997).

Drier areas north and south of the Rio Grande contained a mosaic of thorn scrub, mesquite savanna, and grassland, with both freshwater and saltwater wetlands, especially near the coast. Berlandier (1826–34) described the many small temporary wetlands (*lagunas*), which fill with water during the rainy season and slowly dry out, providing habitat for aquatic, marsh, and even terrestrial species as they dry (Scifres and Mutz 1975). Some isolated small forests (mottes) of live oak occurred in the sandy soil of what is now Kenedy County, north of the Valley (map 2), but the landscape there was almost treeless.

The Coahuiltecans, the early inhabitants of the Valley and adjacent areas, were hunters and gatherers who did not grow crops (Taylor 1972; Gerhard 1982). The closest agricultural fields were probably the small farm plots of the Huastecans south of the Río Soto la Marina, more than 200 miles (330 km) south of the lower Rio Grande (see map 1; Gerhard 1982).

There has been much discussion about the relative abundance of woody plants vs. grasses and other herbaceous plants during the presettlement and early settlement years, both in the Valley and in the region as a whole (Fulbright 2001; to be discussed further later). There may have been few "true" prairies in the sense of the complete absence of woody plants, but there was evidently a lot of very sparsely wooded grassland and savanna (Johnston 1963). These habitats may have been maintained by a combination of light grazing, natural or induced fire, and the relatively moist, cool climates of the Little Ice Age during the 1600s and 1700s (Swan 1981; Lamb 1995). Such mesquite grasslands were luxuriant and open enough to support pronghorn (*Antilocapra americana*) as far south as northern Starr and Hidalgo counties (Schmidly 2002). Although I have seen no records for the Valley, bison (*Bos bison*) occurred in northern Nuevo León and possibly northern Tamaulipas as late as 1840 (Berlandier 1826–34; Coopwood 1900; Taylor 1972). Greater Prairie-Chickens (*Tympanuchus cupido*) may even have nested in Valley coastal prairies, as discussed in the species accounts under Phasianidae.

However, change was coming to the Valley. As early as 1715, Louis J. de St. Denis noted that southern Texas was overrun with cattle and horses descended from those left behind by early Spanish explorers (Jackson 1986). These animals began to change the presettlement landscape, although not nearly to the extent that later, more intensive grazing and intensive agriculture did (Lehman 1969; Jackson 2000).

SETTLEMENT AND BOTANICAL EXPLORATION (1740s–1860s)

The first towns, Camargo, Mier, and Reynosa, were established on what is now the Mexican side of the lower Rio Grande by Jose de Escandón in 1749–52 (map 4). The human population grew slowly, but livestock numbers increased rapidly in good grazing land. For example, in 1757 the 926 Reynosa and Camargo residents already owned 90,000 sheep and goats (Lehmann 1969). Simón Hierro, an early Catholic priest, noted "plenty of timber" and "many small palm trees, useful in thatching the homes" along the Rio Grande near Camargo in 1749 (Castañeda 1938). We learn little else about plant communities during this early settlement time.

Although nearly everyone lived on the south side of the river, ranches had been established by 1761 in what are now Starr, Hidalgo, Zapata, and Webb counties (Jackson 1986; Castañeda 1938). Ranching extended as far north as modern-day Corpus Christi during the 1760s (Jackson 2000). Small farms were established near Camargo and probably other towns to grow corn (*Zea mays*), beans (*Phaseolus vulgaris*), pumpkins (*Cucurbita maxima*), and other foods—the first known agricultural development along the lower Rio Grande (Castañeda 1938). Matamoros, originally called Refugio, was established in 1796 (maps 2 and 4; Sanchez 1994). The whole area was carved up into ranches during the early 1800s, although human population density remained quite low (Scott 1937).

By the 1820s and 1830s, there seemed to be no unclaimed areas on either side of the Rio Grande, but the area was still lightly populated (241 ranches in the Valley in 1830, 356 by 1833; Tijerina 1994). The habitat had probably not yet been altered much, although grazing by livestock had begun to favor thorny plants at the expense of grassland in some areas. There was only a narrow strip of cultivated land, and essentially no irrigated land, in the Valley during at least the early to mid-1800s (Berlandier 1826–34).

We begin to learn more about Valley habitats beginning with the accounts of Jean Louis Berlandier and Manuel Terán from the 1820s and 1830s. General Terán visited the area during a military expedition; Berlandier accompanied Terán on some trips and then stayed in Matamoros. Both men describe a mixture of grassland and savanna dominated by mesquite, huisache (*Acacia minuata*), and prickly pear cactus (*Opuntia engelmannii*, known as *nopal*) in areas not influenced by Rio Grande floods (Berlandier 1826–34; Jackson 2000). "Immense prairies," probably what Escandón called the Llano de las Flores, began apparently a few miles south of Matamoros and Reynosa and continued south in the flat country for about 85 miles (136 km) to San Fernando, broken only by small mesquite forests. Less is known about the north side of the river, but Berlandier mentions riparian forest, thorn forest, and mesquite savanna. Farther north, "a wilderness of plains . . . covered with small forests of oaks" began about 38 miles (60 km) north of the Arroyo Colorado, forming the grassland with scattered oak mottes (what is now northernmost Willacy and Kenedy counties).

Ecological changes occurred first near the Rio Grande, near settlements. In the uplands between Mier and Camargo, old-time residents reported to Berlandier and Terán in the 1820s that formerly treeless prairies were becoming overgrown with "forests" (Berlandier 1826–34). This probably occurred because of seventy-five years of heavy grazing near the river by a variety of grazing animals.

Along both banks of the Rio Grande between Reynosa and Matamoros were "large plains covered with dense forests," with swamps lining the river-banks from Camargo downriver to at least Matamoros. Roads generally avoided such areas, and we may never know the full extent of these riparian forest-scrub-wetland mosaics, but they undoubtedly covered thousands of hectares. Cedar elm, sugar hackberry, Mexican ash, Texas ebony, and anacua were mentioned frequently, along with mesquite and other smaller trees. Varying amounts of flooding and changes in the river's course probably kept most of these riparian habitats in a state of flux (Berlandier 1826–34).

More limited areas were covered by two tree species that are now extremely rare. West of present-day Falcon Dam, Berlandier saw stands of large Montezuma bald-cypress along the Río Salado, a tributary entering the Rio Grande in what is now Falcon Reservoir. This tropical bald-cypress extended downstream into Starr and Hidalgo counties, with some along the Río San Juan near Camargo, but it evidently never was very widespread in the Valley. At the other end of the Valley, Berlandier mentions palm forests on both banks a short distance downstream from Matamoros. The area now called Southmost (in extreme southeastern Brownsville) evidently supported the largest stands of Texas sabal palm, as it does today, but scattered palms probably extended upriver into what is now southern Hidalgo County.

Numerous resacas (old oxbowlike river channels, called *esteros* in northern Tamaulipas) filled with water after floods, as did isolated, poorly drained depressions (*lagunas*). Dense grasses, vines, and fast-growing shrubs formed low thickets as the water receded, with marshes in poorly drained areas. Dense forests and chaparral were noted most frequently along the higher river and resaca banks. Upland (thorn) forests must have been generally quite open, given the abundance of prickly pear and of Northern Mocking-birds (*Mimus polyglottos*) and the scarcity of herbaceous plants (Berlandier 1826–34; Jackson 2000). Hillier areas around Mier and Camargo were covered with lower thorn scrub, except in arroyos where the vegetation was taller and denser. We know much less about the pre-1850 American side, since naturalists and soldiers generally traveled on the south side of the Rio Grande.

We do not learn much about Valley or South Texas birds from early travelers—and some of what we do learn is quirky. As Berlandier noted, "During the march some soldiers of the vanguard lassoed some turkeys which run about on the plains. After its first flight the bird cannot undertake a second, it . . . flees on foot, aiding itself with its wings. . . . As soon as it falls to the ground it can be lassoed if one has a good horse" (1826–34).

We can assume that now abundant birds such as Great-tailed Grackles and Bronzed Cowbirds must have been less common, mainly limited to river and resaca banks where they could forage in shallow water and on mudflats (Berlandier 1826–34; Skutch 1954). Forest birds like Red-billed Pigeon, Tropical Parula, and Audubon's Oriole (*Icterus graduacauda*) must have been more common and widespread than they are today, and birds like Yellow-breasted Chat (*Icteria virens*) and White-collared Seedeater (*Sporophila torqueola*), using moist, viny tangles, must have been more common.

Well-developed coastal prairie, savanna, and more densely wooded areas were found in and around present-day Brownsville, as a Mexican War soldier noticed in 1846 while marching from Point Isabel to Fort Brown (now Port Isabel and Brownsville): "We marched through a wilderness of mesquite and acacia thickets, fragrant with the blossoms of the latter; the grass was rich; the peavine, with bits of delicate blossom, abundant . . . and everything in nature appeared so happy that it was perfectly exhilarating" (quoted in Horgan 1984).

Brownsville and Matamoros were described as being in a relatively tree-less zone. Forests with taller mesquite, Texas ebony, and cedar elm draped with Spanish moss (*Tillandsia usneoides*) pleased Samuel Curtis in 1847 as his troop marched upstream from Matamoros toward Reynosa (Chance 1994).

There were evidently extensive forests along and near the Rio Grande in what is now southern Hidalgo County in the 1850s. Emory (1857–59) described tall riverbank trees and enthused over the agricultural potential that the luxuriant plant growth of the Valley suggested. However, John Woodhouse Audubon (son of the more famous John James Audubon and a naturalist in his own right) described the trees along the Rio Grande from Brownsville to Rio Grande City as being stunted and wondered if much use would ever be made of the land (Audubon 1906). I assume that J. W. Audubon may have seen only scrubby willows growing along the edge of the low-water channel during a time of drought, while Emory must have seen the taller forest during a time of higher water, when trees along the high-water bank were visible beyond the shorter trees.

To soldiers being ferried upriver during the high water of July, 1846, the country along the banks of the river was "decidedly pleasing," being mesquite thickets mixed with cornfields. The Rio Grande, "seen in stretches, had the appearance of so many lakes embedded in green foliage" (Horgan 1984). High water lasted for several months in 1846, but there was evidence of even higher floods earlier in the year, leaving a residue of silt on the land and causing development of dense, low mesquite thickets (Horgan 1984).

On a return trip during the low water of July, 1847, the riverbanks were 12 feet (3.5 m) above the river: "The country along the river is the same everywhere. On one side we have a perpendicular bank and on the other a sandy beach. At very high stages the whole country must be slightly inundated. Thick [chaparral] grows on the bank so thick a man can hardly crawl through it" (Chance 1994).

The "charming verdure" and also the overwhelming mosquito populations noted in river overflow areas by Berlandier (1826–34) were probably still common during the mid-1800s. Mexican ash, cedar elm, and sugar hackberry were likely the dominant riparian trees in the most mesic sites, with a tall thorn forest of Texas ebony, anacua, coma, brasil, and western soapberry on the next terrace. Undoubtedly there were many successional riverbank areas where lush, low vegetation developed as floodwaters receded (Clover 1937; Davis 1940). Areas that the Rio Grande abandoned as it changed courses must have experienced a type of reverse succession, in which tall trees died, providing nest sites for cavity-nesting birds, and thorny plants quickly invaded.

Upstream from Mier and Roma to where Falcon Dam now stands, the riparian forest was probably shorter, narrower, and more open than it is today, due to periodic flooding that would have scoured the banks. Bartlett (1854) mentions narrow strips of gravel or sand flanked by sparse willows and occasionally Montezuma bald-cypress trees. He does not mention Mexican ash, which is now the dominant tree in the dense, tall riparian forests. Today the riparian forest in southwestern Starr County is the most regularly flooded in the Valley due to the frequent release of water for 2 million people and thousands of hectares of farmland downstream. These are controlled "floods," probably best thought of as regular high water and very different from the former violent floods of the untamed Rio Grande. However, this riparian forest is generally the healthiest and richest in the Valley.

The chaparral—thorn scrub or thorn forest—on the south side of the Rio Grande between Cerralvo and Mier was evidently quite dense, as Bartlett describes 30 miles (48 km) of such habitat before reaching Mier. Likewise on the north side of the river, mesquite, Texas ebony, and other thorny trees were abundant. Away from the river, in what was evidently eastern Starr County and western Hidalgo County, Bartlett (1854) describes an "open plain, amid an abundance of grass."

EARLY ORNITHOLOGY AND EXTENSIVE AGRICULTURE (1870s–1940s)

By the time of businessman and ornithologist George B. Sennett's visits in 1877 and 1878, the riparian forest still shaded dirt roads for miles (Havard 1885) and there were plentiful orioles, Red-billed Pigeons, and other birds now rare in the Valley. Lush bottomland riparian forest remained extensive, stretching in a widening band from Rio Grande City to Brownsville. In the wettest spots, black willows reached 50–70 feet (15–21 m) and Mexican ash 50 feet (15 m). In more typical soils stood anacua up to 20–35 feet (6–11 m) and coma and Wright's acacia trees (*Acacia greggii* var. *wrightii*) of 30 feet (9 m), with shorter huisache, retama (*Parkinsonia aculeata*), brasil, tenaza, and granjeno (*Celtis pallida*) making up these forests. We know little about the habitat along the tributaries, but in 1891 William Lloyd, collecting for the Texas Biological Survey, noted particularly large Texas ebonies along the Río San Juan (Schmidly 2002). Sennett and resident army doctor J. C. Merrill, stationed at Fort Brown, provide an excellent early snapshot of Valley bird life.

By the late 1800s overgrazing had presumably converted more grasslands and savannas into thorn scrub, but intensive agriculture was still difficult due to an undependable water supply to dry areas and a good likelihood of flooding in low spots. Jared G. Smith (1899) lamented a dearth of grass and an abundance of dense chaparral with "close thickets" of various kinds of cactus. Likewise, Edward A. Goldman (1951) described abundant thorn forest and thorn scrub in the Camargo-Mier area across from Rio Grande City and Roma in 1902. These habitats were understandably seen as being more hostile to people than were the moister forests and coastal prairies: "There is nothing of the vegetal world on the Rio Grande, but what is armed with weapons of defense and offense" (McClintock 1931).

Much luxuriant riparian forest remained in the early 1900s. Clover (1937) described the taller riparian forest along the river as *monte del río* (dense riparian forest of the river), in reference to its jungle-like nature, with trees 50 feet (15 m) tall draped in Spanish moss, ball-moss (*Tillandsia recurvata*), and Bailey's ball-moss (*T. baileyi*), over dense understory and herbaceous layers (map 5). Such an area, now part of Santa Ana, was studied by L. Irby Davis, who noted breeding White-collared Seedeaters, Yellow-breasted Chats, Orchard Orioles, and Red-billed Pigeons, with Gray-crowned Yellowthroats (*Geothlypis poliocephala*) in more open, weedy resaca habitats (Davis 1940).

A mixed band of thorn forest and thorn scrub (Clover's *mesquital/chaparral*) occurred farther from the river, with taller, denser woody vegetation in eastern Hidalgo and Cameron counties (Havard's "impenetrable chaparral"), and more widely spaced, stunted shrubs in western Hidalgo and Starr counties (Clover 1937). Naturalist Roy Bedichek (1947) wrote about such semi-open habitat in Starr County: "There is a wide expanse of cactus and mesquite country . . . between Hebbronville, Texas, and the Rio Grande. Mixed in with the cactus and mesquite are many other scrubby, semiarid bushes. This kind of country supports more mockingbirds to the acre than any other, I believe."

Even though the Brownsville area had riparian forests near the river, the dominant trees in 1902 were huisache and mesquite (E. A. Goldman 1951). In 1924, ornithologist Herbert Friedmann (1925), famous for his studies of cowbirds, found typical thorn forest birds within walking distance of what is today downtown. Based on what we know now, Olive Sparrows, Long-billed Thrashers, White-eyed Vireos (*Vireo griseus*), Buff-bellied Hummingbirds, and Orchard Orioles must have been common in the tall thorn forest, while Curve-billed Thrashers (*Toxostoma curvirostre*), Cactus Wrens, Verdins (*Auriparus flaviceps*), and Bewick's Wrens (*Thryomanes bewickii*) may have been more common in thorn scrub.

Much thorn scrub and probably some of the thorn forest were produced in many parts of the Valley by intensive grazing of mesquite savanna in the late 1800s and early 1900s: "The invasion of chaparral vegetation is comparatively recent and thought to be the result of over-grazing and drought . . . it covers the greater part of the territory of the Lower Rio Grande Valley" (Clover 1937). Although there are many uncertainties, this may explain why species like Eastern Bluebird (*Sialia sialis*) have now disappeared or are very rare as breeders in the Valley and may be among the reasons why Painted Buntings (*Passerine ciris*) are uncommon.

Farther from the river, Clover (1937) encountered strips of low, semi-open thorn scrub (her *mesquital/nopalera*), which were probably produced by prolonged grazing in what was once grassland. Mesquite savanna (*mesquital/zacatal*) was pushed farther north, in drier areas, followed by grassland (*zacatal*) only in northernmost sections of the Valley (map 5). We know little about the actual bird life of these habitats, but one can assume that Scissor-tailed Flycatchers (*Tyrannus forficatus*), Cassin's Sparrow (*Aimophila cassinii*), and perhaps Botteri's Sparrow (*A. botterii*) may have been among the regular breeding birds. Very dry, rocky uplands supported a desertlike thorn scrub in parts of Starr County, so desert birds such as Verdin, Black-throated Sparrow (*Amphispiza bilineata*), and Ash-throated Flycatcher (*Myiarchus cinerascens*) must have been common.

The earliest mechanical irrigation began in the Valley in the 1870s on a small scale. However, the arrival of the railroad and development of more widespread irrigation in the early 1900s helped set the stage for rapid agricultural development (Robertson 1985). By the 1920s, an extensive irrigation system was being constructed, allowing for large-scale agriculture to begin, mainly in the eastern and southern parts of the Valley. Irrigation canals continued to be built and land was steadily cleared from the 1920s through the 1950s and beyond. Much land was planted in citrus, and fan palms were often planted along roadsides. The Valley was growing fast. Population increased from 85,861 in 1920 to 176,452 in 1930, but the total was still small compared to today's numbers.

The riparian forest and thorn forest in much of southern Hidalgo County and parts of Cameron and Willacy counties was rapidly removed as the "Magic Valley" was cleared for agriculture in the 1920s–1930s (Wynd 1944). In 1938, only 23 percent of the 522,210 acres of irrigable land in the Valley was still "brush," which I assume may have been a mixture of tall riparian forest, thorn forest, and thorn scrub (Matthews 1938). Presumably most of the losses in the early 1900s were in thorn forest in the delta portions of the Valley, where most of the irrigation districts were created. Tall riparian forest might have remained somewhat more intact, as it still flooded regularly and would thus have been harder to irrigate. The drier thorn scrub and grassland of central and northern Hidalgo County and much of Starr County was basically intact at this time.

Habitat on the Mexican side was more intact through the early to mid-twentieth century—it was described in the 1930s as mainly bunch grass and chaparral with narrow strips of dryland cotton (*Gossypium hirsutum*) and small towns (Dicken 1938). In the 1940s the Presa Marte R. Gomez reservoir, also called Sugar Lake, was completed along the Río San Juan about 10 miles (16 km) south of Camargo (map 2). This reservoir greatly accelerated clearing and irrigation of large tracts of cotton and other crops on the Mexican side; first in the delta lands east of Reynosa, and then (mainly in the 1960s and 1970s) in the slightly higher land west and south of Reynosa (Smith 1961; Oberholser 1974).

Up until the 1950s, Red-billed Pigeons, Tropical Parulas, Audubon's Orioles, and Summer Tanagers (*Piranga rubra*) were at least fairly common and widespread in riparian forest, Hooded Orioles (*Icterus cucullatus*) nested in palms or other native trees and flew out into agricultural fields to forage, and White-collared Seedeaters were fairly widespread in grassy, overgrown resaca beds. However, Aplomado Falcons (*Falco femoralis*) disappeared from the Valley early in the century, possibly due to extensive egg collecting as well as poorly known habitat changes.

MODERN DEVELOPMENT AND
FLOOD CONTROL (1950s – 2000)

The construction of Falcon Dam in the early 1950s greatly reduced the frequency of flooding and allowed more land to be settled and cleared for agriculture (Jahrsdoerfer and Leslie 1988; see map 5 in this chapter and map 6 in the color section). "During the last three years, especially, native trees and brush have been destroyed by the thousands of acres in the Lower Rio Grande Valley to open more land for farming," noted Luther C. Goldman (1951), an early refuge manager at the Santa Ana and Laguna Atascosa national wildlife refuges.

In many areas only a narrow strip of vegetation remains on the steep riverbank between large agricultural fields and the Rio Grande. During periods of severe drought since then, such as the 1970s and 1990s, several groves of tall riparian trees have died, and forest has been replaced by thorn forest or thorn scrub (Brush and Cantu 1998). Existing areas of thorn forest have probably become much denser in the absence of prolonged flooding that would kill most drought-tolerant trees and shrubs (John C. Arvin, in Webster 1968a). Resacas have become choked with wetland plants, as there is seldom a scouring effect of extreme flood events (R. J. Fleetwood, in Webster 1972a).

Between the 1920s and 1980s, 91 percent of Cameron County woodlands and savannas were cleared, mainly for agriculture (Thomas A. Tremblay and William A. White, unpubl. data). This severe habitat loss and fragmentation of remaining habitat must have been a factor contributing to the loss of Audubon's Oriole, Varied Bunting, and Vermilion Flycatcher (*Pyrocephalus rubinus*) from the Cameron County breeding avifauna.

The great freeze of 1951 decimated citrus orchards and encouraged farmers to grow other crops like sorghum (*Sorghum bicolor*) and cotton, which were less favorable to birds. Increased pesticide use and increasing sizes of fields could both have hindered nesting efforts of Hooded Orioles, although there is no direct evidence. Continued land clearing favored Great-tailed Grackles and Bronzed Cowbirds while causing declines in Tropical Parulas, Red-billed Pigeons, and Audubon's and Hooded orioles (Oberholser 1974).

Although this effect is not as well documented, large areas of freshwater wetlands have been lost due to greatly reduced flooding (Jahrsdoerfer and Leslie 1988), likely reducing populations of Least Bitterns (*Ixobrychus exilis*), Common Moorhens (*Gallinula chloropus*), Gray-crowned Yellowthroats, and other marsh and marsh-edge birds. Most remaining wetlands are either artificially maintained freshwater marshes, as at Santa Ana; brackish and salt marshes affected by coastal flooding, near the Laguna Madre; or sporadic freshwater wetlands associated with heavy rainfall (Judd and Lonard 2002).

Federal subsidies encouraged the clearing of the drier thorn scrub in northern and western sections of the Valley in the 1960s and 1970s (Longoria 1997). Some of these areas have now grown back into thorn scrub or mesquite savanna, while other areas are used to grow dryland (no-irrigation) crops. Similarly, more than 232,000 hectares of land were cleared on the Mexican side during 1975–79, at the height of land clearing in northern Tamaulipas (Zorrilla and Salinas-Dominguez 1994). Again the effects were not well studied, but common species such as Green Jays, Long-billed Thrashers, and Golden-fronted Woodpeckers must have declined in areas that were so extensively cleared. Such processes continued through the rest of the twentieth century, although beginning to be somewhat balanced in the 1990s by revegetation of farmland purchased for the new Lower Rio Grande Valley National Wildlife Refuge (LRGV NWR) and other newly protected lands.

Mainly toward the end of the twentieth century, various introduced plants began to establish themselves in the Valley. Some of these have had little effect, while others have altered habitats and possibly affected some bird species (either positively or negatively). Some of the more successful Valley invaders have been grasses, such as guineagrass, buffelgrass, and Johnson grass (*Sorghum halepense*). Guineagrass readily invades riparian forest and old agricultural fields and may become dominant, potentially competing with native herbaceous plants and seedlings of woody plants. Buffelgrass may cause similar problems in pastures, on canal banks, and in thorn scrub and mesquite savanna habitat (Lonard et al. 2000; Lonard and Judd 2002). The direct effects, if any, of guineagrass and buffelgrass on Valley bird life are unknown, but these and other introduced grasses may make it harder to maintain or restore native grasslands and wooded habitats. Invading woody plants have had modest impacts thus far, although shrubby salt cedars may eventually be more of a problem in increasingly saline soils. Chinese tallow (*Sapium sebiferum*), a major problem in prairie maintenance and restoration efforts on the upper Texas Coast, is thus far rare outside cultivation in the Valley.

In the 1990s Valley residents became aware of the growing problem of hydrilla in the Rio Grande and irrigation canals. This "perfect aquatic weed" (Langeland 1996) has become dense enough to slow water movement and cause concern to water managers. So far the effects of hydrilla on bird life are poorly known, although casual observations suggest that certain species may benefit: wintering waterfowl such as Gadwall (*Anas strepera*), American Wigeon (*Anas americana*), and American Coot (*Fulica americana*) all are common in areas dominated by hydrilla, and they probably eat some. Migratory shorebirds such as Least Sandpipers (*Calidris minutilla*), Spotted Sandpipers (*Actitis macularus*), and Lesser Yellowlegs (*Tringa flavipes*) all forage by walking on the surface of hydrilla beds. Longer-term impacts of hydrilla on the health of aquatic and possibly riparian ecosystems remain to be determined.

Although not a major focus of this book, coastal land development and dredging to create and maintain ship channels have affected coastal birds and their habitats. Benefits such as creation of new islands for colonial waterbird colonies may be outweighed by deterioration or destruction of sea-grass meadows, intertidal flats, and existing nesting colonies (Tunnell et al. 2002).

While some bird species were declining, those capable of using human-made habitats have increased, and several species have "invaded" the Valley during that time, beginning with Altamira Orioles in the 1950s. Purple Martins (*Progne subis*), Ringed Kingfishers (*Ceryle torquatus*), and Western Kingbirds (*Tyrannus verticalis*) followed in the 1970s; Green Parakeets (*Aratinga holochlora*) and Red-crowned Parrots (*Amazona viridigenalis*) in the 1980s; and Chimney Swifts (*Chaetura pelagica*), Tropical Kingbirds (*Tyrannus melancholicus*), and Cave Swallows (*Petrochelidon fulva*) in the 1990s. Black Phoebes and Lesser Goldfinches (*Carduelis psaltria*) began to be noted around the turn of the millennium.

As is discussed further in the species accounts, "human-tolerant" species continue to increase, while forest species and those needing large tracts of native habitat continue to lose ground.

HABITATS AND BIRDS
OF THE VALLEY

May 20: Birds—birds—birds! Luther Goldman and Roger [Tory Peterson]
showed me more birds today than I have ever seen in any one day before....
Orioles were everywhere—Hooded Oriole, mostly—and their nests must
have been hidden in the Spanish moss.

JAMES FISHER, BRITISH ORNITHOLOGIST

Flat in topography and with a generally uniform climate, the Valley nonetheless presents six distinct habitat complexes. Because individual habitats
usually grade into each other, it seems best to discuss general habitat types
here. In each habitat complex, distinct habitats generally exist as mosaics,
with gradual changes rather than striking differences between them. Exceptions are found in the steeper topography of Starr County bluffs and
in coastal areas, where salinity, wave energy, and soil type may vary more
dramatically.

BARRIER BEACHES, COASTAL WETLANDS,
AND THE LAGUNA MADRE

The salt water of the Gulf of Mexico and the Laguna Madre is a dominant
influence on South Padre Island, other barrier beaches, and the adjacent
mainland. The soil is sandy on South Padre Island, which varies from 0.3 to
3 miles (0.45–4.8 km) in width, and on Brazos Island, currently connected
to the mainland in the Boca Chica area. Typical habitats include broad
sandy beaches, sand dunes, interdune and backdune swales, and high
sandflats, algal flats, and low (intertidal) sandflats. Trees are absent except
where planted and watered. In the shallow Laguna Madre, with an average
depth of only 3 feet (1 m), much area is covered by sea-grasses, particularly
turtle grass (*Thalassia testudinum*), shoal grass (*Halodule beaudettei*), and
manatee grass (*Cymodocea filiformis*). On both sides of the Laguna Madre,

salt marshes of smooth cordgrass (*Spartina alterniflora*) or marshhay cord-grass (*Spartina patens*) are few and far between. High salinity, prolonged ex-posure, high temperatures, and little freshwater input leave vast areas un-vegetated, with only a crust of blue-green algae (Cyanobacteria) in the highly productive algal flats (Tunnell and Judd 2002).

On the mainland side, semitidal clay flats covered sparsely with salt-tolerant plants give way to clay "dunes" (*lomas*) covered with coastal prairie or low thorn scrub. There are many "part-time wetlands" near the coast, de-pending on seasonal and annual rainfall, wind direction, and tidal patterns. Some of these areas are covered with a mat of blue-green algae and perhaps sparse glasswort (*Salicornia* spp.). Others contain a variety of salt-tolerant herbaceous plants and shrubs, such saltwort (*Batis maritima*), sea ox-eye daisy (*Borrichia frutescens*), and saltgrass (*Distichlis spicata*). These wetlands can support high numbers of birds when moist or covered with shallow wa-ter (Brush 1995; Withers 2002).

Several kinds of striking ornithological events occur on the coast. Among the most dramatic are feeding "frenzies" in which several hundred Reddish Egrets (*Egretta rufescens*), from the largest Reddish Egret colony in the world, exploit schools of small fish in shallow water over unvegetated flats. Another spectacle is the gathering of dense mixed-species feeding flocks of shorebirds attracted by wind-driven exposure of many acres of intertidal flats, when a cold front and a wind shift to the north expose mudflats that are normally not available to shorebirds. Long-billed Dowitchers (*Limnodromus scolopaceus*), Black-bellied Plovers (*Pluvialis squatarola*), and Western Sand-pipers (*Calidris mauri*) are particularly abundant, but some of the largest winter numbers anywhere of the declining Piping Plover (*Charadrius melo-dus*) are here. Both Piping Plovers and Snowy Plovers (*Charadrius alexan-drinus*) make great use of algal flats on the bay side of South Padre Island.

Large flocks of wintering ducks, particularly Northern Pintail (*Anas acuta*) and Redhead (*Aythya americana*), winter in the Lower Laguna Madre, eating mainly sea-grass. Fish-eating birds besides the Reddish Egrets already mentioned are abundant in both summer and winter. The Brown Pelican (*Pelecanus occidentalis*), which occurs year-round and has long been on the comeback trail, dives spectacularly into the water when fishing. Wintering American White Pelicans (*Pelecanus erythrorhynchos*) forage in groups, swimming together and forcing their prey up against the shore, where it is scooped out of the water and consumed. Double-crested Cormorants (*Phalacrocorax auritus*) winter in large numbers, and there are breeding colonies of at last six species of terns (*Sterna* spp.), most of them fish eaters.

Peregrine Falcons (*Falco peregrinus*), recently removed from the endangered species list, migrate through and winter in the Lower Laguna Madre, taking advantage of the abundant wading birds and waterfowl to provide food and of the expansive sandflats to provide undisturbed resting areas.

Although woody plants are generally scarce near the coast, tired migratory birds flock to any such areas during rainy weather—to scrubby vacant lots on South Padre Island, the lomas near the mouth of the Rio Grande, and the more extensive thorny thickets on the western side of the Lower Laguna Madre and near the mouth of the river. After such migratory "fallouts" the birds remain only until the weather improves, at which stage they move on.

Coastal prairie with scattered treelike Spanish daggers (*Yucca treculeana*) once supported a breeding population of Aplomado Falcons, but these birds disappeared early in the twentieth century. Reintroduction efforts in the 1990s have begun to establish a breeding population, and there is hope of long-term success. This species and most of the coastal prairie bird life are discussed later under the prairies and savannas habitat complex because of many similarities in the respective breeding bird communities.

Several species thought of as strictly coastal also occur inland areas where their habitats are found. The Salt Lakes area of eastern Hidalgo County and western Willacy County supports breeding Black Skimmers (*Rynchops niger*), Gull-billed Terns (*Sterna nilotica*), Snowy Plovers, and Wilson's Plovers (*Charadrius wilsonia*), the latter perhaps sporadically.

FRESHWATER PONDS, MARSHES, AND RIVERS

Although not covering large areas, these aquatic habitats are vital to many birds. Open water is usually shallow enough to attract wading birds and puddle ducks; diving ducks and cormorants are more common in deeper water. Mudflats are usually quite limited in size, forcing most shorebirds elsewhere. In shallow water and in old river channels, dense stands of cattails (*Typha domingensis*), bulrushes (*Scirpus* spp.), common reed, and other herbaceous plants are suitable for marsh birds. At marsh edges, woody plants (particularly willows) invade, providing rich foraging areas for many bird species. Generally, marshes and ponds are scarcest in Starr County and become more common toward the coast, until one reaches the more saline coastal sections of Willacy and Starr counties. Many ponds and marshes have been drained for flood control, agriculture, and urban development, and the Rio Grande and its distributary the Arroyo Colorado flood much less frequently than in earlier years.

Densely vegetated wetlands provide breeding habitat for Common Yellowthroat (including the declining Cameron County subspecies, the

"Brownsville Yellowthroat"), King Rail (*Rallus elegans*), Least Bittern, and other species.

Abundant fish attract sizable flocks of Neotropic Cormorants, especially near the Falcon Reservoir breeding colonies. Good numbers of wintering Ospreys (*Pandion haliaetus*) and Belted Kingfishers (*Ceryle alcyon*) join the resident Green Kingfishers (*Chloroceryle americana*) and Ringed Kingfishers. The latter two species are rarely found on salt water in the Valley; they depend on suitable freshwater habitats.

Many wintering puddle ducks—especially Northern Shoveler (*Anas clypeata)*, Gadwall, American Wigeon, and Blue-winged Teal (*Anas discors*)—feed and rest on ponds and on stretches of the river with abundant aquatic plants. As is detailed later, several terrestrial birds nest or forage at the water's edge, taking advantage of safe nesting sites over the water, like the Altamira Oriole, or of rich food resources near or in the water, like the Great Kiskadee (*Pitangus sulphuratus*), Couch's Kingbird (*Tyrannus couchii*), and other species.

Small ponds edged with marshes attract breeding Least Grebes—these ponds may be temporary ones, but the water is usually clear—while larger ponds seem to attract more Pied-billed Grebes (*Podilymbus podiceps*) and fewer Least Grebes. Although not truly migratory, the Least Grebe moves around somewhat in response to rainfall patterns. Flocks of up to a hundred sometimes build up on certain ponds, only to disappear as individuals move on.

When mudflats or shallow waters are available during the migration season, large numbers of shorebirds may be attracted—especially Pectoral Sandpiper (*Calidris melanotos*), Stilt Sandpiper (*Calidris himantopus*), White-rumped Sandpiper (*Calidris fuscicollis*), and Wilson's Phalarope (*Phalaropus tricolor*).

RIPARIAN FOREST

Only growing in areas with adequate soil moisture, riparian (streamside) forests contain taller trees and more luxuriant vegetation than do other wooded habitats. Mexican ash, black willow, sugar hackberry, and cedar elm are common in moister sites, while Texas ebony, anacua, and coma grow on higher, drier terraces. Texas ebony, anacua, and coma are absent from or rare in riparian forests farther north, such as along the San Antonio River (Van Auken and Bush 1985), and Valley terrace forest, or Texas ebony–anacua evergreen forest, is considered a globally threatened habitat (McLendon 1991). Spanish moss and ball-moss are common epiphytes if the forest is somewhat open, providing foraging and nesting sites for birds in the more humid forests. When riparian woodlands are limited to narrow strips, often less than 50 feet (15 m) wide along the river, they are less valuable to birds but still provide roosting cover for herons and other large waterbirds. Even a few scattered tall trees can be beneficial, if there is thorn forest nearby.

Of greatest value to birds are the larger stands of riparian forest, especially when well supplied with water, but these are becoming less common due to greatly reduced flood frequency (especially since the 1953 construction of Falcon Dam). Periodic droughts are probably the factor triggering death of many large trees. In these areas, a "reverse succession" allows thorny trees and shrubs—retama, huisache, prickly pear, granjeno, and others—to invade when released from competition with the taller trees for light.

Remaining riparian forests support some of the rarest breeding birds in the United States: Muscovy Duck, Gray Hawk, Red-billed Pigeon, Rose-throated Becard, Northern Beardless-Tyrannulet, Brown Jay, Clay-colored Robin, Altamira Oriole, and Tropical Parula. More widespread North American species at or near the southern edge of their breeding range include Wood Duck, Red-shouldered Hawk, Summer Tanager, and Yellow-breasted Chat. Not all these species are limited to riparian forest, but many depend on it for key nesting or foraging habitat. All these are discussed in the species accounts and summaries.

THORN FOREST AND THORN SCRUB

This mosaic of habitats is more common than riparian forests, although also greatly reduced in coverage, and some former riparian forest has been converted into thorn forest as lack of flooding takes its toll. The habitat many people see while driving on Valley roads is low, semi-open mesquite–prickly pear or huisache-retama scrub. These habitats develop in pastures, abandoned fields, or drainage areas and are of little value to most breeding birds. Rarer but more valuable are dense, mature stands of thorn scrub or chaparral 3–10 feet (1–3 m) high and taller thorn forest 13–20 feet (4–6 m) or more in height. These habitats, sometimes collectively known as *monte,* share honey mesquite, Texas ebony, brasil, coma, guayacán (*Guaiacum angusti-folium*), anacua, colima, Texas persimmon (*Diospyros texana*), and many other plant species. Plant growth form and stature vary, depending on soil type and soil moisture. In some dense thorn scrub, the main canopy is at only 6–10 feet (2–3 m), with emergent trees reaching 13–20 feet (4–6 m) or more in height. In thorn forest, the main canopy may be at 16–20 feet (5–6 m). Thorn scrub is still fairly widespread in Starr County and the northern fringes of Hidalgo and Willacy counties (see map 6 in color section).

Some of the more successful Valley specialty bird species are common in thorn forest as well as in the denser riparian forests; example are the White-tipped Dove (*Leptotila verreauxi*), Golden-fronted Woodpecker (*Melanerpes aurifrons*), Green Jay, Long-billed Thrasher, and Olive Sparrow. Thorn scrub supports a somewhat different bird community than thorn forest, although many species are common in both habitats. Pyrrhuloxias (*Cardinalis sinuatus*), Northern Mockingbirds, and Cactus Wrens (*Campylorhynchus brunneicapillus*) seem particularly characteristic of thorn scrub rather than thorn forest, especially where thorn scrub intergrades with mesquite savanna. Verdins, Bewick's Wrens, and even cavity nesters like Golden-fronted Woodpecker and Brown-crested Flycatcher (*Myiarchus tyrannulus*) may be common. Lark Sparrows (*Chondestes grammacus*) may breed if the thorn scrub has clearings or is open enough. Scaled Quail (*Callipepla squamata*) are common in drier thorn scrub, while Northern Bobwhite (*Colinus virginianus*) are more common in more mesic, grassy thorn scrub or savanna. Ash-throated Flycatcher and Black-tailed Gnatcatcher occur in low thorn scrub dominated by blackbrush acacia (*Acacia rigidula*, also known as *chaparro prieto*) and cenizo (*Leucophyllum frutescens*). Allthorn goat-bush (*Castela erecta*, also called *amargosa*) and fiddlewood (or *negrito*) are particularly common in low thorn scrub near the Laguna Madre.

PRAIRIES AND SAVANNAS

Strictly speaking, prairies are habitats containing only grasses and other herbaceous (nonwoody) plants. Savannas are habitats dominated by grasses and other herbaceous plants but with scattered trees or shrubs. By these definitions, there is more savanna than prairie in the Valley. Most remaining prairies and savannas are along the northern, western, and eastern fringes of the Valley. South Texas grasslands are considered "depauperate" in breeding birds, at least by North American standards. Of North American species for which primary habitat is grassland, only Cassin's Sparrow and Eastern Meadowlark (*Sturnella magna*) are common breeders in the Valley (Johnsgard 2001). However, with the addition of some Mexican species, the Valley's grassland avifauna widens. White-tailed Kites (*Elanus leucurus*) and White-tailed Hawks (*Buteo albicaudatus*) forage regularly over Valley grasslands. Cassin's Sparrow is a widespread breeder, while Botteri's Sparrow occurs only in coastal sections, especially where Gulf cordgrass (*Spartina spartinae*, also called *sacahuista*) forms tall, dense stands. Eastern Meadowlarks are probably the most common breeders in inland treeless grasslands and open savannas, with Horned Larks (*Eremophila alpestris*) in more heavily grazed or saline patches. Mesquite savannas and very open thorn scrub support numerous Common Ground-Doves (*Columbina passerina*), Scissor-tailed Flycatchers, and Lark Sparrows, while Vermilion Flycatchers breed in savannas near water on the northern and western fringes of the Valley.

SUBURBAN, URBAN, AND RURAL HABITATS

Some of these areas are almost useless to the majority of birds. Urban shopping areas are mainly used only by Rock Pigeons (*Columba livia*), House Sparrows, and Great-tailed Grackles, and huge agricultural fields are used by these species plus Red-winged Blackbirds (*Agelaius phoeniceus*) and cowbirds. Well-vegetated suburban or rural residential areas, in contrast, support a great variety of nesting birds, such as Green Parakeet, Red-crowned Parrot, Great Kiskadee, White-winged Dove (*Zenaida asiatica*), Northern Mockingbird, Purple Martin, and kingbirds. Plain Chachalacas (*Ortalis vetula*) seem to be doing well in particularly lush residential areas, but the jury is still out on species like Green Jay and Hooded Oriole. Are their urban populations viable, or are they merely a spill-over for birds coming from nearby native habitats?

THE SPECTACULAR
ANNUAL CYCLE

This region offers an excellent field for the ornithologist. Besides a very large number of northern migrants that either remain throughout the winter or pass farther south, there are many forms characteristic of the river valley, and other Mexican species, either regular summer visitors or stragglers that are new to the United States fauna.

JAMES C. MERRILL, MEDICAL DOCTOR
AT FORT BROWN DURING THE 1870S

Despite the limited annual temperature range and lack of a true winter, the bird life of the Valley shows marked seasonal changes in breeding activity, and there are heavy spring and fall migrations through the area. In general, species breeding in northern and central North America either winter in the Valley or pass through it twice a year on their way to and from their neotropical wintering grounds.

Most Valley breeders are nonmigratory or show partial migration, in which some individuals move south while others remain. A few species completely vacate the Valley in winter, most noticeably the aerial insectivores, which are dependent on a warm-weather food source. Species that capture insects on leaves, branches, or on the ground may have a more stable food supply, although they may have to move south in greater numbers in colder winters. They may also supplement their diet by eating fruits, which are often abundant during fall and winter. Raptors, fish-eating birds, and species that consume seeds have a greater tendency to winter here, because their food supply is more reliable.

WINTER (DECEMBER – FEBRUARY)

When winter comes to the Valley, ducks and geese, cranes, shorebirds, warblers, kinglets, flycatchers, hawks, and sparrows arrive to join the permanently resident kiskadees, kingfishers, orioles, woodpeckers, chachalacas, hawks, and other species. Waxwings, robins, bluebirds, and other wintering frugivores irregularly arrive as well. Many species travel in flocks as they look for abundant sources of seeds, fruits, or insects.

Some permanent residents begin singing in January (Long-billed Thrasher, Northern Cardinal) and others may nest, especially in mild winters (Buff-bellied Hummingbird, Lesser Goldfinch). Strong north winds now (and during spring and fall) expose vast areas of sandflats and algal flats along the Lower Laguna Madre, drawing in large numbers of herons, egrets, plovers, sandpipers, and other species that feed on aquatic invertebrates or fish.

The deciduous trees and shrubs in the Valley generally do not lose their leaves until November or December, even January in mild winters. Many begin leafing out in mid-February to early March, producing a springlike appearance in Valley towns and riparian forests. Generally, leafing out and flowering proceeds from east to west across the Valley. However, coastal spots like South Padre Island and the Boca Chica area lag a little behind Brownsville and Harlingen, probably because of cool winds off the water. Warm February days also induce some wintering cranes and ducks to begin their northward migration, while some herons begin nesting in the Laguna Madre.

SPRING (MARCH – MAY)

The arrival of spring migrants and the increased activity of permanent residents partially fills the void left by the departure of winter residents, but there can be a gap, particularly during March, when fewer birds are seen. Spring migration picks up by late March and April. Broad-winged Hawks (*Buteo platypterus*), Swainson's Hawks (*Buteo swainsoni*), Mississippi Kites (*Ictinia mississippiensis*), and Turkey Vultures (*Cathartes aura*) migrate north in large numbers, often roosting in remnant riparian forests or well-wooded urban areas. Fallouts of migratory warblers, flycatchers, buntings, orioles, and other species during rainy weather can be spectacular along the coast and in prime habitats inland, especially in April and early May.

Winter and spring rains, if they occur, trigger plant growth—flowers spring up in riparian woodlands, thorn forest, and grasslands—and help stimulate the beginning of the breeding season. Permanent residents may begin nesting in March or April, while summer residents do not start until May. Late migrants such as *Empidonax* flycatchers, Mourning Warblers (*Oporornis philadelphia*), and others still are passing through from mid-May into early June, when the nesting season for local species is in full swing.

EARLY SUMMER (JUNE – JULY)

Traditionally considered a "down" time by birders, early summer, especially June, is a time of intense activity for local breeding birds. Many species try to raise one or more broods of young in the face of fairly short days (compared to more northern latitudes), high predation pressure, and an unpredictable food supply. Fascinating nesting behaviors and adaptations can be seen by anyone willing to brave the elements and careful enough not to disturb the nesting birds.

Ground nests are usually just shallow scrapes in the soft ground, with or without any nesting material. Local examples include nests of the Common Pauraque (*Nyctidromus albicollis*), Northern Bobwhite, Snowy Plover, Horned Lark, terns, gulls (*Larus* spp.), and some ducks and herons. I also include "floating nests" built by grebes, since these nests may rest on the bottom in shallow water. Ground nests built in low-lying areas are often flooded, resulting in nest failures.

Burrow nests are excavated in vertical banks of dirt or firm sand. They are often located in erosional banks (cut-banks) of the river, sometimes in areas where gravel, caliche, or sand are being excavated. Some birds use existing burrows, while others make new ones. Local burrow nesters include kingfishers, Bank Swallow, Northern Rough-winged Swallow (*Stelgidopteryx serripennis*), Barn Owl (*Tyto alba*), and possibly Black Vulture (*Coragyps atratus*) and Muscovy Duck. The reduced fluctuations of the river in recent times may have aided some of these species by providing more predictable nesting conditions.

Platform nests may consist of a thin layer of sticks, easily seen through, or a massive accumulation of many sticks added to for several years. Doves, most herons, Neotropic Cormorant, Greater Roadrunner (*Geococcyx californianus*), hawks, and other species build such nests. Usually platform nests are placed in trees.

Cup nests are typically deeper than platform nests and are made of softer materials. Most passerines build such nests, including many flycatchers, warblers, thrushes, and sparrows. Hummingbirds build very small cup nests, often held together with spiderwebs and covered with lichens. Cup nests are usually placed in trees or shrubs, sometimes between narrow twigs and sometimes resting on top of thicker branches. In the Valley, Northern Mockingbirds and Green Jays often incorporate thorny twigs in their nests.

Domed nests are roofed cup nests, better protected from predators and weather than are either cup or platform nests. The Great Kiskadee, Cactus Wren, Tropical Parula, Northern Beardless-Tyrannulet, and Verdin build such nests.

Hanging nests include the long, pendant structures of Altamira Orioles, which sway in the breeze over open space. The shorter, more hidden nests of vireos are technically hanging nests, because only the rim of the nest is attached. However, I include the vireos among the cup nesters because of similar nesting locations. Bullock's Orioles (*Icterus bullockii*), Hooded Orioles, and Rose-throated Becards build typical hanging nests, from 5 inches (13 cm) to more than two feet (0.6 m) in length. The number of suitable nesting trees may limit populations of birds building typical hanging nests.

Cavity nests include those excavated by woodpeckers in wood, and those developing through other natural processes, such as rot or limb breakage. Species using existing cavities include parrots and parakeets, which may enlarge existing cavities, and a variety of other birds, such as Brown-crested Flycatcher, Black-crested Titmouse (*Baeolophus atricristatus*), European Starling (*Sturnus vulgaris*), Bewick's Wren, and some ducks and owls. Cavity nests are cooler in hot weather and warmer in cold weather than are more exposed nests, and they are harder for predators to access. Currently, due to the recent deaths of many large riparian trees, there seem to be plenty of suitable nest sites in locations such as Bentsen and Santa Ana. However, in other times and places, this may not be the case (Gibbs et al. 1993), and nest boxes may be useful to enhance local populations or for studying nesting activities.

Nests in artificial structures may be cup nests built in holes or crevices, mud nests attached to concrete walls, or platform nests placed on towers or buildings. Species mainly or only nesting on artificial structures in the Valley include Rock Dove, Chimney Swift, Black Phoebe, House Sparrow, Cliff Swallow (*Petrochelidon pyrrhonota*), Cave Swallow, and Purple Martin. Most or all of these birds did not occur in the Valley before settlement, and some have apparently invaded within the last ten years.

LATE SUMMER (AUGUST – SEPTEMBER)

While some Valley birds are finished nesting and go into their quiet, postbreeding molt, others (Northern Beardless-Tyrannulet, Red-billed Pigeon, and other doves) are still nesting, especially if rainfall has been adequate. Meanwhile, despite the general lack of "autumnal" weather, migration of both land birds and shorebirds is heavy. The hot, humid weather discourages fieldwork, and the dense foliage allows many forest birds to pass unseen, but this is the peak time for migration of insectivorous neotropical migrants, which are escaping the north woods just before cold weather obliterates their food supply.

In September and early October, large numbers of Broad-winged Hawks and Swainson's Hawks and smaller numbers of other raptors pass through, often coming to roost spectacularly in tall trees, wherever these occur. Meanwhile, tail-less Great-tailed Grackles—waiting for their new tail feathers to grow in—look strange as they fly around towns and agricultural areas. The Valley normally experiences its heaviest rains in September, which help fill ponds and support continued plant growth.

FALL (OCTOBER – NOVEMBER)

October can still be hot, but cool fronts or northers occur with greater frequency as the fall progresses. This ends the nesting season for nearly all local birds, pushing some of them southward to avoid our winter months. Among the species concerned are Least Tern (*Sterna antillarum*), Neotropic Cormorant (most individuals), Groove-billed Ani (*Crotophaga sulcirostris*, nearly all individuals), Scissor-tailed Flycatcher, Common Nighthawk, Brown-crested Flycatcher, and Couch's Kingbird (most individuals).

The second wave of fall migrants arrives, bringing hardier species, many of which will winter in the Valley: sparrows, hawks, ducks, geese, Ring-billed Gull, Sandhill Crane, American Kestrel, Yellow-bellied Sapsucker, Loggerhead Shrike, Eastern Phoebe, Eastern Bluebird, Ruby-crowned Kinglet, Blue-gray Gnatcatcher, Orange-crowned Warbler, Yellow-rumped Warbler, and others. Sometimes fall-like conditions extend well into December, but at some point colder temperatures push out the last of the lingering fall migrants. This leaves the winter and permanent residents to ride out the winter.

BREEDING BIRDS
OF THE VALLEY

Then felt I like some watcher of the skies
When a new planet swims into his ken.

JOHN KEATS, POET

The breeding bird life of the Valley, like the assemblage of woody plants, is a mixture of species typical of quite different habitats and climatic regions. Some birds are widespread temperate species like Bank Swallow, Northern Mockingbird, Red-winged Blackbird, and Lark Sparrow, with ranges extending south into and usually beyond the Valley. Others are more limited in their U.S. distribution—more typically western (for example, Swainson's Hawk), southwestern or non-tropical Mexican (Hooded Oriole), southeastern (White-eyed Vireo), or occurring mainly in the south-central United States (Scissor-tailed Flycatcher). A tropical/Mexican element is strong, with species like Altamira Oriole, Plain Chachalaca, and Red-billed Pigeon barely reaching the United States but having extensive ranges in the tropics.

GENERAL PATTERNS

The ranges of some of our tropical species, like Great Kiskadee, Least Grebe (*Tachybaptus dominicus*), and Neotropic Cormorant, extend all the way to southern South America. Others are limited to Mexico and Central America, like Olive Sparrow, Red-billed Pigeon, and Northern Beardless-Tyrannulet. Desert species like Verdin and Cactus Wren breed within earshot of forest species like Carolina Wren (*Thryothorus ludovicianus*), Red-shouldered Hawk (*Buteo lineatus*), and Clay-colored Robin. Likewise, salt marsh species like Seaside Sparrow (*Ammodramus maritimus*) and Willet (*Catoptrophorus semipalmatus*) may breed within a few hundred meters of the grassland-nesting White-tailed Hawk (*Buteo albicaudatus*) or

Aplomado Falcon and thorn scrub species like Olive Sparrow and Long-billed Thrasher.

Many species, including American Robin (*Turdus migratorius*), Northern Flicker (*Colaptes auratus*), and White-breasted Nuthatch (*Sitta carolinensis*), occur in temperate-zone habitats that extend from the United States into the highlands of central Mexico. Most of these species do not breed in the coastal plains of South Texas and eastern Mexico, although some have invaded this area in recent years, like the Barn Swallow (*Hirundo rustica*) and Loggerhead Shrike (*Lanius ludovicianus*). Thus a birder who grew up in the northern or central United States may find more familiar breeding species by going up into the Mexican Sierra Madre Oriental mountains than by staying in the Valley and nearby lowland areas. Likewise, the birder from coastal Veracruz or Tabasco may find more similar breeding birds by going north all the way to the Valley than going up into the nearby Mexican mountains.

Habitats in which Valley specialties are most prominent include riparian forest (both the deciduous and evergreen varieties), thorn forest, thorn scrub, and freshwater wetlands, with smaller numbers in mesquite savanna, grasslands, and urban/suburban habitats. For example one's first visit to South Texas may be to Santa Ana, which is a mixture of all these habitats except grasslands. Green Jays, Altamira Orioles, Couch's Kingbirds, and Tropical Parulas are just a few of the forest or scrub birds one may see, while Green Kingfishers, Ringed Kingfishers, Least Grebes, and Neotropic Cormorants may be found in wetland areas. Great Kiskadees and Groove-billed Anis may be seen at wetland edges or in scrub and forest. Grasslands and mesquite savanna, especially near the coast, support Cassin's Sparrow, Botteri's Sparrow, White-tailed Kite, and Painted Bunting. Valley cities support a few species not found much in native habitats, notably Green Parakeet and Red-crowned Parrot.

BIOGEOGRAPHY

Despite the tremendous diversity of the bird community, the Valley has no endemic species—that is, species restricted to this geographic area. This is perhaps not surprising, since the Valley's is within 200 miles (320 km) of both the tropics and the temperate zone, with no major geographic barriers in between. Over time, as habitats and climates have changed, species have been able to spread into and through the Valley from all directions.

From one point of view, the Valley can be thought of as an extension of the Gulf–Caribbean Slope zoogeographic region of Mexico and Central America (Stotz et al. 1996). This lowland area has few natural barriers to bird dispersal, so there are relatively few endemic bird species until one reaches the Yucatan Peninsula with its isolated dry forests. The northern section of this region (Tamaulipas, eastern Nuevo León, and northernmost Veracruz) supports several endemic species.

One of these, the Tamaulipas Crow (*Corvus imparatus*), extended its range into the Brownsville area in the 1960s and still barely maintains a tiny breeding population there. Altamira Yellowthroat (*Geothlypis flavovelata*) occurs in southern Tamaulipas and northern Veracruz and is replaced along the Rio Grande by the very similar Common Yellowthroat, represented by a unique Valley subspecies. The beautiful Crimson-collared Grosbeak (*Rhodothraupis celaeno*) occurs in tropical deciduous forest and montane scrub as far north as the Monterrey area of Nuevo León and is an acciden- tal winter visitor to the Valley. The Red-crowned Parrot is a declining regional endemic (in need of continuing protection) in southern Nuevo Leon, central and southern Tamaulipas, and northern Veracruz. Successful invasion of the Valley by Red-crowned Parrots and Green Parakeets and the current status of these birds are discussed in the species accounts.

Although the lower Rio Grande area does not have endemic species, several subspecies are endemic to the Valley or the Tamaulipan Biotic Province (Oberholser 1974). Of these, five have extremely limited ranges:

Common Yellowthroat (*Geothlypis trichas insperata,* sometimes called Brownsville Yellowthroat)—southern Cameron County and possibly adjacent Matamoros, Tamaulipas

Carolina Wren (*Thryothorus ludovicianus lomitensis,* sometimes called Lomita Wren)—Kenedy County, the Valley, and extreme northeastern Tamaulipas

Gray-crowned Yellowthroat (*Geothlypis poliocephala ralphi,* formerly called Rio Grande Yellowthroat)—range is poorly known but probably the Valley and extreme northeastern Tamaulipas

Botteri's Sparrow (*Aimophila botterii texana*)—coastal southernmost Texas and northeastern Tamaulipas

Seaside Sparrow (*Ammodramus maritimus sennetti*)—coastal southern Texas and extreme northeastern Tamaulipas

Several other subspecies occupy various ranges in South Texas and northeastern Mexico, basically in the Tamaulipan Biotic Province and sometimes also in adjacent areas. They add to the uniqueness of our breeding bird community, but many have been studied little, either taxonomically or ecologically. Some may not be valid subspecies; some may be common, while others are rare and in need of protection.

Red-shouldered Hawk, *Buteo lineatus texanus*

Plain Chachalaca, *Ortalis vetula mccalli*

Scaled Quail, *Callipepla squamata castanogastris*

Elf Owl, *Micrathene whitneyi idonea*

Common Pauraque, *Nyctidromus albicollis merrilli*

Buff-bellied Hummingbird, *Amazilia yucatanensis chalconota*

Rose-throated Becard, *Pachyramphus aglaiae gravis*

Great Kiskadee, *Pitangus sulphuratus texanus*

Green Jay, *Cyanocorax yncas glaucescens*

Long-billed Thrasher, *Toxostoma longirostre sennetti*

Eastern Bluebird, *Sialia sialis episcopus*

White-eyed Vireo, *Vireo griseus micrus*

Tropical Parula, *Parula pitiayumi nigriloris*

Audubon's Oriole, *Icterus graduacauda audubonii*

Hooded Oriole, *Icterus cucullatus sennetti*

Olive Sparrow, *Arremonops rufivirgatus rufivirgatus*

White-collared Seedeater, *Sporophila torqueola morelleti*

Species Accounts and Summaries

Bird study in an entirely new country is thrilling, but it is also a bit hard on the nerves. One does not know which direction to turn, which road to take....
One has no way of knowing which species most need to be studied.

GEORGE M. SUTTON, DOCUMENTING AVIFAUNA
OF NORTHEASTERN MEXICO, 1930S–40S

In these species accounts I attempt to list all bird species formerly or currently breeding in the Valley and to describe their history, ecology, and current Valley status. Frequent reference is made to summaries and maps in the Texas Breeding Bird Atlas, to Oberholser (1974), to early ornithologists such as Sennett (1878, 1879) and Merrill (1878), and to other sources of information such as the U.S. Breeding Bird Survey (Sauer et al. 1999). I define current breeders as those species nesting here between 1987, the first year of the intensive Texas Breeding Bird Atlas Program (TBBAP; Benson and Arnold 2001), and 2002.

I have evidence that 171 species have bred at least once in the Valley. Based on the evidence, I am uncertain if five species ever bred here, either historically (Zone-tailed Hawk, Whooping Crane, and Greater Prairie-Chicken), currently (Eurasian Collared Dove), or both (Common Poorwill). Species that currently breed here—although not necessarily every year—number 152, and five more species may also be current breeders, including the Eurasian Collared Dove and Common Poorwill already mentioned. Before 1987, my cutoff for "current" breeding, 146 species bred in the Valley and seven more species may have done so, including those mentioned. The text gives information about their ecology, behavior, and conservation status and about changes in the Valley's breeding bird community.

The species accounts vary in length. My approach is between the behavior and natural history orientation of Alexander F. Skutch, who uses field notes extensively in many of his books, and more standard regional works, which have roughly equivalent amounts of information on all species and have extensive literature references. By using this uneven approach, I wish to highlight gaps in information and also to give a feel for the history, ecology, and natural history of the poorly known bird communities of the Lower Rio Grande Valley of Texas and adjacent areas of Texas and Mexico.

I devote the most space to Valley or South Texas specialties; to those species whose status in the Valley has changed greatly over time; and to certain other species with interesting behavior or ecology. These are treated with separate, titled sections on distribution, habitats, habits, other observations, and outlook. Treatment is less extensive for species that are widespread and well-known in the United States and for other species that I have spent little time studying. Sometimes two or more species are covered in the same paragraph, without distinct sections. Some of the colonial waterbirds and nocturnal birds in particular warrant further study, and even species on which I have spent a fair amount of time need more research.

Scientific names are given when a species is first mentioned, even if given in earlier chapters. I follow the latest revisions adopted by the American Ornithologists' Union (AOU 1998; Banks et al. 2002, 2004). Subspecies are not officially recognized by the AOU, but I mention them to stimulate future research. Unattributed observations are my own.

DUCKS (ORDER ANSERIFORMES)

FAMILY ANATIDAE

Black-bellied Whistling-Duck, *Dendrocygna autumnalis*

Dendrocygna autumnalis, a long-necked, long-legged duck with pinkish-orange bill and legs is a common resident of the Valley, often seen in residential neighborhoods as well as Valley forests and wetlands. One of the first things a visitor notices on the lakes at Santa Ana and Laguna Atascosa are the nest boxes on poles. These are designed for use by Black-bellied Whistling-Ducks and frequently are so used. Barn Owls, honey bees (*Apis mellifera*), and other species also use the boxes. Whistling-ducks, named for their high-pitched calls, were once called tree ducks, an appropriate name for this cavity-nesting species that often perches in trees. They also perch on telephone poles and wires, the latter only when the wind is not strong!

DISTRIBUTION   Black-bellied Whistling-Ducks occur from southern Arizona, central and eastern Texas, southwestern Louisiana, and Florida south through Mexico and Central America through most of South America. In Texas they have expanded from their original range in the Valley and along the coast southward from Corpus Christi to a present range reaching north to Del Rio, Austin, and Dallas and east to southwestern Louisiana (Schneider et al. 1993). Reservoir construction, creating many suitable nesting snags in flooded bottomland forest, may be partially responsible.

In the Valley they occur in a surprising variety of areas, from the expected riparian forests along the southern border north through small towns and cities to the Salt Lakes, and east almost to the low scrub and wetlands of the coast. Although Black-bellied Whistling-Ducks once withdrew from the United States in winter, now they regularly winter in southern Texas, including the Valley. Even so, an influx in March and April likely represents northbound migrants.

HABITAT The Black-bellied Whistling-Duck forages in agricultural fields, shallow wetlands, and grassy shorelines and roosts on islands, on sandbars, and in flooded timber. It can be seen regularly in suburban areas as well, especially in well-wooded residential areas.

HABITS The whistling-ducks are unique in several ways, not least of which is their long-lasting pair bond. Unlike other ducks, in which the brightly colored male departs soon after copulation, male and female whistlers look alike and share most parental duties. Also unique is the flight pattern, as the long legs and neck make for a different flight silhouette. Black-bellied Whistling-Ducks forage primarily at night. They rest for most of the day, unless looking for nest sites or caring for their young. The whistled *pe-ché-che-che* puzzled me as a new resident in the Valley, until I finally figured out what was flying over my house at night. Seeds of corn, sorghum, and various weedy grasses are important items in their diet (James and Thompson 2001).

OTHER OBSERVATIONS The beautifully marked black and yellow ducklings are probably the most attractive of all waterfowl babies (Jean Delacour, in Oberholser 1974). They can be seen in Valley backyards, city parks, and canals, once they hatch and emerge from tree cavities. Merrill (1878) received a report of adults carrying ducklings to water in their bills, but this needs to be confirmed. The chicks may wander through residential neighborhoods, with luck ending up at a nearby pond. If a predator or car kills the parents, the ducklings are on their own to reach a safe area (Tina L. Schiefelbein, pers. comm.).

The white wing patches, black belly, and pinkish-orange legs and bill of the adult are quite conspicuous in flight or when the birds are walking or swimming. Strangely enough, the birds can be hard to see against a colorful background, and I have almost paddled past a pair "frozen" on a gravel bar before seeing them.

Because the species has always been thought of mainly as a cavity nester, with occasional ground nests (Oberholser 1974), it was a great surprise when numerous pairs of Black-bellies were recently found nesting on the ground in one part of the Valley. The nesting population in the Salt Lakes area uses an island that only has low vegetation such as prickly pear cactus (Jeffery R. Rupert, pers. comm.). However, nesting without access to fresh water may lead to nesting failure, as many ducklings may die from drinking salt water (Dorie Stolley, pers. comm.). Breeding pairs seen in coastal Tamaulipas also nest commonly in similar habitat (Markum and Baldassarre 1989a).

OUTLOOK   The outlook for Black-bellied Whistling-Ducks in the Valley is promising, given that they forage and nest commonly in human-dominated habitats. The ninety ducklings produced in 2002 alone at the urban Valley Nature Center in Weslaco give an example of their success (Martin Hagne, pers. comm.). The number of nest sites may be a long-term concern, especially given the loss of trees due to recurring severe droughts. In the short run, nest sites may be more abundant than usual as large trees continue to die, but eventually those trees will fall, leading to a shortage. Nest boxes are a substitute for tree cavities, but such sites may be the objects of strong competition and may experience heavy predation, limiting their value somewhat. Predator guards and proper placement may help ensure that nest boxes are actually a benefit (McCamant and Bolen 1979; James and Thompson 2001).

Muscovy Duck, *Cairina moschata*

Ranging throughout tropical lowlands from Mexico to Argentina, the Muscovy Duck is one of Texas' rarest residents. First recorded here in 1984, it now occurs as a wild species in small numbers in the Valley. Feral and semi-domesticated birds occur fairly commonly in much of the United States, and some occur in the Valley. Wild Muscovy Ducks probably spread north during the 1970s or early 1980s from eastern Nuevo León, Mexico, where Leopold recorded them in La Union in the valley of the Río San Juan in late July, 1945 (Pitelka 1948). The birds would only have had to travel about 70 miles (112 km) to reach the Rio Grande.

DISTRIBUTION   Currently a rare resident of Zapata, Starr, and Hidalgo counties (Texas Ornithological Society 1995), the main Muscovy Duck population is apparently in the Starr County stretch of the Rio Grande. Large numbers have been seen between Chapeño and Fronton, especially in the mid- to late 1990s. Marty Bray and I saw as many as 22 wild birds there in the mid-1990s, and Jeff Rupert saw 28 there on August 9, 1998. This flock may have shifted eastward. On January 6, 2000, Gary Waggerman saw 23 birds along the Rio Grande about 5 miles (8 km) east of Roma. Steven G. Monk, Ray Bieber, and I saw 6–8 birds in the same area on June 11, 2001, confirming their presence below Roma during the breeding season. Small numbers continue to be seen near Salineño, Chapeño, and Falcon Dam.

One or two birds are seen occasionally in Hidalgo County, at Bentsen, Anzalduas, or Santa Ana. The current status of the species in Hidalgo County is poorly known. During March–July, 1997, Marc Woodin and his associates (Woodin et al. 1998) detected a few Muscovy Ducks along the Rio Grande about 40 miles (60 km) upstream from Laredo, suggesting the existence of a small population in northwestern Webb County.

HABITAT   Valley Muscovy Ducks primarily inhabit wooded riverbanks, especially along narrow side channels of the Rio Grande. They can also be seen along the main channel of the river and on resacas and ponds. From such diurnal roosts they presumably fly out to forage in agricultural fields in the evening, although this has not been observed for Valley birds. In the tropics, Muscovy Ducks are common along lowland rivers and in extensive swamps and marshes (Howell and Webb 1995).

HABITS   Quite wary and agile in flight despite their heavy bodies, Muscovy Ducks are often difficult to study in the wild. Frequently one sees a large duck fly swiftly by a river observation post such as Salineño, in the early morning or late evening. Their sharp claws allow them to perch readily on branches, like the smaller Black-bellied Whistling-Duck and Wood Duck. They are often flushed by boaters from such perches along remote side channels or the main channel of the Rio Grande. During the summer breeding season, Muscovy Ducks seem more reluctant to fly, especially if they have ducklings to protect. Once I saw a male swimming back and forth in front of a female, bobbing his head in what seemed to be a courtship display.

Harold Burgess found the first recorded nest of wild Muscovy Ducks in the United States, in a nest box erected for Black-bellied Whistling-Ducks about 1.2 miles (2 km) west of Bentsen. Marty Bray and I examined it on July 21, 1994, when it contained 10 unhatched eggs, one pipped egg, and three hatchlings.

On September 4, 1995, Marty Bray and I saw four independent juveniles along the Mexican shore of the Rio Grande, about halfway between Chapeño and Salineño. These birds were almost as big as an adult female Muscovy, and they were quite wary, at first remaining motionless but then flying off quickly as we came closer. They had dark bills and dark chestnut-brown heads and bodies. The wings had tiny whitish wing patches (in the secondaries).

On September 6, 1999, near Fronton, Jeff Rupert, Kevin Shinn, and I saw five ducklings that were less than $1/4$ grown, two $3/4$-grown juveniles, and one full-grown juvenile. These young birds were accompanied by one adult male and four adult females, which did an apparent distraction display in which they splashed the water with their wings and slowly swam downriver, away from the young birds. The larger young birds flew away from us, while the five smallest retreated quietly into riverside reeds.

Muscovy Ducks are known to consume a variety of plant and animal material from aquatic and terrestrial locations, but as far as I know there is no information on the foraging behavior or diet of Muscovy Ducks in the Valley.

OTHER OBSERVATIONS   Although Muscovy Ducks are usually silent, a female hissed as she extended her head and neck at me from the entrance to the nest box mentioned earlier. In flight, the wings (of at least the large males) make a soft whistling sound, which can be heard when a bird flies overhead.

Nesting has been recorded in tree cavities, nest boxes, and caves (Leopold 1959; Markum and Baldassarre 1989b; Eitniear et al. 1998), and I suspect that Muscovy Ducks may nest in riverbank burrows along the lower Rio Grande. On September 6, 1999, I saw an adult male standing at the entrance to a large burrow along the river between Santa Margarita Ranch and Las Adjuntas. The burrow was of the size used by Ringed Kingfisher, but the entrance looked worn and somewhat enlarged. I could not stay to confirm nesting activity.

OUTLOOK   Wild Muscovy Ducks are so rare in the United States that we cannot be too comfortable about their continued existence. Genetic swamping by feral and tame birds is always a possibility. Currently, nearly all birds in the Starr County population look and act very much like wild birds, and they seem to be reproducing in the wild. Hunting and habitat disturbance are also possible negative factors, although at present there is little evidence that either is a problem for the Texas population.

Other ducks

Given its southern latitude, the number of duck species known to have nested in the Valley us surprising. Some are regular, while others are exceptionally rare or irregular. The **Masked Duck** (*Nomonyx dominicus*) is a rare tropical species that attracts a lot of interest among visiting birders and also causes a lot of frustration among those trying to see one. The first U.S. specimen was taken near Brownsville on July 18, 1891 (Griscom and Crosby 1925–26). There were three successful nesting attempts in Cameron County in the 1930s (Oberholser 1974). A 1968 nest that produced five hatchlings in nearby Brooks County followed Hurricane Beulah in 1967 (Webster 1968b). Like Northern Jacanas, Masked Ducks are very irregular in occurrence in coastal Texas (Blankenship and Anderson 1993). They are most "dependable" during or just after several wet years and may be extremely rare during dry periods. Draining of wetlands for agricultural and urban development may have affected Masked Ducks in the Valley.

In the early 1990s, Masked Duck populations apparently peaked on the central and upper Texas Coasts (Anderson and Tacha 1999; Eitniear 1999). For example, up to 37 birds were seen (and many were photographed) at Welder Wildlife Refuge (San Patricio County), October 8, 1992–August 21, 1993, and a female with five half-grown ducklings was seen there on August 21, 1993 (Blankenship and Anderson 1993). Up to 24 birds (14 adults and 10 young) were at Attwater National Wildlife Refuge (Colorado County), July 29–December 14, 1994. Despite these large numbers at points farther north along the coast, there were no confirmed breeding records for Masked Duck in the Valley during the 1990s.

The early 1990s were a wet period in southern Texas and presumably northeastern Mexico, evidently encouraging either a northward movement or local population increases (or both). For example, up to 81 birds were seen along the Texas coast during 1992–93, including the Welder birds mentioned above (Haynie 1994, 1998). In 1995–96, as the 1990s drought set in, only 21 were seen (Haynie 1998), and only four were seen in Texas in 1998–99, which were extremely dry at least in central and southern Texas (Lockwood 1999, 2000).

Masked Ducks are erratic in their occurrence in the Valley, and they are seen in smaller numbers than in the wetter upper and central Texas coast regions. Like Least Grebes but much less common, Masked Ducks move around as pond quality changes. Individuals may appear on once-dry ponds that have just been filled naturally or artificially. For example, on April 5, 1996, I saw a male in breeding plumage on Santa Ana's Cattail Lake, which had been dry for the previous winter and early spring. Habitat conditions are important: in June and July of 1995, three Masked Ducks resided regularly on Willow Lake at Santa Ana. The lake was then at least 75 percent covered with cattails. They left after the lake was drained and the cattails cleared, as part of normal maintenance (Johnsgard and Carbonnell 1996). The birds would likely have left on their own if the lake had become completely choked with cattails, which is a regular occurrence in the Valley. In coastal

Texas as a whole, Masked Ducks prefer ponds with yellow lotus (*Nelumbo lutea*), yellow waterlily (*Nuphar mexicana*), and water hyacinth, but flooded huisache and sesbania (*Sesbania drummondii*) may be used also (Anderson and Tacha 1999).

There are reliable recent records of Masked Ducks in Cameron County (Brownsville area) and the King Ranch, most occuring on private land. Interestingly, in 1997 a few were seen in stock ponds along the Rio Grande in northwestern Webb County (Woodin et al. 1998), suggesting an inland range extension. More research is needed on this rare, secretive duck, especially to determine whether the species still breeds in the Valley and if there is any way to stabilize the population along the Texas coast.

Red-breasted Merganser (*Mergus serrator*) breeds mainly in the northern reaches of the Northern Hemisphere. It is a common winter visitor on the Laguna Madre, but I never expected to see any breeding in the Valley, since there were no breeding records in Texas or Mexico. However, on May 31, 1995, Jeffery R. Rupert and I saw a female with two full-grown but flightless juveniles on a shallow saline pond on Laguna Atascosa. On that same date we collected a dead juvenile that had washed up onto the shoreline of the lake (confirmed as Red-breasted by location of nostril midway along the bill; Rupert and Brush 1996). Rupert saw a second family group (one female, with five flightless juveniles) in the same area from June 1 to 7, 1995. Since male Red-breasted Mergansers normally abandon the family group, it was not unusual for us not to see any adult males. Perhaps the nearness of a shrimp farm, with abundant food, induced the mergansers to stay and breed, but I have not heard of any further breeding in the Valley.

Wood Ducks (*Aix sponsa*) are beautiful ducks typical of swamp forests in eastern Texas, and they are generally considered uncommon winter visitors in the Valley. However, these cavity nesters do breed in small numbers along the lower Rio Grande, as my field notes for June 8, 1996, indicate: *¹/₂ grown youngster accompanied by nonflying (flightless?) female on river at bluffs below Santa Margarita Ranch—the former flapped around a bit, while the latter watched us carefully.* I saw a full-grown juvenile, almost certainly the same bird, in the same area on July 17, 1996.

Harold Burgess found a Wood Duck nest with seven eggs in a whistling-duck box along Llano Grande, south of Weslaco, on June 27, 1992. This first recorded nesting in the Valley was successful, as the female led seven ducklings into a nearby wetland on the following July 6. Brad McKinney saw a pair entering and apparently nesting in a tree cavity in Brownsville in the summer of 1995, and Jack C. Eitniear and Jeff Breeden saw a family group on the river near Salineño in 2000. Given the 1998 sightings of males, females, and ducklings along the Río Nazas, in eastern Durango, Mexico

(Valdes-Perezgasga 1999), there is apparently a small breeding population in the Texas-Mexico borderland area and northern Mexico.

Mottled Ducks (*Anas fulvigula*) breed commonly along the coast, especially in wet years. I have seen a few broods; for example, six small ducklings at Southmost Preserve near Brownsville on June 13, 2000. They nest in smaller numbers inland to Zapata County but have not yet been recorded nesting in Starr County (Johnson 2001). It has been of interest to me to see both Mottled Ducks and what was formerly called Mexican Duck (now considered the **Mexican race of the Mallard,** *Anas platyrhynchos diazi*) on the river between Falcon Dam and Roma, where neither is confirmed to nest. John C. Arvin has seen some mixed pairs in the Valley. On April 16, 1987, he saw a brood of six ducklings, accompanied by a male Mottled mated with a female of the Mexican race of the Mallard, at the sewage treatment plant ponds in southwestern McAllen. I recorded 35 "Mexican Ducks" on the Rio Grande between Chapeño and Fronton on September 16, 1995, which could have included both local breeders and early fall migrants. "Green-headed" Mallards (typical birds from the midwestern or eastern United States) winter in the Valley in small numbers but do not stay to nest.

Other ducks breed less regularly in the Valley, depending on local and regional water conditions. **Fulvous Whistling-Ducks** (*Dendrocygna bicolor*) breed in the middle and lower parts of the Valley, especially in wet periods when there are more ponds and wetlands. They are much less common breeders than Black-bellied Whistling-Ducks, perhaps because their preferred habitat of rice (*Oryza sativa*) fields is absent from the Valley (Hohman and Lee 2001). **Blue-winged Teal** (*Anas discors*) and **Ruddy Duck** (*Oxyura jamaicensis*) are also confirmed but rare nesters in the Valley (Benson and Arnold 2001).

CHACHALACAS, TURKEYS, AND QUAIL (ORDER GALLIFORMES)

FAMILY CRACIDAE

Plain Chachalaca, *Ortalis vetula*

Our Chachalaca is an impressive Valley specialty that looks rather like a pheasant but acts more like a cross between a roadrunner and a monkey. Chachalacas easily climb from branch to branch, reaching for fruits, leaves, and buds in dense forests and well-vegetated backyards, often making a lot of noise as they jump from branch to branch and push through the foliage. Even more impressive is the loud chorusing *chachalac* song for which they are named. The ear-splitting chant can be heard hundreds of yards away and definitely underscores the tropical feel of the Valley. Once one pair (or group) starts singing, others pick up the beat, until the woods resound with chachalaca noise. Plain Chachalacas are well represented in the fossil record, and they may be survivors from the Mesozoic Era—the Age of Dinosaurs (Cooper and Penny 1997).

DISTRIBUTION   Resident in southernmost Texas, Plain Chachalacas also occur along Mexico's Gulf-Caribbean coastal plain southward into Central America, reaching Honduras and northern Nicaragua. As with Olive Sparrows, there is an isolated population in northwestern Costa Rica (AOU 1998). Plain Chachalacas have been introduced into San Patricio County, Texas, where they persist today, and also into other counties north of the Valley (with varying success; Peterson 2000).

However, chachalacas are basically restricted to the Valley, with birds seen as far upriver as the San Ygnacio area (Zapata County, Texas, and adjacent Mexico; Texas Game, Fish and Oyster Commission 1945; Eitniear and Rueckle 1996). Strangely, birds introduced onto Sapelo Island, Georgia, in 1929 have established themselves there and have spread to a few nearby islands (Burleigh 1958; Peterson 2000).

Even in the Valley chachalacas have not always been widespread. Populations were especially low in the 1950s, when there was concern about their survival (Oberholser 1974). Davis (1966) mentions occasionally seeing chachalacas in central Harlingen. However, the only place where chachalacas were still common in the late 1950s and early 1960s was at Santa Ana, where Raymond J. Fleetwood reported 160 nests in 1964.

Birds from remaining populations such as at Santa Ana were released into more isolated tracts where they did not occur, which greatly helped the species. For example, the Longoria unit of Las Palomas Wildlife Management Area, near Santa Rosa, Cameron County, received 40 birds in 1959–60. By 1964, the Longoria birds were reported doing well (Webster 1964). Chachalacas did so well at Longoria that during the late 1960s, more than 280 birds from there were transplanted to other patches of vegetation in the Valley. Many of these latter reintroductions have been successful, especially in areas where the vegetation was dense enough (Peterson 2000).

Now chachalacas are common in many parts of the Valley, from Falcon Dam to Brownsville. I frequently hear the songs and calls from my home in Edinburg, coming mainly from the direction of the oldest residential neighborhood in town. Most Valley cities have resident flocks now, especially in the wetter eastern half of the Valley. Historically, chachalacas apparently were absent from the grassy northern fringes of the Valley as well as from South Padre Island, and they still do not occur in such areas.

HABITAT   The common feature of Plain Chachalaca habitat in the Valley is that the foliage is dense, providing heavy cover for the birds. Some areas may have a dense understory, while others may be fairly open below the tree layer. Tall thorn forest dominated by Texas ebony supports two to three birds per hectare (Brush and Cantu 1998), but birds are also abundant in tall riparian forest and shorter mixed thorn forest (Oberholser 1974, Peterson 2000). Chachalacas are generally absent from low thorn scrub, mesquite savanna, and abandoned agricultural fields in early successional stages. Although they are not typical rain forest birds, chachalacas do inhabit "viny tangles" along streams and in second-growth scrub in areas dominated by rain forest (Lowery and Dalquest 1951).

HABITS   Chachalacas are the Valley's only leaf-eating (folivorous) bird, and they also eat a lot of fruit. Christensen et al. (1978) showed greatest consumption of the leaves of lazy daisy (*Aphanostephus* spp.) and other composites (*Eupatorium* spp.) and sugar hackberry fruits. Marion (1976) showed moderate to extensive consumption of coyotillo (*Karwinskia humboldtiana*), pigeonberry (*Rivina humilis*), anacua, coma, and chapotillo (*Amyris texana*) fruits, Mexican ash stamens (flower parts), and American nightshade (*Solanum americanum*) leaves. Fruits, leaves, and seeds of a variety of other species were also consumed. It is likely that chachalacas help to disperse many plant species, since they digest only the fruit pulp, not the seed itself (Delacour and Amadon 1973).

In their search for food, chachalacas may venture into open areas where the risk of predation is greater, whether openings in the foliage or clearings on the ground. They seem most alert when on the ground, and they quickly dash for cover if a potential predator comes by. Generally the birds do not get more than 50 feet (15 m) from dense cover, although I have seen them occasionally work their way cautiously across bare fields or even small coastal mudflats. They may hang in precarious positions high in a tree when ripe fruit is available.

Typically for galliform birds, chachalacas do not fly far or for very long; the white muscle fibers in their breast muscles are good for short bursts of power to escape predators, but they quickly tire. Running and climbing do not tire chachalacas easily, and they often flee danger or access new food sources in these ways. When a pair is ready to begin a song bout, they usually ascend by hopping upward from branch to branch, using their wings briefly in "jump-flights" upward.

OTHER OBSERVATIONS   Plain Chachalacas are quite wary birds in the wild, as their large body size makes them desirable especially to mammalian predators like bobcats (*Felis rufus*) and coyotes (*Canis latrans*). They are quick to give their purring low-intensity alarm call or their cackling "immediate-danger" call, as the situation warrants. Chachalacas are extremely alert for hawks. My ornithology students and I frequently see Cooper's Hawks, Sharp-shinned Hawks (*Accipiter striatus*), and Harris's Hawks fly toward and through foraging flocks of chachalacas in mid- to late winter. At that time (late January to mid-February), the tall riparian forests are still leafless, and chachalacas are quite exposed as they eat the opening buds and flowers of Mexican ash.

In my Edinburg yard, there is not enough of a variety of fruits or tender foliage to support a resident pair of chachalacas. However, pairs or individuals sometimes wander through, especially in the fall and spring, when they may be looking for vacant territories. I have seen chachalacas eating fruits of the rare native plant called potato tree (*Solanum erianthum*) as well as sugar hackberry in my yard. Northern Mockingbirds may attempt to drive chachalacas away from such trees, usually without success. One year, a female chachalaca patiently incubated two eggs in our tallest Texas ebony—with apparent success, as the eggshells were neatly opened at about their equators (Marion 1977).

Chachalacas have become tame in several Valley parks and refuges where birdseed is made available and where no hunting is allowed. Especially along the former recreational vehicle area at Bentsen and near the Santa Ana headquarters area, chachalaca numbers are high and the birds allow close approach. However, even in these locations, chachalacas remain wary of predators. At least four times at Bentsen, I have been alerted to the approach of a bobcat through dense brush by the alarm calls of chachalacas (and Green Jays). Chachalacas become quite wary in places where they are hunted, so that it becomes difficult to get more than a fleeting glimpse.

OUTLOOK   As mentioned earlier, Plain Chachalacas have rebounded well from their mid-twentieth-century population low in the Valley, and their prospects are good. Despite high nest predation by snakes and mammals and the harmful effects of rare cold snaps, chachalacas seem to be doing well at present. Although this bird is classified as a game species the Valley, there is currently little hunting pressure. As long as rapid urbanization does not destroy habitat faster than it can be created or can mature, the raucous calls of the Plain Chachalaca should remain common in the Valley.

FAMILY PHASIANIDAE

Greater Prairie-Chickens (*Tympanuchus cupido*) may once have inhabited coastal prairies in or close to the Valley. J. B. Chapa reported the presence of *gallinas monteses,* translated as prairie-chickens, in the South Texas area in the 1600s (Cavazos 1985). Merrill (1878) mentioned a report from a ranch on what is now the Cameron-Willacy county line, about 50 miles (80 km) north of Brownsville. If the species was present, it would have been the Attwater's race, (*T. c. attwateri*), now critically endangered due to loss and fragmentation of coastal prairie. Dresser (1865–66) noted that prairie-chickens were common "after leaving the chaparral and entering the prairie country," but it is not completely clear whether he included the sand plains (Wild Horse Desert of Kenedy County) in the prairie country or not. In the absence of any specimens or confirmed sightings from the Valley, I feel it is best to leave this question open.

Quite local in the Valley today, **Wild Turkeys** (*Meleagris gallopavo*) were once common in riparian forests along the river. John W. Audubon (1906) saw them coming to the river to drink during his visit in 1849, and the first specimen of the "Rio Grande" subspecies was taken at Hidalgo (Sennett 1879). As far as I know, Wild Turkeys are limited now to the northern fringes of the Valley, where they may have originated from the substantial populations farther north. Even as early as the 1920s, the Norias Division of the King Ranch was famous for its turkey populations, which Caesar Kleberg protected (Griscom and Crosby 1925–26). In the early to mid-1990s, a University of Texas–Pan American (UTPA) student told me that a Wild Turkey male had flown into the windshield of her car along U.S. Highway 281 north of San Manuel, Hidalgo County. In the early 1990s I saw a flock of Wild Turkeys on a ranch about 9 miles (14 km) north of Edinburg, and individuals occasionally wander onto Laguna Atascosa.

FAMILY ODONTOPHORIDAE

Two species of quail—much smaller than chachalacas—are common Valley residents. The **Northern Bobwhite** (*Colinus virginianus*) is the common quail of moister rural areas, especially those with a mixture of grassland and brushland (mesquite savannas or open thorn scrub). Bobwhites nest more successfully when grass cover is denser and there is prickly pear cactus nearby. Although bobwhites are well adapted to South Texas, at times the daytime heat is so intense that it reduces nesting activity of adults and may kill developing embryos (Guthery et al. 2001). Dense cover, if available, may help bobwhites survive hot weather in southern Texas (Johnson and Guthery 1988). Generally, wetter periods favor bobwhite reproduction here (Bridges et al. 2001), probably because of increased production of seeds and insects. Somewhat ironically, the replacement of riparian forest by grassy thorn scrub could benefit the Northern Bobwhite. I first noticed bobwhite along the Rio Grande Hiking Trail at Bentsen in 1998, after two years of drought had opened up the thorn forest and encouraged the spread of grass.

The exotic red fire ant (*Solenopsis invicta*) interferes with bobwhite reproduction and even depresses their populations in the Coastal Bend area and in the southeastern United States (Allen et al. 2000; Mueller et al. 1999). Although fire ants have reached the Valley (Allen et al. 1993), so far they are still not at "infestation" levels. Given the long-term decline of Northern Bobwhite in much of the country (Brennan 1991), even in areas without fire ants, maintaining healthy quail populations in the Valley and adjacent areas may be important to the species.

Scaled Quail (*Callipepla squamata*) have always been more local in the Valley than Northern Bobwhite. Sennett (1878, 1879) thought Scaled Quail were limited to the area west of Hidalgo, and those downstream from there were only stragglers. This is certainly true today, as Benson and Arnold (2001) show the species limited to Starr and western Hidalgo counties. Oberholser (1974) indicates that Scaled Quail once ranged throughout the Valley but no longer occur in Cameron or Willacy counties. I have seen them regularly in low thorn scrub about 18 miles (29 km) west of Edinburg. However, an early 1990s location in Edinburg no longer supports Scaled Quail and instead is the parking lot of Edinburg Regional Hospital.

Although Scaled Quail are thought to be more drought-tolerant than Northern Bobwhite, their populations are also strongly correlated with regional rainfall patterns (Bridges et al. 2001). There is an overall downward trend in Scaled Quail populations in South Texas, probably due to continuing habitat loss. Appropriate habitat remains abundant in South Texas, but we need to remain vigilant and continue to monitor the species.

GREBES (ORDER PODICIPEDIFORMES)

FAMILY PODICIPEDIDAE

Least Grebe, *Tachybaptus dominicus*

The Least Grebe is a tiny waterbird of small freshwater ponds and resacas in southern Texas, basically a tropical bird that barely gets into the United States. Interestingly, the closely related Little Grebe (*T. ruficollis*) is widespread in temperate-zone and tropical climates of Europe, Asia, and Africa. Least Grebes are often seen at the Sabal Palm Grove resaca or at Santa Ana, but they are somewhat nomadic and can be difficult to find. Familiarity with the calls—a laughing trill, slowing at the end, and a nasal trumpetlike call— aid greatly in finding this bird in the dense vegetation of ponds and resacas. Once the bird is found, its yellow eyes are noticeable at close range, especially against the darker head coloration of breeding plumage.

DISTRIBUTION   Least Grebes have nested in South Texas north to Webb, Bexar, and Colorado counties (Oberholser 1974), with recent records scattered as far east as Orange on the Louisiana state line (Benson and Arnold 2001). As one would expect, there are few records from drier areas, although this may be partially due to lack of regular observers on many ranches. In Mexico, Least Grebes occur from southern Baja California, Sonora, Nuevo León, and Tamaulipas south through the Yucatán Peninsula, Oaxaca, and Chiapas. They also occur in Central and most of South America, to Argentina. The species has been observed up to about 8,500 feet (2,600 m) above sea level but is most common in tropical lowlands.

Least Grebes are widespread in the Valley, but most records (nesting and otherwise) are from Mission eastward, along the river and in wetter coastal sections. Although the birds are permanent residents, numbers can be erratic. In some cases, this is due to drying up and reflooding of particular ponds. For example, I saw two juveniles at the McAllen sewage treatment plant on June 20, 1997, but the ponds were dry and all waterbirds absent by the end of the 1990s. Charles Castillo (1997) saw a pair of Least Grebes on June 20 and 27, 1997, on Santa Ana's Owl Trail Resaca in an area that had been reflooded after years of being dry.

In other cases, water quality or poorly understood regional movements may be important. For example, at Santa Ana in 1998, numbers ranged from 29 just on Willow Lake on July 24, 1998, to 100 on Willow and Pintail lakes combined on August 29, 1998, to none in a very thorough check of both lakes on November 15, 1998. Willow Lake was dry through much of 2001, but reflooding in early 2002 allowed at least four pairs to settle by April, 2002.

More rarely, Least Grebe populations are affected by severe freezes. During January 10–12, 1962, temperatures as low as 12°F (−11°C) froze many grebes into the ice on Tres Corrales Ranch, eastern Hidalgo County, where they were easy victims for predators (James 1963). Many Least Grebes died that winter, and it must have taken several years for regional populations to recover.

HABITAT   Normally, one expects to see Least Grebes on shallow, small ponds with some aquatic vegetation. Ponds like this can be produced by rainfall or by artificial means. I have also seen Least Grebes in borrow ditches, where removal of soil to make canal banks or levees has created linear ponds. Occasionally Least Grebes occur on the Rio Grande itself. My high river count is five at Santa Ana on December 20, 1997. I noted that the river water was unusually clear on that date, unlike the usual turbidity.

The larger Pied-billed Grebe may aggressively exclude Least Grebes from larger, more permanent ponds, but perhaps differences in prey abundance or foraging conditions are the key factors. John C. Arvin and I have noted independently a strong tendency to use clear pools, which are often created by heavy rain, so perhaps it is important for the grebes to see their prey easily.

HABITS   Least Grebes are seldom seen engaged in activities other than swimming or submerging themselves to hunt for food. They appear to sleep on the water, at which time a bird will tuck its head under a wing. Storer et al. (1976) first described the sunning behavior of the Least Grebe, in which it swims with its tail facing the sun and elevates its short white rump feathers. I have also seen that behavior, especially on chilly but sunny winter days when the temperature is below 50°F (10°C).

Least Grebes commonly eat freshwater insects, and most prey items are captured below the water's surface. Usually underwater activities are out of sight and one never knows where a grebe will pop up. In especially clear water I have watched a grebe swimming underwater, neck outstretched. I have also seen them suddenly rush across the surface of the water, wings flapping and feet paddling, in an attempt to capture a dragonfly. Once I saw a Least Grebe return from a dive with a crayfish claw in its beak, but this is more typical prey of the Pied-billed Grebe with its stronger bill.

Like other grebes, Least Grebes build floating nests, as in Merrill's (1878) description of "a wet, floating mass" attached to cattail or bulrush stalks. This term is somewhat misleading in my experience, as the few nests I have seen have actually rested on the bottom of a shallow area of a pond and were not attached to anything. Nesting is quite prolonged, with young seen from early April through mid-December (Oberholser 1974).

Although they are silent and tolerant of each other in migratory flocks, Least Grebes are noisy, aggressive birds when they are maintaining territories. Territorial Least Grebes chase other Least Grebes and also Pied-billed Grebes out of their territories. This casts some doubt on the hypothesis that Pied-billed Grebes exclude Least Grebes from larger ponds.

OTHER OBSERVATIONS   On January 6, 2000, I saw two Least Grebes possibly conducting a breeding display. Swimming within 50 feet (15 m) of each other, the birds fluffed their rump feathers and held their heads quite erect. I suspect this was a mating display, but the birds were still in nonbreeding (winter) plumage, with white throats. On June 16, 1998, a mated pair simultaneously trilled in the borrow ditch along the northern boundary of Santa Ana, near an active Altamira Oriole nest I was watching. Afterward the grebes both sat on their own nest for a while, but later in June there was no activity at the nest.

Some ponds and resacas are apparently unsuitable for Least Grebes, for poorly understood reasons. For example, I have never seen Least Grebes on the resaca that forms the western boundary of Bentsen, in about ten years of regular visits. This resaca is generally poor in waterbird populations and may have a poor prey base; the water is also quite turbid, which seems to deter the visually foraging grebes, as already noted.

Since I have a mental image of Least Grebes on woodland ponds, I was surprised on May 3, 2000, to see an adult and two juveniles on the borrow ditch along the entrance road to Anzalduas. This pond is flanked by highly disturbed dry grasslands one side and the concrete edge of the road on the other. In no other year have I seen Least Grebes in that pond, which is often dry. Similarly, the Willow Lake complex at Santa Ana is quite erratic in supporting Least Grebes. Often a pair will reside on one or more of the separate ponds, particularly the intermittent woodland pond called Willow 1. These observations provide further evidence of the erratic nature of Least Grebe occurrence and nesting in the Valley.

OUTLOOK   One can never be completely optimistic about the future of any aquatic bird in such a semiarid and rapidly growing area as the Valley. Ponds may be drained or filled for various reasons or may simply fill in naturally due to vegetative succession. In the Least Grebe's case, its ability to find and use small, ephemeral ponds and to recolonize after droughts or freezes will help it survive in the ever-changing landscape of the Valley.

Other grebes

The **Pied-billed Grebe** (*Podilymbus podiceps*), widespread in North America, nests commonly on ponds and small lakes in the Valley. Its loud and drawn-out croaking "song" can be heard for several hundred yards, even when the birds themselves are hidden behind marsh vegetation. I have heard it as early as February 4 (1998, at Santa Ana). The chicks are conspicuous because of their brown and white stripes and their incessant loud begging. Like Least Grebes, Pied-billed Grebes occasionally occur on the Rio Grande, but I have no evidence of nesting along the river itself.

CORMORANTS AND RELATIVES (ORDER PELECANIFORMES)

FAMILY PELECANIDAE

Brown Pelicans (*Pelecanus occidentalis*) once nested commonly along the Texas coast, but the population crashed in the 1950s. The pesticide endrin and disturbance of nesting colonies may have been major causes of the declines in Texas, rather than the DDE and DDT blamed for nesting failures in California (Jehl 1973; King et al. 1977). Brown Pelicans have never been studied intensively in the Valley, but nesting was noted in the Port Isabel area in 1927 and 1928 (Oberholser 1974).

Observers continued to see Brown Pelicans in the Lower Laguna Madre even at their population low point, but it was not until the late 1990s that birds were seen nesting there again. On May 20, 1997, Debbie Jasek saw eight nests with eggs on a spoil island in the Lower Laguna Madre, about 3 miles (5 km) north of Port Isabel (David Blankinship, pers. comm.). More information is needed, but we can hope that Brown Pelicans will continue to recover here, as they have elsewhere in the United States during the twenty-five years (Shields 2002).

As far as I know there are no recent nesting records of **American White Pelicans** (*Pelecanus erythrorhynchos*) in the Valley. American White Pelicans nested in coastal Cameron County in the early 1900s, including a colony of two hundred nests in 1934 in now dry Bahía Grande (Oberholser 1974). They have nested consistently in the Upper Laguna Madre of Texas since 1880, although shifting their nesting island several times since the late 1970s (Chapman 1988). American White Pelicans nested in the Laguna Madre of Tamaulipas in the mid-1970s (Smith 2002) and as recently as 2002 (David Blankinship, pers. comm.).

FAMILY PHALACROCORACIDAE

Neotropic Cormorant, *Phalacrocorax brasilianus*

Sometimes overlooked in the rush to see rare woodland birds, the Neotropic Cormorant is another widespread tropical bird with a range reaching southern Texas. It is most common in summer; the small numbers overwintering can be difficult to pick out within large flocks of Double-crested Cormorants. The grunting, piglike calls of the *pato cerdo* (pig duck) can be heard in breeding-season flocks of hundreds of birds near Falcon Lake, and the species has been increasing in Texas and adjacent states in recent decades (Coldren et al. 1998; Gawlik et al. 1998).

DISTRIBUTION   Well named, the Neotropic Cormorant occurs throughout the Neotropics—South America, Central America, and most of Mexico. The range extends into temperate-zone climate in central and eastern Texas and southern Argentina. In the tropics the birds occur coastally as well as inland, but in the Valley the species is rare on the coast. Neotropic Cormorants regularly occur in small numbers (2–10) wherever there is suitable aquatic habitat, even in urban areas like Brownsville (Teter and McNeely 1995).

In the Valley, breeding has been recorded in Cameron and Hidalgo counties (Oberholser 1974; Benson and Arnold 2001). In 1846 Curtis and fellow soldiers rode through a flooded thicket containing many "water-turkey" nests near Brownsville (Chance 1994). Anhingas and cormorants are both sometimes called water turkeys, but only the cormorants are highly colonial, so Curtis probably saw Neotropic Cormorants.

Breeding numbers are now small and restricted to freshwater sites. One of the larger breeding colonies in southern Texas may be at Falcon Lake, just outside the Valley proper in Zapata County (Wainright et al. 2001; Susan Wainwright and Miguel Mora, unpubl. data). Birds nested in 1997 on trees killed by high water in three different locations there. These must be the birds that often fly downriver below Falcon Dam to forage, making that area one of the strongholds for Neotropic Cormorants in the Valley, at least in some years.

Steve Labuda and David Blankinship reported a breeding colony near the mouth of the Rio Grande in 2002, where the blocked river had spread out and flooded riverside vegetation. This possible recovery in the immediate coastal area may be enhanced if proposed coastal habitat restoration efforts are carried out.

Neotropic Cormorants may nest later than most other colonial waterbirds, like the "thousands" of nonbreeding cormorants Susan Wainwright saw at an active heron and egret nesting colony on May 18, 1997. Wainwright and Blankinship found about 80 cormorant nests with incubating adults (in a different location) on July 15, 1997. This fits with my failure to see cormorants with breeding plumes until July. There may be substantial fluctuations from year to year due to factors such as drought, but this is hard to tell since observer effort around Falcon Lake fluctuates so much.

Other areas farther north may have major concentrations, such as Choke Canyon Lake, a reservoir near Three Rivers (McMullen and Live Oak counties). Willie Sekula saw about 1,600 Neotropics there on June 11, 1995 (Lasley and Sexton 1995), but otherwise little work has been done there.

HABITAT   Freshwater rivers, resacas, ponds, and lakes are all used for foraging sites by Neotropic Cormorants. Usually, birds forage in fairly shallow, slow-moving or still water, with roosting sites nearby. I have never seen Neotropic Cormorants on salt water, although they formerly foraged commonly in the Laguna Madre and possibly shallow Gulf waters (Oberholser 1974). In South America they can be found on sluggish lowland rivers or rushing mountain streams as well as in coastal areas.

HABITS   The Neotropic is a typical cormorant in its running takeoff, steady, somewhat labored flight, and habit of drying its wings after foraging. It appears somewhat more agile in flight than the stockier Double-crested and maneuvers fairly well among trees surrounding small ponds. I often see a group of two or three birds land on a small pond or resaca and start foraging immediately, diving from a swimming position. If undisturbed, the birds may forage for five to ten minutes or more, diving and surfacing repeatedly. Once finished, they look for a spot to perch, preferably on a dead tree emerging from the water, but sometimes on live riverside trees. The birds spread their wings, facing into the breeze, and wait for the water to evaporate from their plumage.

Although they are usually seen in small groups, large foraging flocks are conspicuous (if irregular) features of the Rio Grande between Falcon Dam and Roma. Flying downstream in the morning, the cormorants land in various spots along the river, sometimes in the spillway within 1 mile (2 km) of the dam or down by Salineño, Santa Margarita Ranch, or farther downstream. Several hundred birds forage in a tight group, often splashing the water, leapfrog-flying over one another, and then diving either simultaneously or individually. These birds roost during midday in tall riverside ash trees, with five to ten birds per tree, or they fly back upriver to roost somewhere on the lake. They often grunt when in such large groups; otherwise the species is quite silent.

In Texas as a whole, breeding may occur year-round. In December, 2001, and January, 2002, Tom Langscheid saw about 80 active nests on the King Ranch near Kingsville. In early March, 2003, at High Island on the Upper Texas Coast, Winnie Burkett noted fledglings from a November nesting while a new nesting cycle was under way.

OTHER OBSERVATIONS   The huge flocks that stream downriver below Falcon Dam in late spring and early summer of some years are awe-inspiring. The cormorants fly low over the river, silently following its bends, parting only when they encounter islands or other obstructions such as canoes. On May 23, 1996, I estimated 2,300 birds on the river between Chapeño and Fronton. The largest group (more than 1,000 birds) flew downstream at about 10:10. Marty Bray and I encountered many of the same birds later that day, between Santa Margarita Ranch and the mouth of the Río Alamo. Many birds seemed heavily laden with fish by early afternoon, when they were resting and calling in riverside trees. We disturbed them unavoidably simply by canoeing past them. For this reason, it seems unlikely to me that a breeding colony will become established on the river below the dam. On July 14, 1996, we only saw 14 birds along the same stretch of river, suggesting that most birds were then foraging on Falcon Lake or perhaps farther upstream.

OUTLOOK   The outlook for the Neotropic Cormorant in Texas and probably in the Valley as well is generally favorable. As long as there are safe islands available for nesting and adequate prey (fish) populations, the species should do well. No breeding colonies were recorded in Texas from 1960 to 1967, but the population has increased greatly over years since then, especially since the mid-1980s (Telfair 1995; Gawlik et al. 1998). The Falcon Lake colonies are little studied compared with those on the upper Texas coast, and more research needs to be done on breeding success and consistency of colony occupation, given fluctuating water levels and potential human disturbance. If the Bahía Grande wetland ecosystem (between Port Isabel and Brownsville) is restored, perhaps the species will return and breed there (Friedmann 1925 reported 500 birds there on May 31, 1924). So far there is no anti-cormorant movement in the Valley, but given perceived problems in the Great Lakes involving high cormorant numbers as a possible cause of reduced game-fish numbers (Glahn et al. 2000), we should remain vigilant.

FAMILY ANHINGIDAE

Anhingas (*Anhinga anhinga*) are most common as migrants, and I have seen flocks of 60–100 or more circling to gain altitude as they lift off from Santa Ana and other wooded tracts. Once fairly common as breeders, Anhingas may still occasionally breed in the Valley. During a canoe trip at Santa Ana on July 17, 1997, I saw a female Anhinga sitting on a stick nest in a sandbar willow on the Mexican shore. A male was perched within about 5 feet (1.5 m) of her. The nest had probably been completed that day; green leaves only slightly wilted were still attached to the branches (Baicich and Harrison 1997). Males and females are seen fairly regularly during May–July, but there are no nesting records of Anhinga since 1966 in the Valley proper (John C. Arvin, pers. comm.).

HERONS, EGRETS, AND RELATIVES (ORDER CICONIIFORMES)

FAMILY ARDEIDAE

Herons and egrets can be seen throughout the Valley wherever water is available, but most species occur and nest mainly in coastal areas where nesting and foraging sites are most abundant. Green Island, a natural island protected by the National Audubon Society, supports the largest nesting colony of **Reddish Egrets** (*Egretta rufescens*) in the world (Lowther and Paul 2002) as well as several other ciconiiform species. Mixed-species nesting colonies have also been found on spoil islands in the Lower Laguna Madre and just outside the Valley on Falcon Lake (Wainwright et al. 2001; Susan Wainwright, unpubl. data). **Snowy Egret** (*Egretta thula*), **Little Blue Heron** (*Egretta caerulea*), and **Great Blue Heron** (*Ardea herodias*) nest only coastally, on islands. **Great Egret** (*Ardea alba*), **Tricolored Heron** (*Egretta tricolor*), and **Black-crowned Night-Heron** (*Nycticorax nycticorax*) do nest inland but the vast majority nest in coastal colonies. Great Egrets were thought to nest only along the coast, but Ruby Lopez (unpubl. data) found a small nesting colony south of Pharr (Hidalgo County) in 2002.

Green Herons (*Butorides virescens*) break all the rules for this group, nesting noncolonially in widely scattered nonwetland sites along the Rio Grande and other waterways. Marty Bray and I frequently canoed underneath active nests along the Rio Grande between Chapeño and Fronton between 1994 and 1997. These locations, in trees overhanging the river, may be safer than if the birds had nested in drier locations. We were thankful that neither youngsters nor incubating adults defecated while we were below them. **Least Bitterns** (*Ixobrychus exilis*) are summer residents of cattail marshes, nesting recently in Cameron and Hidalgo counties (Benson and Arnold 2001). I regularly hear and occasionally see them in the Edinburg Wetland Area, at Santa Ana, and in the cattail marsh maintained by treated wastewater outflow at the South Padre Island Convention Center. **Cattle Egrets** (*Bubulcus ibis*) have exploded in numbers in the Valley since the first two pairs were seen at Green Island in 1959 (Alexander Sprunt IV, in Webster 1959).

A great surprise to me in 2001 was to hear of **Yellow-crowned Night-Herons** (*Nyctanassa violacea*) nesting in the city of Weslaco. Martin Hagne and others observed two active nests by one pair that summer in the small nature center woodland in downtown Weslaco. I wondered why the birds were nesting in town when there must have been a few sites within 4–6 miles (6–10 km) of town, such as the Llano Grande wetlands.

However, it turns out that Yellow-crowned Night-Herons are common urban nesters elsewhere in the United States, such as in coastal Virginia (Watts 1995). Nesting over yards in Virginia has prompted concerns about the smell and mess of food remains and droppings. The nest at Valley Nature Center was ideally located, since it was in an accessible natural area but not in a backyard. During 2002, two pairs built four nests and raised a total of nine fledglings there (Martin Hagne, pers. comm.).

FAMILY THRESKIORNITHIDAE

White-faced Ibis (*Plegadis chihi*) and **White Ibis** (*Eudocimus albus*) both nest in coastal colonies in varying numbers. White-faced Ibis also nest in small numbers in Hidalgo County, probably in freshwater habitat (Benson and Arnold 2001). Numbers of White Ibis appear to increase in wet years and decrease in dry years, typical for this somewhat nomadic species (Bildstein 1993). During the wet early 1990s I saw small numbers of White Ibis as far inland as Santa Ana, but since then I have seen them only around the Laguna Madre. **Roseate Spoonbills** (*Platalea ajaja*) nest in coastal sections, but juveniles and immatures occasionally wander inland as far as Falcon Dam.

FAMILY CICONIIDAE

There are no definite records of **Wood Storks** (*Mycteria americana*) breeding in the Valley and very few anywhere in Texas (most recently 1960; Oberholser 1974). However, flocks are regularly seen, beginning in late May, and numbers peak in the hundreds from July through October. These are evidently birds wandering north from breeding colonies in eastern Mexico, unless there are still some Texas nesting colonies.

FAMILY CATHARTIDAE

Despite their similarities to raptors in general body proportion and style of flight, New World vultures have been separated from raptors since 1997 on the basis of studies of DNA, anatomy, behavior, and the chemistry of the uropygial gland (AOU 1998). Although the changing classification makes little difference to the birder or to the birds, it is interesting to think about when searching through flocks of vultures for a rarer species like **Zonetailed Hawk** (*Buteo albonotatus*).

In the 1880s, people living in or traveling through the Valley were likely to see many vultures along the Rio Grande or in the small towns and on ranches, where dead animals were readily available. Today vultures are more likely to be seen soaring high overhead, visiting a garbage dump or landfill, feeding from a road-killed animal, or roosting in large numbers on cellphone towers or high-tension electric lines. In my experience, **Turkey Vultures** (*Cathartes aura*, widely known in Mexico as *aura*) are much more common in the Valley than **Black Vultures** (*Coragyps atratus*, known as *zopilote*). I rarely pass a day in the field or around town without seeing at least one or two *auras* overhead, and larger numbers can be seen in winter or during migration.

Sennett (1878) considered both vultures abundant, the Black Vulture more so, so evidently there have been some significant changes in Black Vulture populations in the Valley. Both species are quite rare as nesters (as far as I know), perhaps due to the shortage of safe nesting sites for these ground nesters. I made a journal note of some apparent nesting activity by Black Vultures in an old Ringed Kingfisher burrow along the Rio Grande: *February 28, 1999: one scraping soil and standing at entrance to what looks like enlarged Ringed Kingfisher burrow—looks at us without flying as we canoe by (Mex. side below Salineño). April 11, 1999: Two at same cavity—one inside nest, legs only visible, while other appears to stand guard just outside entrance.*

Both species are more likely to nest on remote ranches than in smaller refuges and parks along the river. Recent Valley nesting has not been confirmed for the Turkey Vulture (Benson and Arnold 2001). Black Vultures remain more common in areas near unmanaged garbage dumps, such as on the Mexican side, as opposed to sanitary landfills where garbage is quickly covered.

DIURNAL RAPTORS
(ORDER FALCONIFORMES)
FAMILY ACCIPITRIDAE
Hook-billed Kite, *Chondrohierax uncinatus*

The cry "Hook-billed Kite overhead!" generates an immediate frenzy among birders visiting the Lower Rio Grande Valley of Texas. What follows is a scramble for a position from which to see this rare raptor as it flaps or soars briefly over the dense thorn scrub. When it is perched, its long, hooked bill, light-colored eye, and the greenish yellow patch of skin above the eye give the Hook-billed Kite a staring, intense look. The paddle-shaped wings, constricted at the base, seem awkward in slow, flapping flight, but they are used effectively for quick foraging flights in thorn forests. Kites are generally only seen in longer-distance flights because foraging occurs in dense thorn forest. Veteran tropical ornithologist John C. Arvin considers the Hook-billed Kite possibly the most difficult of the regular Valley specialty birds for birders to spot during a short visit.

DISTRIBUTION   Originally described in 1822, the Hook-billed Kite has an extensive tropical and subtropical range. This apparently nonmigratory species ranges from extreme southernmost Texas and northern Mexico southward through Central and South America, mainly in tropical lowlands, all the way to Ecuador, Bolivia, Brazil, and northern Argentina (AOU 1998). Isolated populations in Grenada (in the Lesser Antilles) and Cuba are thought to be separate subspecies or species, respectively.

The Hook-billed Kite was first seen in the United States in 1964, when a nesting pair was discovered at Santa Ana. Its range in the United States is extremely limited (Fleetwood and Hamilton 1967; Delnicki 1978). Although the birds have spread out along the lower Rio Grande, the U.S. population size must still be quite low. Regular sightings occur only between Falcon Dam and Santa Ana, a straight-line distance of only about 72 miles (115 km). In addition to Santa Ana, Hook-billed Kites have also nested in Bentsen,

near Anzalduas, near the small town of Los Ebanos, and in at least two locations between Falcon Dam and Roma. Within this area, Hook-billed
Kites are almost always seen in native habitat along the river, generally
within a strip less than 3 miles (5 km) wide. There are no documented
records from the Brownsville or Harlingen areas or from Laguna Atascosa.
Some Hook-billed Kites occur in northeastern Nuevo León away from the
Rio Grande (Montiel De La Garza and Contreras-Balderas 1990).

HABITAT   For many birders, Hook-billed Kites are associated with the
hot, usually dry thorn forest and thorn scrub of the Lower Rio Grande Valley. *Rabdotus alternatus* snails, its main prey here, are common on retama,
huisache, and other thorny plants of heavy clay soils. I have often seen piles
of neatly opened snail shells, usually in thorn forest near a nest site. The
Greater Roadrunner (*Geococcyx californianus*) frequently eats snails and
leaves small piles of shells, but it breaks the shells apart more completely and
its shell piles are usually near fallen tree trunks in little clearings.

South of the border, Hook-billed Kites are reported to use lowland mangrove swamps, freshwater swamp forests, tropical evergreen and deciduous
forests, and even montane evergreen forests up to about 9,200 feet (2,800 m)
above sea level. For example, William Schaldach (1963) reported a bird in
heavy Mexican fir (*Abies religiosa*) forest on the Volcán de Nieve in Jalisco,
western Mexico. More typical were birds in heavy swamp forest in El Salvador (Dickey and Van Rossem 1938).

HABITS   Although not particularly shy, the Hook-billed Kite is nonetheless difficult to find, both in the United States and in the tropical parts of
its range. Hook-billed Kites do not forage conspicuously, unlike most raptors, and never occur in urban or suburban areas. Tree snails are the main
prey item, which must be sought in dense scrub or forest. In 1962, Francois
Haverschmidt (1962) described the difficulty in seeing the species in Surinam: "A forest hawk living in the lower canopy and dense undergrowth. This
kite is a secretive bird and I never saw it hunting. My encounters with it always happened in the same way. When walking through the forest, my attention would be drawn by a few wing beats and a passing shadow. Following this the bird would alight on a branch where it would sit looking at me."

In Texas I have seen foraging Hook-billed Kites perch on the ground or
a short distance above it, taking off only when approached closely. I estimate
that I have seen Hook-billed Kites on less than one of every fifteen field trips
I have made in the Valley. Although perhaps somewhat more readily seen
during the nesting season, when it is busy foraging for its offspring, this species is never a sure thing.

Nesting is conducted in the hot summer months, usually in areas not visited much by birders. A pair with a new nest 13–14 feet (4 m) up along a trail at Bentsen on June 27, 1996, apparently dismantled the nest once I had seen it—it was completely gone when I returned early the next morning. Most nests in the drier northern part of the kite's range in Texas, Tamaulipas, and Nuevo León have been found in huisache, less than 25 feet (8 m) up (Smith 1982). However, the nest J. Stuart Rowley (1984) found, 45 feet (14 m) off the ground in Oaxaca, southern Mexico, may be more typical of wetter tropical forests.

Like many tropical hawks, these kites raise only one or two young per nest. Both parents attend the nest, and they have been seen bringing in many snails per hour to their youngsters. The nest itself is like a large dove nest, being constructed of a limited number of sticks, so that the eggs or young can be seen through the bottom of the nest. The exact incubation and nestling periods are unknown. Although nesting densities are unknown, Smith (1982) found six nests within 5 miles (8 km) of each other in grazed thorn forest in Tamaulipas, over a two-year period.

Permanent residents throughout their range, Hook-billed Kites may be somewhat nomadic, moving around as snail populations vary. Scott Robinson (1994) saw the species irregularly in marshes and seasonally wet forest in his Peruvian study area, while Dennis Paulson (1983) observed a flock of 25 in Venezuela, perhaps migrating locally in response to a patchy food supply. Both the foraging habits and seminomadic nature of the Hook-billed Kite reduce the chances of seeing it predictably in a particular area. In contrast, the Snail Kite (*Rostrhamus sociabilis*) is easy to see in its open marsh habitat, where it forages on the wing, looking for apple snails (*Pomacea* spp.) below. Interestingly, Hook-billed Kites have been reported eating young apple snails, perhaps gathered from trees in tropical swamp habitats.

In southernmost Texas, Hook-billed Kites seem to forage in particular areas for a few days at a time, during which they follow predictable daily patterns. During my fieldwork in Santa Ana and Bentsen, I typically go for several weeks without seeing one. Then I may see one or two birds at the same time of day flying past the same location, until their pattern changes. Possibly the kites deplete local populations of tree snails and then shift to another section of their territory (or home range).

Typically Hook-billed Kites are seen either within the first hour after sunrise, when moving to their first foraging location, or in midmorning (8:30–10:30), when they may soar briefly. Two or three birds may be seen soaring for five or ten minutes when the air gets warm enough to create thermals, which are also used by soaring raptors and Anhingas. These midmorning soaring periods may include territorial or other social interactions.

Hook-billed Kites seldom call, but I have heard them give a short rattle, like the song of the Northern Flicker (*Colaptes auratus*), when alarmed. A musical, oriole-like call is described from Central America but has not been reported in the United States.

OTHER OBSERVATIONS   Interesting events are seen when enough observers spend enough time in the habitat of poorly known birds, such as the Hook-billed Kite. A number of birders saw eight birds soaring at one time over Bentsen on November 15, 1998, during the Rio Grande Valley Birding Festival. These birds were not likely to have been migrating, as Valley numbers remain constant throughout the year, but the function of such a flock is unknown.

Hook-billed Kites are not very aggressive, although Dickey and Van Rossem (1938) reported a pair chasing a Common Black-Hawk (*Buteogallus anthracinus*). I have observed kites that were flying low over the forest swoop suddenly down and land quickly in a low perch to look at me. Once I saw a possible low-intensity territorial conflict at Bentsen: two typical (gray) males soared together over the trailer loop and then drifted off in opposite directions (July, 1998).

On February 20, 1996, I saw a typical male in a possible mating display over Santa Ana. One sunny morning, the male took off from the tallest remaining stand of Texas ebony, made several deep, slow wing beats, and drifted off to the east toward the Rio Grande. Although the kites are not usually harassed by aggressive territorial flycatchers, on May 7, 1997, a Couch's Kingbird briefly scolded a low-flying female that was protesting my presence in a forest at Santa Ana. Similarly, a full-grown juvenile was briefly chased and scolded by a Couch's Kingbird and a Green Jay at Bentsen.

As indicated earlier, it is difficult to see Hook-billed Kites foraging or even just perching. On one occasion at Santa Ana, a gray male with a bulging throat, likely indicating a crop full of food, flew up from a low retama thicket and landed in a taller deciduous tree in a floodplain forest nearby. I made my only direct observation of foraging on June 6, 1998, while I was driving slowly along a park road at Bentsen. A female flew low across the road, landed in a fairly open stand of mesquite trees, and immediately began turning her head scanning for snails. At least five times in five minutes, she sallied to a nearby branch or to the ground, picked off a snail, and then perched on a fallen log to consume it. On one occasion she seemed quite graceful while briefly hanging onto the underside of a slightly tilted mesquite branch to get a snail. Since it was the nesting season, she may have been putting the snails in her crop to deliver them to an undiscovered nest nearby. This rapid foraging behavior fits in with the rapid snail delivery to nestlings at a Tamaulipas nest, which amazed Snyder and Snyder (1991).

Not seen yet in the United States is the "large-billed" form, which has a bill 1.5 times longer and 3 times larger overall than the "small-billed" form that occurs here (Smith and Temple 1982). Kites with larger, longer bills feed on the larger snails found in western Mexico and several areas in South America, while our kites feed on the smaller snails occurring in the Valley. Birds with different bill sizes show similar plumages and differ in no other body measurements. In Colima, western Mexico, an apparent family group contained an adult female with a large bill and a juvenile with a small bill. There and elsewhere in the tropics, two different sizes of snails apparently support the two bill sizes of Hook-billed Kites, which show no signs of being separate species or subspecies (Smith and Temple 1982).

OUTLOOK   Hook-billed Kites seem to be fairly tolerant of habitat disturbance, given their use of edges, semi-open thorn scrub, and swamp forest, which bodes well for their future in the tropics. Although kites have not been seen foraging in open pastures, the use of grazed thickets and broken forest is encouraging, given habitat trends in the tropics. Obviously when forests have been completely removed, an area can no longer support Hook-billed Kites (Snyder and Snyder 1991).

In Texas, where floodplain forest continues to decline along the lower Rio Grande, Hook-billed Kites may benefit from revegetation of abandoned agricultural fields, since habitat managers usually plant thorn forest species. In addition, the spread of thorn forest at the expense of floodplain forest may benefit Hook-billed Kites, as it has apparently helped the Elf Owl. We should not be too complacent, but the outlook is reasonably good for this fairly recent immigrant.

Other kites

The **White-tailed Kite** (*Elanus leucurus*) is our other breeding kite. For a time known as **Black-shouldered Kite** (*Elanus caeruleus*), this kite is a graceful bird of open country and can regularly be seen over coastal prairies and other grasslands or abandoned agricultural fields. Because of their long wings, light underparts, and grassland habitat, adult male Northern Harriers (*Circus cyaneus*) can be mistaken for White-tailed Kites. However, White-tailed Kites usually hunt 40–50 feet (12–15 m) over fields, whereas Northern Harriers are usually only 5–10 feet (1.5–3 m) up. Kites usually hover when they see a prey item below, again unlike the harrier, which pauses only briefly before attempting to capture its prey. The main prey species in Nuevo León is the hispid cotton rat (*Sigmodon hispidus;* Montiel De La Garza 1978).

Toy kites were named after European kites because of the birds' habit of slowly descending, wings spread and talons extended, to capture their prey.

I have made no particular study of White-tailed Kites but have noticed in a general way their semi-nomadic nature (Gatz 1998). A particular field or grassy marsh edge may support a kite for several months but then be abandoned for months or perhaps a year or two.

Breeding numbers probably vary from year to year in the Valley, in parallel with rainfall. For example, Fleetwood found 22 nests at Santa Ana in 1964, but none in 1965 (Webster 1965). Overall, the species has increased in South Texas over the last thirty years, and breeding has been confirmed all the way to the Houston-Galveston area (Oberholser 1974; Benson and Arnold 2001). The communal winter roosts of 75–100 or more birds in Valley sugarcane (*Saccharum officinale*) fields or mesquite thickets (Clark and Wheeler 1989) may indicate seasonal movement or local aggregation.

Gray Hawk, *Asturina nitida*

The Gray Hawk is a rare woodland hawk of the Rio Grande borderland region of Texas. The dark eyes stand out in the whitish gray face, and the light gray and white barring and gray back and wings make this bird quite attractive. It usually hunts from a low perch in semi-open woodland, sometimes grabbing prey from tree branches. Gray Hawks were once considered buteos, but rarely do they soar high overhead for long periods as most buteos do. Formerly rare in the Valley, Gray Hawks have made something of a comeback since 1970. The highest number I have seen in one day is four, along the Rio Grande between Chapeño and Fronton.

DISTRIBUTION   Gray Hawks are locally common in southern Arizona and much less so in western and southern Texas. They are more generally common south through most of Mexico and Central and South America to Argentina (AOU 1998). In Texas, Gray Hawks have nested since 1988 in Big Bend National Park, West Texas (Lasley and Sexton 1988). In southern Texas, early nesting records (1892 and 1913) were from Webb County, where Gray Hawks have not been seen recently. Nesting was not observed in Texas for much of the twentieth century.

In 1972 Cruz Martinez saw an immature at Santa Ana, and in mid-July, 1973, Wayne Shifflett saw an adult there (Webster 1972b, 1973). Nesting was confirmed in the Valley during the TBBAP (Benson and Arnold 2001).

Currently Gray Hawks occur regularly in small numbers along the river from Falcon Dam to Santa Ana, with nesting records in Starr and Hidalgo counties. The species is a permanent resident in those areas, and individuals occasionally wander into Cameron County in winter and spring (John C. Arvin and Brad McKinney, pers. comm.). I have seen three active nests and one former nest site in the Valley (see Habits). All nests in the Valley have involved two adult Gray Hawks, but in Big Bend National Park in 1989, an apparent female Red-shouldered Hawk was mated with an apparent male Gray Hawk. One downy chick was seen in the nest, but it did not survive to fledging (Lasley and Sexton 1989).

HABITAT Gray Hawks nest in tall trees, which may be in dense or open forest. Usually these forests are quite remote, and I have assumed that seclusion was needed for successful nesting. However, since 1999 a pair has nested successfully in Anzalduas, which is heavily used by picnickers on weekends (see "Other observations"). I have seen pairs using cedar elm, Mexican ash, and black willow for nest sites in the Valley. For foraging, Gray Hawks exploit semi-open riparian forest or drier thorn scrub—evidently wherever their reptilian prey can most easily be found.

HABITS Gray Hawks are relatively long-tailed hawks. They evoke both an accipiter (with a flap-flap-flap-glide flight through the forest) and a buteo (having a fairly heavy body and sometimes soaring above the forest). Apparently based on this hawk's flight style and general size and appearance, an old name was Mexican Goshawk, which has caused some confusion with the true Northern Goshawk (*Accipiter gentilis*), not occuring in the Valley.

The Gray Hawk sits quite upright, often on a low perch, while watching for prey. It is somewhat tame for a hawk, often allowing a fairly close approach. For example, on the overcast, 40–50°F (5–10°C) day of February 5, 1996, a pair of adults roosting side by side in open riparian forest allowed my daughter Elizabeth and me to pass by within about 60 feet (20 m) on a winding trail.

I have been able to study the pair nesting at Anzalduas fairly regularly, since the nest is so accessible. This pair is remarkably silent during the incubation and nestling periods, when one can easily miss seeing or hearing them. During pair formation and nest building, I hear the courtship song, the melancholy descending whistle often repeated three or four times. Adults give the alarm call, *creeer*, when they are upset, and fledglings give a harsher, broken scream.

Young birds are usually on their own by their first fall, but on April 16, 1999, I saw a second-year bird flying toward the active Anzalduas nest, which had at least one nestling. As far as I know the adult did not permit the immature to land in the nest tree, and the young bird was not seen again in the area.

Gray Hawks are harassed less than buteos, evidently because they are not as conspicuous in their habits. In May, 1999, two or three Couch's Kingbirds harassed an adult for a short time along the Resaca Trail at Santa Ana. Two Northern Mockingbirds once scolded a freshly plumaged juvenile at Bentsen.

OTHER OBSERVATIONS Immatures—birds still in the brown-backed plumage with a brown-streaked belly—do not molt until their second fall or winter (Glinski 1998). A bird in molt can look strange, appearing to have a gray head and a brown back, as did the bird I saw at Bentsen in February, 2000. Several visiting birders misidentified this bird as the much-sought-after Roadside Hawk (*Buteo magnirostris*). Identification is particularly difficult if all one gets is a brief glimpse and if there are several hawks in the area.

The Anzalduas Gray Hawks are unusual not only in nesting in such a busy park but in doing so successfully, three years in a row. In 1999, the nest was 49–56 feet (15–17 m) up in a cedar elm, near the eastern edge of the main picnic section of the park. On June 25, 1999, Mel and Arlie Cooksey (pers. comm.) saw a fledgling from this nest being fed by at least one adult. In 2000 and 2001, the birds nested more than 35 feet (11 m) up in a Mexican ash within 50 feet (15 m) of a park road. They must have seen a lot of human activity not far below them, especially on weekends and holidays.

I saw a full-grown nestling on June 21, 2000, and a fledgling in the nest tree on June 24. In 2001 I saw three nestlings there on June 6. The pair seldom foraged in the park itself, and they and most visitors seemed to ignore one another. In 2002, the nest was in a cedar elm within 66 feet (20 m) of the 1999–2000 nest tree, and the birds fledged at least two offspring.

Perhaps more regularly, Gray Hawks nest in remote riparian forests, where they see people less frequently. However, they sometimes encounter Brown Jays, which are large enough to be potential nest predators. On May 25, 1996, a pair of these hawks nesting above Fronton chased three Brown Jays away from the area of their nest tree, which contained two downy youngsters. One adult sat near a nest in the same forest in June, 2002, but river conditions prevented me from stopping to investigate.

OUTLOOK The establishment of Gray Hawks as nesters along the lower Rio Grande is encouraging, and the species may be spreading somewhat along the Rio Grande. However, the total range and number of breeding pairs in Texas are still too small to inspire much confidence. The apparent need for tall nesting trees may be the crucial limiting factor.

Other buteos

I have always associated **Red-shouldered Hawks** (*Buteo lineatus*) with swampy woods and bottomland forests, such as those along the upper Mississippi River. In the early to mid-1990s, I was pleased to see Red-shouldered Hawks fairly regularly in forests and wetlands along the lower Rio Grande. I even saw a breeding pair at Santa Ana and observed the adults searching at the water's edge for snakes and frogs. What I later learned was that most of the birds I saw were only wintering and that the current Valley breeding population is quite small.

A successful Red-shouldered Hawk nest active in the early to mid-1990s at Santa Ana was taken over by Harris's Hawks during the late 1990s (Brush and Cantu 1998). I was not able to tell if this was an aggressive takeover or just one species taking advantage of a good nest site abandoned by another species. In the late 1990s, a pair of Red-shouldered Hawks centered their activity near the northern edge of Santa Ana. Their behavior suggested that they were then nesting on private land just outside the refuge. On October 30, 1997, I saw two adults and one juvenile together at Pintail Lake (Santa Ana). Since winter residents occur singly, I suspected that this was a family group. At least one adult summered in the same area in 1998–2001.

Observations of a summering adult and an immature in 1996 at the mouth of an arroyo between Salineño and Fronton suggested possible breeding in Starr County as well. The immature was molting some flight feathers when I saw it on July 17, 1996, suggesting that it was a second-year bird (first-year birds would be in fresh plumage in July). It is possible that the immature and adult may have been mated, given the small number of potential mates in the entire Valley. I saw an adult in the same area in September, 1998.

Certainly Red-shouldered Hawks have declined since the 1950s. A nesting pair at Laguna Atascosa in 1953 was noted fairly casually (Goldman 1953); today the species no longer nests there. A nesting pair I saw at Quemado, Maverick County, in May, 2002, suggests the upriver range of Red-shouldered Hawks in Texas, and the species occurs along the Nueces River during the breeding season.

Swainson's Hawks (*Buteo swainsoni*), here at the southern edge of their temperate-zone breeding range, migrate in large numbers through the Valley. They often roost on large bare fields at night. During summer, Swainson's Hawk is fairly regular in small numbers and breeds in the western half of the Valley. For example, on June 12, 1997, I saw an adult and immature or subadult in a possible courtship flight over Bentsen. On July 19, 1997, Eric Hopson, Chris Hathcock, and I saw two adults soaring together over private land just outside the southwestern section of Santa Ana. On July 29, 1999, an adult flew over Anzalduas with prey in its talons; the date suggested that it was carrying food to a nestling or fledgling. William S. Clark found an active nest near Anzalduas in 2003, and other territorial pairs in the general area, confirming Swainson's Hawk nesting in the Valley.

The **White-tailed Hawk** (*Buteo albicaudatus*), here near the northern limits of its broad neotropical range, is known to nest in the coastal prairies of the eastern Valley (Benson and Arnold 2001). The species may be more common on large ranches just north of the Valley, and White-tails become more widespread in the area in winter. Many individuals (especially immatures) are attracted to fires, which are regularly set in sugarcane fields in preparation for harvesting. These birds are also attracted to fires in savannas north of the Valley, for example the 56 birds noted at a controlled burn on March 1, 1987 (Lasley and Sexton 1987). Turkey Vultures, White-tailed Hawks, and sometimes Crested Caracaras come in to feast on animals (presumably rodents) killed by the flames.

Other raptors

Ospreys (*Pandion haliaetus*) regularly summer in the Valley in small numbers but have not nested since 1908–10, when Austin P. Smith (in Oberholser 1974) found them breeding at Port Isabel. Ospreys might nest on Falcon Lake, perhaps on a boundary marker, given their regular presence near the dam all year.

The **Common Black-Hawk** (*Buteogallus anthracinus*) is a widespread, water-loving "near-buteo" of the tropics with a limited range in the southwestern United States. It has nested in the Valley in the past (Cameron County, 1937) but is now a rare visitor (Oberholser 1974). During May, 1976, a pair nested unsuccessfully below Santa Margarita Ranch, Starr County (John C. Arvin, in Webster 1976). The Valley does not seem to support enough shallow stream habitat with overhanging trees, which is evidently the kind of habitat Common Black-Hawks need. The nearest recent nesting site in Texas was in the South Concho River drainage (Tom Green County, on the western Edwards Plateau; Maxwell and Husak 1999), about 310 miles (500 km) north-northwest of Santa Margarita Ranch. Common Black-Hawks are still seen in southern Tamaulipas, often in coastal mangroves, but whether the species nests any closer to the Valley is unknown.

Harris's Hawks (*Parabuteo unicinctus*) are quite common as breeders and permanent residents in most parts of the Valley. This social, polyandrous raptor has been studied extensively in Arizona (Bednarz 1987, 1988; Dawson 1998), but South Texas appears to be the heart of its U.S. range. Harris's Hawks are typical of thorn scrub and thorn forest areas, where they often perch on telephone poles at dawn and dusk. They soar only to change foraging areas; in my experience they hunt from perches, often less than 10 feet (3 m) off the ground.

I regularly see two adults foraging over the abandoned fields and roadsides between Edinburg and McAllen, and I suspect that they nest in one of the few remaining patches of brush. During the dry winter of 1999, I saw a subadult attempting to capture shorebirds at Santa Ana's Pintail Lake, indicating both the species' behavioral flexibility and how bad conditions must have been in the thorn forest at that time. The hawk never really came close to capturing a Greater Yellowlegs or Black-necked Stilt in any of its foraging flights.

Young Harris's Hawks may stay in the parental home range for more than one year, and one or two subadults may help raise succeeding broods (Bednarz 1987). However, I have not seen the larger cooperative groups (up to seven birds) observed in southern Arizona (Dawson and Mannan 1989). At Santa Ana in 1999, I and others saw a very tame subadult bird, which often flew toward observers, sometimes startling them if it happened to approach from the rear. This bird was evidently raised in a nest near a ranger's residence, and perhaps frequent contacts with people in that heavily birded area allowed it to lose much of its fear.

In the late 1990s, Harris's Hawks nested in southern McAllen, near the airport and the old floodway (Steve Bentsen and Jane Kittleman, pers. comm.). Here the birds could forage out in the grassland and savanna, so they should not be considered completely urban birds. More urban was the group of three birds residing around the courthouse square in Edinburg during the winter of 2001–2002. Remains of pigeons were found in their rooftop roost sites (Nicholas Parma, pers. comm.). They did not remain to nest.

Other hawks are seen rarely during the summer months, but there is little or no evidence of any of those species currently nesting here. **Red-tailed Hawk** (*Buteo jamaicensis*) has nested in Cameron and Starr counties (Oberholser 1974), but I know of no recent nesting records. This widespread North American breeder is primarily a winter resident here. **Zone-tailed Hawk** (*Buteo albonotatus*) was seen repeatedly in the summer of 1909 in Cameron County by Austin P. Smith, and a specimen was collected there in February, 1912 (Oberholser 1974). I consider it an unconfirmed nester. I saw an adult soaring over Santa Ana on June 6, 1994, and it is a rare but regular Valley winter visitor.

Thus far, **Short-tailed Hawks** (*Buteo brachyurus*) are known to breed in the United States only in Florida. The first seen in Texas was at Santa Margarita Ranch in July, 1989 (Lasley 1991). They have been seen more regularly in recent years, especially at Santa Ana. For example, I saw a single light-morph adult there between June 6 and July 2, 1996, on June 30, 1998, and again on August 22, 2001. I saw a dark-morph juvenile at Santa Ana on September 6, 1996—the teardrop-shaped light marks on the entirely chocolate-brown underparts were a key feature of the juvenile. I also saw light-morph birds at Bentsen on June 27, 1998, and at Santa Ana on August 25, 1999. Brian Wheeler photographed a dark-morph immature at Santa Ana on

May 30, 1995 (Lasley and Sexton 1995). An adult light-morph bird was seen regularly at Santa Ana in June and July, 2002, after I first spotted it on May 31. Our birds doubtless come from northeastern Mexico, where they are resident (Arvin 2001).

I occasionally see juvenile **Cooper's Hawks** (*Accipiter cooperii*) in the Valley in July, but have assumed that these were probably dispersing from the oak forest breeding population in Brooks and Kenedy counties (Benson and Arnold 2001). Cooper's Hawks commonly winter in the Valley. Valley nesting was confirmed by William S. Clark, myself, and Scott Werner in June 2003, when a pair nested at Bentsen, so some birds may be year-round residents.

FAMILY FALCONIDAE

Aplomado Falcon, *Falco femoralis*

Now rare and endangered, the Alpomado Falcon was once a "not very uncommon summer resident" in Valley coastal prairies (Merrill 1878). Aplomados were most frequently seen about halfway between Brownsville and Point Isabel, probably because that was the most accessible section of coastal prairie. Birds were also seen up to 35 miles (56 km) north of Brownsville. Frank Armstrong collected a bird on the Mexican side of the river in the Matamoros region as well as others farther south in Tamaulipas (Phillips 1911). After 1910, the species was basically gone as a nester from Texas (one nest in Brooks County in 1941; Oberholser 1974). No one knows why the species disappeared, since it was gone before pesticides or land clearing could have been significant factors.

Recovery efforts began in the mid-1980s. In 1985 four captive-bred young Aplomados were released on the King Ranch, and in 1986 four were released at Laguna Atascosa (Lasley and Sexton 1986). Twenty-six birds were released at Laguna Atascosa in 1993. In 1995 a pair of previously released birds nested at the Port of Brownsville (Mora et al. 1997). During the 2000 breeding season, 30 territorial pairs were found, 20 of those at Laguna Atascosa and 10 at Matagorda Island in the Texas Coastal Bend. Many of these birds were breeding. Nest depredation by Great Horned Owls and raccoons reduced nesting success; nests atop telephone poles were most successful. A total of 812 fledglings have been released in Texas, and at least 87 wild young had fledged by 2002 (Jenny et al. 2004).

Aplomado Falcons capture a wide variety of birds and insects (Kennedy 1950; Hector 1985). I have seen an Aplomado perched on a roadside fence post gracefully capturing dragonflies, and Perez et al. (1996) found insects to be the main food item for Aplomados in and near Laguna Atascosa. However, Hector (1985) found birds to be the main prey remains at nests in eastern Mexico, including species as large as female Great-tailed Grackles and Yellow-billed Cuckoos. One would think that male grackles are too big to catch, but Aplomados occasionally capture and consume Greater Roadrunners (Montoya et al. 1997). Another possibility is kleptoparasitism, since Aplomados are known to steal prey from other raptors (Brown et al. 2003). Meadowlarks are likely important prey for Aplomados in Valley coastal prairies, as they are in interior grasslands of northern Mexico (Montoya et al. 1997).

While pesticide residues have declined in many prey items, they remain somewhat elevated in meadowlarks and Great-tailed Grackles (Mora et al. 1997). Let us hope that there is enough open coastal prairie with low pesticide levels to support a viable Aplomado Falcon population. The fact that nonbanded (wild-raised) pairs have been nesting regularly is encouraging, and we can hope that the species is back in the Valley to stay.

Other falcons

American Kestrels (*Falco sparverius*) winter commonly in agricultural sections of the Valley, but the closest breeding population is in northwestern Webb County (John C. Arvin, pers. comm.). As an example of the latter, I saw two birds perched on high power poles along U.S. Highway 83 in northwestern Webb County on May 4, 2002. By that time of year wintering American Kestrels have left southern Texas.

Peregrine Falcons (*Falco peregrinus*) regularly summer in small numbers (at least from the 1950s to the present), but there is no evidence of nesting. Two or three times I have seen a Peregrine Falcons stooping down on post-breeding flocks of White-winged Doves that roost near the river.

Crested Caracaras (*Caracara cheriway*), falcons that act more like vultures in their scavenging of road-killed animals, breed in the northern and western fringes of the Valley. In winter, individuals wander more widely, and some are attracted to burning cane fields for their harvest of rodents.

RAILS, COOTS, AND MOORHENS
(ORDER GRUIFORMES)

FAMILY RALLIDAE

King Rail (*Rallus elegans*), **Clapper Rail** (*R. longirostris*), **Purple Gallinule** (*Porphyrio martinica*), **Common Moorhen** (*Gallinula chloropus*), and **American Coot** (*Fulica americana*) all nest in the Valley, in various numbers. The moorhen and coot are by far the most common and widespread, using marshy ponds on public and private lands. Clapper Rails occur in the limited coastal mangrove and salt marsh habitats, and Scarlet Colley has seen chicks accompanied by adults in the Port Isabel area several times in the last few years (June, 2000, for example).

King Rails are rare summer residents of freshwater cattail marshes, with occasional nesting noted. In April, 1993, I regularly saw an adult carrying food into the cattails at Pintail Lake, Santa Ana, indicating nearby nestlings. This bird was also recorded by John Bax in his video *Treasures of the Rio Grande Delta*, but there are no historic breeding records of King Rail in the Valley. Purple Gallinules have nested in Hidalgo and Cameron counties and still nest there in reduced numbers (Oberholser 1974; Benson and Arnold 2001). However, the days of ten pairs nesting at Santa Ana (R. J. Fleetwood, in Webster 1963) seem long gone.

FAMILY GRUIDAE

The **Whooping Crane** (*Grus americana*), now critically endangered, may once have bred in or near the Valley. Henry E. Dresser (1865–66) observed a small number of Whooping Cranes in a lagoon near Matamoros in late June, 1863. He collected one and saw a pair, suggesting possible breeding just across the Rio Grande from Brownsville. There are four nineteenth-century breeding records in Texas (Wharton and Colorado counties; Oberholser 1974), but the species nests only in a small area in Canada today.

SHOREBIRDS, GULLS, AND TERNS (ORDER CHARADRIIFORMES)

The large, busy flocks of sandpipers and plovers that occur in the Valley during migration and winter naturally attract our attention. Hundreds or thousands of shorebirds can be seen at times, especially on the vast coastal mudflats and sandflats along the Lower Laguna Madre (Brush 1995, for example). Piping Plovers (*Charadrius melodus*) winter in coastal southern Texas in numbers that are substantial for this declining species (Drake et al. 2001; Eubanks 1994). However, given the Valley's subtropical latitude, its nine breeding shorebird species—eight current and one former—are of particular interest to me.

FAMILY JACANIDAE

Northern Jacanas are rare visitors from the tropics, and they have bred in the Valley. *Jacana spinosa* acts like a rail or moorhen, foraging by walking on floating aquatic plants and supported by its very long toes. Males incubate the eggs and tend the offspring in this polyandrous species. Merrill saw a pair in August, 1876, and jacanas have bred in Cameron County: at Olmito in 1938 and San Benito in 1951 (Oberholser 1974). Elsewhere in southern Texas, there are breeding records in Bexar (1922), Kleberg (1968), and Brazoria (1971–72) counties. Jacanas apparently are now nonbreeding visitors to the Valley.

The Northern Jacanas that appear in Texas are often in juvenal or immature plumage, recognizable by their whitish underparts and supercilium. Juveniles (first summer birds) and immatures (first fall–first spring birds) are difficult to distinguish, and most observers do not attempt to do so. According to Oberholser (1974), jacanas do not molt into the dark adult plumage until their second fall, but an ornithology class and I saw a bird molting from immature to adult plumage at Santa Ana in April, 1993.

During the last ten years, 10 of the 11 records of Northern Jacanas in the Valley were between 1992 and 1994, between Falcon Dam and Olmito (all records documented and accepted by the Texas Bird Records Committee). The remaining jacana record was on October 21, 2000, after a gap of six years, on the Mexican side of the Rio Grande south of Mission (Jane Kittleman and Billy Snyder). As with Masked Ducks, extended wet periods such as in the early 1990s may encourage northward movement and perhaps even local breeding of jacanas, followed by population declines during dry years. The years 1996–2000 were quite dry overall, the worst extended drought since the 1950s.

Northern Jacanas in Texas have been seen along moist pond edges in managed wetlands dominated by cattails (such as Santa Ana) or along the river's edge in *Phragmites*-dominated habitat (below Falcon Dam, for example). Birds weave in and out among the marsh vegetation, and suitable habitat may be inaccessible to birders; hence some visiting jacanas may go unseen. Jacanas may stay for up to three months or remain for only a day. Birds should be looked for especially during August–October, the Valley's most predictably wet period, when suitable habitat is usually at its annual peak.

FAMILY CHARADRIIDAE

Snowy Plovers (*Charadrius alexandrinus*) are familiar birds along the Pacific and Gulf coasts of the United States, and they occur widely in both the New World and the Old (AOU 1998). They are most easily seen along the coast, often in mixed-species wintering flocks with Piping Plovers (Brush 1995). Snowy Plovers are generally considered to be rare or uncommon breeders in southern Texas, but Jeffery R. Rupert's studies in the mid-1990s revealed both inland and coastal breeders (J. R. Rupert 1997 and unpubl. data). As far as I know, Snowy Plovers do not nest on beaches in southern Texas, but they use old hurricane washover areas and bayside sandflats on barrier islands (Zonick 1997). On the west side of the Laguna Madre, Snowy Plovers nest on mudflats, some of which are a few miles from the bay. Farther inland, the species nests along the shorelines of the Salt Lakes.

Snowy Plovers may nest alone or in small colonies. Nests often suffer from predation or flooding due to sudden downpours. The most successful Snowy Plover nests are those within Least Tern colonies and on higher tidal flats (J. R. Rupert 1997). The terns harass wandering gulls and other potential predators, reducing the chances that nests will be found and robbed. Although human disturbance is a major factor affecting the nesting success of Piping Plovers, Snowy Plovers nesting in southern Texas seem able to avoid areas heavily used by people. Hatchlings, usually attended by one parent, move into partially vegetated areas, as Rupert (1997) found through radiotelemetry and color banding. Such areas may be important so that young can hide from predators.

In terms of plumage matching and habitat selection, **Wilson's Plovers** (*Charadrius wilsonia*) are to dark mud what Snowy Plovers are to light mud or sand. They usually inhabit wet mudflats, often along narrow shorelines. Such areas are often partially vegetated, with scattered black mangrove shrubs and patches of salt-tolerant marsh plants. Wilson's Plovers nest at Laguna Atascosa and nearby coastal areas, mainly along the west side of the Lower Laguna Madre and around South Bay (Oberholser 1974; Bergstrom 1988). Usually thought of as strictly coastal, Wilson's Plovers have been found nesting in the Salt Lakes area and also just north of the Valley, in Brooks County (Greg Lasley, pers. comm.).

Although Wilson's Plovers are resident in the tropics, they are only warm-weather residents (March–October) in southern Texas. Returning males quickly claim a nesting territory by means of calling and chasing, and nesting begins in early April. In wet years, nests may be built on unimproved roads adjacent to mudflats (Bergstrom 1988); in dry years nests are on the flats themselves. Usually one sees two to four birds on a given mudflat, depending on its size, but I once saw a postbreeding aggregation of 143 birds at Laguna Atascosa.

Our most widespread plover is the **Killdeer** (*Charadrius vociferus*), which is common on large expanses of lawn, golf courses, fields, and freshwater shorelines throughout the Valley. I have paid little attention to this common North American species but did record one specific instance: a small Killdeer chick attended by an adult along the Rio Grande near Roma on May 28, 2002.

FAMILY HAEMATOPODIDAE

American Oystercatchers (*Haematopus palliatus*) nest uncommonly along the coast, in my experience close to the water's edge in the southern part of the Lower Laguna Madre. The large, brightly colored adults are conspicuous as they forage on oyster beds and nearby tidal flats. I have seen as many 18 birds in one group on the bay side of South Padre Island in winter. In the breeding season I have seen single juveniles attended by adults on the oyster beds between the former and current causeways on South Padre Island.

FAMILY RECURVIROSTRIDAE

American Avocets (*Recurvirostra americana*) nest both at the Salt Lakes and along the coast, usually in small numbers (Benson and Arnold 2001). They forage in pools, sweeping their scythelike bills from side to side. I know of no recent breeding records along the Rio Grande itself, but Henry E. Dresser (1865–66) saw several family groups in a lagoon at Matamoros in July, 1863. Their numbers increase greatly in winter, when I have seen more than 1,000 at times at Laguna Atascosa (Brush 1995). **Black-necked Stilts** (*Himantopus mexicanus*) are pool foragers, like avocets, but nest in small freshwater ponds and lakes throughout the Valley. A favorite nesting location is at sewage treatment plants, perhaps due to the abundant food resources there. The stilts nest regularly at the McAllen Sewage Treatment Plant ponds, when water is available in an overflow area.

FAMILY SCOLOPACIDAE

Long-billed Curlews (*Numenius americanus*) are intriguing for several reasons: their tremendously long, down-curved bill; their varied foraging habitats, ranging from lawns and golf-courses to coastal bays and prairies; their occasional habit of roosting in trees; and their uncertain nesting status. Long-billed Curlews nest mainly on short-grass prairies of the western United States and southwestern Canada, with substantial numbers wintering in southern Texas and Mexico (AOU 1998). Although some birds can be found year-round, most start returning to the Valley in numbers in late June and early to mid-July. Curlews remain common throughout the fall, winter, and early spring.

Larger numbers occur in coastal sections, where birds can choose between foraging for crabs in shallow bays when the tide is low and picking up grasshoppers from coastal grasslands at other times. A traditional roost on Laguna Atascosa attracts hundreds of curlews from the surrounding area. Strangely, a San Benito bird with only one foot roosted in a tree in a residential area for two or three days in a row in October, 2000 (Liz Bennett de

Luna, pers. comm.). Some birds depart for the north in March, and most follow in April, so that curlew numbers drop noticeably by early May.

There are two definite coastal Texas nesting records from long ago (cited in Oberholser 1974): on June 16, 1877, J. C. Merrill found newly fledged young east of Brownsville; and on June 1, 1910, G. F. Simmons found seven young ("barely able to fly") in Harris County (the Houston area, on the upper Texas coast). In Kincaid's opinion (Oberholser 1974), current nesting was highly doubtful.

Hence it was a great surprise for me to hear evidence that curlews were nesting again in southern Texas. Harold Burgess found two Long-billed Curlew fledglings on July 13, 1990, 4 miles (6 km) west of Laguna Vista, Cameron County, in wet coastal prairie (Benson and Arnold 2001). The curlews were in "early flight," which I assume means that they were barely able to fly. Steve Labuda saw a pair of curlews doing a low circular flight over coastal prairie at Laguna Atascosa on June 6, 2001, suggesting possible continued nesting of Long-billed Curlews in the Valley. As with the Elf Owl, we can only guess at whether curlews had disappeared as nesters for more than a hundred years or had maintained a small, overlooked breeding population, and at what the future will hold.

Willets (*Catoptrophorus semipalmatus*) nest in salt marsh–like vegetation along or within a few miles of the Laguna Madre. They are fairly common nesters, especially in wet years. I have seldom taken the time to look for nesting Willets, but I did see newly hatched young on South Padre Island on May 14, 1994.

FAMILY LARIDAE

Least Terns (*Sterna antillarum*) formerly nested on sandbars in the Rio Grande channel (Merrill 1878). They no longer do so, since such bars no longer exist for long along today's river. Now nesting mainly along the coast, many pairs use islands in the Lower Laguna Madre or adjacent coastal tidal flats. Least Terns also nest inland at the Salt Lakes and sometimes at caliche pits or other ponds that have suitable open nesting habitat. Just outside the Valley proper, Neck and Riskind (1981) found a small colony in 1979 along the Falcon Lake shoreline in the Zapata County portion of Falcon State Park.

Least Terns currently nest in the Laredo area in small numbers. On May 30, 2001, Penny Warren, Jan Earle, and I saw a small Least Tern colony at Bravo Bend along the Rio Grande in Laredo. It included about six adults, one egg and one newly hatched chick. Woodin et al. (2000a) regularly saw Least Terns at Lake Casa Blanca and along the Rio Grande in Laredo during surveys from April to July, 1999, but they did not report any nests. Adults are seen in small numbers, somewhat erratically, over lakes, canals, and the Rio Grande, suggesting that they opportunistically exploit suitable nesting conditions wherever these occur.

Caspian Tern (*Sterna caspia*), **Royal Tern** (*S. maxima*), **Sandwich Tern** (*S. sandvicensis*), **Gull-billed Tern** (*S. nilotica*), **Forster's Tern** (*S. forsteri*), and **Black Skimmer** (*Rynchops niger*) all breed regularly in the Valley. Most nesting colonies are coastal, but Gull-billed Terns and Black Skimmers also nest in the Salt Lakes area, and Forster's Terns have nested at Falcon Lake (Benson and Arnold 2001) and Presa Marte R. Gomez (Sugar Lake) in Tamaulipas (Howell and Webb 1995). **Laughing Gulls** (*Larus atricilla*) commonly nest on islands in the Laguna Madre and fly inland to Brownsville and Harlingen to forage. I see Laughing Gulls occasionally in southern Hidalgo County, and they even reach Falcon Lake in small numbers.

Rare larid species include **Sooty Tern** (*Sterna fuscata*), which nests in small numbers in the Lower Laguna Madre (Benson and Arnold 2001; Smith 2002), and **Herring Gull** (*Larus argentatus*), which nested there in 1989—the only nesting record for the state (Farmer 1990). **Common Tern** (*Sterna hirundo*) nested along the Lower Laguna Madre in the 1920s (Pemberton 1922), but the species' Gulf of Mexico population has declined greatly, and Common Terns no longer nest in Texas (Oberholser 1974).

DOVES AND PIGEONS
(ORDER COLUMBIFORMES)

FAMILY COLUMBIDAE

Red-billed Pigeon, *Patagioenas flavirostris*

The Red-billed Pigeon has a better scientific name than common name, since the bill (*rostrum,* in Latin) has more yellow (*flavus*) than red. In the late 1870s, Merrill (1878) described "this large and handsome pigeon" as abundant, "arriving in flocks of fifteen or twenty about the last week in February." He saw it regularly around Fort Brown—then just east of the city of Brownsville, now surrounded by urban development—but said it was much more plentiful "a few miles upriver" where the tree were taller and the forest denser. Today much scarcer, Red-billed Pigeon is on the wish list of many visiting birders, who must usually travel well upriver to see it. Appearing dark in poor viewing conditions, *paloma morada* shows a beautiful purplish cast when seen in good light.

DISTRIBUTION   Red-billed Pigeons occur from Sonora, Durango, Nuevo León, and southern Texas (Webb, Zapata, Starr, and Hidalgo counties, formerly upstream to Maverick County) south on both slopes through most of Mexico and Central America to Panama (Texas Game, Fish and Oyster Commission 1945; AOU 1998). They are permanent residents in all but southern Texas and northern Tamaulipas. The Rio Grande population is relatively isolated, as the next closest known nesting population is along the Río Corona in central Tamaulipas, about 200 miles (330 km) to the south (Gehlbach 1987). John C. Arvin has seen small numbers in tall trees around ranch houses in the Cerralvo area of Nuevo León, but he has never observed them in the mountain canyons of the nearby Sierra de los Picachos. Small numbers (one to three birds per day) were seen in the summers of 1968 and 1969 on the Norias Division of the King Ranch by Fall (1973), but there is no known nesting population there.

Previously nesting at least as far downriver as Santa Ana and the Brownsville-Matamoros area, Red-billed Pigeons were confirmed nesting during the 1990s only between Chapeño and Fronton and in the vicinity of Bentsen (Brush 1998a). Edgar B. Kincaid saw one at the Sabal Palm Grove near Brownsville in mid-July, 1957, but there was no evidence of nesting (Webster 1957). The last known nest at Santa Ana was in 1970 (Wayne Schifflett, in Webster 1970), and the last known nest in Hidalgo County was in 1996. Red-billed Pigeons have been rare visitors to Santa Ana and Bentsen throughout the 1990s. This is quite a decline at Santa Ana since 1953, when 150 pairs nested there (Luther C. Goldman, in Oberholser 1974). Gone are the days when "the population may gather in large flocks in the fall" (Davis 1966, 1974), ranging throughout the Valley (Texas Game, Fish and Oyster Commission 1945), as far north as Raymondville, Willacy County (Kincaid, in Webster 1957).

Seven out of the ten Red-billed Pigeon nests I have seen were between Chapeño and Fronton, in the heart of the species' current range in Texas. Several other nests were found in the same area in 2000 and 2001 (Jack C. Eitniear and Jeff Breeden, unpubl. data). On June 11, 2001, I saw three pigeons between Roma and Rio Grande City, suggesting a small population in that area, which has remained almost completely unstudied. TBBAP data show Red-billed Pigeons nesting near San Ygnacio (Benson and Arnold 2001). Small numbers were seen in 1999 in northwestern Webb County (Woodin et al. 1999), but no nests have yet been found in Webb County.

HABITAT   A bird of broken forest in the tropics, the Red-billed Pigeon nests in the tallest, densest riparian forests along the Rio Grande. Most nests I have found have been on forested islands, which are sometimes U.S. territory and sometimes Mexican. These islands are dominated by Mexican ash and sugar hackberry, and I consider the ones most heavily used by Red-billed Pigeons to be high-quality riparian forest. Often Brown Jays, Audubon's Orioles, and other forest species are found on the same islands.

Whether this use of islands is to escape predation, as Strong et al. (1991) found for White-crowned Pigeons (*Patagioenas leucocephala*) in the Florida Keys, or for some other reason is hard to say.

Red-billed Pigeons may forage in a greater variety of habitats than just tall riparian forest. For example, on September 6, 1999, I saw 18 scattered along the river between Chapeño and Fronton. Some were in possum-grape (*Cissus incisa*) vines laden with fruit; I assumed that they were eating the fruit. A few others were in possum-grape vines in mesquite trees about 1,000 feet (300 m) from the river.

HABITS   In my Valley experience, Red-billed Pigeons are usually quite wary and fly away just above the treetops, not allowing prolonged observation. Nesting birds may be more reluctant to fly far from the nest, although they have a great knack for staying behind foliage as they fly away. Red-billed Pigeons, like Clay-colored Robins and Audubon's Orioles, readily consume mulberry (*Morus* sp.) fruits. On April 2, 1999, I saw two birds in the understory on an island near Salineño with their bills stained entirely red from the fruits—truly red-billed pigeons. In central Nuevo León, Starker Leopold (1959) found Red-billed Pigeons consuming corn and Johnson grass in winter and brasil (*Condalia obovata*) and wild grape (*Vitis cinerea*) in summer.

Normally one sees Red-billed Pigeons as pairs or individuals, but they can be seen in small flocks either before or after the breeding season. For example, Brush Freeman and Petra Hockey saw 24 come in to roost on an island near Salineño, on February 19, 1999. The birds wander widely in pursuit of abundant fruits and seeds, particularly in the fall and winter (Leopold 1959).

OTHER OBSERVATIONS   Like other doves and pigeons, Red-billed Pigeons sometimes stage a distraction display when flushed from the nest. Nests contain just one egg, which is the complete set for this and some other pigeons. When freshly laid, the eggs have a peachy tinge for about one day. The length of the nesting season (May–September in the Valley) potentially allows birds to nest more than once. Predation is probably high, as with most doves and pigeons.

An incubating adult flies more slowly and noisily than it needs to, to draw attention away from the nest. Then governor George W. Bush and I saw this behavior at a nest near Bentsen on July 11, 1996, when he and his family visited the Valley on a working vacation to promote ecotourism. Unfortunately, the bird disappeared behind heavy foliage before anyone else could see it. Since Red-billed Pigeons can be hard to find in Texas, I was surprised to see one fly across U.S. Highway 83 about 3 miles (5 km) northwest of Zapata, on

March 1, 2002. Interestingly, that area is a location that was known to birders as a "Red-billed Pigeon spot" in the early 1990s (Dunne 1992).

In Sonora, northwestern Mexico, Red-billed Pigeons wander northward in September after they are done nesting, to feed on grapes (*Vitis vinifera*), sorghum, and possibly garbanzo beans (*Cicer arietinum*) in agricultural areas (Russell and Monson 1998). We do not know the immediate destination of birds leaving the Valley in September and October, but there is some evidence of a northeastward movement toward the coast, with a few records from Willacy County and Kenedy County (Fall 1973; Brad McKinney, pers. comm.). Most birds probably winter in Mexico, although small numbers may overwinter along the Rio Grande in Starr County.

OUTLOOK   Red-billed Pigeons apparently benefit from habitat change in tropical areas if some of the forest is removed for agricultural fields or pastures, but of course not if an entire region is deforested. In western Mexico, Red-billed Pigeons occur in tall second-growth and undisturbed tropical deciduous forest, while White-tipped Doves occur in short second-growth as well as taller forests (Hutto 1989).

The largest number of Red-billed Pigeons I have seen or heard in the Valley in one day is 30, along the river between Chapeño and Fronton, on April 15, 1995. This, plus the limited range of the species in the United States, suggests that Red-billed Pigeons are barely hanging on in the Valley. We must protect remaining tall Valley riparian forests and develop additional tall forests.

Other doves and pigeons

At least five other columbid species nest in the Valley, with a sixth likely already nesting as well. The studies of Texas Parks and Wildlife personnel like Gary Waggerman and Steve Benn and faculty and students from Texas A&M University–Kingsville have provided most of our knowledge of population trends and nesting and foraging requirements of the large game species. **Mourning Doves** (*Zenaida macroura*) are common in residential areas, thorn forest, and thorn scrub, being absent only from tall riparian forest and treeless areas. Mourning Doves are the least selective of the large doves in choosing nesting habitat, and they do not occur in dense nesting colonies. **White-winged Doves** (*Zenaida asiatica*) are abundant nesters in thorn forest, and they also nest in residential areas and in thorn scrub. Historically, White-winged Doves have shifted from native habitat to citrus groves to a combination of native habitat and residential areas, as Valley habitats have fluctuated (Small and Waggerman 1999; Hayslette et al. 2000). Both

Mourning and White-winged doves regularly "commute" to foraging sites in fields and also to sources of drinking water. In the 1940s they were limited to the area from San Antonio and Victoria south, but White-winged Doves have spread explosively north to (and beyond) the large cities of San Antonio and Austin, where they are now one of the most common urban birds (Gary Waggerman, pers. comm.).

The **White-tipped Dove** (*Leptotila verreauxi*), on the other hand, is more of woodland and forest bird. Nests are usually hidden in vine tangles or other dense foliage in shady forest, and the bird usually forages under cover as well. The attenuated (narrow-tipped) outer primary on each wing may allow the birds to maneuver well in wooded habitat (Goodwin 1983) or perhaps to lift off from the ground quickly when fleeing from a terrestrial predator (Mahler and Tubaro 2001). White-tipped Doves never seem to fly slowly—they always seem intent on reaching their destination quickly and directly. Some Valley residents with field experience call them "Mourning Doves," because the hollow cooing sounds sad.

They do occur in residential areas, provided that there are some dense, forestlike patches available. They also visit rural residences and woodlots if within commuting distance from larger wooded tracts. In the severe drought of 1998, a White-tipped Dove regularly visited my Edinburg yard to forage, and I see and hear them in a narrow wooded strip along the nearby canal.

Most birders' first experience with a White-tipped Dove is seeing a bird at a feeding station at Bentsen, where the species has become fairly tame, although still somewhat nervous and the first to leave if observers get too close. White-tipped Doves are wary and difficult to see away from feeding stations. Steve Russell, an observer with extensive experience in Sonora, Mexico (Russell and Monson 1998), was pleased to get good looks at White-tipped Doves at feeding stations in Bentsen in the mid-1990s.

Edgar Kincaid, Jr., thought White-tipped Doves would be lucky to survive in remote areas of Willacy and Starr Counties (in Oberholser 1974), so we can be happy that they are persisting across the Valley and spreading northward. For example, on September 6, 1999, John C. Arvin, Brush Freeman and Petra Hockey found three in Calhoun County. On May 30, 2001, I heard three singing in Laredo, and in early May, 2002, I heard small numbers in riparian forest near Quemado, Maverick County, near their upriver range limits. White-tipped Doves (and other species) were introduced to the Hawaiian island of Maui in 1933, but the introduction failed, and they were gone by 1938 (Moulton and Pimm 1983).

The smaller nesting doves are the **Common Ground-Dove** (*Columbina passerina*) and the **Inca Dove** (*Columbina inca*). The ground-dove is common in rural areas, most regularly in mesquite savanna and grassland interspersed with thorn scrub, as Friedmann (1925) noted long ago. The short-tailed ground-dove seems to float along with little effort as it flies, frequently showing the rufous flash in the wings. Males have a rosy tinge to the face and underparts, especially during the breeding season, leading sometimes to confusion with the rare Ruddy Ground-Dove (*Columbina talpacoti*). Common Ground-Doves are browner than Inca Doves and have a much shorter tail, with a small amount of white on the tips of the outer tail feathers. Also, Inca Doves make a characteristic dry, rattling sound with their wings when they take off, while Common Ground-Doves fly almost silently.

I have seen several Common Ground-Dove nests in prickly pear cactus, evidently a preferred nest site (Friedmann 1925). The rising *hooop* song is usually given by a bird well hidden from the observer. One can seldom get a leisurely look at a ground-dove, since they are startled easily and seldom come to feeders. On June 6, 2000, I was surprised to hear a Common Ground-Dove singing in the "mesquite savanna" corner of my yard, but the bird did not stay.

The *no-hope* or *whirlpool* song of the Inca Dove is heard regularly in residential and urban areas, their main habitats. Inca Doves also occur uncommonly in thorn scrub, especially along roadsides or at feeding stations where small seeds are available. Oddly, Merrill (1878) and Sennett (1878, 1879) did not see Inca Doves in the Valley, despite the fact that the birds had been reported in Laredo in 1866 (Casto 2000). Inca Doves may have spread both north and south from Laredo as they invaded the United States, but evidently the rate of increase was slow at first. In May, 1924, Inca Doves were the "least common of all the doves"—including Red-billed Pigeon—in the Brownsville area (Friedmann 1925)! Now this slender dove is common in inhabited areas throughout the Valley, including South Padre Island. Since the mid-1990s I have occasionally seen Inca Doves in the interior of Santa Ana, more than 0.3 miles (0.5 km) from the visitor center. Inca Doves now nest as far north as Amarillo and Dallas and as far east as western Louisiana (AOU 1998).

Two different responses to cold may help the tropical Inca Dove survive the colder temperatures that it now experiences in the United States: on cold days birds may form temporary "pyramids," in which they land on top of one another, forming a dense, heat-conserving pile of doves. At night, Inca Doves save energy by becoming hypothermic (Robertson and Schnapf 1987).

The introduced **Rock Pigeon** (*Columba livia*), formerly known as Rock Dove, has been in the Valley at least since the late 1870s. S. M. Finlay noticed Red-billed Pigeons perching in the same trees as "tame pigeons" in Hidalgo (Sennett 1878). When the birds became truly feral in the Valley— that is, breeding and surviving without the direct help of people—is not known. Still requiring buildings with ledges suitable for nesting, Rock Pigeons can also be seen across the countryside in fast-moving flocks headed for grain storage facilities or harvested corn fields. Sometimes they can be mistaken for Red-billed Pigeons if seen flying in poor light over a Valley park or refuge or along the river.

The **Eurasian Collared-Dove** (*Streptopelia decaocto*) is a recent invader of the Valley, having spread explosively since the late 1970s or early 1980s from Florida along the Gulf Coast to Texas, even reaching the Texas Panhandle by 1996 (Romagosa and Labisky 2000; Seyffert 2001). In October, 1998, at least one was seen at Santa Ana (Bob Behrstock, pers. comm.). In May, 2000, there were four in Rio Hondo, Cameron County (Tom Pincelli, pers. comm.). Brad McKinney saw his first in the Valley on February 4, 2001, in Rancho Viejo. On May 2, 2001, several were seen in display flights at Fort Ringgold (John C. Arvin, pers. comm.), and Katrina Troppy saw one in her Raymondville yard on July 31, 2001.

I saw my first Eurasian Collared-Doves in Edinburg on November 13, 2001, when five or six birds flew around a grain storage facility, evidently one of their favored habitats (Smith 1987). This species has almost certainly already nested in the Valley, given the above sightings and others on the Mexican side during 2001 and 2002: John C. Arvin and Clifford Shackelford saw two birds 12 miles (20 km) south of Matamoros in July, 2000. I saw five birds on January 1, 2002, at a grain storage facility in Pedro J. Mendez, about 53 miles (85 kilometers) south of Reynosa. This species should do well, given the abundance of sorghum here and their earlier invasion of most of Europe (Snow and Perrins 1998), and Valley nesting should soon be confirmed.

PARROTS AND PARAKEETS (ORDER PSITTACIFORMES)

FAMILY PSITTACIDAE

Green Parakeets (*Aratinga holochlora*) and **Red-crowned Parrots** (*Amazona viridigenalis*) are the most numerous psittacids in the Valley and the only Valley psittacid species that are accepted as established in Texas (Texas Ornithological Society 1995). There is considerable debate about the origins of these tropical birds, but I believe that some individuals came across on their own, as have so many other species in recent years, and I agree that they should be considered valid wild species in Texas.

Although usually called frugivores, parrots and parakeets mainly act as seed predators, consuming the seed after discarding or eating the surrounding material (Janzen 1981; Silvius 1995). Nonetheless, they are interesting and valuable components of our Valley avifauna and should be protected (see addition discussion later).

Interestingly, the **Yellow-headed Parrot** (*Amazona oratrix*) may have been the most regular psittacid visitor before 1950 (Davis 1974; Oberholser 1974). However, it has always occurred irregularly and has not become established as a breeding species. L. Irby Davis (1974) mentioned occasional reports of Yellow-headed Parrot flocks by fishermen in the northern Río San Fernando Delta, about 60 miles (96 km) south of Brownsville, as late as 1938. Davis believed that newspaper reports of parrot flocks along the Rio Grande in the late 1800s were Yellow-headed Parrots, and he cites scattered records of individuals in the Valley, one as late as 1964.

I have taken a particular interest in recent years in Green Parakeets because so little is known about them and they are easy to see in my neighboring city of McAllen. This bird is considered a parakeet because of its long tail, but it is much larger than the pet Budgerigar (*Melopsittacus undulatus*) that sometimes escapes from captivity. First reported in the United States at Santa Ana in October, 1960 (R. J. Fleetwood, in Oberholser 1974), Green Parakeets were seen only sporadically for quite a while. They occurred in spots where they are now absent, such as at Laguna Atascosa in late April–May, 1990 (Ken Russell, in Lasley and Sexton 1990).

Green Parakeets currently are urban and suburban birds here, with largest numbers in the cities of Brownsville, McAllen, and San Benito, and they are almost never seen in natural habitats in the Valley. Green Parakeets, like their relatives, are quiet while foraging but become quite noisy in flight. This has allowed my students and me to find regular roosting and preroosting sites, but it has been harder to find nesting or foraging birds.

Small numbers of Green Parakeets were seen in McAllen in the 1980s, for example 8–12 during March–May, 1987 (Sally Weeks, in Lasley and Sexton 1987). By 1989, up to 9 were seen in Harlingen, while 40 were present in McAllen (Lasley and Sexton 1989). Brad McKinney (in Lasley 1995) found 28 nests during a three-week period in July, 1995. Green Parakeets were also confirmed nesting in Weslaco during the TBBAP (1987–92). In late December, 1997, Kim Eckert and Brad McKinney saw more than 150 roosting near Fort Brown in Brownsville.

By the late 1990s, a flock of 150–300 or more was seen on most evenings on some high wires in northern McAllen. I saw about 125 there on December 19, 1999, and UTPA student Juan Hernandez (pers. comm.) reported about 275 on November 20, 2000. The high power lines are preroosting sites, similar to what Wermundsen (1998) saw at the Volcán Masaya in Nicaragua.

The McAllen birds usually end up roosting (sleeping) within 0.5 miles (0.8 km) of the preroosting site, typically in the dense foliage of live oaks.

Small numbers of Green Parakeets now occur upstream from the Valley, in Laredo: for example, I saw about 10 in the downtown historic district on May 29, 2001, some roosting or nesting in an abandoned church. In some parts of the Valley, where food and nest sites may not be present, parakeets are absent or rare. On September 28, 1997, I saw two fly over my house in Edinburg, the first and only time I have seen them in Edinburg.

The high power lines where the McAllen birds gather provide a safe location from most threats. I have always expected a Peregrine Falcon or Cooper's Hawk to make a pass at the parakeets, but so far I have not seen or heard of that happening here. In Nicaragua, both American Kestrels and Gray Hawks attack the closely related Pacific Parakeet (*Aratinga strenua;* Wermundsen 1998). Our parakeets occasionally preen each other or engage in brief squabbles and sometimes fly down to nearby store rooftops to drink water or perhaps chew on mortar between the bricks. Macaws are known to eat clay regularly in South America, probably to detoxify harmful chemicals in the seeds they eat; perhaps mortar serves the same purpose.

At times, some or all the birds may suddenly take off for no apparent reason and fly around a few times, only to land again on the wires. As the sky darkens, the birds fly off to roost. Occasionally the parakeets gather on different and lower wires, but as of 2003 they still usually gather on the high wires at North 10th Street and Violet. In the morning, the birds are difficult to follow, as they split up into smaller groups (5–25 birds) to search for food or nest sites (Carlos Gracia-Manzano, Brian Molina, pers. comm.). Some forage or nest in rural areas between McAllen and Mission, a pattern similar to that of the Olive-throated Parakeets (*Aratinga nana*) that roosted in the center of Huimangillo, Tabasco, and foraged outside of town (Berrett 1962).

Birders have found a few parakeet nests in McAllen. All the ones I have heard of have been in dead palm trees, mainly fan palms that have been killed by hard freezes. Brad McKinney's nests in Brownsville were mainly in dead fan palms. Although most birds may nest earlier in the year, there could be late breeding as well. On September 26, 2000, Brad McKinney saw a pair entering a cavity in Brownsville, and on October 25, 2000, Catherine C. Brush saw similar behavior in McAllen (I found at least five probable nests in McAllen in 2003, all in dead palms).

In Mexico, Green Parakeets nest in limestone caves and sinkholes (Eitniear and Aragon-Tapia 1997), woodpecker-excavated cavities in Montezuma bald-cypress (Gehlbach 1987), and probably rot cavities (like the conspecific or closely related Socorro Green Parakeet, *Aratinga holoehlora brevipes,* which nests in *Bumelia socorrensis;* Rodriguez-Estrella et al. 1995). In Nicaragua, Pacific Parakeets nest in the soft dirt of a volcanic crater wall (Wermundsen 1998).

The food habits of Green Parakeets are poorly known, but in the Valley several observers (including myself) have seen them most regularly eating anacua and sugar hackberry fruits. Buds of cottonwood trees, acorns, and chinaberry fruits are also part of their diet here (Dan Jones and Jorge Mendez, pers. comm.). Green Parakeets eat corn, *Mimosa* seeds, and fruits of Mexican myrtle (*Myrica mexicana*) and nanch (*Byrsonima crassifolia*) in Mexico or Guatemala (Lowery and Dalquest 1951; Edwards and Lea 1955; Forshaw 1977). Pacific Parakeets eat a variety of fruits and seeds during the wet and dry seasons in Nicaragua (Wermundsen 1997), and Green Parakeets probably are opportunistic as well. On October 26, 2002, I saw at about 12 Green Parakeets clinging to the flexible stalks of fan palm fruits, along a busy street in McAllen. At least five were reaching for and consuming the fruits while I drove underneath in heavy traffic. Susan A. Epps (pers. comm.) has seen Green Parakeets eating sunflower and safflower (*Carthamus tinctorius*) seeds at feeding stations in South Florida, where Green Parakeets have become established but are rare.

The successful establishment of Green Parakeets in Valley urban habitats may have more to do with a year-round supply of seeds and fruits than with nest sites (Rodriguez-Estrella et al. 1992). Potential nest sites would probably be more abundant in Valley thorn forest and riparian forest than in our cities, but no Green Parakeets (or Red-crowned Parrots) nest in Valley forests. Growing urban and suburban areas of the Valley provide pecans, acorns, figs (*Ficus* spp.), and palm fruits—which would not have been available in large quantities (or at all) in historic times in the Valley—as well as large, well-watered anacua and sugar hackberry trees. Viewed in a broader context, the spread of Green Parakeets and Red-crowned Parrots into the Valley may be seen as part of a northern expansion of the ranges of several tropical bird species (see table 2 on p. 207). The key is whether the species can successfully breed in current Valley habitats, some of which have changed considerably since the early days.

Red-crowned Parrots are somewhat more desirable as pets than Green Parakeets, and many were smuggled across the Rio Grande, especially in the 1970s and 1980s, before the sale of wild-caught birds was banned in the United States (Walker and Chapman 1992). Because the species is non-native and quite successful in southern California (Garrett 1997) and southern Florida (Epps 2002), some have assumed that Valley birds were also escapees. However, Walker and Chapman's historical research has revealed some early records. In the 1920s and early 1930s, a flock roosted in an abandoned pump house in La Feria. In 1956, at least four apparently wild birds were recorded on a home movie (unknown Valley location).

More significant, Raymond W. Neck (1986) regularly saw small numbers of Red-crowned Parrots wintering near his residence in Brownsville in the late 1970s to mid-1980s. These birds were present in 71 percent of 31 observation periods during October–March but only 16 percent of 19 observation periods during April–September. This pattern suggests that Red-crowned Parrots first overwintered in the Valley and then began to nest, as for example did Fulvous Whistling-Ducks in the Florida portion of their range (Bolen and Rylander 1983).

Larger numbers of Red-crowned Parrots suddenly appeared in the Valley in early 1984, soon after the severe freeze of December, 1983, that affected northeastern Mexico as well as South Texas (Lonard and Judd 1991; Tom Pincelli, in Walker and Chapman 1992). Neck (1986) suggested that conversion of much farmland on the Tamaulipan side from cotton to sorghum and corn during the 1960s may have begun attracting parrots to the Valley and that the freeze of 1983 drove larger numbers here.

Although unproven, this seems no less likely than the popular belief that rapid habitat loss in Tamaulipas drove the birds here (Enkerlin-Hoeflich and Hogan 1997; see also the preceding discussion of Green Parakeets). Perhaps the key is the increasingly diverse food resources provided by Valley cities. Many of the early sightings of lone individuals were at parks or refuges, where birds are rarely seen today. The birds soon discovered the more diverse and abundant food resources and nest sites available in growing Valley cities, and they eventually began nesting.

The first known nest was a successful one in Harlingen in 1985 (Lasley and Sexton 1985), and Red-crowned Parrots became widespread in Valley cities by the late 1980s. For example, a flock of 18–30 was seen in McAllen during January–March, 1987 (John C. Arvin, in Lasley and Sexton 1987). Thirty-five birds were in Harlingen in 1988, and at least some nested successfully (Oscar Carmona, in Lasley and Sexton 1988).

Red-crowned Parrots have nested successfully in Brownsville, where Brad McKinney found 10 active nests in July, 1995 (in Lasley 1995). Those nests were mainly in dead fan palms, but parrots have also used nest boxes (Lasley 1995). In southern Tamaulipas, most birds nest in natural cavities in coma (*Sideroxylon laetevirens*), Texas ebony, and strangler fig (*Ficus cotinifolia*). Nest entrances average 22 feet (7 m) above the ground, and the cavity itself averages about 3 feet (1 m) in depth and 8 inches (21 cm) in diameter (Enkerlin-Hoeflich and Hogan 1997).

Since 2000, Red-crowned Parrot numbers have remained high in the Valley, as the following incomplete survey shows. Roosting flocks may vary in size with local food resources, and birds may shift their roosting sites from time to time (Chapman et al. 1989). The birds' habit of circling over the roost before settling down helps in censusing if one is in the right place at the right time. In 2000–2002, birds still roosted at a traditional site in southern McAllen, in numbers ranging from fewer than 20 to 150 (Ray Bieber, pers. comm.). In 2001, a flock of 100–150 birds was seen regularly in Weslaco, roosting in a dense thicket and spreading out in small groups to forage during the day (Martin Hagne, pers. comm.). In Harlingen 100 Red-crowned Parrots were seen in early 2002, and 60 were regular then in San Benito (Liz Bennett DeLuna, pers. comm.).

In contrast, the flock of seven Red-crowned Parrots that I saw fly over my house on March 19, 1994, was one of my few observations in Edinburg, where there is probably not yet a year-round abundant food supply. I saw 10–12 in Progeso Lakes on June 14, 2000, where large anacuas, sugar hackberries, and Texas ebonies offered a rich food supply in a lush residential area along a resaca. I wondered if these birds commuted from Weslaco, only 7 miles (11 km) away. They are still common in Brownsville, but I have few recent counts.

The diet of the Red-crowned Parrot, like that of most psittacids, includes a variety of seeds and fruits. In southeastern Tamaulipas, the birds most frequently eat fruits of strangler fig, coma, and anacua, and seeds of Texas ebony (Enkerlin-Hoeflich and Hogan 1997). They eat acorns, pecans, walnuts, pine seeds, chinaberry fruits, and other items in southern California or southern Florida (Garrett et al. 1997; Epps 2002) and perhaps here as well.

Known staple items in the Valley include anacua and Texas ebony. Red-crowned Parrots have also been seen in the Valley eating green mesquite and huisache seeds, cottonwood leaf or flower buds, prickly pear fruits (*tunas*), oranges, Mexican olives, mulberries, Vasey adelia (*Adelia vaseyi*), and even tiny, low-growing chilipiquin (*Capsicum annuum*) peppers and sunflower seeds (*Helianthus* spp.; Marty Bray, Martin Hagne, David L. Handy, Cristina Mild, pers. comm.).

We may never know the precise story of origin of the Valley's parrots and parakeets, but in any case these birds should be protected and encouraged, given their endangered status in Mexico. In 1992 Brownsville declared the Red-crowned Parrot its city bird and gave it special protection, to help prevent capture of adults or nestlings.

The known populations of Red-crowned Parrots closest to the Valley are near the mouth of the Río Soto La Marina, near La Pesca, Tamaulipas, and at General Terán, Nuevo León (John C. Arvin, pers. comm.). Whether there is any interchange between Valley and Mexican populations is unknown, but at least the potential is there. The acceptance of both Red-crowned Parrot and Green Parakeet as "official" Texas birds during the 1990s may help further proect these welcome additions to the Valley avifauna. More complete surveys of Valley parrot and parakeet populations and nesting habits are needed, the better to predict and document future population trends.

CUCKOOS, ANIS, AND ROADRUNNERS (ORDER CUCULIFORMES)

FAMILY CUCULIDAE

Groove-billed Ani, *Crotophaga sulcirostris*

This all-black member of the cuckoo family is widespread in the humid tropics, but in the United States it is usually sought in southern Texas. A Groove-billed Ani looks rather like a Great-tailed Grackle at first glance, but the grooved, high-arched bill, weak flight, and skulking habits soon distinguish it. Also, the distinctive, high-pitched *tee-ho* or *pi-hui* calls help alert one to its presence and confirm its identification. The grooves in the bill can be seen at close range, but their function is unknown. Birders often look for anis on winter trips to the Valley, but the birds are much more easily seen from May through September, when they are common in suitable habitat. Indeed, as far as I can tell, Groove-billed Anis appear to enjoy hot weather, often sunning themselves on warm, humid Valley mornings.

DISTRIBUTION The Groove-billed Ani occurs regularly in South Texas, from Del Rio, San Antonio, and Goliad south to the Rio Grande. Groove-bills are widespread in Mexico, occurring from southern Sonora, Coahuila, and Tamaulipas south mainly along the Pacific and Gulf-Caribbean slopes through Central and most of South America. Although they occur up to 5,900 feet (1,800 m) above sea level, they are characteristic permanent residents of hot, tropical lowlands. In the Valley, the Groove-billed Ani occurs regularly, in numbers, from April to October. Individuals wander regularly in winter to the upper Texas coast and farther east along the Gulf Coast. Winter birds in the Valley are quite rare but tend to occur from Santa Ana eastward to the coast.

HABITAT Most common in dense thickets near water, the Groove-billed Ani also occurs in drier thorn forest and thorn scrub. Our anis sometimes forage in pastures with cattle, a habit that is well-developed in tropical populations as close as southern Tamaulipas. In the Valley anis usually forage in or within easy flight distance of dense cover; one does not see them commonly in large pastures far from natural habitat. Thorn forest dominated by huisache and retama along canals or at the edge of ponds is excellent ani habitat, for example near Pintail Lake in Santa Ana. Such areas are often successional habitats, maintained by periodic disturbance, but otherwise eventually developing into taller riparian forest less used by anis. Although I tend to associate with anis with moister areas, they may also occur in thorn forest and thorn scrub (Carter 1986).

Unexpected to me was how common anis are in dense riparian forests and thickets right at the water's edge. Evidently they seek dense foliage adjacent to productive open habitats, but I did not learn this until doing several summer canoe trips.

HABITS   A flock of anis is amusing to watch as they fly and hop erratically around a shrub or tree. The large bill is used to capture large insects, such as grasshoppers, which the birds often pursue down to the ground. At least during fall migration, anis readily consume small fruits such as granjeno and seeds like *Urvillea*. The species is an occasional nest predator (Eitniear and Aragon-Tapia 2000), and I have seen other bird species pursue and harass anis in open fields in Belize. Valley birds do not seem to recognize anis as predators, so perhaps that habit limited to tropical areas.

Anis are famous in the ornithological literature for being cooperative breeders (Vehrencamp et al. 1986). Several adults may cooperatively build a nest, incubate the eggs, and bring food to the nestlings. Juveniles from earlier nests often stay to help raise their potential siblings from a later nest. With all the cooperators involved, there may be as many as 15 eggs laid, although later-laying females may toss out some eggs laid earlier by other females. Even in the tropics, there are many ani territories that have only one breeding pair (with or without helping juveniles) present. Thus far there is no evidence of communal breeding in Texas, but the species has not yet been the subject of a focused study here.

OTHER OBSERVATIONS   Despite their usual preference for thorny thickets, groove-bills sometimes wander through suburban yards during migration. I have seen a small flock of three birds foraging in my mesquite trees and shrub garden on a few occasions. The birds are wary when foraging out in the open like this; I could watch them only from inside the house. I have seen as many as 16 anis in a flock during fall migration (September).

Anis seem uneasy when not in a flock. On two or three occasions, I have heard an unusual call, consisting of a long series of *huh* notes, in tall forest habitat. With some investigation, this call proved to be given by a lone Groove-billed Ani, which appeared to be wandering through unsuitable habitat (where I do not normally see anis). I suspect that these are individuals looking for a partner, for suitable habitat, or both. Such wandering birds seem restless and continue quickly through the forest.

Anis can raise two broods during their long breeding season. Fledglings are regularly seen in June (Oberholser 1974). On July 12, 1996, three different groove-bills sat tightly on nests along the Rio Grande between Santa Margarita Ranch and Fronton. A factor that may speed up nesting is the fact that young anis can leave the nest quite early in their development.

OUTLOOK   The prospect for Groove-billed Anis in the Valley and Texas as a whole are good. The species seems fairly common in currently protected areas, and anis should be able to use revegetated areas as these mature into thorn scrub and thorn forest. Anis seem to be unaffected by the cowbird brood parasitism that has such an impact on many species. Population trends have been generally positive in Texas for the last thirty-five years, as measured by the U.S. Breeding Bird Survey (Sauer et al. 1999).

Other cuculids

The **Greater Roadrunner** (*Geococcyx californianus*) is a fairly common breeding resident of thorn scrub, thorn forest, and mesquite savanna. It occurs in both semi-open and denser habitats, but is much easier to see in the former. Roadrunners disappear quickly and silently into thorny thickets, where one may hear the hollow, cooing song or the rapid bill-rattle. Roadrunners are tough to see during rare, prolonged cold spells, but they may hide in dense thickets, relying on stored body fat to see them through (Geluso 1970).

Yellow-billed Cuckoo (*Coccyzus americanus*) breeds across the Valley in thorn forest, thorn scrub, and riparian forest. Despite serious declines in the western United States (Rosenberg et al. 1991), Yellow-billed Cuckoos remain abundant summer residents in remaining Valley habitats. They breed quickly when caterpillars, cicadas, or other large food items are abundant: incubation is 11 days or less, and fledging occurs within 7–9 days—very short periods for a bird of this size (Potter 1980; Hughes 1999).

OWLS (ORDER STRIGIFORMES)

FAMILY STRIGIDAE

Elf Owl, *Micrathene whitneyi*

The sparrow-sized Elf Owl is poorly known in the Valley, except for the birds regularly using certain snags in Bentsen. Detail on these locations has been passed from birder to birder for several years. One tends to think of Elf

Owls as Sonoran Desert birds: a tiny bird emerges at dusk from a cavity originally excavated by a Gila Woodpecker (*Melanerpes uropygialis*) in a saguaro cactus (*Cereus giganteus*) in Arizona. However, even in Arizona, substantial populations of Elf Owls inhabit canyon riparian forests and other habitats (Henry and Gehlbach 1999).

Strangely, although Elf Owls were first found in the Valley in 1888 by Sennett (1889), the species "disappeared" for about seventy years. Finally, in the late 1950s and early 1960s, a breeding population was located at Bentsen and Santa Ana (James and Hayse 1963; Oberholser 1974). Nest boxes were set up on power poles in La Grulla, southeastern Starr County, by Pauline James in the late 1970s. They were used into the mid-1980s, when the habitat was cleared (Dewayne Hodges, pers. comm.).

DISTRIBUTION Elf Owls are widespread summer residents across southern Arizona and Sonora. They also occur in northern Sinaloa, the Trans-Pecos region of western Texas, small areas of adjacent Chihuahua and Coahuila, Mexico, and on both sides of the lower Rio Grande (AOU 1998; Henry and Gehlbach 1999). In the late 1980s, singing males were found as far north as Devil's River State Natural Area, Val Verde County, and Kickapoo Caverns, Kinney County (Lasley and Sexton 1989). In the Valley Elf Owls have not spread east of Santa Ana or north along the coast (Benson and Arnold 2001). A few individuals winter in the Valley, although most leave during August (Gamel 1997).

The range of the Elf Owl in the Valley is poorly understood because of its nocturnal habits and the questionable nature of access to many areas along the river at night. We know that Elf Owls regularly occur at Bentsen; at Santa Ana the birds are fairly numerous but less accessible to birders. Elf Owls have been reported from relatively large Lower Rio Grande Valley NWR tracts adjacent to Bentsen and Anzalduas. However, they may prove sensitive to habitat quality and fragmentation, as they are absent from a 17-acre (7 ha) tract of thorn forest less than 3 miles (5 km) east of Bentsen (John C. Arvin, pers. comm.) and from the early successional Marinoff tract of the LRGV NWR immediately west of Santa Ana (Gamel 1997).

In Hidalgo County Elf Owls have only been detected less than 2 miles (3 km) from the river. They have not been found on a large ranch north of McCook in western Hidalgo County despite repeated nocturnal tape-playbacks (Steve Bentsen, pers. comm.). Small numbers of boxes designed for Elf Owls were set up at two sites in southwestern Hidalgo County in early spring 2000 but were not used by Elf Owls in 2000–2002 (Lisa Williams, pers. comm.; and the author).

Elf Owls evidently occur (or have occurred) along and within a short distance from the Rio Grande in Starr, Zapata, and Webb counties (Pauline

James and Edna Rodriguez Silverman, unpubl. data; Steve Benn, pers. comm.; Woodin et al. 2000b; Benson and Arnold 2001), and such populations need further study. The Webb County population inhabited the Galvan Ranch, about 37 miles (60 km) upriver from Laredo, during 1998 (Woodin et al. 2000b).

HABITAT   Radiotelemetry and nocturnal point-count surveys at Santa Ana revealed that Elf Owls prefer thorn forest with a fairly open canopy and moderately dense understory (Gamel and Brush 2001). Birds were absent from low, dense thorn scrub and also from taller riparian forest with an open understory. Elf Owls may have increased at Santa Ana since the 1970s, due to xerification (drying out as a result of the lack of periodic flooding) of tall riparian forest and its conversion to open thorn forest. For example, at least two territories were found in 1995 and 1996 in Fred Gehlbach's old study plots, which were formerly closed-canopy forest and are now a mixture of semi-open thorn forest and thorn scrub (Gehlbach 1987; Brush and Cantu 1998; Gamel and Brush 2001). Gehlbach had noted Elf Owls only on the edge of his study plots in the 1970s. In low thorn scrub farther upriver, woodpecker holes in wooden utility poles may provide the only nest sites for Elf Owls. We need to do more research on the foraging habitat, population density, and distribution of Elf Owls in the Valley since so little is known.

HABITS   Elf Owls are strictly nocturnal, unlike some other owls, among them Eastern Screech-Owls (*Megascops asio*) and Great Horned Owls (*Bubo virginianus*). Typically an Elf Owl waits until it is completely dark to emerge, and peak foraging activity and calling are just after dusk and before dawn (Henry and Gehlbach 1999). I was surprised on July 5, 1997, to see one sleeping in the open, at eye level, along a trail in Bentsen.

Home range sizes are quite small for an owl, averaging 2.5 acres (1 ha) at Santa Ana (Gamel 1997), compared to 2–150 acres (1–60 ha) for breeding Ferruginous Pygmy-Owls in Kenedy County (Proudfoot and Johnson 2000). The small areas used by Elf Owls at Santa Ana are likely due to their insectivorous habits and the greater abundance of such prey.

OTHER OBSERVATIONS   Despite their small size, Elf Owls are known to mob the much larger Great Horned Owl (*Bubo virginianus*) as well as gopher snakes (*Pituophis melanoleucus*) and ringtails (*Bassariscus astutus*), all nocturnal predators. A nesting pair and one to four other Elf Owls called and flew at the head of a nearby Great Horned Owl (Boal et al. 1997).

An apparent territorial encounter was seen by Gamel at Santa Ana. An intruding bird was chased out of a territory by an owl that had been calling and that was assumed to be the territory owner. As the observer watched while lying on his back in the middle of the road, the latter bird chased the former across a narrow refuge road and then returned to its territory (Christopher Gamel, pers. comm.).

OUTLOOK   Although it is encouraging that Elf Owls have proven to be fairly common at Bentsen and Santa Ana, their absence from other smaller tracts is a concern. The presence of tall dead trees in places like Bentsen and Santa Ana may provide abundant nest sites at present, but perhaps declines will occur in the future as those large snags deteriorate and fall. Although nest boxes can be helpful, better yet would be maintenance of suitable thorn forest habitat. Eventually, former agricultural fields that have been revegetated may provide additional suitable habitat.

Other owls

Ferruginous Pygmy-Owls (*Glaucidium brasilianum*) once occurred regularly along the lower Rio Grande, even as far downstream as the Matamoros area (Phillips 1911). This tiny owl mainly eats insects, lizards, and small birds but has been known to take Gambel's Quail (*Callipepla gambelii*) in Arizona. Unfortunately, Ferruginous Pygmy-Owls became quite scarce and local in the Valley during the late twentieth century, probably due to habitat loss and fragmentation (Proudfoot and Johnson 2000). The best-known Valley location until recently has been the thorn forest below Falcon Dam, where many birders looked for the species for their U.S. lists. The Ferruginous Pygmy-Owl that Marty Bray and I saw and heard singing along the Rio Grande between Salineño and Santa Margarita Ranch on April 15, 1996, may have been part of that remnant population (Oberholser 1974).

Recent research and ecotourism development has revealed that Ferruginous Pygmy-Owls breed regularly in the live oak forests in Kenedy County. This includes the famous pair nesting since the mid-1990s (and seen by thousands of birders) at a bed and breakfast lodge in southern Kenedy County. This population has evidently extended (or has been discovered to extend) into northeastern Hidalgo County, where nesting has been confirmed (Glenn A. Proudfoot, pers. comm.).

As far as I know, there are no breeding Ferruginous Pygmy-Owls currently along the Rio Grande in Cameron or Hidalgo counties. The two birds found by Red and Louise Gambill at Bentsen on September 18, 2002, were surprising, given the absence of recent reports in that intensively birded park. I saw one of those birds in October, and others saw and heard them through the rest of 2002 and 2003 (John C. Arvin, pers. comm.).

Eastern Screech-Owls (*Megascops asio*) are common residents of the

Valley, occurring regularly in tall riparian forest and thorn forest and somewhat less commonly in thorn scrub and residential areas. They readily use nest boxes as well as woodpecker holes and other natural cavities. Gehlbach (1987) suggests that screech-owls may exclude Elf Owls from nesting territories. I heard a screech-owl whinnying in my neighborhood on October 27, 1997, but have otherwise seen individuals only in natural habitats. Frequently a bird roosts in an old woodpecker hole in one of the dead palm trees at the old refuge headquarters site of Santa Ana.

Great Horned Owls (*Bubo virginianus*) are also fairly common residents in the Valley, and they do nest here (Benson and Arnold 2001). As expected for a species that breeds while snow is on the ground in the northern United States and Canada, I once saw a bird sitting on a nest (apparently incubating) at Santa Ana, during a Christmas Bird Count. They seem to need larger tracts of land than smaller owls, and I am not aware of any nesting in residential areas in the Valley. Occasionally, one is heard or seen on a golf course or nearby residential area (Steve Monk, pers. comm.).

FAMILY TYTONIDAE

Barn Owls (*Tyto alba*) are common permanent residents of the Valley, but I have made only a few casual observations of this highly nocturnal species: *July 19, 1997: 5 essentially full-grown nestlings (brownish facial disks) in large burrow near top of bank on Mex. side across from SE Santa Ana (possibly old Ringed Kingfisher burrow?). May 13, 1998: full-grown tawny-faced indiv[idual] on duck box in SE part of Pintail.*

As these notes suggest, Barn Owls breed in burrows and large nest boxes. They also breed in elevated deer blinds and abandoned buildings. Their tolerance of agricultural habitats makes their rodent-eating habits particularly valuable (Oberholser 1974).

NIGHTHAWKS, PAURAQUES, AND POORWILLS (ORDER CAPRIMULGIFORMES)

FAMILY CAPRIMULGIDAE

Centuries ago, it was commonly thought that these large, big-mouthed, nocturnal birds obtained milk from grazing animals at night; hence the common name "goatsuckers." The Valley has a good diversity of these insectivores, with three species definitely breeding and one probably nesting here. No nightjars build nests; instead they lay their eggs on bare ground or leaf litter. These are beneficial birds to have around, despite their strange calls which may be alarming to some.

The **Common Pauraque** (*Nyctidromus albicollis*) occurs year-round in the Valley and is limited to South Texas in its U.S. range. One usually hears a pauraque before or instead of seeing it. The bird is harder to find in chilly winter weather, but it can be found roosting on the ground in thick forests or woodlands (Bendire 1895). The loud *poweer, gaweer,* or *who-are-you?* (Beebe 1923) call is not rapidly repeated like that of a Whip-poor-will or Chuck-will's-widow.

Typically pauraques roost by day in forest or scrub and then come out to clearings to forage at night. They "jump-fly" up from the ground to capture night-flying beetles, moths, and other insects. One bird ate a large number of fireflies (Bendire 1895). The reddish brown eggs are usually quite conspicuous on bare soil or leaf litter (Rowley 1966) but are better hidden when the mottled adult incubates.

One does not see Common Pauraques flying high in the sky in the manner of nighthawks; in fact they are seldom seen by the casual observer. Their eyes shine reddish in lights at night, which is a characteristic relied upon by birders looking for the birds by driving along roads at night. I occasionally hear Common Pauraques from the narrow strip of woods along the canal in my neighborhood, mainly in winter. This suggests that some pauraques wander in winter or even migrate short distances (Latta and Howell 1999). As Ingels and colleagues (1999) noted in South America, pauraques use human-created habitats such as clearings, roadsides, and rural houses, but they do not persist where dogs and cats are common.

One of my observations suggests that other birds may mistake the mottled, large-headed Common Pauraque for an owl: *July 16, 1998: one flies up, prob. flushed by me, and had landed in open leaf litter along Terrace Trail [Santa Ana]. Then scolded by 6 titmice and 1 white-eyed vireo—some get within 1 m of motionless goatsucker.*

In contrast to the seldom-seen Pauraque, **Common Nighthawks** (*Chordeiles minor*) and **Lesser Nighthawks** (*C. acutipennis*) are often conspicuous birds. Both occur throughout the Valley, although Commons are mainly restricted to the eastern two thirds. They are indeed common foraging at night over the larger cities and towns, and they are also common in coastal sections of Cameron County, such as at Laguna Atascosa. Lesser Nighthawks have been confirmed nesting throughout the Valley, and they nest in towns (John C. Arvin, pers. comm.). I have heard the soft trill of this species regularly in recent summers in Edinburg, and I once saw one trilling individual chase another in broad daylight. However, Lesser Nighthawks may be most common in the drier northern and western fringes, such as the

Salt Lakes area and Starr County. The **Common Poorwill** (*Phalaenoptilus nuttallii*) summers regularly in Starr County and breeds in Webb County (Arnold 1977), but no one has yet reported a nest in the Valley.

SWIFTS AND HUMMINGBIRDS (ORDER APODIFORMES)

FAMILY APODIDAE

Chimney Swifts (*Chaetura pelagica*), although more closely related to hummingbirds than to swallows, are similar to swallows in their tireless search for flying insects. Swifts were formerly common migrants through the Valley. A few pairs of swifts summered in Pharr in 1966 (John C. Arvin, in Oberholser 1974). I saw two or three swifts regularly in summer in the mid-1990s and once saw a bird try to enter a neighbor's chimney, only to be repelled by wire mesh. The only definite breeding records are of nestlings that have fallen down chimneys and died: San Benito, August, 1990 (TBBAP files); and McAllen, July 12, 1999 (dead nestling brought to me by Mary Lou Escobedo).

As of the late 1990s, the species was still spreading in the Valley. Brush Freeman reported several Chimney Swifts over Fort Ringgold in Rio Grande City in mid-June, 1998, and John C. Arvin saw swifts breaking twigs (nesting material) there on May 2, 2001. Brad McKinney reported his first-ever summering birds in Rancho Viejo (one on June 14, 1999) and Brownsville (a pair, June 20–26, 1999). In Hidalgo County, Dick Heller reported hearing Chimney Swifts in July, 1999, in his uncapped chimney in Mission. There are still no confirmed breeding records for Mexico, although the species may well nest in cities like Reynosa or Matamoros, provided that chimneys are available. On a trip to the Ciudad Victoria area in early June, 2003, small numbers were seen and heard over the small town of Güemez, Tamaulipas.

FAMILY TROCHILIDAE

Buff-bellied Hummingbird, *Amazilia yucatanensis*

Tikk ... tikk ... tikk is how a Buff-bellied Hummingbird announces its arrival at a backyard feeding station or favored patch of flowers. If other hummingbirds are there, they will likely be chased away, since Buff-bellied Hummingbirds are quite aggressive. This species occurs in the Yucatán Peninsula of southeastern Mexico and ranges northward along the Gulf Coastal Plain of Mexico all the way to southern Texas, where it was first found in 1876 (Merrill 1877). Buff-bellied Hummingbirds are common in parts of the Valley, especially in summer; they have also spread along the Texas Gulf Coast most of the way to Houston and regularly occur in Louisiana in winter.

As with most hummingbirds, seeing the iridescent bright colors depends on the light and the angle at which one sees the bird. In shade, the Buff-bellied appears dark and seems to disappear into the thickets it inhabits, while in a straight-on, sunlit view the greenish head, back, and throat glisten. The throat of adult males shows a bluish tinge overlaying the green. The somewhat forked, rust-colored tail is also striking, although not iridescent. Perhaps the bird should have been named Rufous-tailed Hummingbird, but that name was already in use for *A. tzacatl*. The buffy-colored belly is not very noteworthy, but it does help distinguish this species from similar species. Most individuals of this partially migratory species probably winter in Mexico; the species has been little studied in either the United States or Mexico.

DISTRIBUTION   Buff-bellied Hummingbirds occur regularly in coastal southern Texas from Beeville and Victoria south to the Rio Grande. They frequently wander north to San Antonio, and one spent the summers of 1998–2002 in a yard in Chappell Hill, Washington County (Marcia Effinger, pers. comm.). In the Valley, Buff-bellied Hummingbirds occur regularly only from around Anzalduas eastward along and near the Rio Grande, through most of the towns and cities in Hidalgo and Cameron counties.

Although I have not done enough field work to see whether Buff-bellies ever occur in the towns of Starr and western Hidalgo counties, I can say that I have never detected the species along the Rio Grande in those areas. In contrast, I have found the species regularly during the smaller number of canoe trips I have made along the river in the Santa Ana area. In Mexico, Buff-bellied Hummingbirds occur from southern Coahuila, Nuevo León (nesting confirmed in Monterrey area; Chavez-Ramirez and Moreno-Valdez 1999), and Tamaulipas south along the Gulf Slope to the Yucatán Peninsula, Belize, and northern Guatemala.

HABITAT   Scrubby or broken forest, forest edges, gardens, and parks with abundant flowers are the easiest places to find Buff-bellies and seem to be preferred habitat. In the Valley, the species regularly inhabits thorn forest with an understory of tropical sage or riparian forest with tropical sage, Turk's-cap, or coralbean. Especially during the breeding season, Buff-bellied Hummingbirds frequently occur in places that do not appear to have suitable flowers, such as shady riparian forest or retama-huisache or dryland-willow scrub. They may be using such flower-poor habitats to forage for insects (riparian forest) or do their territorial display (scrubby areas). In towns, well-vegetated suburban neighborhoods usually support Buff-bellied

Hummingbirds. Open, coastal oak forests with abundant Turk's-cap support Buff-bellies in Kenedy County, and the species may occur in bottomland forest farther north in Texas.

In wetter Veracruz in eastern Mexico they inhabit the more arid end of the habitat spectrum, such as gardens, orchards, and scrub in an area dominated by tropical evergreen forest (Toledo 1975). This pattern is also seen in other tropical species like Red-billed Pigeon and Tropical Parula, which inhabit the wetter end of the moist-dry gradient in semiarid South Texas and the drier (or more open) end in wetter tropical forests.

HABITS   In the wild, Buff-bellied Hummingbirds use mainly the red tubular flowers of Turk's-cap, coralbean, and tropical sage as nectar sources, and the species does not often occur where none of those plants can be found. Even as early as 1919, Turk's cap was found to be common only along the lowermost Rio Grande in thickets and palm groves (Hanson 1921), and it is still common today.

In towns and around isolated houses, the exotic firecracker (*Russelia equisetiformis*), shrimp-plant (*Justicia brandegeana*), scarletbush (*Hamelia patens*), and Cape honeysuckle (*Tecomaria capensis*) add to the diversity and abundance of nectar sources, and hummingbird feeders expand the food supply. In central Veracruz, Buff-bellies have been seen foraging at a cactus (*Neobuxbamia scoparia*), giant Turk's-cap, tropical sages (*Salvia coccinea* and *S. purpurea*), and some *Tillandsia* species (Ortiz-Pulido and Diaz 2001).

Most of the flowers mentioned are ornithophilous (bird-loving) — they depend on birds for pollination (McGregor 1899). According to Oberholser (1974), Buff-bellied Hummingbirds obtain nectar from mesquite, Texas ebony flowers, and anacahuita flowers. In my experience they usually ignore those insect-pollinated flowers.

Like most hummingbirds, Buff-bellied Hummingbirds are quite aggressive and frequently chase other hummingbirds away from food sources. In a good territory with plenty of nectar, an individual may become territorial and try to keep all other hummers out. The resident usually perches above the preferred food source in between foraging bouts, preening and keeping careful watch for intruders. The aggressive strategy can work at low or moderate levels of intrusion, when the resident simply flies at and chases away the intruder, usually a smaller Ruby-throated (*Archilochus colubris*) or Black-chinned (*A. alexandri*) Hummingbird.

However, during the spring and fall, when many migratory Ruby-throated Hummingbirds are present, the Buff-belly may give up on being territorial, since it becomes impossible to keep all intruders out and still forage. When only a small number of flowers are present in any one area, Buff-bellies become "trap-liners," having a regular route through a park or neighborhood, along which they stop to forage and then quickly move on (Feinsinger 1976). Especially during the hot summer months, Buff-bellies frequently hover-glean tiny arthropods from the bark or spiderwebs of Texas ebony trees, and they also capture insects in midair.

Hummingbirds are known for their mating displays, in which the males may sing or do a spectacular flight display in a regular location. These displays help males to attract females for the purposes of mating. No long-lasting pair bonds are formed; after copulation the female is on her own to build the nest, lay and incubate the eggs, and raise the youngsters. Displays vary: Anna's Hummingbird (*Calypte anna*), for example, sings regularly from a favorite song post, while Costa's Hummingbird (*C. costae*) makes a *zing* noise as it makes repeated flights in the shape of an oval. Buff-bellied Hummingbirds have been suspected of having a breeding display (Howell and Webb 1995), but there has been some confusion in this regard and little study.

My journal records my first observation of the breeding display, near the maintenance yard of Santa Ana on March 17, 1994: *6:40–7:00 A.M.— Unknown hummingbird at Santa Ana maintenance area. I hear a high-pitched, somewhat whining "seeee" falling slightly, as it "bounces" and twists a little [in flight] over 5–8 foot Baccharis just west of the ware yard. Flares tail as it flies . . . medium-sized hummingbird, hard to see well in half light. Stays low in display flights . . . and perches in coralbean between flights.*

Two days later, on March 19, I saw and heard a similar display at the Santa Ana parking lot and was able to identify the bird as a male Buff-bellied Hummingbird; it had a pinkish-buff bill with a blackish tip, as opposed to the more extensively blackish bill of the female. The bird perched in a flowering coralbean plant in a well-vegetated median strip of the parking lot, calling *sit-che* while perched and also while doing its bounding display flight over the parking lot. The bird always returned to the same perch at the end of each flight.

Since those early observations, I have observed similar display flights, mainly at Santa Ana and in my neighborhood in Edinburg, between March and October. Displays are always given in the dim phase between first light and sunrise, stopping as soon as the light gets strong enough to see colors. On various occasions, I have recorded the call as *sit-che, ts-ik, si-we, see,* and *tsi-we* (the latter being the most common). Sometimes the bird's display area contains abundant food resources (especially coralbean or Turk's-cap), but on other occasions there is no obvious food source available. Actual copulation has been recorded only once, in an ash tree in a residential area in Edinburg, late on a cloudy afternoon just before a storm (Antonio de la Peña, pers. comm.). Early on April 1, 2002, I heard two simultaneously displaying males from my yard in Edinburg, but by April 3 only one displaying male remained.

Other calls are given in response to intrusion by other hummingbirds (rapid, angry-sounding *see-see-see-see-sur-sur,* usually followed by a chase), to announce the bird's arrival in a foraging area (*tik-k*), or for other reasons. The *tik-k* call was also given by a female defending her nest tree on the UTPA campus against a male Great-tailed Grackle that was foraging on the ground underneath. I saw a stub-tailed recent fledgling and heard another in this tree on June 29, 2001. The *tsii* call given in response to potential predators such as hawks is similar to the mating display call but is given at any time of day, not during a regular display flight. Seemingly fearless, as most hummingbirds are, Buff-bellies harass raptors, including the tiny but dangerous Ferruginous Pygmy-Owl (Proudfoot and Johnson 2000). Nests have been found opportunistically, mainly in southern Texas, but little study has been made of the breeding habits.

OTHER OBSERVATIONS   Buff-bellied Hummingbirds apparently have a long potential breeding season in the Valley: I saw two recent hatchlings in a nest in a backyard in McAllen on February 15, 2000. In March, 2001, in an urban nature center in Weslaco, a nest with young almost ready to fledge was emptied by a predator, probably a Great-tailed Grackle (Martin Hagne and Richard Lehman, pers. comm.). I have seen dependent fledglings fed by females from June 19 to October 1, and I have heard the territorial display as early as March 17 and as late as October 8. I see full-grown, independent juveniles most regularly in August. Given the long dependent period of many tropical hummingbirds (Skutch 1976), the August juveniles could have been produced as early as June.

Although Valley winters are generally mild, Buff-bellies sometimes have to endure chilly, rainy weather for a day or two. From January 12 to 14, 1997, the temperature was consistently less than 41°F (5°C) with strong north winds and intermittent rain. Rain froze on bridges briefly on the morning of the thirteenth. During this cold spell an adult regularly visited a feeder at our home, resting between foraging bouts in a dense, sheltered *Pittosporum* bush within 3 feet (1 m) of the feeder.

The Buff-belly is usually top dog in conflicts with other hummingbird species around flowering plants, mainly because it is the largest hummingbird regularly occurring in the Valley. The Green-breasted Mango (*Anthracothorax prevostii*) that briefly visited Santa Ana from August 18 to 20, 1993, however, was larger and dominant; Buff-bellies had to wait their turn. Surprisingly, the smaller Rufous Hummingbird (*Selasphorus rufus*) sometimes chases Buff-bellies.

OUTLOOK   Hummingbirds are difficult to census; we have no quantitative data on population levels or changes. The highest single-day count of which I am aware is 13, recorded by 11 observers in 5 different parts of Santa

Ana on International Migratory Bird Day, May 14, 1994 (Eric Hopson, pers. comm.). I saw 10 birds (including at least 3 juveniles) on at Santa Ana on August 29, 1998, just in the area around Willow and Pintail lakes and the visitor center at Santa Ana—on that day, most birds were near a lush bed of Turk's-cap at the visitor center.

Such data suggest that we can be cautiously optimistic about this species, given its apparent spread along the Texas Gulf Coast and its extensive use of suburban gardens. This may counterbalance earlier losses due to clearing of riparian forests and scrub in the Valley. We have no information on trends in Mexico but can only assume that similar factors are at work there as in the United States. Planting flowers that hummingbirds favor is something that can be done easily and reliably provides nectar even when the human residents are out of town for a while.

Other hummingbirds

Black-chinned Hummingbirds (*Archilochus alexandri*) nest uncommonly in the Valley. I studied a nest apparently of this species in a live oak tree in my yard in Edinburg in 1994. A male had a regular perch high on a dead willow branch within about 330 feet (100 m) of my yard, and he displayed regularly over my yard near flowering plants. The female had quite a dull crown and a long bill, both of which suggest a Black-chinned rather than a Ruby-throated Hummingbird, which is an abundant migrant but has never nested in the Valley. A single nestling hatched, but I was not able determine if it fledged. Similarly, I saw a nestling apparently of this species (with buffy tips to the growing back feathers) in southern McAllen on June 29, 2001. I also saw a displaying male in 1993 along the Arroyo Colorado in Harlingen, indicating possible breeding in Cameron County. We are near the southeastern edge of the Black-chinned Hummingbird's range, but it is common in the Texas Hill Country.

KINGFISHERS (ORDER CORACIIFORMES)
FAMILY ALCEDINIDAE

Two tropical species of kingfishers nest commonly in the Valley. Until 1970 there was only one nesting species, the **Green Kingfisher** (*Chloroceryle americana*). Early naturalists (e.g., Merrill 1878) thought that species rare because the muddy Rio Grande water made fishing too difficult. However, Griscom and Crosby (1925–26) list Green Kingfisher as a fairly common permanent resident, mainly along remote resacas. Green Kingfishers are now fairly common along the lower Rio Grande. I suspect that they have increased as nesters because Falcon Dam prevents sudden rises in river level, which would have flooded river-bank nests.

Despite being fairly common, Green Kingfishers are harder to find than larger kingfishers because they fly and perch low over the water, their call notes are relatively soft, and their burrows are usually hidden behind overhanging leaves and branches. Once I learned the bird's calls and songs, it proved much easier to find. Probably most common along the Rio Grande itself, Greens can also be seen along the Arroyo Colorado as well as canals and drainage ditches. During periods of low water Green Kingfishers are easy to see along the main channel of the Rio Grande. During peak releases they forage mainly in flooded forests and side channels, especially between Falcon Dam and Roma, where peak releases have their greatest effect on river levels.

I occasionally see Green Kingfishers in unusual situations: *June 29, 1996: Bird quickly flies through our back yard [in Edinburg] from neighbors' yard [with pool]—too quick to see anything before it flies toward canal. . . . May 13, 1999: At 19:00, on University Drive across from UTPA campus, saw juvenile male (whitish tips to greater wing coverts) sitting on "cement walk" immediately in front of big front window of convenience store. Seemed stunned—nictitating membrane over both eyes, bird not moving. Gone when I returned 20 minutes later.*

Ringed Kingfishers (*Ceryle torquatus*) created quite a stir in 1970, when the first nest was found at the Falcon Dam spillway (Webster 1970). That year two nests were also found on the Mexican side in the stretch immediately below Falcon Dam. This was eighty-two years after the first U.S. record, an adult female collected near Laredo (Bendire 1895). Ringed Kingfishers are now fairly common and widely distributed along watercourses in the Valley, mainly along the Rio Grande itself. I sometimes see one along the Edinburg Canal in my neighborhood, particularly in the nonbreeding season. It probably needs exposed banks at least 15 feet (4 m) high in which to dig its large nesting burrows.

As with the Green Kingfisher, clearer water and reduced flooding after the construction of Falcon Dam may be important factors (Kincaid, in Oberholser 1974). This huge kingfisher is always conspicuous because of its loud calls, bright colors, large size, and habit of sitting on exposed perches high above the water.

WOODPECKERS (ORDER PICIFORMES)

FAMILY PICIDAE

Although I originally thought I would not be writing anything about these common, widespread birds, there are several interesting aspects to mention.

The Valley is poor in woodpecker diversity, with only two nesting species, but it supports high population densities of at least one species. By far the more abundant and widespread species is the **Golden-fronted Woodpecker** (*Melanerpes aurifrons*), which is common in suburban and natural habitats across the Valley.

Often foraging low or even on the ground, Golden-fronted Woodpeckers regularly eat both arthropods and fruit. Their fruit-eating behavior has not yet been studied in the Valley, but in tropical habitats Golden-fronted Woodpeckers may be among the most important frugivores for particular plant species (e.g., Howe and Vande Kerckhove 1979; Coates-Estrada et al. 1993). I have seen some unusual foraging methods and sites in the Valley: *May 26, 1997: One repeatedly captures moths near boatramp at Bentsen, from tree trunks and branches. June 17, 1997: 3 forage on mud and moist algal mat at Willow 1* [the woodland pond at Santa Ana].

Their habit of digging nest holes in telephone poles and fence posts has allowed Golden-fronts to live in large areas of low thorn scrub where no natural nest sites are available (Synatzske et al. 1999). In habitats with larger trees, my casual observations suggest that soft-wooded black willow and sugar hackberry may be preferred over hard mesquite and huisache (as with the similar Gila Woodpecker in Arizona; Brush et al. 1990).

In towns, Golden-fronted Woodpeckers often excavate nesting cavities in dead palm trees. These excellent nest sites may stand for several years, and Valley parrots and parakeets regularly use abandoned palm tree cavities. On the King Ranch, Ferruginous Pygmy-Owls often use old Golden-fronted Woodpecker cavities as nest sites (Proudfoot and Johnson 2000). Night-blooming cereus (*Acanthocereus tetragonus*) reaches 7 feet (2 m) in height here, but its stems are evidently not quite thick enough to attract nesting woodpeckers.

During the twentieth century, Golden-fronted Woodpeckers expanded their range about 2500 miles (400 km) north, into the Texas Panhandle and southwestern Oklahoma, and west into the Big Bend region of Texas (Husak and Maxwell 2000). Their numbers may have increased in coastal areas after trees were planted. For example, Dresser (1865–66) noticed no Golden-fronted Woodpeckers in Matamoros in the 1860s, but the species is common there and in Brownsville and smaller coastal towns today.

The somewhat smaller **Ladder-backed Woodpecker** (*Picoides scalaris*) is less common but nevertheless widespread in the Valley. Both it and the larger Golden-fronted Woodpecker may end up providing nest sites for the tiny Elf Owl as well as Bewick's Wrens and Tufted Titmice. Ladder-backed Woodpeckers are becoming regular suburban residents of Edinburg, and I strongly suspect that they have nested there. Currently there are no documented cases of Ladder-backed Woodpeckers nesting in urban or suburban habitats, although they have occurred in well-vegetated trailer parks along the lower Colorado River in Arizona (Rosenberg et al., 1987, 1991). Much less common in urban and suburban habitats than Golden-fronted Woodpeckers, Ladder-backed Woodpeckers can tolerate smaller trees as nest sites and thus occur more commonly in low thorn scrub and mesquite savanna.

PERCHING BIRDS
(ORDER PASSERIFORMES)
FAMILY TYRANNIDAE

Northern Beardless-Tyrannulet, *Camptostoma imberbe*

Unlike many of the tropical birds of the Valley, the Northern Beardless-Tyrannulet is a dull, somewhat secretive bird that usually does not draw attention to itself. Finding a tyrannulet usually requires knowledge of the song or calls or careful observation of a winter mixed-species foraging flock. Once found, this tiny bird shows a personality of its own, with a loud voice and aggressiveness justifying the name tyrannulet. Juvenile Northern Beardless-Tyrannulets can be distinguished from adults by the younger birds' more rounded, less "bushy" crown, buffy-cinnamon eye-ring, and unique *bee* begging calls (Brush 1999a).

Rare in the Valley, tyrannulets occur regularly northward to Kenedy County. In the Valley they are easiest to find at Bentsen, where at least two territories occur in heavily birded areas (the former recreational vehicle area and the beginning of the Rio Grande Hiking Trail). One frustrating habit of the bird is to sit still for several minutes, usually in fairly dense foliage, and then to fly suddenly away and out of the immediate area. The *pier* calls, apparently given nearly exclusively by males, are given frequently enough to make it fairly easy to track down a singing bird. We know little about the habitat use of tyrannulets. While Sennett (1878) and Smith (1910) both noted a tendency to forage in low bushes outside the forest, in my experience the bird seldom leaves thorn forest or riparian forest.

DISTRIBUTION   In the United States, this tyrannulet occurs from Zapata County (where it may be only an occasional winter resident) and Kenedy County south to the Valley and also in southeastern Arizona and extreme southwestern New Mexico (Texas Ornithological Society 1995; AOU 1998). They birds summer residents throughout much of that range except in the Valley, where they are permanent residents at Santa Ana and Bentsen.

The species' winter status in the vast expanses of Kenedy County ranches (where they summer regularly) is unknown. Wintering birds have been seen, especially during recent mild winters, in small patches of brush along the Arroyo Colorado in Harlingen and near the Laguna Atascosa headquarters. A very out-of-range bird was photographed in Presidio County, western Texas, on July 28, 2001, far from any known population (Barry Zimmer and Victor Emmanuel, in Sexton 2001). Tyrannulets also occur on the Pacific and Gulf-Caribbean slopes of Mexico and northern Central America, to Nicaragua and northern Costa Rica.

Although found early by Sennett (1878), near Hidalgo on April 24, 1878, this tiny flycatcher was not found breeding for another sixty-two years, and it was seldom even reported during that time. Finally, in 1940, L. Irby Davis found a nest with young in riparian forest in what is now Santa Ana. On June 15 of the same year Davis found another nest, this one with eggs, in Harlingen (Oberholser 1974). In my intensive study at Santa Ana and Bentsen from 1996 to 1998, I found 11 nests, and there were some other territories where I was unable to find nests. Tyrannulets likely have bred southwest of La Joya in extreme southwestern Hidalgo County, as evidenced by my June 14, 1996, observation of a juvenile following and begging from an apparent female.

Tyrannulets may breed as far west as the Fronton area, based on a few detections during the early breeding season of 2001, but this has yet to be confirmed. One has to wonder where they would build their nests in the Fronton area, given the absence of ball-moss and Spanish moss from the riparian forest upstream from Bentsen. The "nests" of tent-caterpillars, which I have seen in southwestern Hidalgo County, may be used, as they have been in southeastern Arizona (Brandt 1951).

HABITAT   Tyrannulets inhabit riparian forests and woodlands in the United States and northernmost Mexico, but farther south they occur in tropical deciduous forest, partially evergreen tropical forest, disturbed tropical evergreen forest, and tropical savannas (Sutton and Pettingill 1942; Russell and Monson 1998). In the Valley, this species usually occurs in forests with ball-moss, which is the usual site where the small domed nest is built. However, they may wander into *Tillandsia*-less habitat in winter. Tyrannulets do not occur in mesquite savanna or successional thorn forest dominated by huisache and retama in the Valley. In Kenedy County, they are fairly common in live oak forests with dense thickets of mesquite and prickly-ash (*Zanthoxylum* spp.; Fall 1973).

HABITS   Although they are difficult to follow in their dense, thorny habitat, tyrannulets seem to forage almost entirely by gleaning, a behavior whereby a perched bird picks small arthropods from twigs or branches. The somewhat arched, narrow bill may make it easier to glean from rough surfaces, and bristles (absent in this species, hence the "beardless") are likely not needed to detect escaping ants or scale insects. Tyrannulets occasionally take small fruits or seeds, but they seem to be mainly insectivorous. The species forages at all heights from the canopy to the understory.

Solitary during the breeding season, tyrannulets sometimes join mixed-species flocks of warblers, titmice, kinglets, and gnatcatchers during the winter. Such flocks wander over several hectares of forest or scrub, but tyrannulets may drop out before long.

During the breeding season tyrannulets seem to have large territories, with males (more conspicuous because of their loud, piercing song) often covering more than 655 feet (200 m) during thirty minutes or less. This seems unusual for such a small bird, which would be expected to use an area much smaller than that. Specific foraging requirements or interactions with neighboring territory holders could be involved, but much further study is needed.

Tyrannulets, as the name implies, can be aggressive when defending their nest tree. I have seen one chase a foraging Ladder-backed Woodpecker or Tufted Titmouse that (probably unknowingly) got too close to an active nest. However, since titmice often poke their heads into various crevices, clumps of ball-moss, or even nests, they could be a threat to eggs or nestlings. Tyrannulets sometimes briefly chase Orange-crowned Warblers (*Vermivora celata*) in mixed-species winter flocks.

Mated pairs interact frequently and seem to keep in contact mainly by calls. Males often alternate trill calls with their songs, and females respond with trill calls that are indistinguishable from those of the males (at least to me). Twice I have noted an exchange of trill calls, the departure of the female from the nest (where she was probably incubating), and then apparent copulation on a high branch. Females give *peeuk* calls when approaching the nest with food, and males likewise give the *pier*-series song. Both sexes work their way to the nest indirectly, usually landing near the top of the nest tree, and then working their way down in a series of short flights.

Dawn songs are a feature of the territorial behavior of many flycatchers, including the tyrannulet. The male perches high up in an open location and gives its emphatic dawn song from first light until perhaps half an hour after sunrise. This song is not given at other times of day, and tyrannulets seem particularly quiet toward dusk, at a time when other species may be singing. In cases where I knew the nesting location, the dawn song might be given more than 300 feet (100 m) from the nest, and the male usually approached the nest tree and gradually switched over to the normal song (the *pier* series) as the sky brightened.

OTHER OBSERVATIONS   On two occasions an adult of this normally retiring species flew quite close to me after I had "shushed" in an attempt to attract woodland birds. This method works by attracting birds to what may sound like predator scolding, and if a predator is found, harassment or mobbing may occur to drive the predator away. In both cases involving tyrannulets I knew that there were recent fledglings in the area, and the adult may have been especially interested in any potential predators nearby.

Nestlings beg fairly loudly from the nest, especially during the last three or four days before fledging. The two or three nestlings may take turns poking their heads a little way out of the nest entrance, although they withdraw when an adult approaches with food. Nestlings may fledge within an hour or less of each other or on consecutive days. A recent fledgling has some sparse downy feathers on top of the head and a stubby tail; it flies weakly. Family groups seem to stay together for a week or two, and they can be located most easily by the juveniles' begging call.

Usually seeming to move randomly from tree to tree, tyrannulets sometimes appear to pick out particular species of woody plants for foraging. I once saw a bird descend to less than half a meter above the ground to forage in a shrubby Vasey adelia, which was covered with ants and scale insects. Smith noted a preference for a certain shrub species (unknown to him) along the Arroyo Colorado in Harlingen.

Once I saw a tyrannulet crouch down onto a horizontal cedar elm branch and remain frozen for several minutes when a Harris's Hawk flew over. Although I thought it unlikely that the hawk would actually take such a tiny bird, Sutton (1951) records finding a tyrannulet in the stomach of a Bat Falcon (*Falco rufigularis*) in Tamaulipas. Sometimes birds avoid discovery by remaining in the hidden nest when potential nest predators are nearby: *May 8, 1998: At Anzalduas, female sits in nest while 4 Green Jays and 1 grackle are perched within 5 m of nest (apparently without noticing the nest!)*.

In Texas, active nests have been found from April through September, with some nest building in March. The August and September nests occurred during rainy periods, and it would be interesting to see if late nesting also occurs in years without much rain during those months.

OUTLOOK   Given how little we know about the historical abundance and distribution of tyrannulets in the United States, it is premature to draw conclusions about population increases or declines. However, we do know that the smallest tract on which breeding has been confirmed is Bentsen at 588 acres (235 ha). Anzalduas is smaller than Bentsen, but the Anzalduas birds regularly forage in the adjacent large Gabrielson tract of the LRGV NWR. Only three pairs have been recorded each at Bentsen and Santa Ana, so this is not a common bird. We have to be somewhat concerned about the future of the Northern Beardless-Tyrannulet in the Valley, given its low population density in large tracts and apparent absence from many small tracts.

Also, although tyrannulets may find ample nest sites in dead or dying cedar elms, once all the tall elms are dead, the area may no longer be suitable for nesting. I have occasionally seen ball-moss and Spanish moss plants on thorny species such as Wright's acacia, coma, and Texas ebony. We can only hope that such a trend will continue, since thorn forest will likely continue to replace tall riparian forest in many parts of the Valley. The continued existence of *Tillandsia*-rich forests of live oak on the sand plains of coastal Kenedy County may prove crucial in retaining Northern Beardless-Tyrannulet populations in South Texas.

Black Phoebe, *Sayornis nigricans*

Common along southwestern rivers in some of our country's most dramatic canyons and mountains, Black Phoebes joined the Valley breeding avifauna in 1999. Oberholser (1974) considered the species a rare winter resident in all of South Texas. However, birders' reports on which I was able to follow up led to the discovery of a small breeding population in Hidalgo and Starr counties.

DISTRIBUTION   In West Texas, Black Phoebes are common residents along the Rio Grande and in other water's-edge habitats. The species also occurs in the southwestern Edwards Plateau near Del Rio (Val Verde County) and Uvalde (Uvalde County), and Black Phoebes are known to winter occasionally as far downriver as Zapata (Benson and Arnold 2001; Texas Ornithological Society 1995). The overall range is large, extending from southwestern Oregon, California, southern Nevada, southern Utah, southeastern Colorado, central New Mexico, and Texas south through Mexico and Central and South America to Argentina (AOU 1998). Northern populations migrate to the tropics and tropical highland populations shift in part to lowland areas in winter.

Black Phoebes are still very local in the Valley, with a small nesting population known from around Chapeño east to Weslaco (Brush 2001). Mel and Arlie Cooksey saw one immediately below Falcon Dam on May 30, 1989, the first indication of possible breeding (Lasley and Sexton 1989). I saw my first Valley Black Phoebe along the Rio Grande about 2 miles (3 km) east of Santa Ana on July 14, 1994, livening up a hot canoe trip. This bird may have been an early disperser from farther upstream, and there was no direct evidence that it was nesting.

The year 1999 brought evidence of an expanding population. In late

March a pair was observed carrying nesting material to a hidden location underneath the Highway 1015 bridge over Llano Grande, a resaca south of Weslaco. At least one of those birds stayed through mid-May. I saw a pair on the Mexican side of the Rio Grande near Chapeño on June 19 and a juvenile Black Phoebe, accompanied by a pair of adults, at Anzalduas on July 11, 1999.

HABITAT   Black Phoebes are almost always associated with running water—in the Valley mainly with the Rio Grande itself. Pairs are territorial around artificial structures, such as bridges or water-intake structures, and in one case were seen carrying nesting material under a low bridge (Mark and Sandy Turner, Pat and Bob DeWenter, pers. comm.). Presumably the birds are nesting under bridges and on water-control structures.

HABITS   Like other phoebes, this species regularly "wags" or flicks its tail, raising the tail higher and wagging it more rapidly than the Eastern Phoebe (*Sayornis phoebe*). It forages by sallying to the ground from a low perch at or near the water's edge or by hawking insects in midair (Oberholser 1974). At Anzalduas, I have seen Black Phoebes forage in open, park habitat less than 200 yards (183 m) from the water's edge but perhaps still benefiting from the proximity of water with its insect emergences.

Originally Black Phoebes nested in crevices and on ledges of cliffs, but now they nest widely on shelves or ledges of artificial structures. This has likely allowed the species to increase its geographic range, at least in the United States (Wolf 1997).

OTHER OBSERVATIONS   Other duties and interests prevented me from spending much time following up on the 1999 observations in the Valley. However, the presence of two singing males at Anzalduas on April 24, 2000, a bird there on February 3 and July 2, 2001, and also a bird along the Rio Grande between Roma and Rio Grande City on June 11, 2001, suggest the continued presence of Black Phoebes in the Valley.

On May 30, 2001, I saw a Black Phoebe along Zacate Creek in Laredo. This observation, plus those in Laredo in 1999 (Woodin et al. 2000a), suggest a nesting population there also. The most likely series of events is that Black Phoebes have worked their way down the Rio Grande from the Trans-Pecos region. Perhaps they spread from nearby Mexican rivers, as Couch found two at Cadereyta, Nuevo León, in April, 1853 (Baird 1859). Their breeding status in Nuevo León, Tamaulipas, and Coahuila is still poorly known.

OUTLOOK   It is likely that Black Phoebes will consolidate their breeding range in the Valley, given the abundance of bridges and other nesting substrates near water. They could also spread along the Arroyo Colorado to the Harlingen–Rio Hondo area. A similar range expansion occurred in the lower Colorado River valley in Arizona and California between the 1950s, when the species was a rare breeder, and the 1980s, when it was considered fairly common (Rosenberg et al. 1991). Even in severe droughts, there is still water in the Valley's waterways, given urban and agricultural needs.

Brown-crested Flycatcher, *Myiarchus tyrannulus*

This is the common breeding crested flycatcher of the Valley, especially in denser forest and scrub. Historically, many Valley birders have been unaware of how common Brown-crested Flycatchers are, probably because the birds are present only in the breeding season, when few birders are present. Once one learns to listen for its loud *ha-whik* and *beer, beer* calls, Brown-crested Flycatchers appear to be everywhere. Like several Valley species, they are easiest to see when attending their nests, usually woodpecker-excavated cavities. They become more conspicuous as they enter and leave nest holes, chase off possible competitors, and protect and feed their young.

DISTRIBUTION   In the United States Brown-crested Flycatchers are birds of the Southwest, being summer residents in much of Arizona and the fringes of adjoining California, Nevada, Utah, and New Mexico and in southern Texas north to the southern fringes of the Edwards Plateau. In Mexico the species is mainly a permanent resident, occurring from Sonora, Durango, Zacatecas, Coahuila, Nuevo León, and Tamaulipas south to Oaxaca, Chiapas, and the Yucatán Peninsula. This widespread tropical species also resides in most of Central and South America, up to 5,576 feet (1,700 m) above sea level, reaching to Peru, Bolivia, and northern Argentina. Brown-crested Flycatchers occur throughout the Valley except on South Padre Island.

HABITAT   In Arizona, a large race of the Brown-crested Flycatcher is restricted to habitats with sizable natural cavities or those excavated by large woodpeckers, and it would not be expected to occur in thorn scrub habitat there (Brush 1983). In the Valley, the somewhat smaller race is able to use smaller natural cavities and woodpecker holes and is thus more widespread. The presence of wooden fence posts and telephone poles provides nest sites for woodpeckers even in otherwise unsuitable low thorn scrub. Even fence posts treated with creosote to repel wood-boring insects are used by Brown-crested Flycatchers and other cavity nesters, at least after several years of weathering have reduced the creosote levels (Synatzske et al. 1999). As a result, Brown-crested Flycatchers are common in thorn scrub as well as tall riparian forest and thorn forest. They also nest in small numbers in well-vegetated residential areas in the Valley. In the tropics this adaptable flycatcher occurs in mangrove forest, tropical deciduous forest, and even broken tropical rainforest (Howell and Webb 1995).

HABITS Although easy to hear, Brown-crested Flycatchers can be harder to see due to their foraging behavior of hover-gleaning, in which a bird pauses in flight to grab an arthropod from a leaf or twig surface within a tree's canopy. Brown-crests usually perch in shady locations while watching for their next meal. They do not typically perch in the open as do kingbirds, which are very similar in size.

Nesting takes place out of sight for the most part, with eggs being laid in a tree cavity. The few nests I have seen in Texas were almost all in cavities that appeared (from their size) to have been excavated by Golden-fronted Woodpeckers. Brown-crests probably wait until the woodpeckers are done with a cavity before using it, as in Arizona (Brush 1983). Nesting pairs will aggressively defend nest-cavities against nearby Fox Squirrels (potential nest predators), as on June 27, 1996, at Bentsen.

Like some other cavity nesters, such as Tufted Titmice, Brown-crested Flycatchers seem curious about nests of other species. On July 27, 1996, on the LRGV NWR Marinoff tract, a worn adult looked into an active Altamira Oriole nest (with nestlings) while the adult orioles were away. A returning Altamira chased the Brown-crest briefly, but Brown-crest later chased the Altamira and looked into the nest again (from the entrance). Such behavior may help keep cavity-nesting birds aware of the status of other nests in their area, in case something happens to their own nest.

When their youngsters have fledged, Brown-crests keep a careful watch on them, even when they are full-grown and apparently able to feed themselves. Any bird of kingbird size or larger is harassed if it lands in the same tree where the Brown-crest fledglings are. Once nesting is over and the young have dispersed, Brown-crests become harder to find. I saw two molting birds, in the process of growing new tail feathers, at Santa Ana on August 29, 1998.

OUTLOOK The prospects for Brown-crested Flycatchers in the Valley are good, given their habitat flexibility, safe cavity-nesting habit, and aggressiveness. As an example of the latter, in western Arizona Brown-crested Flycatchers were the only cavity-nesting species that were able to maintain control of nest cavities in competition with European Starlings. I suspect that the same occurs here, although local starling populations are not yet much of a problem. On the northern fringes of the South Texas brush country, perhaps competition with the similar Great Crested Flycatcher (*Myiarchus crinitus*) is a limiting factor.

OTHER OBSERVATIONS   At Santa Ana in June, 1995, a Brown-crested Flycatcher entered an abandoned Altamira Oriole nest and remained inside for at least thirty minutes, suggesting possible nesting. They are known to use unusual nesting sites such as iron pipes (which must become quite hot in the noonday sun) and creosote-laden fence posts (Synatzske et al. 1999) but so far no nesting in hanging nests has been confirmed.

Brown-crested Flycatchers readily accept nest boxes such as those designed for small owls, even if these are only a meter or so above the ground. There one can easily see the fur, strips of bark, and bits of snakeskin along with the usual fibrous nesting materials. The incubating adult sometimes remains on the nest until the box is about to be opened, startling the investigator as it flies out.

All *Myiarchus* flycatchers (and most tyrannid flycatchers) have distinctive dawn songs, which are given before and shortly after first light. To me, Irby Davis (1972) describes its dawn song well: an alternating *three-for-you* and *wit–will–do.*

Great Kiskadee, *Pitangus sulphuratus*

Although very limited in range in the United States, the Great Kiskadee makes a strong impression on all who see or hear one. I am frequently asked by both by newcomers and long-time Valley residents: "What's that noisy bird in my backyard that has a striped head and bright yellow underparts?" Tropical naturalist William Beebe (1923) summed up the impression it makes: "The kiskadee has nothing of delicacy or dainty grace. It is beautiful in rufous wings and brilliant yellow under plumage, it is regal with a crown of black, white, and orange. . . . It is the harbinger of the dawn, but so is an alarm clock."

Great Kiskadees have a variety of common names in different countries, among them *Cristofue* and *bem–te–ve,* deriving from their common *kis-ka-dee* call. The kiskadee's somewhat shrikelike shape evidently led Linnaeus to call it *Lanius sulphuratus* (sulfur-yellow shrike). The loud, raspy calls of this "supreme generalist" (Fitzpatrick 1980) are regularly heard along jungle rivers, rural roadsides, and urban streets in the New World tropics and subtropics.

DISTRIBUTION   The Texas range of the Great Kiskadee was once thought to be limited to the area from Valley north to Corpus Christi (Oberholser 1974). It was sufficiently uncommon in the Valley for the presence of four nests at Santa Ana in 1970 to be considered noteworthy (Webster 1970). Griscom and Crosby (1925–26) saw less than 10 per day of active fieldwork in the Brownsville area.

Now Great Kiskadees occur regularly north to Del Rio (Val Verde County), Fort Clark Springs (Kinney County), Goliad (Goliad County), and from Calhoun County south to the Rio Grande (Texas Ornithological Society 1995). They have also become substantially more abundant in the Valley. I can find four nests on or near the University of Texas–Pan American campus without much difficulty, and I have seen more than 50 Great Kiskadees in one day along the lower Rio Grande.

Great Kiskadees continue to spread, with a bird wintering in southeastern New Mexico and a few nests built in the Houston area and in the Mississippi Delta of Louisiana in 2000 and 2001 (Brush and Fitzpatrick 2002). On June 1, 2002, David Dauphin (pers. comm.) saw two adults feeding two fledglings in Baytown, Harris County, indicating successful nesting in the greater Houston area, where Great Kiskadees are still very rare.

In Mexico kiskadees occur from central Sonora, southern Durango, southern Zacatecas, northeastern Coahuila, northern Nuevo León, and northern Tamaulipas south to Oaxaca, Chiapas, and the Yucatán Peninsula and through Central and South America to central Argentina (AOU 1998). In the Caribbean region Great Kiskadees are also found in Bermuda, where they were introduced in 1957 to control the *Anolis* lizard population, and in Trinidad, where they are native (Amos 1991; AOU 1998).

Great Kiskadees occur regularly throughout the Valley, except in huge agricultural fields and the immediate coastal area. They may even be invading residential areas of South Padre Island, given the nest found there in spring 2001 (Oscar Carmona, pers. comm.).

HABITAT   In Texas, kiskadees are common in riparian forest and thorn forest, especially near the edges of ponds, lakes, or rivers. They also are common in residential areas and tree lines along irrigation canals or drainage ditches. Less commonly I have seen them in thorn scrub or mesquite savanna, usually within a few hundred meters of water. Kiskadees are less common on big ranches dominated by vast areas of dry thorn scrub. In tropical areas kiskadees are common in banana and shade-coffee plantations, disturbed riverside forests, urban areas, and other semi-open habitats. They even forage at the water line on beaches in Bermuda, where populations have soared (Amos 1991).

HABITS   It is great fun to watch Great Kiskadees at any time of year. Whether gleaning fruit in flight, chasing off a grackle or cowbird that comes too close to the nest, or making a shallow dive into the water to capture a fish or aquatic insect, kiskadees are always doing something interesting.

Nests are large football-shaped domes, usually placed securely in a tree fork or wedged between a transformer and wooden telephone pole. Nests built among the smaller branches of the outer canopy sometimes are pulled apart by strong winds, a regular condition in the Valley (Gorena 1995).

Strange but evidently safe nesting locations include the superstructure of an electrical substation, the top of a Purple Martin nest box, woodpecker holes, and niches in the facade of a Brazilian church (Brush 1993; Lago-Paiva 1996). In tropical banana plantations, the birds wedge their nest in between clusters of fruit (Bendire 1895). Kiskadees also nest in "ant-acacias" in Mexico and Central America, where the aggressive ants vigorously repel intruders (Janzen 1969; Young et al. 1990). Wasps often nest in ant-acacias and provide an additional degree of protection (Young et al. 1990).

Kiskadees may nest inside partially destroyed or incomplete "oven" nests of the Rufous Hornero (*Furnarius rufus*) or the large stick nests of Plain-fronted Thornbirds (*Phacellodromus rufifrons*) in South America (Belton 1985; Lindell 1996). Three times, Floyd Hayes has seen kiskadees building their nests on top of old Tropical Mockingbird nests in Trinidad. Conversely, Bay-winged Cowbirds *(Molothrus badius)* and House Sparrows sometimes nest in old kiskadee nests (Fraga 1988; Lago-Paiva 1996), evidently once the kiskadees are done.

Both males and females build the nest, often bringing in streamers of Spanish moss, various grasses, or even smaller nests of other birds. Sometimes Spanish moss becomes established on kiskadee nests and grows in its new location long after the kiskadees are finished nesting. Only the female incubates, but the male is an excellent sentinel, on the lookout from perches near the nest.

Nesting adults readily take on an intruding hawk, snake, Great-tailed Grackle, human, or monkey that may be trying to rob the nest (Skutch 1987; Gorena 1995; Robinson 1997). Kiskadees fly close to the intruder, giving a stuttering "chase-chutter" if the intruder flees or a sudden loud *reep* if the intruder is stationary (Gorena 1995). They also chase Bronzed Cowbirds away from the nest area, avoiding brood parasitism by that species (Friedmann and Kiff 1985; Gorena 1995). However, Shiny Cowbirds (*Molothrus bonariensis*) have parasitized Great Kiskadees on a few occasions (Friedmann and Kiff 1985).

Given the large, stout bill and aggression of kiskadees, it is odd that a passerine bird is able to raid kiskadee nests. In Amazonian Peru, a wren, the Black-capped Donacobius (*Donacobius atricapilla*), enters and robs Great Kiskadee nests, even though the kiskadees may try to fight them off (John W. Fitzpatrick, in Brush and Fitzpatrick 2002). It is unclear whether the donacobiuses wanted to take over the nests for their own use, as happens with House Wrens (*Troglodytes aedon*) and other cavity nesters.

The broad black eye-line of the kiskadee (and several other tropical flycatchers) may allow more accurate sighting of moving prey and thus more accurate foraging attempts. It may also help to reduce the effect of the strong glare of open tropical and subtropical habitats, by reducing the amount of reflected light entering the eye (Ficken et al. 1971). In any case, kiskadees readily capture small fish, freshwater shrimp, tadpoles, and dragonfly nymphs in the water, a favored foraging site.

Great Kiskadees eat many fruits, usually taking them by snatch-gleaning, in which they grab a fruit as they fly by. In the Valley, kiskadees mainly glean insects and fruits from leaves and branches and make shallow dives into water for aquatic insects and small fish (Gorena 1997).

More unusual feeding habits include scavenging dead fish (Fitzpatrick 1980) and eating refuse in garbage dumps (ffrench (1976). In drier terrestrial habitats, kiskadees may take small lizards, snakes, and even mice (Palmer 1986; Gorena 1995). In addition to wild-caught food, kiskadees also visit feeding stations to eat bread, cooked rice, or bananas, and they even take dog food out of bowls placed on back porches (Robin Restall, pers. comm.; Brush and Fitzpatrick 2002).

Great Kiskadees have occasionally seen robbing nests, for example the Bananaquit (*Coereba flaveola*) nestling being carried off by a Great Kiskadee in Trinidad (Floyd Hayes, pers. comm.). As a result, smaller birds sometimes chase Great Kiskadees away from their nest or territory (Skutch 1976; Dyrcz 2000). Kiskadees also rob food items from other bird species, such as Limpkin (*Aramus guaruana*) and White-faced Ibis (*Plegadis chihi*), as well as from other Great Kiskadees (Llambias et al. 2001; Hayes 1992, respectively).

OTHER OBSERVATIONS   Great Kiskadees normally occur as single individuals, in pairs, or in family groups, and individuals normally forage on their own. I was quite surprised on November 5, 1999, to see a flock of 15–20 kiskadees moving through Anzalduas. These birds appeared to be covering a lot of ground in a loose flock. They harassed some Eastern Meadowlarks that were foraging in an open grassy area, and the meadowlarks soon moved on. I suspect that these kiskadees were nonterritorial juveniles, but viewing conditions did not allow me to see the short, thin yellow line visible along the inner edge of the bill, which is typical of young birds.

Unlike most tropical birds, Great Kiskadees have been used in a few lab and field studies of predation (Smith 1977, 1978). Juvenile Great Kiskadees hand-raised in captivity in Costa Rica by Smith (1977) showed an innate fear of sticks painted with the same color pattern as shown by coral snakes. They readily pecked at sticks with a variety of other patterns, but they shrank back and gave alarm calls when presented with coral snake "models."

Free-ranging Great Kiskadees in Brazil showed a preference for the more palatable bullfrog (*Rana catesbeiana*) tadpoles over the distasteful black tadpoles of the Creole frog (*Rana semilineata;* D'Heursel and Haddad 1999). However, they readily ate Creole frog tadpoles when bullfrog tadpoles were not available (Vaira and Coria 1994). When foraging in aquatic habitats, kiskadees evidently pick up internal parasites such as nematodes and flukes, at least in South American riverine habitats (Brush and Fitzpatrick 2002).

It is not easy to catch these birds off guard, so the observation of a Great Kiskadee sunbathing must be one of the rarest of sights. The bird in question, seen in Port O'Connor, Calhoun County, Texas, first pecked at the head of a pocket gopher, driving it back underground, and then sunbathed on the bare soil of the gopher mound (Petra Hockey, pers. comm.). We need more such observers scattered throughout the subtropics and tropics to document the behavior and ecology of tropical birds like the kiskadee in various parts of their range.

OUTLOOK   The prospects for Great Kiskadee in the Valley are excellent, given their current numbers, previous range expansions, and general success in human-dominated habitats. The only question is how far north they will be able to establish themselves. Will the species continue to expand and consolidate its range, perhaps becoming highly migratory, as the Great-tailed Grackle has in its expansion into the northern Great Plains (AOU 1998)? Or perhaps kiskadees will simply fill in gaps in their current South Texas range and be limited from expanding farther north by recurring winter cold spells.

Couch's Kingbird, *Tyrannus couchii*

George B. Sennett (1878) confirmed in 1877 that "Couch's Flycatcher" did occur in the United States: "On May 8th, I saw a number of this species at Lomita Ranche [sic], on the ebony-trees." Named for Lieutenant Darius N. Couch, who discovered the birds in eastern Nuevo León, this attractive kingbird quickly sank into relative obscurity—as did Couch, who became a little-known general in the American Civil War (Rhodes 1899). Couch's Kingbird was considered a subspecies of the similar and more widespread Tropical Kingbird (*T. melancholicus*). However, L. Irby Davis noted the marked vocal differences between Couch's and Tropical kingbirds (Davis 1972). With the more detailed studies of Smith (1966) and Traylor (1979), the species were recognized to be distinct.

DISTRIBUTION   Couch's Kingbird is a species of the Gulf-Caribbean slope, occurring in southern Texas from Del Rio, Brackettville (Kinney County), and Victoria (Victoria County) south to the Rio Grande. In Mexico, Couch's Kingbirds occur from Coahuila, Nuevo León, and Tamaulipas south to the Yucatán Peninsula, Belize, and northern Guatemala. Although poorly understood, the species evidently expanded northward out of the Valley during the twentieth century, and its breeding range now almost reaches San Antonio. It is mainly a lowland bird, and northern populations are partially migratory.

Couch's Kingbirds occur throughout much of the Valley, from Falcon Dam to beyond Brownsville. In drier parts of Starr and northern Hidalgo County, the species may occur mainly in taller trees along arroyos and around rural homes. In mesic and wetter areas, Couch's Kingbirds are quite common, and one is seldom out of sight or sound of a kingbird during the breeding season. The only area they seem to be missing from is South Padre Island and the salty shoreline of the Laguna Madre (although migrants may pass through that area).

HABITAT   Couch's Kingbird inhabits thorn forest, riparian forest, well-vegetated residential areas, and sometimes thorn scrub. It seems to require some tall trees for both foraging and nesting purposes. Occasionally, Couch's Kingbirds occur in pastures with scattered trees, but Western or Tropical kingbirds are more common in such areas. Couch's Kingbirds are common along the Rio Grande itself, as long as there are some trees to provide perches for foraging and nesting.

HABITS   Like other kingbirds, Couch's Kingbird is an aggressive, conspicuous bird of treetops and open spaces. Often seen hawking insects (its main foraging method), Couch's Kingbird is often also the first species to detect a passing raptor, and it chases raptors and other large birds from its territory. The first indication of an intruding raptor is the repeated *kip* calls with an occasional *breeeer* mixed in. If one looks up, there is usually a Swainson's Hawk, Harris's Hawk, or White-tailed Kite flying over. I was alerted to my first Short-tailed Hawk in Texas by calling Couch's Kingbirds.

The next steps after a hawk is spotted are takeoff, direct flight toward the hawk, and chasing it out of the area, sometimes riding on its back or even striking it on the nape of the neck (Robinson 1997; Brush 1999b). The kingbird does not seem to be in much danger during these chases. If, however, the raptor is a Peregrine Falcon, which is much more maneuverable in flight, the kingbirds remain perched and merely continue to give alarm calls (Brush 1999b).

Couch's Kingbirds often place their nest in open locations in treetops, exposed to the full force of the subtropical sun. In such locations, an adult remains on the nest for extended periods both during cold weather, to incubate or brood the young, and during hot weather, when the adult shades the nest contents. Bronzed Cowbirds and Great-tailed Grackles usually avoid landing in or within 66 feet (20 m) of nest trees. Although I once saw a Couch's Kingbird feeding two Bronzed Cowbird fledglings (Santa Ana, July 17, 1994; Clotfelter and Brush 1995), cowbird eggs are usually ejected and brood parasitism is extremely rare (Carter 1986).

Couch's Kingbirds are part-time frugivores, consuming a variety of native and exotic fruits. I have seen them eating fruit most regularly in fall and winter. Both Eastern and Couch's kingbirds consume possum-grapes in September. In winter, I have seen several bird species, including Couch's Kingbird, eating exotic Chinese tallow (*Sapium sebiferum*) fruits in a residential neighborhood.

OTHER OBSERVATIONS   Couch's Kingbirds are sympatric in the Valley with both Tropical and Western kingbirds, and there are a few areas where all three species nest within a few meters of each other (see Tropical Kingbird account following). So far, I have not seen Couch's Kingbirds nesting on artificial substrates like a substation, but the other two kingbirds have done so. Kingbirds are not strongly territorial away from the nesting tree, so aggressive interactions are uncommon. Hybrids between Couch's and Tropical kingbirds are known from Oaxaca in southern Mexico (Binford 1989), but I have never seen any mixed pairs.

There is a distinct habitat segregation among the three nesting kingbirds, with Couch's being commonest in relatively dense forest and scrub, Westerns being common in agricultural areas and around rural homes and other open inhabited areas, and Tropical Kingbirds most frequent on golf courses, in city parks, and on the open campuses of some Valley schools.

I have twice observed apparent copulation of Couch's Kingbirds. At the edge of the forest, the presumed male flew toward the presumed female and fluttered briefly on her back, before retiring to a nearby tree. Once the birds are mated, the greeting ceremonies are conspicuous: as one partner flies back toward the nest tree, the other gives an excited series of calls and rapidly flutters its wings. The returning bird calls similarly, lands, and then also flutters its wings as the ceremony is completed.

OUTLOOK   The outlook for the species is excellent, given its success to date in invading urban areas in the Valley and spreading northward. The birds' aggressiveness, main diet of flying insects, and habit of ejecting cowbird eggs are all in their favor. It will be interesting to see how far north the species gets.

Tropical Kingbird, *Tyrannus melancholicus*

Once confused with Couch's Kingbird, the Tropical Kingbird is a more widespread tropical bird, which we can now say has successfully invaded the

Valley. Although not yet established throughout the Valley and still much less common than Couch's Kingbird, Tropical Kingbirds seem to expand their range every year, with nesting records in Hidalgo and Cameron counties and Río Bravo, Tamaulipas. One now has to take into account the strong possibility of a Tropical almost anywhere in the Valley, not just in the Brownsville area as in the early 1990s.

In my opinion, all observations must be confirmed by hearing the birds, since visual characteristics are difficult to see and may overlap (see also Howell and Webb 1995). I say "saw," "seen," and "sighted" in the following sections for simplicity—in every case where I have noted Tropical Kingbirds, they have been calling.

DISTRIBUTION   Ranging from southeastern Arizona, Sonora, San Luis Potosí, southern Texas, and Tamaulipas south to central Peru and central Argentina, Tropical Kingbirds are truly widespread tropical birds. In Texas, Tropical Kingbirds have nested since 1996 in Brewster County, first and most regularly at Cottonwood Campground along the Rio Grande in Big Bend National Park, and in 1999 in northern Brewster County.

Farther east, Tropical Kingbirds have been sighted in a number of southern and eastern Texas counties. They were first seen in Brownsville in 1990, and the first known nest there was in 1991. During 1991–95 they expanded their range in Cameron County. They nested at the Rangerville electrical substation south of Harlingen in 1992, at Port Isabel in 1994, and also established themselves in Harlingen and Rancho Viejo (Haynie 1992–95).

Tropical Kingbirds soon spread upriver into Hidalgo County. I saw one along the river about 3 miles (5 km) east of Santa Ana on May 27, 1994. On June 29, 1995, I saw two adults tending at least two fledglings in Progreso Lakes, southeastern Hidalgo County. On July 8, 1999, a pair attended a nest under construction in the municipality of Río Bravo, Tamaulipas, right across the river from Santa Ana. On June 14, 2000, I heard Tropical Kingbirds in at least three different locations in Progreso Lakes. In 2001 I observed a pair nesting successfully twice at Bill Schupp Park in northern McAllen. Repeated observations of birds in 2001 and 2002 around McAllen, Edinburg, Mission, and La Joya (by Jane Kittleman, John Arvin, Steve Monk, myself, and others) suggest that Tropical Kingbirds are becoming well established in southern Hidalgo County. So far there have been only a few sightings in Starr County and none that I am aware of in Willacy County. I am awaiting the first Anzalduas Park nesting pair, since the habitat appears suitable, but thus far only Couch's Kingbirds have nested there.

HABITAT   Tropical Kingbirds occur in quite open habitats with scattered trees, at least in Texas. Birds have nested mainly in city parks, school grounds, golf courses, electrical substations, and football fields so far. Tropical Kingbirds seem particularly attracted to well-watered lawns, golf courses, or pastures near water. The one nesting site right along the Rio Grande was in a narrow strip of trees between the river and a large field.

In Belize, where Tropical Kingbirds are quite common, they may be more tolerant of scrub, as I have seen them along rivers with no fields nearby. Although fledglings sometimes end up in thickets, they do not usually go far in, and adults and older juveniles generally stay out in the open. The only Tropical Kingbirds I have ever seen at Santa have been at Pintail Lake or in the headquarters parking lot, both quite open areas within easy flight of fields.

Tropical Kingbirds overlap little in habitat with other kingbirds. Never have I detected one in forest or thorn scrub, despite many hours spent in such habitats at Santa Ana and Bentsen. In semi-open areas near Santa Ana, I have had Tropical Kingbirds briefly visit fruiting trees, usually being chased off quickly by the more numerous Couch's Kingbirds. I have never seen a Tropical Kingbird in agricultural areas with scattered houses and occasional wooded fencerows—situations where Western Kingbirds would be common breeders.

HABITS   Tropical Kingbirds forage mainly by hawking insects from midair, which is typical for kingbirds. They often make flights of more than 50 feet (15 m) from a high, exposed perch. I have seen them eat mistletoe berries and Chinese tallow fruits in Texas, and they probably consume other fruits, especially in winter. Limited observations (by Brad McKinney, John Arvin, myself, and others) indicate that a greater percentage of the Valley's Tropical Kingbirds remain here in winter, compared to Couch's. Groups of two to five are seen throughout the fall and winter, probably family groups staying together until the following breeding season.

Calling is most regular during the breeding season, early in the morning, and when one partner greets the other around the nest. Both adults and younger birds normally give a rapid "metallic" trill, in which it is hard to distinguish the individual notes. There is a dawn song, as in most flycatchers, which is a somewhat irregular series of trills. Nestlings and dependent fledglings give shorter trills, still recognizable as Tropical. Interestingly, Western Kingbirds have a song consisting of a rapid series of slurred notes, though it lacks the metallic quality of Tropical's song and tends to speed up toward the end.

Tropical Kingbirds are quite aggressive toward predatory raptors in the tropics (Robinson 1997), but I have spent too little time observing them in Texas to see any chases. One would expect that they would interact most with White-tailed Kites and other open-country raptors.

Pairs probably sometimes raise two broods in a year, such as the Bill

Schupp Park pair in McAllen in 2002. I have seen nest building in early May and nestlings still being fed in mid-August, plenty of time for two broods.

OTHER OBSERVATIONS   The variety of flycatchers nesting together at some spots is remarkable, as I saw at the Rangerville Substation. *May 4, 1995: At Cannon Rd., Tropical Kingbird pair vocalizing at Rangerville electric substation. They are finishing a nest on the south side of the structure, about 16–17' up on a horizontal bar. Heard short, metallic trill and saw birds carrying nesting material and adding it to nest. One bird was starting to shape the nest cup with its body but the nest has a ways to go.*

Calls given when one or both individuals returning to the substation greet one another. These calls are short trills, not the longer series (the latter of which may be the song). A Great Kiskadee pair was feeding nestlings about 25–30' away on the substation, and an Altamira Oriole nest was just being begun on a nearby power pole guy wire 15–20' away from the kiskadee nest and about 30' away from the kingbird nest. A Couch's Kingbird called chi-beer from a wooded area 150 yards away (heard as I drove through area on dirt road).

Nests are built in trees or on artificial structures, as noted. The Port Isabel nest in 1994 was about 90 feet (21 m) up, on top of a football stadium light pole. Perhaps the Tropical Kingbird's greater use of golf courses, sports fields, and other habitats with few trees has induced it, like the Western Kingbird, to use artificial structures. In contrast is the Couch's Kingbird, which mainly occurs in denser forest and scrub, where plenty of natural nest sites are available.

OUTLOOK   Although we must be somewhat cautious, given the short length of time that Tropical Kingbirds have been in Texas, I am optimistic about their future here. There should be more suitable habitat created in the future, as more schools, golf courses, and similar habitats are made. It will be interesting to see what happens when colder winters return. Will the birds become more migratory, as Couch's are, with most individuals leaving during winter, or will they try to tough it out? I do not expect that Tropicals will have much impact on Couch's Kingbirds, given their different habitat preferences. Tropical Kingbirds could affect Western Kingbirds somewhat, but the Western's use of residential neighborhoods and rural and agricultural areas should allow for coexistence.

Rose-throated Becard, *Pachyramphus aglaiae*

This beautiful tropical bird (whether it is a tyrant-flycatcher or cotinga has not yet been decided) has always been rare or uncommon in the Valley. Even before 1950 when there was more tall riparian forest, becard records were relatively few. In 1943, L. Irby Davis (1945a) found two nesting pairs in the Valley—one near Harlingen, the other in what is now Santa Ana. The Santa Ana pair produced at least one fledgling. Davis's Harlingen site was open riparian forest, while he described his Santa Ana site as a "jungle."

George M. Sutton (1949) found becards and some old nests around a pond 6 miles (9 km) south of McAllen in December, 1948, but the trees were being cut during his visit and there is no forest there today. Becards nested at Bentsen and in another location near Mission in 1959 (Webster 1959) and at Santa Ana and Anzalduas in the 1970s. The most recent successful nesting at Anzalduas was in 1972 (John C. Arvin, in Oberholser 1974). Becards nested at Santa Ana in 1975, the first successful nesting at the refuge in more than fifteen years (Wayne A. Schifflett, in Webster 1975).

Until 1999, the most recent nesting at Santa Ana was an unsuccessful attempt in 1977 (Gehlbach 1987). Becards have occasionally been seen since, mainly in winter, and recent nesting efforts are described in the next section.

DISTRIBUTION   Rose-throated Becards occur from southeastern Arizona, Nuevo León, and southernmost Texas south along both slopes of Mexico and Central America to northwestern Costa Rica (AOU 1998). Today they are rare sporadic nesters and winter visitors in Hidalgo County. My first Valley becard was a subadult male at Santa Ana on July 30, 1997. The bird stayed into October, but no female ever was seen.

In 1999, a female becard built at least one nest at Anzalduas in the absence of a male, between May 8 and June 3. A subadult male was first seen at Anzalduas on June 3, and he immediately paired with the female. I suspected that incubation was under way during June, but the nest was abandoned by June 24. The becards built a second nest between June 24 and July 2, with the female doing most of the work, but it also was abandoned, by July 15. Female Bronzed Cowbirds were observed approaching each nest on one occasion, but it is not known if nests were parasitized (Brush 2000a).

In late July the becard pair wandered around Anzalduas, possibly inspecting potential nest sites, but no additional nests were built. By early fall the male had finished his molt into full adult plumage. In 2000 only the male returned (or remained), and despite repeated calling and some mating displays during April 4–May 2, no female was ever seen. No becards were known to nest in the Valley in 2001. A female built a nest at Santa Ana in late May 2002, but the nest failed, in the absence of a male.

In addition to the above locations, becards wander occasionally to Cameron County (Laguna Atascosa in 1999, Los Fresnos in 2000; McKinney 2002). Despite the presence of tall riparian forest along the Rio

Grande in Starr County, becards have not been recorded there, perhaps due to the absence of suitable nesting material (Spanish moss or vines).

Rose-throated Becards nested in a citrus grove in Linares, southern Nuevo León, in the 1940s (Eaton and Edwards 1947), and they may still be common in remaining riparian forests in that area. I found two abandoned becard nests in November, 1999, in Las Estanzuelas Park, southeastern Monterrey, Nuevo León. Since the only other becard in Nuevo León (Gray-collared, *P. major*) builds a nest supported from below by branches (Russell and Monson 1998), I judged that the hanging nests in Las Estanzuelas must have been built by Rose-throated Becards.

In Tamaulipas, becards still nest along the Río Corona, where I saw at least two old nests and detected six birds in December, 2001, and several nesting pairs and nests in June 2003. Whether populations are as high as Gehlbach's (1987) "nests about every 100 m along the river" during the 1970s remains to be seen.

HABITAT   The becard is usually noted as occurring in open forests, such as along streams, and at the edges of fields or even around inhabited areas or in areas partially cleared for agriculture. The nest apparently needs to be built with some open space around it, to reduce the chances of predation, as is the case for the Altamira Oriole. In the Valley, becards have usually been seen close to water, but the association is probably between the bird and the riparian forest, which in turn depends on water for its existence.

Becards usually avoid dense forest, although Davis noted that the 1943 fledgling was difficult to see in heavy junglelike growth at Santa Ana. Usually they occur in parklike open forest here. In wetter areas such as eastern Mexico and Central America, becards may occur far from surface water, wherever there is suitable open forest (often created by partial clearing of tropical forests for pastures or remote resorts).

HABITS   The hanging nest of the Rose-throated Becard usually swings freely from an isolated branch, over a clearing. However, few observers besides the indomitable Alexander F. Skutch have spent much time observing their nesting behavior. He observed that female becards spend an average of 12 minutes on the nest (incubating), and 9 minutes off, with a lot of variation in both (Skutch 1976). In the brief time that I observed the 1999 Anzalduas nest, I noted that the female shot in and out of the nest so rapidly that I easily missed it if distracted even for a moment.

The male often remained within about 165 feet (50 m) of the nest, calling, preening, foraging, and sometimes bringing material to the outside of the nest, so his behavior was not much of a clue to nest status. The male accompanied the female on distant flights, leaving the nest unattended for several minutes, as Rowley (1984) also has observed. An unusual nest (attached to and resting on a horizontal branch of an orange tree) was evidently successful at least to the nestling stage. However, ants were able to reach and injure at least one of the nestlings, which were only 4 feet (1–1.5 m) off the ground (Eaton and Edwards 1947).

Adults are difficult to see if not calling, since they spend a lot of time perched quietly in dense foliage. One typically hears the sharp *tsee* or the very high-pitched *tee-tee-tee* calls before one sees the bird. Becards are easier to see when they are nesting, as they make frequent trips to gather nesting material, and the male regularly accompanies the female to and from the nest. Becards continue to add nesting material throughout the nesting cycle, making it difficult to tell what stage they are in (Rowley 1984). The nesting season in the Valley may not be quite as long as in Oaxaca, where nest building was seen from late March through early July (Schaldach et al. 1997), but it may last from May through July. Males give a territorial or courtship display in which they call *sit-chee,* elevate the crown and throat feathers, and sway back and forth a few times. I observed this behavior on April 4, 2000, and on at least one date later in the month, when the unmated male at Anzalduas was making his last stand to attract a female.

OTHER OBSERVATIONS   Once the 1999 Anzalduas pair had abandoned the two earlier nests, I saw them checking out potential nesting sites near some Great Kiskadee nests and attempting to steal nesting material from at least some of these. The kiskadees chased the becards away, as did a Couch's Kingbird also nesting in the area. Rose-throated Becards are known as regular robbers of nesting material (Rowley 1984), but once or twice I have seen Great Kiskadees returning the favor and robbing material from old becard nests.

Rose-throated Becards (particularly the males) vary tremendously in the darkness of their plumage across their extensive range. In general, birds from arid northwestern Mexico and southeastern Arizona are palest, and the females do not have any rusty color in their wings. Birds from the wet forests of southeastern Mexico and Central America are very dark, and adult males have a smaller rosy throat patch (or none at all). Valley birds are intermediate: males have a bright, rosy red throat patch and a blackish cap and nape, and females and subadult (second-year) males are quite rusty on the back. The males at Santa Ana in 1997 and at Anzalduas in 1999 were both subadults. The latter bird gradually molted new gray back feathers during summer 1999.

OUTLOOK   The outlook for Rose-throated Becard in Texas is poor, given its small starting numbers and current erratic status. Open riparian forests with tall trees are rare in the Valley, and it will take some effort to maintain existing forests or create new ones. For better assessment of the likelihood of recolonization, we need to know if becards currently nest any closer to the Valley than Monterrey. The Río Alamo and Río San Juan watersheds of Nuevo León and the Río San Fernando watershed of Tamaulipas should be checked to see if there is a nesting population of becards, as should other river systems farther south.

Other tyrannids

Ash-throated Flycatcher (*Myiarchus cinerascens*) is the other summer resident *Myiarchus* in the Valley, besides the Brown-crested Flycatcher. They have nested on the northern fringes of the Valley (Benson and Arnold 2001) and probably also nest in the desertlike arroyos and uplands of southwestern Starr County. For example, I saw and heard one on top of the Santa Margarita Ranch river bluffs on May 25, 1996, at which time there were several Brown-crested Flycatchers in the riparian forest below.

Given the limited distribution of the Ash-throated Flycatcher in the Valley, I was surprised in May–June, 2001, to hear the familiar *kabrick* and the drawn-out "police-whistle" calls and to see the paler Ash-throated Flycatcher in an area dominated by Brown-crests, about 18 miles (30 km) west of Edinburg. The habitat was dense thorn scrub, in which I had detected no Ash-throats in 2000. Evidently the species is somewhat erratic at the fringes of its range.

Despite careful study, I have never seen or heard an Ash-throat at Bentsen or Santa Ana, although a few individuals may pass through during migration. Great Crested Flycatchers are quite common in those locations, and I usually hear their familiar, rising *wheeep* call regularly during spring migration.

Western Kingbird (*Tyrannus verticalis*) is another success story among North American birds, being a common open-country bird throughout most of the western United States. It has benefited from the spread of irrigated farmland in some areas and from clearing of forests in other areas. Western Kingbirds worked their way south and east from the Panhandle and Southern Plains area, reaching the Valley in the late 1960s (Oberholser 1974). They are now widespread summer residents in the Valley wherever there is suitable habitat: the edges of large agricultural fields, open residential areas, and open pastures. Interestingly, Sennett (1878) found small numbers at Lomita, southern Hidalgo County, in early May, 1877, but these may have been transient migrants.

Nests are placed in large trees, on the cross-braces of telephone poles, or on electric substation girders (in the Houston area, they are most easily found at substations; Honig 1992). The birds are not usually seen right along the river or in forest or scrub. For example, I have never seen a Western Kingbird at Santa Ana, although the species is common along the Military Highway (U.S. Highway 281) just outside the refuge. On two or three occasions I have seen one at Bentsen, in places like the former recreational vehicle area where the death of large trees has opened up the habitat. But those were wandering individuals and they stayed only a day or two. In towns, Western Kingbirds seem most common in newer residential areas, which are often interspersed with agricultural fields.

Like other kingbirds, Westerns effectively keep Great-tailed Grackles and Bronzed Cowbirds away from their nests, greatly reducing the chances of nest predation or brood parasitism. One frequently sees chases, with the more agile kingbird repeatedly flying close to intruder and swiftly moving back out of reach again. Hence it was a great surprise to me on July 9, 1993, to see a pair of Western Kingbirds feeding two fledgling Bronzed Cowbirds in Edinburg (Clotfelter and Brush 1995). Although Western Kingbirds are known to eject cowbird eggs, evidently this pair had failed to do so.

Another common nesting *Tyrannus* in the Valley is *T. forficatus,* the **Scissor-tailed Flycatcher.** *Tijeras* (scissors) have much longer outer tail feathers than "true" kingbirds, but there are great similarities in foraging behavior and general lifestyle. Hawking is the predominant foraging mode during their summer residence in the Valley. Interestingly, like many kingbirds, Scissor-tails consume a variety of fruits during the nonbreeding season in Mexico (Ortiz-Pulido 1997). This includes Barbados cherry (*Malpighia glabra*) and probably coyotillo, both of which are trees in moist Veracruz but shrubs in drier Texas.

Scissor-tailed Flycatchers build simple cup nests in exposed locations, and their calls are similar to those of Western Kingbirds. Differences include greater use of extremely open habitats and a twisting courtship flight by Scissor-tailed Flycatchers.

Scissor-tailed Flycatchers are common summer residents in agricultural and thorn savanna habitats in the Valley, but their time of greatest abundance here is during the spring and fall migrations. Then one can see 50–100 or more birds foraging gracefully over a sugarcane field, perched on telephone wires, or streaming overhead in loose groups. Scissor-tailed Flycatcher migrations are an obvious foreshadowing of marked seasonal changes in temperature. The species is aggressive, takes well to human-altered habitat, and is a known ejector of cowbird eggs (Peer and Sealy 2000), so its future looks bright in the Valley.

Vermilion Flycatchers (*Pyrocephalus rubinus*) nest on the fringes of the Valley, in the thorn scrub and mesquite savanna of Starr County, northern Willacy County, and northern Hidalgo County (Sexton 1999; Benson and Arnold 2001). I am aware of only pre-1950 nesting records for Cameron

County. In winter, Vermilions are fairly common near ponds on golf courses and in other similar habitats, but Valley golfers seldom get to see the butterfly-like display flight of the breeding male. On June 8, 1996, I saw an adult male at Starr County Park near Falcon Dam, and I have seen several displaying males in spring on the Norias Division of the King Ranch (southern Kenedy County).

Sulphur-bellied Flycatcher (*Myiodynastes luteiventris*) is currently one of the rarest and most irregular of the nesting flycatchers in Texas. On May 29, 1976, John C. Arvin saw a pair fight with a pair of Golden-fronted Woodpeckers for a nest cavity at Santa Margarita Ranch, Starr County. The flycatchers remained until July 11, but the dead tree containing the cavity was felled by a violent thunderstorm on June 3. The pair returned for two more breeding seasons (McKinney 2002).

Acadian Flycatchers (*Empidonax virescens*) breed commonly south to central Texas, and they migrate regularly through the Valley. Irby Davis found a nest with eggs at Santa Ana on July 1, 1940, a record that has not been duplicated in the Valley (Oberholser 1974).

FAMILY LANIIDAE

The **Loggerhead Shrike** (*Lanius ludovicianus*), a rare but increasing nesting bird in the Valley, is best known for its habit of impaling prey (insects, spiders, lizards, birds, or mammals) on thorns or barbed-wire fences. This may allow storage of the prey away from scavenging ants or mammals, always on the lookout for a carcass, or it may be a way of storing food captured during times of plenty for hard times (Oksanen et al. 1985). In the Valley I have seen fiddler crabs (*Uca* spp.) impaled on yucca spikes, a true South Texas sight.

South Texas is known to be an important wintering area for Loggerhead Shrikes, and northeastern Mexico probably is also. However, shrikes have not been thought to nest anywhere from the Valley south along the Gulf coastal plain of Mexico (Phillips 1986). For example, Roth (1971) did not record any during his fieldwork in South Texas in 1969. In fairly recent times, this has begun to change. A pair nested successfully near Alamo in 1988 and 1989 (Bert Wessling, in Lasley and Sexton 1988, 1989). Larry Ditto found at least one shrike nest in McAllen in 1999, and shrikes have been nesting regularly in the Kingsville area (Benson and Arnold 2001; Felipe Chavez-Ramirez, pers. comm.). In 2002, John S. Brush saw a family group of shrikes at McAllen High School, and I found a nest with an incubating adult near the University of Texas–Pan American campus. Earlier, Ro Wauer (1998) was surprised to find a pair of shrikes near Rancho Nuevo (coastal southern Tamaulipas) during late April–early May, 1978, suggesting the first breeding effort in coastal Tamaulipas.

I do not know why shrikes are doing so well in South Texas while declining in several regions of the United States (Cade and Woods 1997). Certainly the growing tolerance of suburban habitats is a factor. So far imported fire ants do not appear to be a problem for the shrikes, although the treatment methods may be in some areas (Yosef and Lohrer 1995). We should be pleased that shrike nesting is on the increase here but remain vigilant in monitoring future trends.

FAMILY VIREONIDAE

Bell's Vireos (*Vireo bellii*) were probably never common in the Valley, but they declined to the vanishing point in the late twentieth century. The species formerly bred as far east as Cameron County (Oberholser 1974), but there are no recent breeding records. Bell's Vireos are known to be heavily parasitized by Brown-headed Cowbirds in California, where the local race is endangered (Kus 1998). Brown-headed Cowbirds are probably a major problem in South Texas also: in 1972, nine of 10 nests were parasitized in the study area of Mr. and Mrs. O. C. Bone in Brooks, Duval, Jim Hogg, Jim Wells, and Zapata counties (Webster 1972b).

    Yellow-green Vireos (*Vireo flavoviridis*) have nested in small numbers since at least the 1940s (Davis 1945b). They nested in Brownsville in 1974 and probably fledged one youngster (Maxine Wigington, in Webster 1974). In 1988 and 1989, a pair nested at Laguna Atascosa (Mike Farmer and Tom Pincelli, in Lasley and Sexton 1989). A pair was present again in 1990 (Lasley and Sexton 1990), but it was not known if they nested. Usually, I hear one or two singing males during the course of a Valley summer. In 2002, at least two were present for more than one week, one at Santa Ana and one at Bentsen.

    While other small passerines such as Tropical Parulas and Varied Buntings have declined or disappeared as breeders in the Valley, **White-eyed Vireos** (*Vireo griseus*) are still fairly common. For example, I heard 13 singing birds along the Rio Grande between Pharr and Donna on May 27, 1994. In the Valley, vireos use both thorn scrub and thorn forest, and they are not dependent on the successional scrub they use in much of the United States (Robinson and Robinson 1999). They use areas under reverse succession, where small thorny plants are invading areas formerly dominated by riparian forest or tall thorn forest (Brush and Cantu 1998). White-eyed Vireos seem especially common in low thorn scrub with abundant fiddlewood at Laguna Atascosa. Based on their frugivorous habits in Mexico (Greenberg et al. 1995), the vireos could be important dispersers of fiddlewood fruits.

    Vireo nests are difficult to find, but Christopher Hathcock found a few during his graduate research at Santa Ana in 1997–99. I have seen some family groups and independent juveniles there. On June 16, 1999, Hathcock showed me a nest right along the paved tour road at Santa Ana, with one vireo egg and one Brown-headed Cowbird egg. This vireo is probably not parasitized by the larger and more abundant Bronzed Cowbird, which may be one of the reasons why it seems to be holding its own here.

This widespread vireo has several subspecies, and ours (*V. g. micrus*) is duller and sings shorter songs than northern subspecies. However, it is brighter than the little-studied *V. g. perquisitor* of northern Veracruz (Borror 1987; Howell and Webb 1995). Undoubtedly, some northern birds winter here and may still be present when local birds are beginning to sing. Juveniles have dark eyes and may sing a "whisper" (or practice) song during their first summer, as did a bird at Santa Ana on July 26, 1997.

FAMILY CORVIDAE

Green Jay, *Cyanocorax yncas*

The Green Jay is a beautiful but reclusive bird of tropical and subtropical forest and scrub. Difficult to study in its dense Valley habitats, the Green Jay has been a challenging species for me to get to know. This noisy blue, black, green, yellow, and white jay regularly visits feeding stations in winter, but like other corvids it becomes quiet and inconspicuous during the nesting season (Rowley 1966). Its behavior and ecology have been the subject of only a few studies, notably Doug Gayou's work at Santa Ana in the 1970s (Gayou 1986). Green Jays deserve more attention, given their own attractiveness and in light of the interesting breeding behaviors and intelligence shown by other jays, crows, and ravens (e.g., Heinrich 1999).

DISTRIBUTION   Green Jays occur widely in the Neotropics, in two disjunct (separated) ranges: from Nayarit, Coahuila, and southern Texas south through low and mid-elevations of Mexico to Guatemala, Honduras, and Belize; and in northern and central South America, mainly east of the Andes (AOU 1998). Although some have speculated that disjunct ranges imply introduction by people, there is no direct evidence that Green Jays were introduced anywhere.

Green Jays occur throughout the Valley wherever suitable habitat exists; they are absent from grassy South Padre Island. There is some confusion concerning the northern limits of the Green Jay's range in Texas and some evidence of northward range expansion. Oberholser (1974) shows Green Jays occurring regularly only from Webb, Brooks, and Kleberg counties south to the Valley. More recently, the Texas Ornithological Society (1995) lists the Green Jay as uncommon north to the southern edge of the Edwards Plateau (presumably Val Verde, Kinney, and Uvalde counties) and rare north and east to Goliad, Victoria, and Calhoun counties. This is confirmed by recent records in Val Verde and Maverick counties to the northwest (Sylvestre Sorola, pers. comm.) and in Live Oak and Goliad counties to the northeast (mainly by Mark Elwonger, pers. comm.).

HABITAT   Like Olive Sparrows and Long-billed Thrashers, Green Jays are primarily birds of dense thorn forest and thorn scrub. More than the sparrow and thrasher, Green Jays are also common in tall riparian forest, especially if there is some understory. In the early and mid-1990s, I thought Green Jays were at least regular in well-vegetated residential areas, but more recently those populations seem to have declined somewhat. They still do occur in residential areas and also citrus groves, I suspect mainly when there is a patch of native habitat with dense foliage nearby. Although common in thorn scrub at Laguna Atascosa and in live oak–mesquite forests farther north, Green Jays do not occur in mesquite savanna or coastal prairies or large agricultural fields.

HABITS   Green Jays are inquisitive birds, alert to any changes in their environment. They often are the first to respond to predators, especially those remaining low in dense vegetation or on the ground. The scolding call is an intensification of the normal *eh-eh-eh-eh* calls used in jay interactions. Often a snake, bobcat, or owl is the object of the jays' loud attention, but they may also give the same calls during territorial conflicts.

The effects of predator harassment vary. Sometimes, Green Jays and other species drive a predator completely out of an area for the time being. For example, at Bentsen on June 24, 1999, three Green Jays scolded an adult Harris's Hawk from a perch low in a hedgerow at the end of the dump road. The hawk then flew out across the nearby agricultural field, where three Couch's Kingbirds harassed it until it again moved on. Rarely, a predator will hold its ground, as in Glen Proudfoot's observation of a fledgling Ferruginous Pygmy-Owl, which was knocked from its perch by two Green Jays, which then continued pecking it on the ground (Proudfoot and Johnson 2000). On another occasion, I saw a basking snake near the old Santa Ana headquarters area ignoring a group of four or five Green Jays scolding it.

At least in the Valley, Green Jays make nests of thorny twigs, which are strong because of how the twigs interlock. Sometimes these nests are within reach of a person standing on the ground, but usually they are 10–20 feet (3–6 m) up. In mild winters, such as 1996–97, I have seen nest building in late January. Most nesting is probably done between April and July, and I have seen fledglings between late May and late August.

Female Bronzed Cowbirds follow foraging Green Jays during the nesting season, evidently in hopes of following them back to the nest (Carter 1986; Joe Ideker, pers. comm.) Brood parasitism by Bronzed Cowbirds is frequent, at least in the Valley: I have seen at least 20 different family groups of one to three Bronzed Cowbird juveniles being fed by adult Green Jays (see table 1 on p. 186). Such groups are easy to find because of the loud begging by the young cowbirds, while young Green Jays give a soft *waah,* only audible for a short distance.

Green Jays maintain group territories, in which young from the previous breeding season remain with their parents. These immatures do not breed or bring food to their parents' next set of offspring, but they do help defend the territory against other Green Jay groups (Gayou 1986). Once the current young have fledged, the parents drive off their older offspring, which must then decide where to live.

OTHER OBSERVATIONS   Green Jays are suspected of preying upon the nests of other birds, but I have little evidence of this. The only year in which I observed other birds chasing Green Jays away from their nests was 1998. Even then the observations were few: I once saw an Altamira Oriole harassing a Green Jay from the oriole nesting tree, which was at the edge of a small Great-tailed Grackle colony. The grackles (themselves known nest predators) followed the Green Jay as it worked its way through their colony, giving alarm calls but not attacking it.

Green Jays seldom allow themselves to get more than 20–30 feet (6–9 m) away from cover, which at times restricts their movements to narrow corridors connecting larger patches of forest. Many times I have seen one jay lead off, followed within a few seconds by another, and another, until the whole group has flown. Green Jays cross the Rio Grande occasionally. Gayou (1995) once found a banded Green Jay near Reynosa, 9 miles (15 km) from the Santa Ana banding location. I suspect that accipiters (Cooper's and Sharp-shinned hawks) would be the main predators on Green Jays in the Valley. In tropical areas Aplomado Falcons, Bat Falcons, and Collared Forest-Falcons (*Micrastur semitorquatus*) probably take some Green Jays.

OUTLOOK   I am cautiously optimistic about Green Jays in and near the Valley. In their favor is their ability to maintain high population densities in thorn forest and in places where Bronzed Cowbird parasitism is highest (Santa Ana and Bentsen). Their ability to detect and avoid aflatoxin-tainted grain at feeders (Perez et al. 2001) may be beneficial. Negative factors include rapid human population growth and the possible harmful effects if xerification continues in the Valley.

Brown Jay, *Cyanocorax morio*

The Brown Jay is a tropical bird that reaches the northernmost limits of its distribution along the Rio Grande in southern Texas. In a very limited area, one can see this impressive jay and hear its explosive *pow!* and *kee-ow* calls.

Full adults have all-dark bills, while nestlings have yellow bills. Birds two to four years old usually have bills blotched with varying amounts of yellow and blackish. The Brown Jay's omnivory and general success in disturbed areas in the tropics makes it hard to understand why Brown Jays have not been more successful in the Valley. I cannot say that I know the species well, but I have been fortunate to make a few nesting and foraging observations and to peruse the literature.

DISTRIBUTION   The Brown Jay is a permanent resident from Zapata and Roma south through eastern and southern Mexico to Panama. Populations in the Valley are limited to the immediate area of the river, and many birds regularly cross back and forth. Although the species has been observed as far east as Rosita, Starr County (Dick Heller, in Benson and Arnold 2001), in my experience it is limited in the Valley to the riparian forest between Falcon Dam and Fronton.

The first U.S. report was of two birds seen between Falcon Dam and Chapeño on April 28, 1969, by L. B. Cooper and Paul Schulze (Oberholser 1974). A group of two adults and three immatures was seen west of Roma on June 8, 1974. On July 14, 1974, an active nest (with a nestling) was found and photographed about 2 miles (3 km) downstream from Salineño by John C. Arvin (Webster 1974). Since then, the species has spread upstream to the San Ygnacio area, where it may be irregular (Jack C. Eitniear, pers. comm.), and somewhat downstream in Starr County, as already mentioned.

The Starr County Brown Jays likely spread north from nearby populations in Nuevo León, Mexico. At one time there was a "more or less regular" population at China, Nuevo León, along the Río San Juan (Oberholser 1974). The species currently occurs regularly in the Monterrey area of Nuevo León (Selander 1959), where I saw them in 1999, and along the Río Corona, Tamaulipas (Gehlbach 1987).

Not as well known is the fact that there may have been a Brown Jay population along the lower Rio Grande in the late 1890s and early 1900s. On February 27, 1897, Austin P. Smith collected a subadult in Brownsville, and on April 25, 1902, a Brown Jay egg set was collected there (Hubbard and Niles 1975). On January 16, 1902, two females (adult and immature) were collected at Camargo, which is along the Río San Juan within 3 miles (5 km) of the Rio Grande (Selander 1959). These early records suggest that the lower Rio Grande has been at or just beyond the extreme northern edge of the Brown Jay's range for some time, but the exact history remains unknown.

HABITAT   In the Valley, Brown Jays inhabit tall riparian forest and adjacent thorn forest. In my experience they inhabit shady ash forest most of the time, but others have seen them regularly in semi-open riparian forest and even thorn scrub at times. In the tropics, Brown Jays are common in banana plantations, small roadside clearings, and second-growth forests, and the species increases as old-growth forest is cleared.

HABITS   Brown Jays travel in small flocks much of the time, with one breeding pair and a few nonbreeders. In the Valley they are most easily seen at feeding stations (in Chapeño and Salineño), often showing up within the first hour or two after sunrise and staying for just a few minutes. On April 25, 1998, five Brown Jays flew up to a bird-feeding platform at Chapeño before sunrise, putting on the desired show for an American Birding Association field trip. Based on where I see and hear them, they must obtain most of their food from wild sources, but it is good for birders that they visit feeders.

As they fly, Brown Jays look like big-headed chachalacas with slower wing beats. Despite their large size, Brown Jays can hide easily in the dense foliage of the *monte* and tall riparian forest. Their loud calls may be their only giveaway, and the species even has a "nest call," a far-carrying *pee-ah* given only by the breeding female or the nestlings (Skutch 1960). Once I heard that call emanating from a small island near Chapeño, but Marty Bray and I were unable to find a nest.

Marty Bray and I did find a Brown Jay nest on May 9, 1996, at the river's edge in a shady ash forest on the U.S. side, less than 1 mile (1.6 km) above the confluence of the Río Alamo and Rio Grande. We heard the *pee-ah* call as we approached. A dark-billed (adult) bird sat on the nest, 20–22 feet (6–7 m) up in the fork of a small ash, while two other adults perched nearby. The birds moved quietly off into the underbrush when they saw us. We were unable to see into the nest at any time. The nest appeared disturbed the next time we checked, on May 25, 1996, and we suspected predation. Sharon Bennett saw an adult feeding two recent fledglings at the Salineño feeding station on April 11, 12, and 14, 1995, indicating how early they may start nesting.

OTHER OBSERVATIONS   In Belize, I once watched and listened to at least two Brown Jays scolding a Spectacled Owl (*Pulsatrix perspicillata*) outside a cave entrance at Blue Hole National Park. The jays did not attack the owl, but it eventually moved off after at least ten minutes of noisy scolding. Presumably, Brown Jays would be effective mobbers even of large owls such as the Great Horned Owl, but I have not seen that behavior.

Brown Jays are known to be nest predators at least in some parts of the tropics. Alexander Skutch (1960) saw Brown Jays eat two newly hatched Grayish Saltators (*Saltator coerulescens*) and a well-developed Clay-colored Robin nestling in the Costa Rican highlands. However, he believes that this habit may be less common in the food-rich lowlands, where he has not seen nest depredation by Brown Jays. In Salineño on April 6, 1996, Sharon Bennett (pers. comm.) saw some Brown Jays looking into an iron pipe that contained an active Tufted Titmouse nest. The jays were unable to reach in and get the nestlings. The normally retiring Audubon's Oriole has been observed chasing a Brown Jay away from an oriole nest that was under construction (Sutton and Pettingill 1942).

OUTLOOK   Given the limited range and small U.S. population of the Brown Jay, we cannot be confident about its long-term persistence in the United States. In its favor are its large size, its success in the tropics, and the fact that it has successfully nested in the United States. A negative is the possible fragmentation of its habitat just south of the Rio Grande. As less water flows in the Río San Juan and possibly the Río Alamo, and as more habitat is cleared or xerified, the Brown Jay may lose its direct connection to the central Nuevo León population. The long-term drought of the mid- to late 1990s has reduced the already small Brown Jay population between Falcon Dam and Roma (John C. Arvin, pers. comm.).

Other corvids

One of the first birds I remember seeing as a beginning birder in New Jersey was the **Blue Jay** (*Cyanocitta cristata*), an unmistakable and common bird of eastern and central North America. Its loud *thief!* or *jay!* calls resound through cities, suburbs, and rural areas alike, but in Texas it breeds no farther south than the Rockport area, Aransas County (Benson and Arnold 2001). Blue Jays are partially migratory, and one was found dead on the University of Texas–Pan American campus in Edinburg on October 21, 1967 (Brush 2000b).

It was a surprise to me on October 25, 1995, to hear and then see a Blue Jay in a flock of four or five Green Jays in my neighborhood in Edinburg. Over the next five years, I fairly regularly saw and heard a Blue Jay in my neighborhood but made no special effort to look for a nest. On April 6, 2000, Anne H. Toal saw a Blue Jay building a nest in a live oak in her Edinburg yard. Over the next two months she saw the Blue Jay finish the nest, bring food to the four nestlings, and chase off intruding Great-tailed Grackles, Great Kiskadees, and Plain Chachalacas. The nest was judged to have been successful on or before May 23, 2000. On October 23, 2000, Anne found a dead first-year Blue Jay in her yard, evidently one of the young from the earlier nest. This series of observations established the first nesting record for the Valley (Brush 2000b). Since then I have regularly heard and seen a flock of four to six birds in the same part of Edinburg.

The **Chihuahuan Raven** (*Corvus cryptoleucus*) is the common black corvid of the Valley, occurring regularly in the less-populated ranch country and in coastal prairie sections of the Valley. The largest numbers can be seen in winter, especially at landfills in Brownsville and Matamoros. The old name, White-necked Raven, was a good one, but had already been given to an African species (*C. albicollis*).

I have seen pairs of ravens evidently searching for nesting sites in April at Laguna Atascosa, but during the breeding season the birds are hard to find near towns, even small ones. Sennett (1878) and Merrill (1878) did not record any ravens in the Hidalgo and Brownsville areas in the late 1870s. On May 9, 1996, I saw a raven carrying an egg in its bill over the river near Fronton. It was being pursued by a male Great-tailed Grackle, which suggested that the egg had come from a grackle nest.

The enigmatic **Tamaulipas Crow** (*C. imparatus*), a Valley invader, was split off from the Sinaloa Crow (*C. sinaloae*) based mainly on striking differences in their calls (Davis 1958, Hardy 1990). It is high on the list of "most wanted" Valley birds, because of its very limited Valley and total range. The mystery with this bird is why it has done so poorly here, given the tremendous success of species like the American Crow in the United States and the recovery of Common Ravens (*Corvus corax*) in much of North America.

A hint that Tamaulipas Crows were headed north toward Texas was a December 28, 1960, observation of three birds at Moquetito, Tamaulipas, in flat delta land about 35 miles (56 km) southwest of Brownsville (Edgar B. Kincaid Jr. and others; in Oberholser 1974). This was the first known observation of Tamaulipas Crows in the Mexican portion of the Rio Grande Delta; before that the species had seemed limited to the rolling ranch country just outside the delta proper, another 35 miles (56 km) southwest of Moquetito.

In 1968, Tamaulipas Crows reached the United States. On August 2, John C. Arvin saw three birds 3 miles (5 km) inland from the mouth of the Rio Grande. By September 1, about 200 birds were foraging on a ranch east of Brownsville (Oberholser 1974). On September 4, 1968, Bruce Fall (1973) saw a flock of 30, flying south, near Rudolf, Kenedy County. He saw apparently the same flock of 30 one hour later, in Willacy County, 5 miles (8 km) north of Raymondville. Fall stated that the birds appeared confused and disoriented, and individuals stayed close together.

For the next few years, Tamaulipas Crows were winter residents, with a high of 480 on October 14, 1971, at the Brownsville Landfill (Howard H. Axtell, in Oberholser 1974). A few birds spread farther inland, with one bird seen on the Falcon Dam Christmas Bird Count (December 28, 1971, in Oberholser 1974).

Once here, Tamaulipas Crows were slow to nest. A pair was seen east of Brownsville on July 8, 1987 (Mitch Heindel, in Lasley and Sexton 1986). They first nested in the Valley in 1989, when four nests were built at the Port of Brownsville (Arnold Moorhouse and Mike Farmer, in Lasley and Sexton 1989). Mike and Rose Farmer found one nest at the Brownsville dump in April, 1990 (Lasley and Sexton 1990). Birders were able to see the crows fairly easily at the Brownsville Landfill through most of the 1990s, but nesting success was uncertain. Declines were noted in the late 1990s, and by 2000 Tamaulipas Crow was added to the Texas Bird Record Committee Review List because of its increasing rarity. Nesting still is reported near the Brownsville Airport (at most one nest per year, 1998–2002), but the species seems to be barely hanging on in the United States.

We do not know whether changing landfill practices—in which garbage is covered sooner—are responsible, or the lingering drought of the mid- to late 1990s, or some unknown factor. Tamaulipas Crows are still common in parts of their limited range in northeastern Mexico, as shown by the more than 50 roosting at the Matamoros dump in 2001 (Mel Piñeda, pers. comm.). However, Tamaulipas Crows may have declined in northern and central Tamaulipas during the last five to ten years (John C. Arvin, pers. comm.). Whether birds are still present at China, Nuevo León, formerly the northwestern corner of the species' range, is unknown (Davis 1958). On three visits to the Ciudad Victoria area, Tamaulipas (2001–2003), I have yet to see one.

FAMILY ALAUDIDAE

Horned Larks (*Eremophila alpestris*) are common residents of open habitats in the Valley, mainly bare or sparsely vegetated agricultural fields. They also occur in barren shoreline habitats along the Lower Laguna Madre and the Laguna Madre of Tamaulipas. Horned Larks have nested in coastal prairies since at least the early 1900s, but during the Texas Breeding Bird Atlas surveys they were also confirmed nesting in Hidalgo and Starr counties (Oberholser 1974; Benson and Arnold 2001). Undoubtedly, agricultural development in the Valley has allowed Horned Larks to spread inland.

FAMILY HIRUNDINIDAE

The changes in the aerial insectivore community have been striking during the last forty to fifty years, and at least three species of swallows have expanded their range into the Valley (or South Texas as a whole) from the north. All the invading species have been helped by artificial nesting surfaces, whether provided purposefully by people or not.

In Sennett's and Merrill's time, the late 1870s, at least one swallow species bred in the Valley: **Cliff Swallow** (*Petrochelidon pyrrhonota*), which nested in a dense colony in the Hidalgo County Courthouse, in what is now Hidalgo. However, Cliff Swallows were then absent from areas downriver and upriver (Sennett 1878, 1879), and Merrill (1878) thought this was the only swallow that bred in the Valley. One wonders if even Cliff Swallows originally bred in the Valley, given the general scarcity of natural nest sites except for a few small cliffs in Starr County. Currently, Cliff Swallows nest widely under bridges and culverts throughout the Valley, except for the South Padre Island area. They also nest at Anzalduas Dam, the only location at which I have seen fledglings, but I simply have not looked in the many other colonies.

Sennett (1879) thought **Bank Swallows** (*Riparia riparia*) possibly nested along the river, as he saw them regularly through May. In 1891, there was a nesting colony of Bank Swallows in Brownsville (Oberholser 1974). Bank Swallows quickly colonize new excavations for sand or gravel (Oberholser 1974), and they also nest in natural dirt banks along the Rio Grande. I know of at least river bank sites frequently used in the 1990s, all on the Mexican side of the Rio Grande between Chapeño and Fronton. On June 11, 2001, I canoed past a large group of Bank Swallows, associated with a gravel pit on the U.S. side of the Rio Grande about 2 miles (3 km) downstream from Roma. I could not see the walls of the pit from the river, but the birds acted as though they were nesting. The TBBAP (Benson and Arnold 2001) found a colony in the Mission area of Hidalgo County, the farthest downstream site of which I am aware.

The widespread **Northern Rough-winged Swallow** (*Stelgidopteryx serripennis*) is not mentioned in early accounts. It could have bred in the Valley during the late 1800s, but even Oberholser (1974) shows it summering only in Starr County, with no nesting records south of the San Antonio area. This widespread swallow may have been overlooked, as even today it is present only in small numbers, and the species' solitary nesting habits do not attract attention. I have seen recently fledged young on several occasions at Anzalduas, and the birds seemed to be using artificial cavities as nest sites.

Species that definitely invaded the Valley during the twentieth century include **Barn Swallow** (*Hirundo rustica*), **Cave Swallow** (*Petrochelidon fulva*), and **Purple Martin** (*Progne subis*). Barn Swallow nested only as far south as Laredo and Corpus Christi as of the early 1970s, but during the Texas Breeding Bird Atlas work of 1987–92 the species was confirmed breeding from Starr County to Cameron County (Benson and Arnold 2001). Barn Swallows are now fairly common, regular breeders on highway bridges and culverts and other artificial surfaces throughout the Valley. In 1995 and 1996, a pair bred at least three times (total) in the open second-floor breezeway of the old Science Building on the University of Texas–Pan

American campus. I regularly see a pair foraging over the cattail marsh near the South Padre Island Convention Center (as on June 13, 1999), where they likely nest on an electrical substation.

The Cave Swallow has spread explosively through southern Texas during the last twenty-five to thirty years. Cave Swallows originally nested only in caves and sinkholes, mainly in the southwestern Edwards Plateau area. In 1973, over 600 nests were found in culverts as far south as Maverick County, as the species reached far beyond its cave habitat (Martin 1974). Cave Swallows reached Webb County by 1976 and Duval County by 1977 (Martin and Martin 1978).

In addition to the Valley nesting records following, Cave Swallows have expanded as nesters to easternmost Texas (1989), Oklahoma (1996–98), and southwestern Louisiana (1997–99), so the species is clearly doing well (McNair and Post 2001). Some interbreeding between Cave and Barn Swallows was noted, especially during the expansion years of the 1970s (Martin 1980), but overall the species have kept separate.

During the 1987–92 TBBAP, Cave Swallows were noted nesting in Starr County (Benson and Arnold 2001), but they now nest throughout the Valley. I saw a small colony of Cave Swallows repeatedly entering and leaving nests under Route 1015 south of Weslaco on May 13, 1999, and June 14, 2000, but I am unaware of the timing of the invasion of Hidalgo County. On July 4, 2001, I saw about 20 independent juveniles resting and foraging under a large, open-sided pavilion at the Edinburg Municipal Park.

Purple Martins are well known to many Americans, given their striking purplish color, their insectivorous habits, and most of all their readiness to accept nesting structures such as gourds and nest box apartments. A colony was reported at Rio Grande City long ago: June 5–10, 1891. This was not long after the only specimen records of Gray-breasted Martins (*Progne chalybea*) in the Valley (Rio Grande City, 1880, and Hidalgo, 1889, in Oberholser 1974), so the two species may have occurred together for a brief time in the United States.

Purple Martins may have been absent from the Valley for almost a century, but John Arvin estimated about 200 nesting in Cameron and Hidalgo counties in 1975 (Webster 1975). Today Purple Martins breed almost wherever nest boxes have been put up. I know of several small colonies in McAllen, Edinburg, and Brownsville. Competition with House Sparrows for nest sites is ongoing, although the martins are aided by nest box managers who often remove sparrow nests. In June, 2000, I saw a martin repeatedly enter a cavity in the top of a light tower at a baseball field in southernmost McAllen. Although I was not able to confirm that the martin was carrying food, this observation suggests that Valley martins occasionally nest in locations other than nest boxes.

FAMILY PARIDAE

The changing taxonomy of the **Black-crested Titmouse** (*Baeolophus atricristatus*) has caused confusion. For much of the second half of the twentieth century, it was considered a subspecies of the widespread Tufted Titmouse (*B. bicolor*), which has probably decreased the interest level. The existence of a stable hybrid zone in Central Texas, despite the frequency of intermediates within that zone (Dixon 1990), was reinterpreted to mean that the two groups are separate species.

In the Valley, Black-crested Titmice are common in tall riparian forest, thorn forest, and thorn scrub, and they occur regularly in well-vegetated suburban areas. I hear singing males frequently in March and early April, and first broods are off the nest in late April or May, at a time when many species are just getting around to building nests and laying eggs. Second broods appear to be common as well, given the abundance of family groups in June and early July. I have seen active nests in woodpecker holes in dead trees and fence posts.

FAMILY REMIZIDAE

The **Verdin** (*Auriparus flaviceps*) has been studied fairly extensively in Arizona, where its small, domed nests are built in conspicuous locations in the Sonoran Desert (Phillips et al. 1964). They are confirmed nesters in thorn scrub across the Valley, but I have spent little time studying them. Verdins are uncommon to rare in thorn forest, but I sometimes see juveniles or adults appear suddenly in June or July in such habitats. I suspect that Verdins wander somewhat after a nesting attempt is over, as they do in Arizona (Rosenberg et al. 1991).

FAMILY TROGLODYTIDAE

Carolina Wrens (*Thryothorus ludovicianus*) have had an interesting history in the Valley. Once common along the river from Brownsville to at least the Bentsen area, the species declined in the 1960s. In 1972, John C. Arvin estimated that fourteen pairs resided in the Santa Maria tract, in extreme southwestern Cameron County, but he stated that none then remained at Santa Ana (Oberholser 1974). While this is not an abundant species today, I have had no difficulty finding Carolina Wrens at Santa Ana or the Sabal Palm Grove. Smaller numbers live in riparian forest between Chapeño and Fronton, where John Arvin reported the first record in modern times on May 15, 1976, at Santa Margarita Ranch (Webster 1976), and I heard some during canoe trips in the 1990s. Breeding has not yet been confirmed for Starr County. The apparent rebound is encouraging but should be further studied, since the Lomita Carolina Wren is an endemic subspecies that is poorly known.

Bewick's Wren (*Thryomanes bewickii*) is quite a common breeder in the western Valley, in drier habitats than those chosen by Carolina Wrens. I have had a few nests in my nest boxes west of Edinburg (2000–2001), and these wrens also nest in woodpecker holes, other cavities, and even skulls of cattle (Steve Bentsen, pers. comm.). There is some evidence that Bewick's Wrens decline in small habitat fragments (John C. Arvin, in Webster 1972b), but this has not been studied. There are no confirmed nesting records for Santa Ana (Benson and Arnold 2001).

According to the Texas Breeding Bird Atlas (Benson and Arnold 2001), **Rock Wren** (*Salpinctes obsoletus*) does not breed anywhere south of 29°N, thus excluding most of southern Texas. However, Rock Wrens formerly bred in the Valley, with the most recent records being in 1919, when R. W. Quillin saw two nests in southeastern Cameron County, in the loma region east of Brownsville (Oberholser 1974). In 1966, John C. Arvin found a nest containing young Rock Wrens at Falcon Dam (Webster 1966), but I am unaware of any recent nesting.

Cactus Wren (*Campylorhynchus brunneicapillus*) is a common breeder in southern and western Texas and has been confirmed breeding in all four Valley counties (Benson and Arnold 2001). Nests are normally placed in large cacti, such as prickly pear. Once at Santa Ana I saw a nest under construction in a cedar elm, in lush riparian forest, but only about 600 feet (about 150 m) from open thorn scrub habitat. Despite remaining fairly common in the Valley, Cactus Wrens have declined in recent decades in southern Texas, probably due to continued brush clearing.

FAMILY SYLVIIDAE

Blue-Gray Gnatcatchers (*Polioptila caerulea*) are common winter residents and migrants, often joining mixed-species foraging flocks. Although once nesting in the Valley (confirmed for Cameron and Hidalgo counties; Oberholser 1974), gnatcatchers are now scarce breeders in all of South Texas, and they apparently no longer nest in the Valley. The closest confirmed nesting location was Refugio County in the Coastal Bend (Benson and Arnold 2001). Some early fall migrants pass through the Valley in late June or July, confusing their breeding status. Heavy brood parasitism by Brown-headed Cowbirds may have had a major impact; in 1971 the last known nesting pair in Zapata County had all their eggs destroyed by cowbirds (O. C. Bone, in Webster 1971).

Black-tailed Gnatcatcher (*Polioptila melanura*) is an uncommon resident of the driest thorn scrub of Starr County, but its current breeding status is poorly known. The only known nest was discovered by Frank B. Armstrong on April 13, 1892, near Brownsville (Oberholser 1974). In April, 1998,

I saw an adult scolding a Crested Caracara in Starr County Park near Falcon Dam, suggesting possible breeding.

FAMILY TURDIDAE

Clay-colored Robin, *Turdus grayi*

"No other bird is so conspicuous, to ears as well as eyes, in gardens and dooryards throughout much of continental Middle America" (Skutch 1981). As well as being the national bird of Costa Rica, where it is said to "bring the rains," the Clay-colored Robin is an increasingly common sight and sound in the Valley. Its first recorded nests in the United States were in 1986 and 1988 at Bentsen (Lasley and Sexton 1986, 1988) and in 1992 at Anzalduas (Brush 2000a). Since then the birds have established a modest population scattered along the lower Rio Grande. The peak flock size so far is eight birds at Salineño on January 7, 2000 (Nick Block et al., pers. comm.). Clay-colored Robins have clearly come a long way since the first U.S. sighting in 1940, and their soft, melodic song is likely to be heard even more frequently in the near future.

DISTRIBUTION   The species is a year-round resident in small numbers from Laredo southeast to Harlingen, but it has been recorded nesting only in Hidalgo and Webb counties so far. Clay-colored Robins nested successfully at Bentsen in 1986 (John Pace, in Lasley and Sexton 1986). Intensive fieldwork in Hidalgo County in 1999 revealed breeding pairs at Anzalduas and Santa Ana and a singing male at Bentsen (Brush 2000a). At least once in the last ten years, I have seen or heard Clay-colored Robins during the breeding season in Laredo, Chapeño, Salineño, La Joya, McAllen, Edinburg, and Laguna Atascosa. Others have reported robins in Roma, Rio Grande City, Weslaco, Harlingen, Laguna Vista, and Arroyo City (the latter two sites in winter only). Interestingly, this robin's status in Brownsville is uncertain despite apparently suitable habitat, and I am not aware of any records. Likewise, I have no records yet from little-birded Willacy County.

The ten birds detected on a canoe trip between Roma and Rio Grande City on June 11, 2001, may represent the largest Valley breeding population. On that trip, eight birds were heard singing (on both sides of the river), one gave the *meeyoo* call, and one was seen flying across the river.

Laredo and Nuevo Laredo probably also support a small resident population, as evidenced by a singing male I heard on May 30, 2001, at the Nuevo Laredo sewage treatment plant, a bird calling in response to a tape on January 3, 2001 (John C. Arvin, pers. comm.), and some birds found there in spring 1999 (Woodin et al. (2000a). Ron LaDuque showed me an active Clay-colored Robin nest near International Bridge 2 in Laredo on May 1,

2002 (he saw one large nestling on May 28, 2002, which fledged in late May or early June).

In Mexico, Clay-colored Robins occur from at least central Nuevo León (Sada de Hermosillo et al. 1995) and northern Tamaulipas south along the Gulf-Caribbean slope through southern Mexico and Central America to northern Colombia. Although Clay-colored Robins occur up to 8,200 feet (2,500 m) above sea level, they are most common in tropical lowlands.

HABITAT   In the Valley, which is drier than most of their range, Clay-colored Robins mainly occur in well-watered residential areas or parks and moist riparian forests and adjacent mudflats. In Central America they also forage in plantations, willow and reed thickets, shady pastures, and light, open woods (or even dense rain forest within a few hundred meters of a clearing; Skutch 1981). Clay-colored Robins seem to forage in more open habitats during the breeding season, while they may spend more time in forests and thickets the rest of the year. Fruiting trees may be an important component of their nesting habitat.

HABITS   Clay-colored Robins act like a cross between the tame American Robin of U.S. towns and cities and a shy thrush of the forest. Sometimes they even join flocks of American Robins, whether in a fruiting tree or on a well-watered lawn. Clay-coloreds look much like brown-backed, brown-tailed versions of American Robins in flight, although the wings are shorter and more rounded, and the flight is somewhat "bounding." Such intermittent flight may help tired flight muscles recover in between wing beats. This may be important for nonmigratory species, which have wings that are shorter and less useful for sustained flight than are those of their migratory relatives (Kramer and McLaughlin 2001; Rayner et al. 2001).

I have seen them hopping tamely on lawns in the familiar robin manner, presumably looking for insects. Earthworms (Annelida, Oligochaeta) are rarely seen aboveground in the Valley, and I have never seen a bird of any species eat one here. Clay-colored Robins also forage on moist mudflats at the edge of woodland pools, where they are easily disturbed.

They are quite frugivorous both in winter and summer. A common way to find one in winter is to find a tree laden with fruit and then wait for the birds to visit. An individual may not stay long, but it will likely soon return for more fruit (Coates-Estrada and Estrada 1986). Anacua and coma fruits seem quite attractive to Clay-colored Robins in the Valley, and I have also seen them eating fruits of sugar hackberry and mulberry. In tropical areas they consume a variety of fruits (Skutch 1981).

Male Clay-colored Robins sing loudly while trying to attract a mate and before the eggs are laid, and they can be heard for more than 650 feet (200 m) at those times. Even so, their habit of singing 10–20 feet (3–6 m) up in dense foliage can make the male hard to spot. Once incubation begins, males sing much more softly, and sometimes they are hard to hear more than 50 feet (15 m) away. Nests can be found most easily by watching adults with nesting material, as they readily fly to the nest. The nest is large and contains mud, and it seems to need a firm support. At Anzalduas most nests were on the strong, nearly horizontal branches of live oak.

Later in the nesting cycle, when the male is quieter and the female is incubating, it can be quite difficult to get a good look at the birds or to find the nest. Although Skutch (1987) has noted being followed and scolded by his "garden thrushes," he and I have both noticed that they may simply refuse to go to the nest when observers are anywhere around (Skutch 1983). Adults bring fruit or arthropods to the nestlings and recent fledglings, and they can be quite bold in driving off intruding fox squirrels at such times.

OTHER OBSERVATIONS   At Anzalduas on May 8, 1998, I heard a Clay-colored Robin include a pauraque-like *poweer* regularly in its song. Northern Mockingbirds regularly imitate the Clay-colored Robin in areas where the latter is most common in the Valley, and one has to listen carefully to the quality of the song, the number of repetitions, and the mockingbird's eventual switchover to other phrases.

In April–July, 1999, a pair of Clay-colored Robins nested successfully at Anzalduas, despite being observed by hundreds of birders during that time. An early nest was abandoned (April, 1999), possibly due to the large number of birders during a bird festival. Without nest locations being known (which itself can attract unwanted attention), groups of birders often walked right under the nest without knowing it. At least one later nest was successful, possibly because of fewer disturbances, and one fledgling was seen on June 24, 1999. Evidently predation can be high, both in the tropics (Morton 1971) and in Texas.

OUTLOOK   Although there are likely fewer than fifty pairs currently in the United States, Clay-colored Robins continue to establish themselves as permanent residents, as noted. Much of the range expansion has occurred during a series of years with relatively mild winters, so it will be interesting to see what happens when colder weather returns. My belief is that the Clay-colored Robin is here to stay, given the number of other tropical species that have expanded into and beyond the Valley during the late twentieth century.

Other thrushes

There is one other thrush breeding in the Valley. **Eastern Bluebirds** (*Sialia sialis*) once bred in the Valley (John C. Arvin, in Webster 1957), and they still breed regularly in the open live oak forests just to our north (Benson and

Arnold 2001). For example, I saw a female carrying nesting material on May 8, 1994, near Encino, Brooks County. A few recent summer observations of bluebirds in western Starr County and northeastern Hidalgo County suggest that there may be a small breeding population in the Valley itself. Karen Hunke confirmed that Eastern Bluebirds used nest boxes at her ranch in northeastern Hidalgo County in 2002. In May, 2003, John S. Brush and I saw a pair feeding three small, weakly flying fledglings on a savannalike golf course in Edinburg, indicating nearby breeding. The species is much more regular and widespread in winter, particularly in mistletoe-infested mesquite. In 1986, four pairs of **American Robins** (*Turdus migratorius*) nested successfully at Falfurrias, Brooks County (A. W. O'Neil, in Lasley and Sexton 1986). There was no evidence of American Robins nesting any farther south than Victoria (Victoria County) during the Texas Breeding Bird Atlas Program (Benson and Arnold 2001).

FAMILY MIMIDAE

Long-billed Thrasher, *Toxostoma longirostre*

This species comes close to being a poster child for the Tamaulipan Biotic Province of southern Texas and northeastern Mexico, as the ranges match almost perfectly. However, showing the dynamic aspect of ecology, the thrasher has recently expanded its range into the Trans-Pecos region of western Texas. Long-billed Thrashers spend most of their lives on the ground, as does the closely related (and much better known) Brown Thrasher (*T. rufum*).

They can be difficult to watch for extended periods of time in their dense *monte* habitat, as Sennett (1878) noted: "One day in April [1887], while concealed in a dense thicket close by some heavy timber, a pair of this species gave me pleasure for a full half hour. This, I think, was the only time I ever saw them for more than a moment at a time."

DISTRIBUTION   Common from Del Rio, the San Antonio area (although not in urban habitats), Goliad (Goliad County), and Rockport (Aransas County) south to the Rio Grande, Long-billed Thrashers are also common south through eastern Coahuila, eastern Nuevo León, and Tamaulipas to central Veracruz (Tweit 1997). Although mainly a lowland bird, the species does occur in suitable habitat up to about 4,900 feet (1,500 m) in the mountains of northeastern Mexico. Even in Sennett's time (the late 1870s), Long-billed Thrashers were regularly seen as far north as Corpus Christi (Sennett 1879), so the species has not spread north as dramatically as other Valley specialties like Couch's Kingbird.

Strangely enough, a few vagrants of this nonmigratory species have shown up in Colorado, revealing their potential for dispersal. There have been some signs of range expansion, with birds nesting in Midland and Presidio counties of West Texas (Tweit 1997) and also occurring in Big Bend National Park (Wauer 1996). Long-billed Thrashers occur throughout the Valley wherever there is suitable habitat.

HABITAT   The *monte* (dense thorn forest and thorn scrub) is classic Long-billed Thrasher habitat. When the canopy is 10–15 feet (3–5 m) high, the understory may be fairly open, as in stands of Texas ebony, coma, or Texas persimmon, but in other cases only a rabbit or thrasher would seem able to squeeze through the thorny brush. Usually there are some trees greater than 20 feet (6 m) tall in nesting territories. Thrashers are found in lower densities in tall riparian forests, mainly in areas with some understory (Fischer 1981; Carter 1986).

In fall 1991 I saw a bird in a long narrow strip of scrubby riparian forest along a canal in Edinburg, but this was evidently a dispersing individual, as it did not stay. Long-billed Thrashers do not occur in mesquite savanna and are quite rare in open thorn forest, where Curve-billed Thrashers are so common. Long-billed Thrashers inhabit reforested tracts, but it is not known how old or well developed the vegetation must be for birds to enter.

HABITS   Long-billed Thrashers earn their name by "thrashing"— picking up sticks and flicking small objects out of the way to find food items in the leaf litter on the forest floor. Sometimes a bird becomes so focused on its foraging that it may approach to within 10 feet (3 m) of a quiet observer. Thrashers are like Olive Sparrows in seldom coming far out from cover. Even when they visit feeding stations (mainly in winter), Long-billed Thrashers usually stay within a meter or two of dense brush, ready to run or fly quickly back inside. They eat quite a variety of foods, with snails, beetles, and ants being prominent animal items. They also consume a variety of fruits, such sugar hackberry, granjeno, brasil, anacua, and Texas persimmon (Fischer 1983; Carter 1986, Tweit 1997).

Individuals of this species, like other thrashers, perch in trees at times. They often find a somewhat hidden perch from which to sing their rich, varied song during the long breeding season. I have not made a careful comparison of the similar songs of Long-billed and Curve-billed thrashers, but the easiest way to distinguish them is to wait for the unique *whitwheet* call of the Curve-billed Thrasher. Long-billed Thrashers also have some unique calls, such as a whistled *cleeooeep* and a gruff, low-pitched call given at all times of year.

Nests are fairly small cups, usually placed in the densest foliage available. In a riparian forest in the Valley, nests were mainly 7–13 feet (2–4 m) up, often in viny tangles in small trees such as huisache or sugar hackberry (C. E. Rupert 1997). In thorn scrub habitat farther north, nests were only 3–6 feet (1–2 m) up in thorny shrubs (mainly colima; Fischer 1980). Nests are well shaded, reducing the need for the parents to shade their young from the intense subtropical sun. Predation rates are fairly high during the incubation period but less so during the nestling period, probably due to active nest defense by the parents (Hathcock 2000). Young leave the nest able to run and climb but not fly (Fischer 1980).

OTHER OBSERVATIONS   Long-billed Thrashers begin singing early in the year, like Northern Cardinals. I usually first hear their song in February in the Valley. Individuals may be territorial all year, but winter and breeding territories may be in different locations (Fischer 1981), requiring reestablishment of breeding territories each spring. The breeding season is probably over by the end of July, but I occasionally heard birds singing in September or October.

Juveniles have whitish yellow eyes and their tails take some time to grow out to full length. They apparently do not beg loudly, as I cannot find any records in my field notes. Adults too can be quiet, especially from August through December, and at times one can walk through an area where the species is common and not hear or see a single bird.

OUTLOOK   Long-billed Thrashers are still quite abundant in suitable habitat in the Valley. In a five-year banding study at Santa Ana 123 thrashers were banded—only the totals for Brown-crested Flycatcher (213) and Olive Sparrow (208) were higher (Gallegos 2001). Thrashers do suffer from moderate to high brood parasitism by Bronzed Cowbirds in the Valley. In 1980–81, 96 percent of 26 nests were parasitized, with an average of about 2.5 Bronzed Cowbird eggs per parasitized nest (Carter 1986). However, in 1997–99, only 68 percent of 19 nests were parasitized, with about 2.8 Bronzed Cowbird eggs per parasitized nest (Hathcock 2000). Bronzed Cowbirds may not be as much of a problem in less fragmented habitats north of the Valley, where cowbird parasitism is rare (Fischer 1980; Tweit 1997). The second broods of Long-billed Thrashers probably produce more cowbird offspring than the first brood, which is laid before the main Bronzed Cowbird breeding season.

Although the species seems currently fairly stable, and has actually increased in southern Texas over the last thirty-five years, we need to watch this thrasher carefully. There is such a limited amount of excellent habitat left in the Valley that we do not want to be misled by high Long-billed Thrasher densities in places like Santa Ana. Revegetation of agricultural fields offers promise for species like the Long-billed Thrasher.

Other mimids

Curve-billed Thrashers (*Toxostoma curvirostre*) are common permanent residents, mainly in much more open habitats than those Long-billed Thrashers inhabit. Curve-billed Thrashers are especially common in areas with abundant prickly pear cactus, where nests are often placed. This thrasher even nests occasionally on artificial structures such as the beams of open-sided sheds, inside the valve cover of a butane tank, and even inside a nest box (Casto 1999). Curve-billed Thrashers nest in residential areas in Arizona (Rosenberg et al. 1987); they also do so in the Valley but less predictably.

In 2001, they nested for the first time in my yard in Edinburg, perhaps because of the growth of my largest prickly pear cactus to more than 6 feet (2 m) in height. A partial nest was built in the same cactus in November, 2002, after a rainy late October and early November, but was never completed.

As larger trees die due to drought, and prickly pear and thorny shrubs take over, Curve-billed Thrashers seem to become locally more common, such as along the Rio Grande Hiking Trail at Bentsen. On the other hand, they have become rarer at Santa Ana, now occurring only in the most open habitats in the central and southwestern parts of the refuge. Despite the species' occurrence in suburban habitats in the Valley and most ranchland in the Tamaulipan Biotic Province, Curve-billed Thrasher numbers are declining overall in South Texas. As with Verdins and Cactus Wrens, continued clearing of thorn scrub habitat may be taking its toll.

Northern Mockingbirds (*Mimus polyglottos*) have been abundant birds in the Valley since at least 1828, as noted by Terán in the 1820s (Jackson 2000) and Bedichek in the 1940s (Bedichek 1947). Despite raising many Bronzed Cowbird youngsters in some years, mockingbirds remain abundant today. In suburban habitats, thorn scrub, and mesquite savanna, the varied songs of this excellent mimic are hard to escape!

Mockingbirds tend to mimic what is around them, and this habit can (with caution) be used to suggest where other species may be found. For example, at Santa Ana and Bentsen, I have heard mockingbirds imitating Black-bellied Whistling-Duck, Plain Chachalaca, Chuck-will's-widow, Groove-billed Ani, Ferruginous Pygmy-Owl, Great Kiskadee, Couch's Kingbird, Brown-crested Flycatcher, Northern Beardless-Tyrannulet, Green Jay, Verdin, Curve-billed Thrasher, Altamira Oriole, Bronzed Cowbird (begging call), Northern Cardinal, Olive Sparrow, and House Sparrow.

All of those species except Blue Jay breed within earshot of these spots, sing regularly as they pass through on migration, or have occurred there in the past fifty years. Only in Starr County have I heard mockingbirds imitate

Clay-colored Robins, which apparently are most abundant along the river between Roma and Rio Grande City. Interestingly, on May 19, 1997, at Bentsen, I heard both the first begging Bronzed Cowbird fledgling of the year and the first mockingbird imitation of that call for the year.

Recent fledglings have been seen from mid-April through mid-August. Early and late breeding may help them raise their own young instead of Bronzed Cowbird young. Mockingbirds sometimes eject cowbird eggs and defend their nests against cowbird intrusion, increasing their chances of nesting successfully.

Northern Mockingbirds are well known for their frugivorous (fruit-eating) habits. Valley residents sometimes call them *chileros,* for their regular habit of consuming the native chilipiquin peppers (fruits). Their aggressiveness even keeps the larger Great Kiskadee away for a while.

FAMILY STURNIDAE

The **European Starling** (*Sturnus vulgaris*) is one of the most abundant birds in North America, having multiplied exponentially and spread widely since its introduction to New York City in 1890. Starlings compete with native grassland birds for food and with native cavity nesters for nest sites, form large roosts, and are generally considered a pest species. Early evidence of Valley starlings was in Cameron County, with the first sighting in Port Isabel in 1936 (L. Irby Davis, in Oberholser 1974). The first confirmed nesting in the Valley was at Laguna Vista in 1971, when John C. Arvin saw two pairs carrying food into woodpecker-excavated holes in telephone poles (Webster 1971). Although certainly a common bird now in the Valley, starlings are not yet overwhelmingly abundant, and they have not penetrated far beyond the border into Mexico (Howell and Webb 1995).

Nesting mainly in woodpecker holes and other natural cavities, starlings so far are limited to urban and rural habitats around human dwellings and businesses. A favorite nesting site is in cavities excavated in palms by Golden-fronted Woodpeckers. Sometimes the starlings use abandoned holes, but they also evict woodpeckers from freshly excavated cavities.

Starlings seem to avoid forests and brushlands as nesting habitat. For example, at Santa Ana starlings have nested in dead fan palms at the abandoned refuge headquarters site and also in telephone poles along the tour road between the former and current headquarters areas. As of 2002, I have noticed no use by starlings of woodpecker-excavated cavities in native trees even within about 330 feet (100 m) of the starling nest sites. So far all I have seen is a starling briefly "fluttering" at the entrance to an active Ladder-backed Woodpecker nest and then flinching and flying away (June 3, 1998, Santa Ana). We can hope that the European Starling will remain uncommon in native habitats of the Valley.

FAMILY PARULIDAE

Tropical Parula, *Parula pitiayumi*

A brightly colored gem of the forest, the Tropical Parula was once a common breeder in tall riparian forests in the Valley. Although difficult to see, it can be easy to hear, as Sennett (1879) indicates: "It is truly a bird of the forest, and delights to be in the upper branches of the tallest trees. The song of the male is almost continuous as it flits about, and is so clear that it can be heard at a long distance . . . yet the small size and forest habits of the bird would account perhaps for its being so long concealed from observation."

Birders who visit the Valley often list this bird as a priority, and many go home disappointed because of limited numbers and yearly variation in locations of birds, the season at which people visit the Valley, and the difficulty in seeing a small bird high in dense foliage. Once seen well, the bluish head and back and yellow underparts make the Tropical Parula a very attractive bird. Its typical habitat of lush riparian forest with abundant Spanish moss or ball-moss adds to the overall experience of seeing this bird, but unfortunately such forests have declined greatly in southernmost Texas.

Recently, birds have been seen in the southwestern Hill Country of Texas and farther north and west in Texas. There is some evidence of possible hybridization with Northern Parulas in Texas (Tony Gallucci, unpubl. data). In the Valley, I have noticed a female Tropical Parula with light eye-crescents (typical of Northern), and several of the fledglings had whitish eye-crescents and also whitish underparts (also typical of Northern).

DISTRIBUTION   Outside the United States the Tropical Parula is widespread, occurring regularly along the Pacific and Gulf-Caribbean slopes of Mexico and south through much of Central America and South America. However, the species is more of a foothill and montane species south of the U.S.-Mexican border. Tropical Parulas were common in June of both 1995 and 1996 in the Sierra de los Picachos of northern Nuevo León (Ernesto Enkerlin-Hoeflich and Andres Sada, unpubl. data), and they occur as far north as the Serranías del Burro mountains of northern Coahuila (Benson et al. 1989; Charles W. Sexton, pers. comm.). In May–July, 2001, a pair nested (unsuccessfully) in Davis Mountains State Park, Jeff Davis County (Sexton 2001), quite a surprise since that was a first park record for the species.

As with the Northern Beardless-Tyrannulet, Tropical Parulas are found in the Valley and also in Kenedy County, generally in tall riparian forest and coastal live oak forests. The species is known to summer from Bentsen downstream to Santa Ana. It occurs in a few spots farther downstream, such as the LRGV NWR tract in extreme southeastern Hidalgo County, near Santa Maria, and along the Rasaca de la Palma near Brownsville (Mitchell

Sternberg and Carrie Cate, pers. comm.). J. C. Merrill found a nest about five miles from Fort Brown, in July, 1877 (Sennett 1878).

Upstream, despite repeated canoe trips between Chapeño and Fronton in Starr County (particularly during 1994–97), I have not recorded Tropical Parulas. This is probably because there are no *Tillandsias* so far west to provide nest sites. Although the ash, willow, and sugar hackberries are tall enough, perhaps lower atmospheric humidity or isolation prevents the establishment of epiphytes even in well-watered forests in Starr County. The westernmost confirmed nesting record in the Valley is at Anzalduas, where the species does not breed regularly, while the easternmost definite breeding locality is Santa Ana. The species may have nested historically at Bentsen but no longer does so.

Tropical Parulas maintained two to five territories per year at Santa Ana during 1996–98, when I carried out research on the species there. Territories were generally in the healthiest, largest stands of riparian forest available. I observed several family groups and one active nest. The most consistently occupied territory was in tall riparian forest in a deep resaca that evidently collects enough runoff to maintain large ash, sugar hackberry, and Texas ebony.

I saw family groups in that forest in 1996: June 20, when four stub-tailed fledglings were fed by an adult female and male; and in 1997: July 8, when four fledglings were fed by an adult female while male sang 33–100 feet (10–30 m) away. Volunteers running the banding station regularly recorded singing birds in the forest there, but they did not capture any in their nets, probably because the parulas stay so high in the trees.

Other territories that were less consistently occupied at Santa Ana were in narrow strips of cedar elms and in Texas ebony-ash-cedar elm forest with a partially closed canopy. The latter territory held an active nest in 1999 (found under construction by Steve Phillips on June 13). This nest had reached the nestling stage by June 22, but conflicting fieldwork prevented me from returning to check for fledglings. In the southwestern part of Santa Ana, Chris Hathcock saw a female feeding a single fledgling, on June 19, 1999. On July 8, 1997, a pair fed a single Brown-headed Cowbird fledgling in the south-central part of Santa Ana, in one of the few instances of brood parasitism for the species.

Three singing males maintained territories at Anzalduas in 1999, and there were at least two productive nests (single recent fledglings in June and July). In 2000, there were at least two territories at Anzalduas (one of which contained a mated pair), but there was no evidence of successful breeding. However, in 2001, no singing males or other Tropical Parulas were seen at Anzalduas.

At Bentsen only individual singing males have been reported (in 1998 and 1999), in the tiny remnants of tall riparian forest remaining from the drought of the mid- to late 1990s. Despite careful, repeated searching, no females, nests, or family groups have been seen at Bentsen. In general, Tropical Parulas seem highly threatened in the Valley, although the populations in the Sierra de los Picachos and in Kenedy County may provide a source of dispersing birds to help maintain the Valley population.

HABITAT   As noted, Tropical Parulas are usually restricted to *Tillandsia*-rich forests in the U.S. portion of their range. However, in Mexico and other countries, the species occurs regularly from sea level to about 5,900 feet (1,800 m) above sea level. In western Mexico, Tropical Parulas occur in arid thorn forest and also in mangroves (Howell and Webb 1995). *Tillandsias* may be present in some of these habitats, or other nest sites may be available. In winter, our partially migratory Tropical Parulas often show up in suburban resaca forests in the eastern Valley, in places where they do not stay to breed.

HABITS   The Tropical Parula is a methodical forager, hopping and making short flights to nearby branches as it searches for arthropods. Often, I find that a bird has remained in a particular tree and is just quietly foraging in a different section of the crown foliage. As Sennett (1878) noted, males forage while they sing, unlike other species (like Long-billed Thrasher and Northern Mockingbird), which do either one or the other.

The Tropical Parula is apparently mainly a stationary gleaner, like the Northern Beardless-Tyrannulet. I have occasionally seen one hover-gleaning (gleaning from a hovering position) or sally-gleaning (flying down to the ground) to get a caterpillar that had fallen or let itself down by a thread to avoid predation. Foraging heights in the Valley usually range from 20 to 35 feet (6–11 m) above the ground. Birds forage on occasion in mesquite, acacias, or other smaller trees in thorn forest, despite their general restriction to tall riparian forest.

If two or more males are present in a patch of woods, they sing more regularly, apparently to maintain their territorial boundaries. On the other hand a lone male may sing quite irregularly, especially if he has succeeded in attracting a mate. Thus one may need to visit an area several times during the potential breeding season to confirm whether Tropical Parulas are present. Although the song of Texas birds is quite similar to that of the Northern Parula, this is not so in western Mexico or Central America.

Wintering individuals may join mixed-species flocks (which may contain a Northern Parula) or forage on their own. Once I saw a singing male fly to the ground and bathe in a puddle left by irrigation—under such circumstances I had a good chance to see the olive-yellow patch on the upper back, which is often difficult to see.

OTHER OBSERVATIONS   The nesting female at Santa Ana in 1999 showed remarkable restraint when intruders landed near the nest. She stayed in the nest for 38 minutes on June 22, looking out occasionally but sitting tight when a Bronzed Cowbird perched briefly within 7–10 feet (2–3 m) of the nest and when a Great Kiskadee landed within 3 feet (1 m). In both cases, the female parula did not even look out of the nest while the other birds were present. Such restraint may help keep the nest site hidden and the nest contents safe. However, I have seen a male Tropical Parula chase other small birds from the nest tree when the nest itself was in little immediate danger of discovery.

OUTLOOK   The species' dependence on tall, epiphyte-laden riparian forest does not bode well for the future.

Common Yellowthroat, *Geothlypis trichas*

Breeding in marshes, swamps, and wet meadows over vast areas of North America, the Common Yellowthroat is a familiar species to many birders. Although it is attractive, with a black mask and bright yellow underparts, this bird is usually overlooked in the Valley by birders looking for rare tropical birds. Ironically, it turns out that one of the few endemic birds of the Valley is the little-known yellowthroat subspecies *Geothlypis trichas insperata*, a valid subspecies of the Common Yellowthroat (Zink and Klicka 1990). The "Brownsville Yellowthroat" is similar in appearance to other subspecies but has a distinctive song (discussed under Habits). Migratory Common Yellowthroats swell the species' numbers in fall, winter, and spring, but the following sections deal only with breeding birds.

DISTRIBUTION   Common Yellowthroats are scattered through the Valley where suitable wetland habitat occurs, but nowhere do they occur in large numbers. The "Brownsville Yellowthroat" was discovered in 1930 in marshes about 12 miles (20 km) east of Brownsville (Van Tyne 1933). Formerly known to breed in Cameron and Hidalgo counties, the "Brownsville Yellowthroat" was considered at or near extinction by 1951 (Oberholser 1974). Fieldwork by John Klicka in the Brownsville area in 1988 and 1989 suggested an estimated 100–150 pairs in southern and central Cameron County, with most birds along the Rio Grande itself (Klicka 1994). Klicka did not find any Common Yellowthroats in Hidalgo, Starr, or Willacy counties. The TBBAP (1987–92) shows the species as probable in the Valley at a small number of locations, both near the Rio Grande and away from it.

My own fieldwork on Common Yellowthroats in the Valley has been opportunistic, as I have recorded singing birds that I encountered while participating in field trips or doing field studies of other species. There are many gaps in my coverage of the species, and I base my identification of subspecies on song alone, so my statements should be treated cautiously.

Throughout the 1990s and around the turn of the millennium, I regularly heard singing Common Yellowthroats in wetlands at Santa Ana. I generally have found three to four singing males on territory at Pintail Lake in the easternmost part of Santa Ana: for example, three on June 9, 1997, and four on June 2, 1999. I have never seen any nests and I do not recall seeing any female Common Yellowthroats at Santa Ana during the nesting season, but focused fieldwork might achieve greater success. Common Yellowthroats also summer in small numbers along the Rio Grande in Starr County. I believe that all the Hidalgo and Starr County birds are of a different subspecies, possibly the upriver subspecies, usually called *G. t. chryseola*.

In limited fieldwork in the Brownsville area, I have heard what I believe to be "Brownsville Yellowthroats" on a few occasions. At the Sabal Palm Grove, I heard one singing on April 21, 1996, and four there on June 13, 2000. The June 13 male that I saw had a wider grayish white upper border to its black mask. To the east, at the Southmost Preserve on the same date, I heard at least two "Brownsville Yellowthroats" singing. These two sites were Klicka's main study areas in the late 1980s, so it was good to confirm that the birds were still present.

HABITAT   Common Yellowthroats inhabit three distinct wetland habitats in the Valley during the breeding season. At Santa Ana, birds are almost always in cattail marshes, such as that occurring at Pintail or Willow Lake or along the borrow ditch on the northern refuge boundary. In Starr County, where there is almost no cattail marsh, the Common Yellowthroats are in river-edge reeds (usually common reed). In Cameron County, the habitat is mainly resacas, which are flooded in winter but dry in summer. Weedy vegetation springs up in such areas, with grasses and other herbaceous plants among the scattered black willow trees. Birds may be in weedy upland fields as well, as were two of the four birds at the Sabal Palm Grove on June 13, 2000.

HABITS   Common Yellowthroats generally stay less than 6 feet (2 m) off the ground, whether for foraging or singing. The "Brownsville Yellowthroat" sings a less distinct, more run-together version of the species' normal song. Although this follows the same general pattern as those of other subspecies, I do not hear it singing the distinct *wichity* phrases so characteristic of Common Yellowthroats elsewhere.

During the residency of the male Gray-crowned Yellowthroat at Santa Ana in March–May, 2000, other birders and I occasionally saw it briefly chase some male Common Yellowthroats from its territory. Since the Gray-crown's territory, which it patrolled regularly, was mainly in cattails, it is not surprising that the bird encountered some Common Yellowthroats. Usually the species are separated by habitat, with the Common Yellowthroat inhabiting wetter areas.

OUTLOOK   Wintering Common Yellowthroats will likely always be common in the Valley, especially in riverside common reed or cattail marshes. However, continued existence of the "Brownsville Yellowthroat" is in doubt, given development pressures in its limited range in Cameron County. Resaca management is challenging, given conflicting goals and uncertain water availability and rainfall. Although the species does persist on private sanctuaries in the Brownsville area, we need to know more about the actual requirements of this Valley bird and then how to maintain such habitats.

Other warblers

The **Gray-crowned Yellowthroat** (*Geothlypis poliocephala*) is something of a mystery bird in Texas. Once a fairly common breeder in the Valley, at least in southernmost Hidalgo and Cameron Counties, it is now accidental. What is surprising is that in Mexico and Central America this is a bird of disturbed habitats such as overgrown pastures and weedy marsh edges, which are still available in the Valley. This is not a bird of lush riparian forests like the Red-billed Pigeon, a species in which we can clearly link decline to the loss of habitat.

There are old nesting or specimen records from the Lomita area (along the river near Anzalduas) east to Brownsville, with the last breeding record in 1894 and the last specimen from 1927 (Oberholser 1974). Friedmann (1925) saw a pair on Green Island in May, 1924, near the mouth of the Arroyo Colorado. Perhaps the loss of extensive freshwater marshes around Brownsville was a contributing factor, but this is not a true marsh bird like the Common Yellowthroat. Birds occurred in areas with tall grass and scattered shrubs. In Tamaulipas, Wauer (1998) saw them in coastal scrub habitats with glasswort, saltwort, and sea ox-eye daisy. Similar locations in the Valley would probably be too open or dry for Gray-crowned Yellowthroats.

At least some of the sightings in the last three years have been of singing males in marsh-upland edge habitat, such as around Pintail Lake at Santa Ana. Typically, a male establishes a territory, sings regularly for several weeks, eventually fails to attract a female, and leaves. For example, a male present June 17–22, 1999, was heard singing from a much broader area just before it disappeared, as if it was trying harder to find a female (Lockwood 2001). The 1999 bird looked and sang like a typical Gray-crowned Yellowthroat, but the first couple of phrases of the 2000 bird (present March 24 – May 26; Lockwood 2002) sounded a bit like a Common Yellowthroat's *wichity*. This bird looked normal, however, and the rest of the song was normal. In both cases, I noticed the longer, bicolored bill with a curved culmen, and the generally "elongated" look of the bird compared with nearby Common Yellowthroats. The 2000 bird gave a *tsee* call occasionally, which sounded intermediate between a Redwing's *chee* and a becard's *tsee* in quality.

In both cases, the male had favorite singing posts in cattail, retamas, or other woody plants near the upland edge of a marsh, and it would be easy to see for the five to ten minutes or so when it sang. In between song bouts, the bird would disappear down into the dense vegetation, although it could sometimes be seen foraging low in cattails or other herbaceous plants.

Yellow-breasted Chat (*Icteria virens*) was once quite a common breeder: "At Hidalgo, nearly every night, when through our work, we went to the river to bathe, and never did we fail to hear the sweet melody of the Chats, in a thicket and brush fence across the river" (Sennett 1878). It has now vanished as a breeder from the Valley, and the closest confirmed recent breeding location is the Eagle Pass–Del Rio area, about 250 miles (400 km) to the northwest (Benson and Arnold 2001). Cowbird parasitism was light in the late 1800s and early 1900s but may have become a problem later in the twentieth century, as with other cowbird-sensitive species. Likewise, the lack of flooding may have allowed drier thorn forest to invade former lush successional riverine habitat favored by chats.

I was pleasantly surprised to hear and see a singing male on July 2, 1999, southwest of Mission, Hidalgo County. The habitat was a small patch of dense shrubs between a dirt road and railroad tracks, along an outflow from a small reservoir. The male did the usual chat display flight under dense cover. On May 29, 2001, I heard a chat singing along the Rio Grande near San Ygnacio, Zapata County, and on May 30, 2001, one sang at Father Mc-Naboe Park in Laredo. Visits to the Eagle Pass–Quemado area in early May, 2002 and 2003, revealed chats to be common in riparian thickets.

Chats are still common as migrants in the Valley, but they apparently do not sing while migrating; thus a bird I heard and saw on April 14, 2001, near Salineño may have been a local breeder. These observations suggest a small breeding population scattered along the river between Roma and Laredo, perhaps continuous with the upstream population and with the poorly known central Nuevo León population (Behrstock and Eubanks 1997).

There is one record of **Northern Parula** (*Parula americana*) nesting in the

Valley, a bird that nested near the Anzalduas flood control levee in 1966 (John C. Arvin, in Oberholser 1974). Given the intermediate appearance of some Valley birds (see Tropical Parula account) and the distance from the normal Central Texas breeding range, it is hard to know what to make of this report. Perhaps a pair stopped migrating sooner than usual, as evidently happened to the Acadian Flycatchers nesting at Santa Ana in 1940.

FAMILY THRAUPIDAE

Another of the once regular breeders that have declined greatly this century, the **Summer Tanager** (*Piranga rubra*) remains a common migrant and occasional winter resident in the Valley. Evidently Summer Tanagers were fairly common in tall floodplain forests, at least from Hidalgo County eastward (Sennett 1878). Summer Tanagers still were nesting successfully at Santa Ana in 1940 (Davis 1940), but I know of no nests there since then. The last evidence of nesting in the Valley was obtained by John Arvin on May 2, 1971, when two pairs were carrying nesting material in the area that is now Anzalduas County Park.

On July 2, 1999, Chris Hathcock and I examined a nest southwest of Mission, Hidalgo County, the same location and date on which I found the singing Yellow-breasted Chat mentioned earlier. The nest was built directly on a sloping limb of a sugar hackberry tree, suggesting a tanager, but we were uncertain as to the identity of the nest builder, and the nest (now in the University of Texas–Pan American collection) appeared to be abandoned. A yellowish breast feather taken from the abandoned nest was identified as being from a female Summer Tanager (Carla Dove, Smithsonian Institution, pers. comm.). An incomplete nest in a similar position within 65 feet (20 m) appeared to have been made by a tanager as well.

Summer Tanagers still breed in the open oak forests of Brooks and Kenedy counties just to the north of the Valley. Perhaps the openness of the forest is important, as the few remaining tall riparian forests in the Valley usually have dense understories. Cowbird parasitism, grackle nest depredation, and habitat clearing may also have been important. Since the tall riparian forest with an open understory where Sennett (1878) first found these tanagers is now almost gone, we cannot expect tanagers to recolonize the Valley successfully.

FAMILY EMBERIZIDAE

White-collared Seedeater, *Sporophila torqueola*

Once a fairly common resident of moist grassy areas and resaca edges, the White-collared Seedeater has become a rare, highly sought-after bird, apparently no longer nesting in the Valley. Oddly, for a bird that uses highly impacted scrubby roadsides and pastures in the tropics, seedeaters have vanished from the Valley, which has plenty of disturbed scrubby country. However, some areas just upriver from the Valley support resident populations.

DISTRIBUTION   South of the border, White-collared Seedeaters are common on both the Pacific and Gulf-Caribbean slopes of Mexico and Central America, from Sinaloa and Tamaulipas all the way to Panama. They expanded their range within Costa Rica and Panama during the twentieth century as deforestation created suitable habitat (Eitniear 1997).

Once fairly common breeding residents of the Valley, White-collared Seedeaters declined severely in the 1950s and 1960s (Oberholser 1974). The last Valley breeding records I know of are at Santa Ana in 1963 (Greene 1966) and at Anzalduas in 1971, when two pairs nested "with limited success" (S. Johnson and W. A. Shifflett, in Webster 1971). By the 1980s, seedeaters were seen regularly in San Ygnacio (Zapata County): two pairs plus one singing male were seen there on June 12–13, 1986 (Guy Tudor, in Lasley and Sexton 1986). Keith A. Arnold (1980) collected a male specimen from a ranch 30 miles (50 km) northwest of Laredo in Webb County. During the 1990s, the known range of seedeaters in Texas remained upriver from the Valley: from northwestern Webb County downriver to northwestern Zapata County (Woodin et al. 1999; Eitniear 1997). Seedeaters have nested successfully in the Zapata and San Ygnacio areas (Eitniear and Rueckle 1995).

Despite Arnold's 1980 specimen and three collected by George M. Sutton in 1948, also in Webb County (Oberholser 1974), the "rediscovery" of the Webb County population in 1997 was a pleasant a surprise to ornithologists and birders. On May 4, 2002, I saw at least one White-collared Seedeater in riparian giant reed farther upriver, near Quemado, Maverick County. This could represent a significant range expansion, but further work will be needed to confirm their continued presence and possible nesting location.

HABITAT   Seedeaters readily use pastures and roadsides, with low grass and scattered trees and shrubs, in moist tropical areas. In drier South Texas, seedeaters appear more restricted to areas near water, because that is where their habitat is. In Hidalgo County, seedeaters were once fairly common in open floodplain forests of black willow. These areas were regularly flooded, and grass and other herbaceous plants sprang up as the waters receded (Davis 1940). Currently seedeaters are seen mainly in areas with common reed or giant reed, adjacent to low meadows with shorter grasses (Eitniear 1997; Woodin et al. 1999).

Seedeaters do not seem to use common reed or giant reed habitats much if these are at the bottom of steep banks covered with riparian or thorn forest or if there are only vast agricultural fields nearby. In one area dominated by such habitat, the Chapeño-Fronton stretch of the Rio Grande, I found a seedeater only once in about twenty-five canoe trips between 1993 and 1997. It was a singing immature at the edge of a large agricultural field on the Mexican side near Fronton on May 7, 1994. However, seedeaters may occur in marshes with stands of cattail fringed by dense, low grass, even if such areas are surrounded by golf courses or other expanses of open lawns. For example, on May 29, 2001, I saw a male in such habitat in Zapata, at the golf course/library spot well known to birders.

HABITS   Seedeaters are generally not wary birds, but these tiny birds may be difficult to see in their dense habitats. My limited experience suggests that seedeaters may use reeds or cattails mainly as refuges from predators, emerging to gather seeds from shorter grasses. Likewise, birds often perch in black willows in open riparian forest in between foraging bouts in nearby grass (Woodin et al., 1999).

While foraging, seedeaters frequently land on grass stems, causing them to bend under the weight of the bird. This allows the bird to eat seeds while in a vigilant, upright position. Seedeaters have been observed consuming the small (less than 2 mm) seeds of barnyard grass (*Echinochloa cruz-pavonis*), Louisiana cupgrass (*Eriochloa punctata*), spreading panicum (*Panicum diffusum*), and even the widespread invasive guineagrass in Texas (Eitniear 1997). Little is known of seed preferences (if any) and whether food resources are limiting factors.

During the breeding season, male seedeaters spend much time patrolling territory boundaries, while females only fly as needed to obtain food and water (Eitniear 1997). In tropical areas, White-collared Seedeaters are among the most persistently active species, continuing to sing, call, and forage even in the heat of the day. Nests may be built quite low, as was a seedeater nest with eggs less than 1.5 feet (0.5 m) above a mown lawn at the headquarters of Blue Hole National Park, Belize (March 1997).

OTHER OBSERVATIONS   Individuals wandering outside the species' normal range are usually males looking for suitable breeding territories and mates. They may sing from a number of perches over a broad area, since they are not yet tied to a particular nesting territory. For example, on June 30, 1998, I found a male of the more colorful *S. t. torqueola* group in the Willow Lake area of Santa Ana. On July 10, 1998, probably the same male sang along Rio Grande within 0.6 of a mile (1 km) of Willow Lake. On July 15, 1998, an unseen bird sang again in the Willow Lake area. I concluded that this individual was an escaped cage bird, because it was of the western Mexican subspecies. I never saw it again.

Birds near a known population center may use habitats that would not attract the species in an outlying area. For example, in Laredo on May 30,

2001, I heard two seedeaters singing in habitat that did not appear any different from much of the Valley: a narrow strip of reeds between the river and a sparsely vegetated park in Laredo. Laredo is between the two known breeding areas (Galvan Ranch and San Ygnacio–Zapata), and it probably has breeding seedeaters of its own.

OUTLOOK   The regular presence of White-collared Seedeaters along about 72 miles (115 km) straight-line distance of the Rio Grande is encouraging. However, as there is no evidence of expansion away from the Rio Grande or back into the former Valley range, we can expect that the species will remain uncommon to rare in the United States. The importance of particular grass species as food resources should be investigated further, as a possible habitat management tool. Given that reasons for the seedeater's precipitous Valley decline remain uncertain, we cannot predict whether seedeaters will ever reoccupy their former range. The possible significance of pesticides (Oberholser 1974) remains unclear.

Olive Sparrow, *Arremonops rufivirgatus*

The Olive Sparrow is a common permanent resident of South Texas, lowland Mexico, and northern Central America (south to Guatemala, Belize, and northwestern Costa Rica). The geographic range is very disjunct, and some of the isolated populations have been considered separate species in the past. In the United States, Olive Sparrows occur only in the Tamaulipan Biotic Province of semiarid South Texas. Their name here was once Texas Sparrow. Preferring dense brush or chaparral, Olive Sparrows are common but difficult to see, as they forage on the ground in shady areas. As Bent and Sutton both noted, the way to see Olive Sparrows is to sit quietly for a time in the right habitat and wait for the birds to become active. Populations may be quite dense, but birds can be very quiet, and their numbers can only be appreciated when the territorial males are singing.

DISTRIBUTION   In Texas, Olive Sparrows occur from Uvalde, Beeville, and Rockport south to the Rio Grande. Birds occur from Sinaloa and Coahuila south in low and middle elevations to northern Guatemala and northern Belize, with an outlying population in northwestern Costa Rica (AOU 1998; Brush 1998b). Olive Sparrows do not occur in easternmost sections of the Valley because of lack of suitable habitat in coastal prairies and on barrier islands, but otherwise they are widespread.

HABITAT   Olive Sparrows primarily inhabit dense thorn scrub and thorn forest (Oberholser 1974; Brush 1998b), but they avoid mesquite savanna and grassland (Roth 1977). Riparian forest and oak forests are inhabited, particularly if some shrubs occur in the understory. Olive Sparrows avoid coastal prairie, salt marsh, and barrier islands but occur within easy earshot of barren coastal flats when dense brush is present nearby (Brush 1998b). Singing males occur occasionally in narrow, field-margin brush lines, but I have no evidence that they nest in such narrow strips.

Olive Sparrows benefit from revegetation of old agricultural fields or pastures. Such areas more than thirty years old may support densities as high as in mature thorn scrub (Wright 1996). A layer of leaf litter may be important, since Olive Sparrows do most of their foraging on the ground, and they frequently scratch noisily in the dead leaves like a towhee (*Pipilo* spp.). Urban and suburban residential areas are avoided, but birds use isolated patches of dense thorn scrub of 50–75 acres (20–30 ha) or less, surrounded by residential areas or open fields.

HABITS Olive Sparrows spend most of their lives gleaning exposed and hidden prey under cover. They do not flock or move around very far, and several banded individuals remained in the same few hectares of thorn scrub for at least five years (Laguna Atascosa banding data, in Brush 1998b). I do not think I have ever seen an Olive Sparrow fly across the Rio Grande, although they must do so occasionally. Parkes (1974) found two subspecies of Olive Sparrows living within 6 miles (10 km) of each other in the Yucatán Peninsula, with intergrades only in a narrow zone between coastal scrub and tropical deciduous forest. This is another indication of how sedentary they must be, since with most species there would be too much intermingling for subspecies to be maintained.

In the Valley, nests may be placed on the ground in shady understory or (more often) in a low shrub or cactus. Ground nests are domed, with the entrance from the side, while aboveground nests are more like cones set at an angle. I have seen birds picking up nesting material from the ground, and most Valley birds evidently use mostly grass (which is abundant in most areas). The nesting season is long (May–September in the Valley), so that if a nest is lost to a predator or to cowbird competition, there is plenty of time to rebuild and try again.

Nestlings and fledglings beg quietly, probably to reduce the chances of predation. A fledgling Bronzed Cowbird that I saw at Bentsen, in contrast, begged quite loudly from the attending Olive Sparrow pair. Adults watch fledglings carefully, and twice I have seen an adult fly at a fledgling, chasing it away from an open perch and into protective cover. I suspect that pairs remain together year-round and that juveniles leave their natal territory within a month or so after fledging, but a careful banding study is needed.

OTHER OBSERVATIONS While leading field trips for students or visiting birders in my early years in the Valley, I sometimes had great trouble locating a singing Olive Sparrow. I would tend to look mainly within 3 feet (1 m) or less of the ground, with no luck, until I noticed that birds would often go higher up to sing. Typically singing from 7–15 feet (2–4 m) up, they may go as high as 26–30 feet (8–9 m) to sing. Singing birds go particularly high to sing during hot weather, whether as a way to escape the hotter lower levels or for some other reason I do not know.

As a species that spends most of its life less than 3 feet (1 m) above the ground, Olive Sparrows are vulnerable to ground-based predators. Twice I have seen Olive Sparrows mildly scolding a snake. The birds chipped repeatedly but did not harass the snake physically. On the Mexican side of the Rio Grande, a coachwhip snake (*Masticophis flagellum*) has been seen with its head in an Olive Sparrow nest, apparently having already eaten the eggs or young (Amadon and Eckleberry 1955). Similarly, Chris Hathcock (2000) saw a Mexican racer (*Coluber constrictor*) with its head inside a nest that had contained small nestlings a few days earlier. Overall, Olive Sparrows do suffer higher nest predation rates than Altamira Orioles, which have a nearly inaccessible nest (Hathcock 2000). The sedentary ways of these sparrows, remaining in the same small patch of brush, may allow them to become familiar with the hazards of their home range.

Free-standing water is often unavailable to Olive Sparrows for weeks or months at a time. Like many dry-country birds, they probably obtain all the water they need to ingest through eating fruits, insects, and other animal prey. To clean the plumage and keep external parasite populations down, Olive Sparrows may dew-bathe. In the early morning, David H. Fischer (1978) and I have separately seen Olive Sparrows rub their bellies, flanks, and wings against foliage wet from the overnight dew, which is dense even in drought years. They then fluff their plumage and preen themselves before going back to foraging or singing.

OUTLOOK Although Olive Sparrows remain common in suitable habitat in South Texas, there is little information regarding population trends. U.S. Breeding Bird Survey data show conflicting patterns, with increases during the 1966–79 period followed by decreases during 1980–94. With fifteen or fewer survey routes having Olive Sparrows, any trends should be treated with caution. Some declines may have occurred due to massive brush clearing following World War II (Oberholser 1974), but conversion of prairie or savanna grassland to brushland (Rhoads 1892; Johnston 1963) may to some extent have counterbalanced any declines.

On a local basis, the density of breeding Olive Sparrows increased on a study plot in Santa Ana as the area changed from Texas ebony evergreen woodland in the 1970s (Gehlbach 1987) to Tamaulipan thorn scrub by the 1990s (Brush and Cantu 1998). Both Bronzed and Brown-headed cowbirds parasitize Olive Sparrow nests, but the intensity of parasitism varies from year to year (Hathcock 2000). Limited data suggest that once parasitized, Olive Sparrow nests generally raise only cowbirds (Carter 1986). Since cowbirds often find nests by following adults to them (Carter 1986), dense cover may be crucial in allowing some Olive Sparrow nests to go undetected and to produce young Olive Sparrows.

In years with good spring rains, Olive Sparrows produce good numbers of offspring. Compare 1997, in which 18 inches (47 cm) of rain fell in March–April and forty-nine juveniles were captured during the immediately following nesting season, with 1995, in which only 4 inches (10 cm) of rain fell in March–April, and only five juveniles were later captured (Brush 1998b). Both dense cover and abundant food during wet years may contribute to success.

Other emberizids

A big surprise of the summer of 2002 was the first nesting attempt of a **Yellow-faced Grassquit** (*Tiaris olivaceus*) in the United States (Brush 2003). A common neotropical resident species ranging from northeastern Mexico south to northern South America, the Yellow-faced Grassquit was first seen in Texas in 1990 (Haynie 1992). The species is currently considered accidental in Texas and Florida, and there have been no breeding records anywhere in the United States (Texas Ornithological Society 1995; Bruce H. Anderson, pers. comm.).

On June 11, 2002, visiting birder Kenny Nichols found a singing male at Bentsen, along the Rio Grande Hiking Trail. The bird was in semi-open thorn forest, in an area where dying hackberries have opened up space for huisache, granjeno, and other thorny plants as well as guineagrass. The male sang his soft, insectlike song regularly from one of several dead trees. Another vocalization, probably a call, was similar to the soft, slow trill often given by Olive Sparrows.

On the following June 15, I saw the grassquit repeatedly carrying short pieces of grass into a nest that it was building within 50 feet (15 m) of the trail. To avoid disturbing the bird, I watched the nest only from the trail, and it showed no signs of nervousness. The grassquit usually sang or called before and after visiting the nest. It stayed under cover as much as possible during the approach, remained in the nest for five to ten seconds, and then left the nest area in a low, rapid flight.

On June 22 I did not see the grassquit approach the nest, but it was still singing regularly in its territory. The nest walls appeared thicker than on June 15, and the male may have completed the outer shell of the nest. I saw the grassquit occasionally following a singing Olive Sparrow from tree to tree, within about 66 feet (20 m) of the nest. This may have been an expression of territoriality in this sociable bird: "But all that the territorial male does is to fly mildly in the direction of the intruder, who retreats without necessity of conflict" (Skutch 1954:39).

The nest was domed, with a roof and a side entrance, and was attached to some guineagrass stems 3–6 feet (1–2 m) from the nearest woody plant and about 1.3 feet (42 cm) above the ground. The nest was made primarily of plains bristlegrass (*Setaria leucopila*), a common grass of disturbed habitats (Lonard 1993). Some strands of the coarser guineagrass were woven into the outside.

During the last week of June 2002, the grassquit was seen more erratically. On June 25, Bruce Crider saw it in semi-open thorn scrub farther along the Rio Grande Hiking Trail, within about 165 feet (50 m) of the Rio Grande, but the bird was not reported after June 30. At no time was a female grassquit observed. Unlike most passerines, the male Yellow-faced Grassquit typically starts building the nest and may complete the outer shell, leaving it to the female to complete the nest and add lining material (Skutch 1976). On September 6, 2002, I collected the nest, having determined from two visits in the previous week that no grassquits were around. The nest did not have any lining, eggs, shell fragments, or droppings, further confirming that the nest was not completed and eggs were never laid.

Despite the failure of the 2002 nesting attempt, Yellow-faced Grassquits may eventually breed successfully in the Lower Rio Grande of Texas, as have other tropical species now established in Texas (Oberholser 1974). Grassquits are common in disturbed grassy and brushy habitats, increasingly common habitats in central and southern Tamaulipas (Wauer 1998; Arvin 2001). Similarly, grassquits have been seen in higher elevations than before in central Nuevo León (Behrstock and Eubanks 1997), again suggesting that a larger, nearby source than previously known exists for dispersing individuals. However, regular fieldwork will be needed, since Yellow-faced Grassquits can easily be overlooked, given their secretive habits and soft song.

Seaside Sparrows (*Ammodramus maritimus*), once thought to be only winter residents in the Valley, have been shown to nest here. John Arvin found a singing male at the mouth of the Rio Grande on June 2, 1978 (Webster 1978). I saw a pair at Laguna Atascosa on September 3, 1993, and July 11, 1994 (in the same location). Later, two groups of researchers independently discovered breeding evidence of Seaside Sparrows in the Valley. Mark Conway and Jim Irvine made the exciting discovery of a breeding population at Laguna Atascosa in August, 1999, and thereafter. At least fourteen juvenile Seaside Sparrows have been banded, mainly in salt marsh vegetation dominated by saltwort. No nests have been found there yet, but adults have been seen carrying food to hidden locations. In July, 2001, Mark Conway and I watched an adult carrying food over a dense saltwort marsh near the southern boundary of Laguna Atascosa, but the bird was too wary to go to the nest while we were anywhere nearby. Also exciting to us was the nearby rattlesnake, perhaps driven into the salty environment by the long-running drought.

In 1999, Steve Phillips and Gerald Einem documented that Seaside Sparrows also breed near the mouth of the Rio Grande. They saw a flightless fledgling and some probable nests (inactive). Given earlier sightings, this population may have been present since 1989 (Phillips and Einem 2003). Given the general shortage of coastal marshes and lack of attention, I cannot be sure whether the recent breeding is a new phenomenon. The total population for the Valley must be small, but it is significant, given problems that Seaside Sparrows have faced in Florida and the fact that recent discoveries extend the breeding range south all the way from Corpus Christi to the Mexican border.

Two of the secretive *Aimophila* sparrows breed in the Valley, but I have not gathered much information on them. **Cassin's Sparrow** (*A. cassinii*) is much more common and widespread in Texas as a whole, where it breeds west of the 97th meridian. In the Valley, it has been confirmed breeding in coastal and interior grasslands, but it avoids the heavily agricultural and urban areas. I have heard Cassin's Sparrows singing even in small patches of grasslands at the edges of developed areas, but whether they attract mates and nest successfully there is unknown.

More typical habitat is a large, dry grassy field with widely scattered shrubs, such as a spot about 18 miles (29 km) west of Edinburg, where I have found them during the springs of 2000–2002. Singing birds seem to pop up after rains or with warm weather in late winter, but whether they have recently arrived or wintered in the area is hard to determine. Except for Laguna Atascosa and coastal tracts of LRGV NWR, most birds are outside officially protected areas. On July 1, 1997, I saw one in dense guineagrass along the Rio Grande Hiking Trail of Bentsen (the only time I have ever seen one there). Oberholser's (1974) failure to show Cassin's breeding in the Valley is probably due to lack of fieldwork in hot, chigger-infested grasslands.

Botteri's Sparrow (*A. botterii*) is much rarer than Cassin's, both in the United States and in the Valley, but is confirmed as a historic and current nester. This predominantly Mexican species breeds in coastal grasslands in the Valley and Kenedy County (Benson and Arnold 2001) and also in southeastern Arizona. Botteri's Sparrows sing from April through September, but they are usually silent and hard to find during periods of drought. Almost nothing is known of their nesting success or population levels, but they are most common in dry grassland with scattered yuccas or moister Gulf cordgrass (*sacahuista*) stands (Webb and Bock 1996).

Lark Sparrows (*Chondestes grammacus*) breed commonly in open thorn scrub, mesquite savanna, and citrus orchards across the Valley. They may even breed in or near cotton fields, as I have seen them regularly in such habitat, in Cameron County, during U.S. Breeding Bird Survey censuses. Lark Sparrows do not nest at Santa Ana, but my notes indicate that they must breed nearby: *July 11, 1997: 2 juveniles at Pintail Lake [Santa Ana]— otherwise have never seen them right here. July 26, 1997: juv. on W. edge of Santa Ana, at edge of . . . field.*

I had seldom seen Lark Sparrows at Anzalduas, so it was interesting on July 22, 1999, to find a nest with four eggs there. Ardath L. Egle (pers. comm.) found a Lark Sparrow nest in an unusual spot in the late 1990s: the nest was placed at the base of a fern in a basket hanging from the eaves of her house in Mission. The citrus orchards nearby may explain the birds' presence.

Black-throated Sparrows (*Amphispiza bilineata*) are the common desert sparrow of much of the U.S. Southwest and adjacent Mexico, but surprisingly they have declined in and near the Valley. Oberholser (1974) shows the species nesting in all four Valley counties plus Kenedy, Kleberg, and Nueces counties, and L. Irby Davis (1974) considered it common in all Valley grasslands. However, the Texas Breeding Bird Atlas Program recorded Black-throated Sparrows only in the western half of the Valley, and McKinney (2002) agrees. Thus the species is apparently gone from Laguna Atascosa, the coastal tracts of the LRGV NWR, and most other coastal habitats.

To our north, Tom Langschied (pers. comm.) has seen less than five Black-throated Sparrows on the vast King Ranch, despite numerous field trips. What is odd is that the coastal thorn scrub and savannas seem relatively untouched compared to more inland areas, at least in the Valley, so it is not clear what caused this apparent range contraction. Perhaps the isolation of such areas from other such habitats was a factor. Black-throated Sparrows remain common in Starr County. At least a few still breed in coastal Willacy County (Land 1999), suggesting that additional fieldwork is needed to determine their current range.

FAMILY CARDINALIDAE

Northern Cardinal (*Cardinalis cardinalis*) males in this region are a more intense red than those of much of the eastern and central United States. However, they are harder to see in their dense thorn forest habitat and are less common in urban areas, making them unfamiliar to most Valley residents. Cardinals and **Pyrrhuloxias** (*Cardinalis sinuatus*) coexist in many areas of thorn scrub. One has to know the songs and calls to appreciate how many of both species may be present. Pyrrhuloxias are abundant in mesquite savanna, where cardinals do not occur (Roth 1971), and cardinals are most common in dense thorn forest or open riparian forest. Pyrrhuloxias occasionaly gather into flocks of fifty or more birds in winter, and varying numbers wander into areas where they do not nest. Cardinals are not abundant enough in the Valley to flock, as they do elsewhere (Halkin and Linville 1999). Brown-headed Cowbird nestlings do not do well in competition with the larger cardinal nestlings. Northern Cardinals raise a good number of Bronzed Cowbirds, and Pyrrhuloxias may do so also. Populations of both cardinalids nest in the Valley (Benson and Arnold 2001) and seem to be doing well.

Painted Buntings (*Passerina ciris*) are common migrants but uncommon breeders in riparian forests and thorn forests in the Valley. Breeding numbers seem to vary from year to year, with more birds seen and heard in wetter years. Typically I hear a singing male work his way along a forest edge, singing regularly in an attempt to attract a female. For example, on June 28, 1996, July 1, 1997, and June 12, 1998, respectively, I heard the first singing male of the breeding season along the Rio Grande Hiking Trail of Bentsen. These were obviously not spring migrants but may have been males that failed in a breeding attempt elsewhere. During all three years I was doing regular fieldwork in that area, but only in 1998 did the male stay around for more than one week. In 1999, the first male was heard on the same trail on May 24, and I found a full-grown juvenile there on July 2. This bird still had tiny remnants of flanges on its bill, suggesting that it was raised at Bentsen or on the immediately adjacent LRGV NWR tract.

I hear singing males occasionally at Santa Ana and along the Rio Grande between Chapeño and Fronton, but the main center of abundance in southern Texas is much farther north (in the central and northern sections of South Texas). Painted Buntings breed commonly in the southern Edwards Plateau–Hill Country area of Central Texas and in eastern Texas as well (Benson and Arnold 2001). They probably were more common in the late 1800s and early 1900s along the lower Rio Grande, but I have found little direct evidence of any declines.

Varied Buntings (*P. versicolor*) are quite rare both as breeders and as migrants in the Valley. They were once regularly seen in thickets in the coastal prairies near Brownsville (Merrill 1879). Two pairs nested at Laguna Atascosa in 1973 (George A. Unland, in Webster 1973). A singing male was on territory in 1959 near Harlingen (Webster 1959). This bunting no longer breeds in coastal areas, perhaps due to habitat loss or fragmentation (Wolfe 1968).

The only definite recent breeding records for Varied Bunting are both near Sullivan City, on the border between Starr and Hidalgo counties. On June 4, 1991, Dick Heller saw at least one fledgling on an LRGV NWR tract (Benson and Arnold 2001), and in early May, 1992, David Blankinship (pers. comm.) and others saw a nest with eggs on a different tract in the same area. Observers reported Varied Buntings in other parts of Starr County and adjacent areas to the north and west, during the Texas Breeding Bird Atlas Project (Benson and Arnold 2001).

As well as being rare, Varied Buntings are quite wary during the breeding season, often dropping from high song perches when the observer is more than a hundred yards away (Dick Heller, pers. comm.). Varied Buntings are more common in the Trans-Pecos region, and there is also a breeding population in the Edwards Plateau near Del Rio (Lockwood 1995). Varied Buntings are widespread in foothill scrub in northern Mexico (Groschupf and Thompson 1998), but this subtly beautiful bunting deserves more study. Its breeding range overlaps extensively with that of the more widespread Painted Bunting, but I suspect that Varied Buntings occur in drier scrub than Painted Buntings.

Blue Grosbeaks (*P. caerulea*), widespread in the southern and central United States and northern Mexico, are uncommon breeders in the Valley. Nesting has been confirmed, but birds are present in low densities. I usually hear one or two singing males per day, in early successional thorn forest at the edge of Santa Ana and Bentsen. A thick grass cover between scattered shrubs and trees appears most attractive to Blue Grosbeaks in the Valley.

Dickcissels (*Spiza americana*) breed erratically (Benson and Arnold 2001).

FAMILY ICTERIDAE

Great-tailed Grackle, *Quiscalus mexicanus*

One of the most abundant and conspicuous birds in the Valley, the Great-tailed Grackle forages in agricultural fields, suburban and urban areas, and along salt- and freshwater shores. Grackles have expanded their range dramatically in the United States. In 1864 they were found only in southern Texas, south of the Nueces River (Dresser 1865). Today they are common across the southwestern United States and have spread from there. This large icterid is a major success story of the U.S. Great Plains, with first nesting records in Austin (Texas) in 1915, Oklahoma in 1958, Kansas in 1969, Nebraska in 1977, and Iowa in 1983 (Dinsmore and Dinsmore 1993). Great-tailed Grackles have been seen in at least three Canadian provinces and twenty-one U.S. states (Johnson and Peer 2001). South of the Valley, they have spread into the Mexico City area during the twentieth century, as a growing urban population provided abundant food and nesting sites (Christensen 2000). Grackles are still quite successful birds in the Valley also, and one can count on seeing or hearing them on almost any field trip or just around town.

DISTRIBUTION Great-tailed Grackles are common breeders throughout most of the southern Great Plains and in much of the U.S. Southwest and Central America. In easternmost and westernmost Texas, grackles are limited to the vicinity of farms, homes, and businesses by widespread forests and deserts, respectively. But elsewhere, including the Valley, Great-tailed Grackles are common to abundant permanent residents. For example, there may be more than 500,000 birds roosting in sugarcane fields by late winter (Tipton et al. 1990a), and large numbers roost in urban areas as well. Populations are highest in urban and agricultural areas, but the species does occur regularly on more remote sections of river and on South Padre Island.

HABITAT Irrigated farmland, residential areas, and adjacent small woodlots seem to support the highest densities of grackles. Birds nest in high densities in huisaches in colonies of White-winged Doves and also higher up in tall residential ashes or Texas ebonies. Brush-covered islands in the Rio Grande or Laguna Madre support nesting grackles as well, especially if there is a colony of egrets, herons, spoonbills, and ibis present. Cattail marshes with standing water are used mainly for roosting sites, but birds nest there at times. Most roosts I have seen are in urban areas, where the bright lights and human activity may reduce nocturnal predation. Grackles seldom forage in larger tracts of dense thorn forest or taller riparian forest, but they use more open thorn forest and thorn scrub, particularly when grasshoppers are abundant.

HABITS Sennett's (1878) remarks capture the habits of the Great-tailed Grackle in the early years in the Valley: "In the towns and about the ranches, he knows no fear; is always noisy, never at rest, and in all places and positions; now making friends with the horses in the barns or the cattle in the fields, then in some tree pouring forth his notes . . . then following close behind the planter, quick to see the dropping corn. With all his boldness and curiosity, the boys of the streets say they cannot catch him or trap him in a snare."

In the modern Valley, Great-tailed Grackles continue to forage opportunistically in human-created habitats. They readily fly distances of several kilometers between feeding areas and roosting or nesting sites. Grackles forage commonly in grain fields, especially sorghum. Landfills are prime foraging sites for grackles, on both sides of the border, and birds look for food scraps in parking lots of supermarkets and fast-food restaurants. They love to bathe in flooded fields or yards, and they also forage in shallow water. Grackles take dog food from suburban yards (Casto 1996).

Nesting females in particular respond to the sound of the lawnmower to capture grasshoppers and emerging beetle larvae that have been exposed as the grass is cut. Females forage underneath cars, where they remove dead insects from the grille. Males too may forage underneath cars, and they definitely sing there, standing on the pavement in the shade. To the dismay of farmers, grackles poke holes in grapefruits and oranges, either causing blemishes that reduce the value or destroying the fruit entirely. This is a particular problem in isolated citrus groves near good roosting sites, such as sugarcane fields (Johnson et al. 1989).

Grackles forage also in more natural habitats, such as sandy beaches, where they search along with Laughing Gulls for arthropods in piles of sargassum weed that has washed up. Grackles search for food on mudflats (in both fresh and salt water) — perhaps more like their original Valley habitat, before extensive European settlement. They consume newly hatched sea turtles on some tropical beaches (Peña 1998). Grackles have been known to consume eggs and nestlings of both colonial and solitary-nesting birds, but the overall impact of this behavior must be verified, not assumed (Hayslette et al. 2000).

Grackles are polygynous, meaning that one male mates with two or more females. As in many other polygynous species, females do all the work of building nests, incubating the eggs, and feeding the young. Nests are made of coarse grasses with a lining of mud and are usually placed high in a tall tree. Often one sees three to five grackle nests (or more) in a single tree, and a single male may defend the entire tree as his territory. Other males may wait in the area for an opportunity to mate with a female (Johnson et al. 2000). The grackle nesting season is long in the Valley, and I have regularly seen begging fledglings attended by females from early May to mid-September. The fact that they reject Bronzed Cowbird eggs is greatly in their favor (Carter 1986; Peer and Sealy 2004).

OTHER OBSERVATIONS Most species in the blackbird-grackle-oriole group have ritualized displays, such as the "bill-tilt," in which males face each other and point their bills upward, meanwhile sleeking their plumage (Jaramillo and Burke 1999). I have sometimes seen Audubon's and Altamira Orioles do this display, just for a few seconds at a time. Great-tailed Grackles regularly do the bill-tilt, much as Sennett (1878) observed: "Two males will take position facing each other on the ground or upon some shed, then together begin slowly raising their heads and twisting them most comically from side to side, all the time steadily eyeing each other, until their bills not only stand perpendicular to their bodies, but sometimes are thrown over nearly to their backs. After maintaining this awkward position for a time, they will gradually bring back their bills to a normal position, and the performance ends." I have never seen these displays lead to fighting, but they may allow individual males to determine their position in a dominance hierarchy, without having to fight.

Male grackles follow females as they fly between nesting and foraging areas, and often display to them and chase other males away. In these courtship displays, a male fans his tail, puffs out his body feathers, and droops and quivers his wings as he points his bill downward and gives a rapid series of *cheat* calls (Jaramillo and Burke 1999). I often see the male running around the female while doing this display, as she moves slowly across a lawn. Males flying toward females to give such a display may almost hit pedestrians along their flight path. Despite grackles' abundance and conspicuous behavior at roosts, there are few observations of predatory birds capturing Great-tailed Grackles (Johnson and Peer 2001). I have never seen even an attempted capture in the Valley.

OUTLOOK   Great-tailed Grackles have been abundant in the towns and agricultural sections of the Valley since at least the 1870s. Expansion of agriculture and cities undoubtedly allowed grackle populations to increase during the twentieth century. U.S. Breeding Bird Survey data show continued increases in South Texas from the mid-1960s through the late 1980s and early 1990s, after which the population leveled off. Some attempts have been made to control grackle populations and damage in citrus groves by scaring them off with reflective tape or fireworks or killing them using shotguns or chemical poisons (Rappole et al. 1990; Tipton et al. 1990a, 1990b). All these measures have had very local effect, if any, and the outlook for Great-tailed Grackles is highly favorable in the Valley and adjacent areas.

Bronzed Cowbird, *Molothrus aeneus*

Bronzed Cowbird is one of the most common "blackbirds" in the Valley. The hunchback outline created by a thick ruff of feathers that make the bird appear neckless, the powerful bill, and the red eyes all give male Bronzed Cowbirds a vaguely menacing look; the species was formerly called Red-eyed Cowbird. Females look like males but with less prominent ruffs, duller red eyes, and less iridescent plumage.

A large, whistling flock of Bronzed Cowbirds makes an impressive sight and sound, whether roosting, flying overhead, or jostling for position at a water source. For some reason birds roosting on wires tend to cluster on top of and near the wooden support poles, perhaps interpreting the pole as a tree. Other Valley blackbirds tend to spread out more on wires and are less likely to roost in such dense groups. Although not studied yet in much detail, the Bronzed Cowbird is becoming increasingly known for its habit of laying eggs in the nests of various host species, which may have their reproductive efforts thwarted.

DISTRIBUTION   Bronzed Cowbirds were once limited in the United States to southern Texas, but they now occur in southeastern California, central Arizona, southern New Mexico, western and Central Texas, and southern Louisiana. Their distribution is irregular within this range. For example, Bronzed Cowbirds are still quite rare in the Houston area of Texas but better established in New Orleans, Louisiana (Nancy L. Newfield, pers. comm.).

The species also occurs in most of Mexico, except Baja California, and in Central America south to central Panama (AOU 1998). Although most common in agricultural lowlands, Bronzed Cowbirds occur as high as about 9,800 feet (3,000 m) above sea level, following population growth and habitat clearing up the mountains. Bronzed Cowbirds occur in almost all parts of the Valley, although like many land birds they do not regularly occur on South Padre Island. The species is a permanent resident here, but individuals and flocks move around a good deal.

HABITAT   During the nesting season, Bronzed Cowbirds are common in riparian forest, thorn forest, thorn scrub, and agricultural fields. Individuals probably move back and forth between feeding areas—especially in short grass and sorghum fields—and nest-searching areas in native habitat (Carter 1986). Despite their name and reputation, Bronzed Cowbirds appear to be more common in places dominated by irrigated agriculture than where the dominant land use is grazing (Steve Monk and author, unpubl. data). Populations are fairly low in residential areas, probably due to the reduced number of potential host species (mainly Northern Mockingbird and Hooded Oriole).

In winter, Bronzed Cowbirds flock up, often segregating by sex, and they become more common in urban areas and nearby farmland. They disappear from native habitats at such times, and birders visiting in winter may have to look for Bronzed Cowbirds in town. Large roosts develop, usually in well-lit urban areas such as college campuses, medical centers, shopping centers, and town plazas. I suspect that feedlots are an important habitat feature in winter, even in the Valley, but do not have observations to confirm this suspicion. Males begin returning to native habitats in late March and early April, followed within a week or two by females.

HABITS   Bronzed Cowbirds forage mainly on the ground or on crop plants in fields and other open areas, getting seeds of grain crops such sorghum and several noncereal grasses. Birds are regularly seen foraging with cattle, mainly in nonagricultural areas. They probably consume arthropods disturbed by the cattle but occasionally perch on cattle and wild game, perhaps to remove ticks. Females regularly consume snails during the nesting season, presumably as a source of calcium for their developing eggs, but second-year males (presumably nonbreeders) also do so (Carter 1986).

I have seen winter flocks eating seeds of weedy grasses such as goosegrass (*Eleusine indica*) and introduced liverseed grass (*Urochloa panicoides*) on schoolyards and native Texas signalgrass (*Urochloa texana*) in recently abandoned agricultural fields (Wipff et al. 1993; Hatch et al. 1999). Bronzed Cowbirds frequent urban parking lots, where they may be picking up grit to help digest the seeds they have eaten.

In the tropics, Skutch noted Bronzed Cowbirds turning over stones in riverbeds, evidently getting arthropods from underneath. I have not seen this behavior in the Valley, probably because of a general lack of stones and extensive use of other habitats. I suspect that birds once used riverine habitats more extensively in the Valley, as Giant Cowbirds still do in the tropics (Robinson 1988). Different riverbank and mudflat areas may have become suitable at various times, but cowbirds would have been free to fly considerable distances in search of such habitats. As residential areas, pastures, and agricultural fields were developed, cowbirds must have begun to use such habitats and to increase in numbers.

Of great interest to me and also a few others are the effects Bronzed Cowbirds have had on local bird populations (see Audubon's Oriole and Hooded Oriole accounts, for example). High parasitism rates have been observed in the past on orioles, tanagers, chats, and other medium-sized passerines in the Valley (Friedmann 1963). I suspect (as did Carter 1986) that the dramatic decline of Audubon's Oriole, Orchard Oriole, Hooded Oriole, Summer Tanager and perhaps other birds was partially caused by high Bronzed Cowbird parasitism. Other species, such as Olive Sparrow and Long-billed Thrasher, were seldom parasitized in early years (Friedmann 1929; Amadon 1940). Growth of irrigated agriculture and fragmentation of remaining native habitats probably allowed the growth of larger cowbird populations, which then needed host nests to parasitize and expanded beyond "preferred" species' nests to use those of other species as well.

Today the main Bronzed Cowbird hosts in the Valley are different. Green Jay, Long-billed Thrasher, Northern Mockingbird, and Northern Cardinal are the species that Chris Hathcock and I have most regularly observed feeding fledgling Bronzed Cowbirds. Olive Sparrows are frequently parasitized in the Valley but may not successfully raise cowbirds as regularly as larger, higher nesting species (Hathcock 2000). Hooded Orioles still raise Bronzed Cowbirds (Brush 2000c), and Altamira Orioles have now been confirmed to raise and feed fledgling Bronzed Cowbirds (see Altamira Oriole account). It was once thought that Bronzed Cowbirds would avoid the long, saclike nests of Altamira Orioles and other orioles, due to fear of being trapped inside by a returning parent. However, Bronzed Cowbirds have parasitized the even longer nests of the larger and colonial Yellow-winged Cacique (*Cacicus melanicterus;* Dickerman 1960; Rowley 1984) as well as those of most of the orioles that build long, hanging nests.

New hosts for Bronzed Cowbirds are still being discovered, especially in tropical areas, as more habitat is cleared and more research is done. For example, Sealy et al. (1995) documented five new host species for the Bronzed Cowbird, which included two yellowthroats, a tanager, a saltator, and the House Wren (*Troglodytes aedon*). The wren is one of the few cavity-nesting species to be parasitized by Bronzed Cowbirds. I expect that Dickcissel and Common Yellowthroat will soon be added to the list in the Valley, and others in Mexico and Central America, such as the flycatchers that build hanging nests (Thurber and Villeda 1980).

OTHER OBSERVATIONS   Skutch (1996) suggested that there was a great cost to the host in being parasitized by Bronzed Cowbirds, in that no one had seen a mixed family group of Bronzed Cowbird and host fledglings. Of twenty-eight cases compiled by Sealy et al. (1995), all involved only Bronzed Cowbirds (no host young) being fed by host adults. Evidently the host nestlings or fledglings do not survive in competition with the larger Bronzed Cowbird youngsters. Possible counterstrategies include guarding the nests, particularly during the early morning when most cowbird eggs may be laid, or ejecting the cowbird eggs once they are present, but both these behaviors have their costs (Rohwer et al. 1989; Peer and Sealy 1999).

Jimmy Jackson's observations of an Audubon's Oriole nest in a wooded residential area in Beeville (Bee County) in 2002 provided one example of the cost of Bronzed Cowbird parasitism. The nest, in which one Bronzed Cowbird egg and two Audubon's Oriole eggs hatched, fledged only the cowbird. The cowbird fledged before the orioles were able to do so, and the small oriole nestlings died, evidently due to starvation. My guess, as Skutch suspected, is that the adult orioles must have spent most of their time following and feeding the Bronzed Cowbird fledgling, at the cost of failing to raise their own young.

Data that I collected during 1996–98 in the Valley generally showed a

Table 1. Family groups attended by host adults and containing Bronzed Cowbird fledglings, 1996–98.

Host	Average No. adults attending	Average No. host young	Average No. Bronzed young	No. family groups
Green Jay	1.5	0	1.4	20
Hooded Oriole	1.6	0	1.1	7
Long-billed Thrasher	1.5	0	1.7	6
Northern Mockingbird	1.5	0	1.5	4
Northern Cardinal	2.0	1.7	1.7	3
Altamira Oriole	1.6	0	1.7	3

similar pattern (table 1). I never saw a mixed family group except for the Northern Cardinal, which evidently was able to raise both its own young and cowbirds; perhaps the reason is its mainly granivorous diet, good for cowbirds and for its own young. Since cardinals are sometimes known to feed other fledglings that they did not raise themselves (Skutch 1976), and since brood parasites are sometimes fed by birds other than their foster parents (Sealy and Lorenzana 1997), confirmation is needed.

Although sample sizes are small, the information suggests that Bronzed Cowbirds are indeed excellent competitors for food. The loud, persistent begging of Bronzed Cowbirds may be important. One wonders how Green Jays and Long-billed Thrashers, in particular, maintain their currently healthy populations in Valley brushlands—perhaps early or late broods escape cowbird parasitism, since cowbirds seem to have a shorter breeding season than their hosts.

Bronzed Cowbirds have been reported to approach their own young occasionally, in a possible vestige of parental behavior (Kay McCracken, cited in Lorenzana and Sealy 1998). Although I cannot refute this, my own observations suggest another explanation. On at least two occasions, I have seen a male Bronzed Cowbird fly over toward a begging juvenile (being attended by Green Jays) and then proceed to do some partial courtship behavior, involving inflation of the ruff and some bowing. I suspect that the male was simply treating the full-grown juvenile as a potential mate, perhaps being programmed to display to any Bronzed Cowbird that is not an adult male.

The bright red eyes of the male are striking at close range. Several carotenoid pigments produce the intense scarlet to crimson color, and red blood cells may add to the color (Hudon and Muir 1996). Dickey and Van Rossem

(1938) stated that El Salvador males developed brownish orange or orange-brown eyes in the nonbreeding season. I have seen red eyes all year in the Valley, although possibly not quite as bright in winter. The dietary source of the carotenoid pigments is unknown, but it must be readily available given the tremendous number of bright-eyed Bronzed Cowbirds here.

Icterids such as the Bronzed Cowbird seem particularly likely to have deformed bills. Easterla and Wauer (1972) report a Bronzed Cowbird with unusually long crossed mandibles, seen June 9, 1969, in Big Bend National Park, and Small and Pruett (1998) discuss a bird with an unusually long, decurved upper mandible. A specimen in the UTPA collection (undated, Falcon Dam, Starr County) has a very short lower mandible, which looks as if it was broken, allowing the upper mandible to grow into a long, twisted shape. Bill deformities also occur in other icterids (Sharp and Neill 1979) and other birds and may prevent birds from foraging or preening normally.

OUTLOOK   The outlook for Bronzed Cowbirds remains excellent. The species is well established in the Valley and is expanding in Central and eastern Texas and southern Louisiana. There seems to be no shortage of hosts or foraging sites for this flexible species. More research is needed on the impacts of Bronzed Cowbird parasitism throughout its range, especially on forest-edge and scrub species like Altamira Oriole that were once thought to be "cowbird-proof."

In tropical areas such as central Belize, my limited fieldwork during the dry season (March–May) suggests that Bronzed Cowbirds appear to be fairly uncommon and limited to pastures within 0.5 of a mile (1 km) of water. This pattern might suggest a limited impact on potential hosts. However, they likely spread out away from water after the rains come in June and the main nesting season begins, thus being able to find a greater number of nests. The lack of large sorghum or corn fields in countries such as Belize probably helps keep Bronzed Cowbird populations lower in less developed areas, but undoubtedly numbers will increase as human population growth and habitat alteration continue.

Other cowbirds

The **Brown-headed Cowbird** (*Molothrus ater*) is the only other cowbird so far recorded in the Valley, although the first record of **Shiny Cowbird** (*M. bonariensis*) could happen any day now. Although widespread in the Valley, Brown-headed Cowbirds are much rarer than Bronzed Cowbirds during the breeding season. They generally are found in riparian forest and scrub, and I cannot recall seeing one in residential habitat during the breeding season.

In the late 1800s and early 1900s, their eggs were often found in nests of smaller orioles, such as Orchard and Hooded, as well as those of other species (Friedmann 1963). Currently, the Brown-headed Cowbird is a rare brood parasite of small species like White-eyed Vireo, Tropical Parula, Olive Sparrow, and Hooded Oriole (Chris Hathcock, pers. comm.; Brush 2000c). The species is more common as a breeder just north of the Valley, in Laredo, Kingsville, and areas farther north. Usually I see fewer than five Brown-headed Cowbirds per day during the breeding season. Although larger numbers may winter in the Valley, the estimated 500 that I saw at Delta Lake on July 28, 2001, was phenomenal. Those birds had apparently gathered to take advantage of a swarm of midges that had emerged from the lake, along with about 300 Bronzed Cowbirds, 50 Red-winged Blackbirds, and 40 Great-tailed Grackles.

Blackbirds and meadowlarks

The extremely widespread **Red-winged Blackbird** (*Agelaius phoeniceus*) is a common bird in the Valley at all times of year. During the nesting season, Valley Redwings are more limited to marshes and the river's edge than are birds of the wetter eastern and midwestern United States, which often nest in fields and meadows. Valley birds may nest in small cattail marshes along road or canal margins but few do so out in pastures or other fields. Despite the species' abundance in winter, many urban Valley residents are surprisingly unfamiliar with the Red-winged Blackbird. This lack of familiarity may reflect how rare Red-winged Blackbirds are in residential areas and city parks.

Redwings nest low over water, in cattails or wetland shrubs. For example on June 8, 1996, I saw six active nests (at least two with nestlings) along the Rio Grande between Chapeño and Fronton. Red-winged Blackbirds are always alert to possible danger, and their high-pitched calls warn other species like Audubon's Orioles of approaching raptors.

Eastern Meadowlark (*Sturnella magna*) is a common year-round resident, and it does breed regularly in the Valley (Oberholser 1974; Benson and Arnold 2001). One regularly hears the *spring-o-the-year* or *tortilla-con-chile* song, particularly in spring and summer. However, like Sennett (1878), I have found that most of my time "was spent among the timber, and the birds of the prairies were neglected." The domed nest would be hard to find, concealed in thick grass. Short-grass pastures or similar large mown fields, coastal prairies, and savannas all support meadowlarks. **Western Meadowlarks** (*Sturnella neglecta*) winter in the Valley, but there are no breeding records.

Altamira Oriole, *Icterus gularis*

The symbol of the Frontera Audubon Society, headquartered in Weslaco, is the Altamira Oriole, formerly known as Black-throated or Lichtenstein's Oriole. A Valley invader, it was rare or absent in the days of the early ornithologists Couch, Merrill, Sennett, Grissom, Crosby, and Friedmann. Although there is an 1890 specimen from Cameron County, no others were noted until 1938, when T. D. Burleigh collected a specimen near Brownsville. The fact that Merrill and Sennett both missed the species in the late 1880s, despite their extensive field work, suggests that Altamiras were at best extremely rare then. Following the first recorded nest in 1951 (near Santa Maria), Altamira Orioles rapidly increased, becoming the most common breeding oriole at Santa Ana by the 1960s, as other orioles declined (Oberholser 1974). Today this large, flashy species is still the most common breeding oriole at heavily visited Valley birding areas like Santa Ana and Bentsen, despite some declines since the 1970s.

DISTRIBUTION In the United States, the Altamira Oriole regularly occurs only in Starr, Hidalgo, Cameron, and possibly Willacy counties, from the Falcon Dam area east to Arroyo City, Los Fresnos, and the Brownsville area (at least downstream to the Southmost Preserve, where I saw nests, adults, and fledglings on June 13, 2000). The species is most common along the Rio Grande and within 1–2 miles (3–5 km) of the river itself, where most of the suitable habitat is. However, nesting pairs are also scattered in resacas, patches of brush, and along the Arroyo Colorado in Cameron County.

Farther north the range is patchy and somewhat changeable. Altamiras have nested along the river near San Ygnacio, Zapata County, on both the U.S. (Eitniear and Rueckle 1996) and Mexican sides (Ron LaDuque, pers. comm., 2001). The northernmost nesting locations have been around Premont (Jim Wells County) and Kingsville (Kleberg County), where Altamiras probably do not occur regularly. Even in the Valley, the exact distribution of Altamiras is patchy and is still being worked out. In 2001, Chris Hathcock found two Altamira nests along Highway 186, 6–8 miles (10–12 km) from Port Mansfield, thus confirming their presence in that part of Willacy County. However, Altamiras have never been recorded at Laguna Atascosa, even though they nest less than 3 miles (5 km) from the refuge border and in similar habitat in coastal Tamaulipas. The species has never been documented to occur on the King or Kenedy ranches.

In Mexico, Altamiras are largely a Gulf-Caribbean slope bird, occurring mainly in the lowlands all the way south through the Yucatán Peninsula to northern Belize. I saw two nests, at least one of which was active, on July 21,

2001, at Laguna Blanca Ranch, south of Matamoros. Altamiras also nest at Rancho Rincon de Anacahuitas, in the same area. Both these ranches contain coastal thorn scrub habitat that looks similar to that at Laguna Atascosa.

Altamira Orioles also occur on the Pacific slope of southern Mexico from Guerrero and Oaxaca south to northwestern Nicaragua. They have been reported from the state of Mexico high on the central plateau, but this seems unlikely to me, given the species' preference for lowland habitats below 4,920 feet (1,500 m) above sea level (AOU 1998).

HABITAT   Like Baltimore Orioles (*Icterus galbula*) in the central and eastern United States, Altamiras are birds of broken forests and forest edges. Although often seen in large trees, Altamiras also forage extensively in thorn scrub and riparian thickets, and a suitable nesting area may include only one or two large trees or electric lines (for nesting sites) amidst a "pygmy forest." The scrubbiest site where I have seen Altamiras nesting is Falcon State Park, dominated by low thorn scrub, where they nest in blackbrush acacia. Only a few kilometers away, Altamiras nest in the narrow band of moist riparian forest below Falcon Dam, where Mexican ash provides most of the nest sites. Overall, the birds tend to be most common within a couple of hundred meters of the edge of dense riparian forests rather than in the interior.

Pairs occasionally nest over suburban or rural yards in the Valley, provided that at least a few hectares of native habitat is available for foraging. The success of such nests is doubtful, as nesting seldom continues for more than three years in suburban habitats. The subadult bird I saw at Lake James, Edinburg, on July 17, 2001, may have been a wandering bird looking for a suitable nesting area, as there is little native habitat immediately nearby.

In Mexico and northern Central America, edges of or openings in tropical deciduous forest or even evergreen forest provide suitable nesting habitat. Tropical swamps, palm forests, savannas, and dry tropical scrub are also used. Altamiras are common in places with a patchwork of small agricultural fields (*milpas*) or pastures and wooded sections, but they avoid extensively cleared areas.

HABITS   Altamira Orioles are large, often conspicuous orioles, and they forage in a variety of unusual ways. Although the usual oriole fare of small fruits and insects is consumed, this species regularly captures and carries larger insects like grasshoppers and stick insects; the latter are frequently given to older nestlings. The large bill and associated strong jaw musculature allow the Altamira Oriole to tear vines and strips of bark loose, for use as nesting material, and also to squeeze small branches to see if there are insects hidden inside. Inside the mouth is a palatal knob, found in no other orioles (Wetmore 1919). This ridge in the roof of the mouth (also found in grackles) evidently allows Altamiras to crack seeds like those of sunflower and safflower, which they may obtain from plants or at feeding stations (Beecher 1950; John C. Arvin, pers. comm.).

Like many icterids, Altamiras also forage by gaping, in which they insert the bill into a small hole or crack in a branch or a fruit and open it up, exposing what is inside. In tropical Mexico, they have been seen opening the swollen thorns of the bull's-horn acacia to get the ants that live inside—but only during cool weather, to avoid a fierce defensive response (Janzen 1969).

Altamira Orioles take nectar from flowers, sometimes by removing the whole flower from a plant and carrying it off (as I saw an Altamira do with the flower of a giant Turk's-cap, *Malvaviscus arborea,* on February 29, 1996). The variety of foraging techniques is probably a major factor allowing Altamiras to live year-round in the subtropical Valley, while most other orioles migrate south for the winter. Interestingly, the other main gaper among Valley orioles is the Audubon's Oriole, which is also a permanent resident.

Even the casual visitor to Valley parks and refuges often notices the long, hanging nests of the Altamira Oriole. As Sutton and Pettingill (1943) noted in northeastern Mexico more than fifty years ago, the birds seem to build their nest in the most conspicuous location possible—on telephone wires along roads and on isolated trees at the edge of fields or villages or along rivers and arroyos. This is one of the few species that one can survey by looking for nests; surveying most species requires early morning censuses of singing birds. I once saw two Altamira Oriole nests while visiting a rest area along a limited-access Mexican toll road between Monterrey and Reynosa— not the kind of place usually thought of as a prime bird study area.

Altamira Orioles and a few other orioles of Mexico and Central America that make similar nests are often called *bolseros* (purse makers), and the nest does somewhat resemble a coarsely woven purse. The long bill and strong jaw muscles allow Altamira Orioles to obtain tough nesting materials not available to most other birds (Leisler 1995). Materials such as the inner bark of cedar elm trees and the living fibrous leaves of retama may help keep the nest from breaking in the strong South Texas winds.

As among other orioles, only the female builds the nest, while the male sings and preens nearby, keeping watch for intruders. Sometimes the female waits for the male to return to the nest area before she enters the nest with food, as Ricklefs (1980) noted for a tropical flycatcher. The male may follow the female while she gathers nesting material, but often he waits or forages near the nest.

Early nests may take more than three weeks to complete (Sutton and Pettingill 1943), but Altamiras can complete later nests in less than one week. Once or twice I have seen an Altamira of different plumage take over the building of a particular nest in the early stages of construction. It is possible, as Sutton and Pettingill suggested, that occasionally the male may start the nest and leave the majority of work to the female, but in the great majority of cases I suspect that the female builds the nest from beginning to end.

Nests are usually suspended from flexible, slender terminal branches over open space at least 16 feet (5 m) above ground level. Although a great variety of tree species have been used for nest sites, those most often used are common riparian species like Mexican ash, cedar elm, sugar hackberry, and black willow. Montezuma bald-cypress is occasionally used, particularly in areas where large Mexican ashes have died due to beaver chewing or soil compaction. Thorny species like huisache or Texas ebony may be used if tall and emergent, but they seem less favored. Honey mesquite is usually not used, given its low, spreading growth form and failure to provide open enough sites for nest construction.

Altamira Orioles most frequently begin their nests in spots where two or three thin branches are close enough together to serve as attachment points. For this reason palms (with larger but more widely spaced fronds and no true branches) are seldom used. I have occasionally seen nests in exotic fan palms, but usually birds find alternative sites if their territories are in palm groves. In the strong South Texas winds it may be difficult to start nests on telephone wires. I have seen such start-nests blow back and forth as much as 10 feet (3 m); such nests are generally not finished, although those on the northwest side of a utility pole may be better protected. Perhaps this is one of the reasons why nesting on telephone wires is less common in the Valley than in certain areas of eastern Mexico, where winds may be lighter during the breeding season. Alternatively, nest sites may be less abundant in parts of eastern Mexico.

Young birds (subadults) sometimes build weaker nests of more irregular form, sometimes in undesirable locations, and these may be more likely to break and fall than those built by adults. As with the young Village Weavers (*Ploceus cucullatus*) studied by Collias and Collias (1984), practice makes perfect.

Altamira Orioles nest in a variety of trees in Mexico, although there may be preferences for particular tree species. Near Aldama in southeastern Tamaulipas, most nests found by Ernesto Enkerlin-Hoeflich and Jack Eitniear (pers. comm.) have been in gumbo limbo trees (*Bursera simaruba*). The smooth trunk of gumbo limbo (also called *chakah*) may make it more difficult for snakes to reach oriole nests. Near El Encino and Gómez Farías, southwestern Tamaulipas, most nests have been in *orejón* trees (*Enterolobium cyclocarpum*), perhaps because of their large size, numerous horizontal branches, and tendency to grow as isolated trees (Nancy J. Flood, unpubl. data).

While most nests are over fields or streams, John C. Arvin noted a nest over a busy Mexican highway near El Encino; the nest swayed wildly every time a large truck passed a few feet below—certainly a safe site, if a noisy one. Altamira Orioles frequently build nests low in ant-acacia trees in Mexico, with the ants and thorns both providing protection (Janzen 1969); African weaver birds use such protection as well (Collias and Collias 1984).

Like the oropendolas (*Psarocolius* spp.) that Gonzalo Fernandez de Oviedo (1526) noticed in the West Indies in the early 1500s, Altamiras probably nest at the tips of branches in isolated locations to make the nests harder for predators to reach. Regardless of which tree species are used, the Altamira Oriole's exposed nest locations do seem quite safe from predators. Chris Hathcock (2000), in his Santa Ana study, noted no predation of Altamira nests once they reached the nestling stage, unlike the higher predation rates suffered by open-cup nesters like Long-billed Thrashers and Northern Mockingbirds nesting in the same habitats. This is a great advantage for the Altamira in subtropical and tropical habitats with abundant nest predators such as snakes and mammals.

Drawbacks of the Altamira Oriole's nesting habit are the need for a tall tree that is either isolated or at the edge of a forest; the time and skill it takes to build the nests; and, in the Valley at least, the need to build the nest on the northwest side of the tree so that it does not blow around too much. I have seen a few active Altamira nests break loose and fall. At least some of these were built by less experienced second-year birds and were either less carefully constructed or not built in the northwest quadrant of a tree. In the strong southeasterly winds and occasional heavy rains such nests may break loose, carrying their occupants to the ground. However, well-built and well-positioned nests can withstand day after day of strong, gusty winds, and the majority last through the breeding season.

There is no evidence of reuse of old nests by Altamira Orioles in the following year, and in fact they usually do not reuse nests even within the same year, at least in the Valley. A new nest may be constructed in the same tree as the earlier nest, sometimes on the same branch. As Skutch (1987) noted with Montezuma Oropendolas (*Psarocolius montezuma*), Altamira Orioles do not repair a nest in danger of falling but rebuild quickly if the nest does fall or fails due to predation or brood parasitism.

Other species sometimes use Altamira Oriole nests, particularly cavity-nesting species for which nest sites may be in short supply. I once saw a Brown-crested Flycatcher enter an Altamira nest and remain inside for at least fifteen minutes, suggesting that it may have been incubating eggs. House Sparrows occasionally take over Altamira Oriole nests in the Valley, although we do not know if they evict the orioles or wait until the orioles are done nesting (Mark Conway, pers. comm.). House Sparrows enlarge the entrance area of an Altamira nest so that it looks like a keyhole.

Strangely enough, the cavity-nesting Masked Tityra has used Altamira nests on two occasions in Tamaulipas: once in a nest left over from the year before, and once in a current-year nest that had already been used by Altamiras (Will Carter, pers. comm.). Skutch (1983) has seen tityras take over active nest cavities from woodpeckers and aracaris in the tropics, but there is no record of them using a hanging nest.

On September 6, 1999, I saw a juvenile Cactus Wren chase four Bronzed Cowbirds when they tried to approach an Altamira Oriole nest near Fronton. There were three juvenile Cactus Wrens gleaning from the outside of the nest—whether they were using the nest in any other way I could not tell.

Owls may sometimes use oriole hanging nests. David Watson (1999) saw a Ferruginous Pygmy-Owl exiting an abandoned Streak-backed Oriole (*I. pustulatus*) nest on May 23, 1997, in Oaxaca, Mexico. At Bentsen in the mid-1990s I found a dead Eastern Screech-Owl that had caught one of its feet in a loop of monofilament fishing line used by Altamiras in nest construction. I do not know for what reason the screech-owl was interested in the nest, since the bird would seem too large to roost inside.

OTHER OBSERVATIONS   The bright colors and overall rarity of the Altamira Oriole in the United States make it a bird attracting great interest among Valley visitors. Confusion sometimes results when people see a bright adult paired with a duller bird and assume that the duller bird is the female and the brighter bird the male. This may be true, but second-year birds of both sexes are noticeably duller than adults, which themselves brighten between their third and fourth years (Dickerman 1986). Adults of both sexes can be almost equally bright, although the male usually is slightly brighter around the face in direct comparison.

Observers have noticed some interesting habits, like the gleaning of dead insects from radiator grilles of vehicles, especially in cold weather, or the tendency for Altamira nests to be built near nests of other conspicuous birds, like Great Kiskadee or Couch's Kingbird (Dickey and Van Rossem 1938; Rowley 1984). These nesting associations are thought to benefit mainly the less watchful species like Altamira Oriole or Rose-throated Becard. Great Kiskadees and Couch's Kingbirds do appear to be better "watchdogs" than Altamiras, because one of the flycatcher pair usually remains within about 65 feet (20 m) of the nest and aggressively chases away intruding predators or brood parasites (Gorena 1995). Altamiras are more likely to leave the nest unguarded, and they have been known to abandon nests due to cowbird parasitism or to accept cowbird eggs and raise the young cowbirds instead of their own young (Brush 1998c; Hathcock and Brush 2004). But I have seen several pairs of Altamiras successfully raise broods when nesting on their own, and I have seen nests close to kiskadee or kingbird nests fail, so other factors are involved. This needs to be better investigated to test whether there is either active association or any actual benefit to the orioles (Richardson and Bolen 1999).

Despite great similarity between the sexes in appearance, male and female Altamiras respond to predators and brood parasites in different ways. Male Altamiras (distinguished, with care, by their brighter plumage and failure to build nests or incubate eggs) fly directly toward and chase away fox squirrels, which have been seen entering Altamira nests and robbing Green Jay nests. Once, a male bird came within 3 feet (1 m) of an "intruding" nest-checking device, but he did not attack it. In contrast, females typically land within 10 feet (3 m) of a squirrel and quiver their wings, giving a soft *keeer* call. This display—similar to one given by female Red-winged Blackbirds (Nero 1984)—usually attracts the attention of the male, which then drives the squirrel away.

Females are as aggressive as males in chasing away Bronzed Cowbirds that may land within about 3–6 feet (1–2 m) of the nest. The female Altamira may emerge from the nest and chase the cowbird away, then returning to the nest. If a male Altamira sees a cowbird, he flies at it and chases it and then either returns to his high perch near the nest or flies away on another foraging trip. Females seldom stand guard near the nest. They are either inside—building the nest, laying or incubating eggs, or brooding young in chilly weather—or bringing in food or removing fecal sacs. While males do participate equally in feeding nestlings and may care for fledglings while the female is building a second nest, they otherwise function mainly as guards.

Altamiras sometimes remove (eject) Bronzed Cowbird eggs, by impaling them on the bill, which has been seen on three occasions in the Valley (Brush 1998c; Hathcock 2000). I saw something very surprising along the Rio Grande Hiking Trail at Bentsen on July 8, 1998: *7:26—Alt. to nest from E., enters (can't see any food in bill). 7:42—Alt. still inside nest—other has been calling off to E. a ways. 7:43—nest shakes, then inside bird emerges with egg in foot—out and away, drops it about 15–20 m from nest. I hear it crack as it hits a downed branch (later picked up piece with scrawls typical of Alt.—has yolky material attached to inside).*

An intruding adult had been seen within 10 feet (3 m) of the nest and had been chased away by the nesting pair—it may have entered to lay an egg before I arrived for my observation period. I concluded that this was most likely a case of attempted intraspecific brood parasitism, not known before in Altamiras. Even more interesting about this egg removal incident was the use of the foot to remove the egg. This may be the only passerine besides the Common Raven (*Corvus corax;* Owen 1950; Heinrich 1999) known to carry anything in its feet. Whether Altamiras ever use their feet to remove cowbird eggs is unknown, but I would think it would be easier than puncturing the tough cowbird egg with the bill. The eggs of Altamiras are long and narrow (for an oriole), and are probably more easily damaged than the more spherical, thicker-shelled cowbird egg (Picman 1989).

Another use of the legs may be to help cool off after a long incubation bout on a hot summer afternoon. Although the birds usually keep their legs and feet covered by their outer belly feathers (as do most birds), I have seen incubating females emerge from the nest with feet dangling down and brood patch exposed. The bare feet and legs are thought to help cool various birds in hot weather, especially in flight (Udvardy 1983; Ward et al. 1999).

There is some evidence of hybridization with Audubon's Orioles, as for example the unusual oriole that others and I saw at Bentsen in 1998 and 1999. This bird had the overall pattern of an Altamira, but the black of the throat patch extended up onto the cheeks (although it was not solid black) and the bill was somewhat narrower than a typical Audubon's bill. The black area of the upper back had short orange streaks in it, especially where the back met the hind neck. This bird (apparently a male) mated with a normal-looking female Altamira and attended at least one nest in 1998 and 1999; a bird looking very much like this bird is pictured in Perrigo 2002. A second possible hybrid bird was seen at Bentsen in the early 2000s (John C. Arvin, pers. comm.).

OUTLOOK My outlook for Altamira Orioles in the Valley is cautiously optimistic. Although Altamiras have done better than any other oriole species at maintaining a breeding population in the face of habitat change and high cowbird parasitism, there have been disturbing signs in the last ten to fifteen years. There are now at least three cases of Altamiras raising Bronzed Cowbirds, and as mentioned earlier, nests are regularly abandoned during the early stages, which I suspect is mainly due to cowbird disturbance or parasitism.

This is a marked change from the more than 150 nests examined in Mexico by Travis Meitzen, of which only two had Bronzed Cowbird eggs in them (Friedmann 1963). In the best-studied case of Altamiras raising Bronzed Cowbirds to fledging, Chris Hathcock (2000) noted seven Bronzed Cowbird eggs in the nest at one point during incubation. All eggs but one were removed (presumably by the orioles), leaving one to hatch and be raised to fledging.

The number of Altamira pairs at Santa Ana has declined since the highs in the 1960s and 1970s, and most nests are now located toward the perimeter of the refuge. This may be due to death of suitable large nesting trees in the interior of the refuge, where Barbara Pleasants found many nests in 1974

(Pleasants 1981). Xerification of foraging areas may also be a factor, causing birds to spend more time away from the nest and making it easier for cowbirds to enter unnoticed (Brush 1998c; Hathcock and Brush 2004). Bronzed Cowbird parasitism could be more intense near the edge, although I do not have any direct evidence of that.

The death of large trees is also a concern at Bentsen. Bentsen has a higher density of breeding pairs than Santa Ana, but the total is still fewer than eight pairs. Currently the largest contiguous population of Altamiras in the United States is along the Rio Grande in Starr County and adjacent Mexico, where twenty to twenty-five pairs nested in the mid-1990s (Brush 1998c). These birds nest mainly right over the river in large Mexican ash trees and then forage either in the narrow strip of tall riparian forest or in thorny habitats nearby. I suspect that these birds suffer less from Bronzed Cowbird parasitism in this less heavily agricultural area and that they have higher nesting success than downstream birds.

Audubon's Oriole, *Icterus graduacauda*

Formerly known as the Black-headed Oriole, Audubon's Oriole was named by J. P. Giraud for his friend John James Audubon (Stone 1919), who visited Texas but probably never saw the species in life. Audubon's Oriole is attractively patterned in black and yellow with white trim, but it is usually the song that attracts attention to the bird. Sutton (1951) wrote: "I was completely fooled by whistles that I thought were those of a small boy on his way to a favorite fishing hole . . . pleasing enough to the ear, but a bit 'off-key' and without definite pattern."

DISTRIBUTION   In the United States Audubon's Oriole occurs regularly from Webb, LaSalle, Live Oak, McMullen, and Bee counties south to the Rio Grande, except in highly agricultural or urban areas (Brush 2000d). More of a foothill and montane bird in Mexico than in the United States, Audubon's Oriole occurs from Nayarit south to Oaxaca on the Pacific slope and from northern Coahuila south to central Veracruz on the Gulf slope (AOU 1998; Benson et al. 1989; Chuck Sexton, pers. comm.). Perhaps most surprising is the 1940 specimen from the Sierra del Carmen mountain range across from Big Bend National Park (Dallas Museum of Natural History). The species is still there. John Karges of the Nature Conservancy of Texas (pers. comm.) noted "pairs of Audubon's Oriole, including singing males, at elevations between 7000 and 8500 feet in pine-fir-oak forests, on the 10th–11th June 2000. We heard them first, and out of context, I did not recognize the song until we actually saw a tree-top male singing."

In the Valley, Audubon's Oriole occurs regularly along the Rio Grande from Falcon Dam almost to Los Ebanos (southeastern Starr County) and also in areas of Starr County away from the river, as well as northernmost Willacy County (Steve Monk, unpubl. data) and northern Hidalgo County (Steve Bentsen, photo).

Despite intensive fieldwork in both Bentsen and Santa Ana, I have not found any individuals there during the breeding season. Wayne Shifflett suspected that four pairs of Audubon's Orioles nested at Santa Ana in 1970 and 1971 (Webster 1971) and three pairs nested there in 1975 (Webster 1975). One pair was followed by three fledgling Bronzed Cowbirds in 1975, and the last known territorial pair at Santa Ana was in 1976 (Gehlbach 1987). The last nest of which I am aware in Cameron County was in the 1920s (Friedmann 1963), although they may have occurred there for another thirty years or so. Audubon's Orioles occasionally show up in winter at Bentsen—for example, a pair during February 17–26, 1999 (Petra Hockey and Laura Moore, pers. comm.), which I also saw.

HABITAT   In the Valley, Audubon's Orioles occur most commonly in tall, shady riparian forests, but they also occur in thorn forest and even thorn scrub. Populations in thorn scrub may be more nomadic, with birds abandoning such habitat during prolonged drought (Vega and Rappole 1994). In Mexico, the species inhabits tropical deciduous and semi-evergreen forests, cloud forest, moist and dry pine-oak forest, and thorn forest. In the Sierra Madre Oriental of Nuevo León, Audubon's Orioles occur in apple (*Pyrus malus*) orchards at about 3,940 feet (1,200 m) above sea level and pine-oak-fir (*Abies*) forests at about 7,870 feet (2,400 m) above sea level (Gracia-Manzano 1988). Throughout its range, there is usually dense foliage at some level, whether it be 10–20 feet (3–6 m) in thorn forest or 40–50 feet (12–15 m) or higher in cloud forest, but open pine-oak forest is also used extensively in Mexico. Flowering and fruiting trees or vines may attract Audubon's Orioles into otherwise unsuitable habitat. The species seems particularly common in scrub and forest near citrus groves, at least near Gomez Farías, Tamaulipas.

HABITS   Early ornithologists such as D. B. Burrows commented on the "shyness" of the species, and I concur. I have never seen such a shy, skulking oriole as the Audubon's Oriole. Generally seen as pairs or individuals, the birds forage quietly in dense foliage. Even when gathering fruit, which often brings birds into full view, they seem to keep in the shade somehow. John H. Clark (quoted in Cassin 1856) noticed their shyness as well: "It was noticed most frequently while feeding on the fruit of the hackberry; but whenever exposed in picking off the berries, it always showed signs of uneasiness, and would immediately seek refuge in places affording greater con-cealment." Both females and males sing regularly, usually from hidden perches, and females may even sing or call from the nest, communicating with the unseen male nearby (Flood 1990).

Audubon's Orioles are easiest to see in winter, when leaves may be off the trees and the orioles often join conspicuous mixed-species flocks of Altamira Orioles, Great Kiskadees, Green Jays, and other medium-sized passerines (Gehlbach 1987). In winter they visit feeding stations in wooded areas of southern Texas, to eat fruit, seeds, or even marshmallows. I have seen Au-dubon's Orioles fly across the Rio Grande to visit the feeders at Salineño, where up to six individuals may be seen at one time. Since birders today are happy to find a pair of Audubon's Orioles, early reports of wintering flocks of 15–20 birds in South Texas seem fantastic (Burrows 1918).

With their strong bills, Audubon's Oriole often engage in "gaping," a for-aging behavior in which a bird inserts its bill into some sort of hole, crack, or soft spot and then pries the material open to get at something inside. I have seen birds open up common reed leaf sheaths and orange sections and flake off sections of mesquite bark from dead branches. Birds also consume fruits (such as mulberry) or insects by simply gleaning them from branches. Couch (in Cassin 1856) saw a pair picking insects from pads of the prickly pear cactus, and I saw a bird in pine forest near Monterrey, Nuevo León, foraging only 1–2 feet (0.5 m) above the ground. The species may also for-age high up in tall oaks, bald-cypress, ashes, or other trees.

Nests are usually well hidden by dense foliage of trees such as mesquite or Texas persimmon or by epiphytic *Tillandsia* in cedar elms or hackberries (Burrows 1918; Oberholser 1974). In Mexico, other species have been used (Flood 1990). Audubon's Orioles are apparently not inclined to nest near other species as other orioles are, thus they tend to nest solitarily (Dickey and Van Rossem 1938; Howell and Webb 1995).

OTHER OBSERVATIONS   In places where a species is rare, mismat-ing may occur. A mixed Audubon's-Altamira pair was seen in 1988 in Kle-berg County. This pair attended a nest, which was the long sac typical of Al-tamiras, so it was concluded that the Audubon's was a male and the Altamira was a female. This nest was apparently not successful, and it was uncertain whether eggs were laid (Paul C. Palmer, pers. comm.; Jaramillo and Burke 1999). See Altamira Oriole account for discussion of possible hybrid birds.

In frontier Mexico during the 1800s, Audubon's Orioles were thought to consume strips of meat put out by Mexican ranchers (Lieutenant Darius N. Couch, in Baird 1859). The species was known as *calandria iquimite* in the Jalapa area of central Veracruz, evidently for the habit of eating the fruits of

Erythrina americana, locally known as *iquimite.* The seeds of *iquimite* (also known as coralbean or *colorín*) contain an alkaloid toxic to humans (Bob Mugele and David Riskind, pers. comm.). I do not know if Audubon's Orioles also eat the fruits of the coralbean (*Erythrina herbacea*) that occurs in the Valley.

An Audubon's Oriole lived year-round at suburban Lake James, Edinburg, in 2000 and 2001 (Tom and Donna Peterson, pers. comm.). It sometimes sunned itself in backyard trees and often foraged in the tops of tall palms. This bird may have been a remnant of the 1980s population, when there was a patch of old-growth thorn forest and a small Audubon's Oriole population in the area (John C. Arvin, pers. comm.). I saw the bird at Lake James on May 9, 2001, in live oaks and fan palms.

OUTLOOK   The outlook for Audubon's Oriole in southern Texas is questionable. Although it does use a greater variety of habitats than was once thought, it does not do well in areas with a growing human population. Habitat loss and fragmentation lead to a variety of problems. Bronzed Cowbird parasitism has probably been particularly harmful to this species, as these orioles accept cowbird eggs and then raise cowbird young at the expense of their own. Even in 1918, Burrows wrote: "The bird is imposed upon by the bronzed cowbird to such an extent that it is difficult to find a full set [of five eggs]. I have only one perfect set . . . in one instance there are two eggs of the oriole and four of the cowbird."

Earlier yet, Bendire (1895) stated that orioles seemed to "be especial victims of the Bronzed Cowbird, and among these Audubon's seems to be the worst sufferer. In the nine sets of this species in the U.S. National Museum collection there are only two which contain the usual number of eggs, 4." Of course, cowbirds increase as natural habitat is altered and cleared, so it is habitat degradation that is the heart of the problem.

Several large ranches in southern Texas currently contain large blocks of forest and scrub habitat and Audubon's Orioles. We should encourage current land management practices that have maintained the species in some areas, and also continued land acquisition to prevent future fragmentation along the Rio Grande. A hopeful trend in Mexico is the increasing numbers of Audubon's Orioles in the mountains near Gómez Farías, Tamaulipas (Webster and Webster 2001; John C. Arvin, pers. comm.).

Other orioles

Three other oriole species once bred in the Valley. **Orchard Orioles** (*Icterus spurius*), once common in forest and scrub, have retreated north several hundred miles, to the San Antonio area. A "small nesting colony" near Matamoros in the 1950s may have been the last hurrah for nesting Orchard Orioles, of the typical form, at least, in northeastern Mexico (Davis 1957).

Orchard Orioles also declined rapidly on the U.S. side during the 1950s and 1960s. On July 25, 1970, Wayne Shifflett saw a flightless youngster at Santa Ana—the last successful Valley nesting that I know of (Webster 1970). Orchard Orioles were commonly parasitized by both Bronzed and Brown-headed Cowbirds in the Valley (Friedmann and Kiff 1985), which may have been an important factor in their decline. However, they are still common migrants through the Valley, with spring migrants passing through in April and May and fall migrants from late June to September.

Interestingly, a male "Ochre Oriole" (currently considered to be *Icterus spurius fuertesi*) summered along the Arroyo Colorado, near the small town of Arroyo City, Cameron County, April 15–July 17, 1998, and April 11–July 17, 1999 (Lockwood 2003). This bird sang throughout the summers it was present and interacted with locally breeding Hooded Orioles (M. Kay Baughman, pers. comm.). "Ochre Orioles" breed as far north as southern Tamaulipas. Way back on April 3, 1894, a male similarly overshot its normal range and ended up near Brownville (Dickerman 1964).

Hooded Orioles (*Icterus cucullatus*) still are widespread in the Valley, although nowhere do they occur in high density. Once the most common nesting oriole along the lower Rio Grande (Sennett 1878, 1879), Hooded Orioles regularly nested in Spanish moss and in palm trees (Oberholser 1974). Valley farmer and naturalist Charles E. Hudson (in Webster 1958) noted: "Ten years ago, every brush line, row of palm trees, and patch of brush had Hooded Orioles. They were in the country and in the towns. The only place I know of now with a fair population of them is the Santa Ana Refuge."

After the freeze of 1951, Hooded Orioles declined almost to the vanishing point in riparian forest, and the species now nests in residential areas in small numbers. Cowbird parasitism may have been a major problem for this species, and this continues today (Brush 2000c). Their former habit of feeding in agricultural fields such as cotton plantings may have become detrimental once pesticides came into common use (Oberholser 1974). Palm trees are the main nest sites now, with occasional use of banana trees. Small numbers of Hooded Orioles breed at or near Santa Ana: for example, a pair nested in a palm tree at the old refuge headquarters in 1970 (Wayne Shifflett in Webster 1970).

More recently, Eric Hopson saw a male carrying food to a hidden location in a Mexican fan palm just outside the northern boundary of Santa Ana (June 6, 1996). I have seen territorial males in the same area regularly during the 1990s, and I saw fledglings in the area on June 26, 1997. Valley birds sing rather infrequently, and they can be difficult to detect unless an active nest or family group is found.

202 SPECIES ACCOUNTS AND SUMMARIES

Hooded Orioles have spread north of the Valley, almost to San Angelo (Tom Green County), the Pleasanton area (Atascosa County), and near Corpus Christi (Nueces County; Benson and Arnold 2001). They have become common in live oak–mesquite habitat such as the Norias Division of the King Ranch and the Kenedy Ranch, and perhaps Valley populations are regularly supplemented by birds dispersing from such populations. They do winter occasionally in the Valley, usually at a nectar source such as a hummingbird feeder or a consistent patch of tubular flowers.

Bullock's Oriole (*Icterus bullockii*) is a common oriole of the western United States and north-central Mexico (AOU 1998). This ejector of cowbird eggs seems to be doing fairly well in the western Valley. The species once bred downstream to present-day Hidalgo (Sennett 1878) and as late as 1940 was still breeding in Cameron County (Samuel Grimes photo, in Bent 1958). I saw a female feeding a recent fledgling along the Rio Grande in extreme southwestern Hidalgo County on June 14, 1996, the farthest downstream location in recent years. Farther west, the species is fairly common in tall riparian forest and thorn forest between Falcon Dam and Roma. Males can be surprisingly hard to see as they forage in dense foliage, but they call and sing regularly and also forage in more open situations, such as bushes at the water's edge.

The hanging nests (less than half the length of a typical Altamira Oriole nest) are often placed in conspicuous locations over the river, such as ash or cypress branches. In at least two cases, Bullock's and Altamira Oriole nests were in the same tree, once only about 2 feet (0.5 m) apart on the same branch. Bullock's Orioles often use artificial nesting materials, such as orange or blue baling twine, especially in ranch country away from the Rio Grande. They are common in drier areas well away from the river in Starr County and northward through southern Texas, the Trans-Pecos, the Panhandle, and adjacent areas.

FAMILY FRINGILLIDAE

Lesser Goldfinch, *Carduelis psaltria*

The Valley's breeding goldfinch is widespread in most of the western United States and north-central Mexico. It has been a regular winter resident in the Valley but has recently begun to nest. The species is common in the live oak belt just north of the Valley in Brooks and Kenedy counties (with an old breeding record in Oberholser 1974). I commonly see more than ten birds at the state roadside rest area along U.S. Highway 281 in the oaks near Falfurrias, in summer. However, the closest confirmed breeding during the TBBAP was in Corpus Christi (Benson and Arnold 2001). Over the last five years, I and others have found summering goldfinches in residential and riparian areas of the Valley. Finally, on March 24, 2000, I was able to confirm breeding in the Valley when I saw a male and female attending a weakly flying fledgling near my home in Edinburg.

DISTRIBUTION   Lesser Goldfinches breed regularly from southwestern Washington, southern Utah, central Colorado, and western Oklahoma south through most of the western United States and the highlands of Mexico and Central America to northwestern Central America. They are listed by the AOU as resident throughout their range, but Oberholser mentions that varying numbers head south from their breeding range in Texas.

Since the mid-1990s, I have regularly heard and seen small numbers in summer along the Rio Grande in Starr and Hidalgo counties, and during the last half decade in urban areas of Hidalgo County. So far all four nesting records have come from Hidalgo County, but I expect that the birds breed in all four counties, at least in small numbers.

HABITAT   In the Valley, Lesser Goldfinches inhabit well-vegetated yards and college campuses, and also open forest and woodlands near water. Small flocks (3–11 birds) visit wetland areas with scattered trees, such as the Edinburg Wetland Area, the fringes of the sewage treatment plant in southern McAllen, and the wetlands at Santa Ana. Just to the north of the Valley, goldfinches are common in open oak forests. These forests often contain clearings of various sizes, and the giant, endemic silverleaf sunflower (*Helianthus argophyllus*) may be an important component of the habitat there. In the Valley, Lesser Goldfinches consume seeds of common sunflower (*Helianthus annuus,* known as *mirasol*) and sow thistle (*Sonchus oleraceus*); thus old fields, roadsides, and weedy lawns are important foraging habitats. The only times I have seen Lesser Goldfinches in dense forest are in the late winter, when small numbers of birds visit cedar elms to eat the seeds (and possibly flowers).

HABITS   Like other goldfinches, Lesser Goldfinches are mainly granivorous. They probably consume a variety of small seeds across their North American range, although they have been little studied outside California (Linsdale 1957; Watt and Willoughby 1999). They often eat niger (*Guizotia abyssinica*) seeds at bird feeders (Martin Hagne, pers. comm.), but overall, Lesser Goldfinches seem to visit feeders less regularly than do American Goldfinches (*C. tristis*). Lesser Goldfinches fly hundreds of meters to and from food sources, and one often hears the plaintive *tee-yee* and *ch-ch-ch* call notes as a bird flies over. Lesser Goldfinches regularly visit bird baths for drinking water, perhaps because of the dry seeds that they eat (Oberholser 1974).

Males sing from perches high in trees in gardens or similar habitats with scattered trees. They also sing during display flights, in which the male flies slowly in a circle with a radius of less than 50 feet (15 m) and then returns to the original tree. Sometimes two to four males display in a grove of trees. I have seen two males displaying at the same time, but generally these are leisurely displays without much chasing. The long, rambling song often contains mimicked songs and calls, such as that of the Eastern Phoebe.

Nesting could occur almost year-round in the Valley, with displaying males seen as early as January 23, 2000, and single recent fledglings seen on March 24, 2000 (southwestern Edinburg), September 18, 2001 (Valley Nature Center, Weslaco, by Martin Hagne), and October 13, 2001 (University of Texas–Pan American campus). The nest is small and is placed in the fork of a tree.

I have seen two Valley nests, both on the UTPA campus and both about 10 feet (3 m) up. The first was in a peach (*Prunus persica*) tree. The male and female were looking into that nest when I found it on August 30, 2001, but the nest contained a dead nestling and an unhatched egg on August 31, when I was able to look into it. I suspect that heavy rains on August 28 may have killed the embryo and the new hatchling. The other nest was in an ornamental conifer (species undetermined) in the summer of 2002. On September 5, 2002, a male and female attended a begging fledgling, within 30 feet (9 m) of this nest. Across their U.S. range, nests have been found at widely varying heights in trees and shrubs but generally limited to spring and summer months.

OTHER OBSERVATIONS Lesser Goldfinches are difficult birds to study, perhaps surprisingly. Although they are vocal and occur regularly in residential areas, they are not very territorial, and they appear to wander widely in search of food. I have not learned the meaning of most of their call notes and rely primarily on luck to find nests or youngsters. Interestingly, when looking for the fledglings, the female gives a series of soft notes that sound more like calls that a fledgling would make. The fledglings make a louder call (*cheedee*), which sounds to me like a contact note given by adults. Finally, the birds perch for long periods, sometimes hidden by foliage, making them more difficult to locate than more active warblers, vireos, or kinglets would be.

OUTLOOK Given their adaptability to suburban gardens and broken forest, Lesser Goldfinches should continue to do well. I expect continued growth of the Valley population and eventual confirmation of nesting in most Valley towns. The planting of large numbers of live oaks in Valley residential areas is likely a major factor triggering the colonization of the Valley, given the birds' abundance in oak forests in much of Central Texas

(John C. Arvin, *pers. comm.*). It will be interesting to see if they ever nest on South Padre Island, which has some lush gardens and yards but may not sustain an adequate seed supply for breeding.

Nesting is to be expected (if not already in progress) in northern Tamaulipas, and eventually there may be continuous breeding range where habitat allows in northeastern Mexico. The species is already common in the Sierra Madre Oriental in places such as Chipinque Ecological Park and adjacent suburban areas of the Monterrey metropolitan area in Nuevo León (Sada de Hermosillo et al. 1995). Strangely enough, given their abundance elsewhere in Texas and the United States, **House Finches** (*Carpodacus mexicanus*) are rare in the Valley and have never nested, despite being common in much of Texas and northern Mexico.

FAMILY PASSERIDAE

The **House Sparrow** (*Passer domesticus*), omnipresent in the United States, is common also in the Valley. First brought to Texas in 1867, House Sparrows had spread to Nuevo Laredo, Tamaulipas, by 1901 and Brownsville by about 1905. However, the first Valley specimen was not collected until 1924 (Oberholser 1974). Although they are known to use Bank Swallow burrows for nests, House Sparrows are almost entirely restricted to the immediate vicinity of humans for nesting. They build nests in crevices in buildings, nest boxes, holes in light poles and traffic lights, old woodpecker holes in posts or trees, and possibly in Altamira Oriole nests. Their main food sources are human-derived, such as seeds at bird feeders, feedlots, and chicken coops and scraps at fast-food restaurants, However, I have seen them gleaning and hawking insects in trees and shrubs, particularly during the nesting season, when the growing youngsters need protein. House Sparrows occur in large natural areas only when feeding stations attract them—such as along the former recreational vehicle area at Bentsen and at the Santa Ana headquarters.

Northern Mockingbirds generally are good indicators of species present within earshot of their territories, so I was interested to hear a Northern Mockingbird imitating the weak song of the House Sparrow at Santa Ana on May 28, 1997. The mockingbird was near the southern end of the Vireo Trail, more than 0.6 of a mile (1 km) from the nearest Santa Ana feeding station, but I assume the mockingbird had heard House Sparrows on cattle ranches on the Mexican side of the river.

Concluding Remarks

To do science is to search for repeated patterns, not simply to accumulate facts.

ROBERT H. MACARTHUR, GEOGRAPHICAL ECOLOGIST

The more than 170 past and present breeding species in the Valley all have their own particular habitat needs and current status, which I have attempted to summarize. In these concluding remarks I outline changes in the Valley breeding bird community and make suggestions for future research and conservation efforts regarding birds and their habitats. I focus on rare species, especially those limited to the South Texas region within the United States, but I also address overall diversity issues.

CHANGES IN THE VALLEY'S BREEDING AVIFAUNA

Since the earliest ornithological research of Sennett and Merrill in the 1870s (and Dresser's briefer visit in the 1860s), the Valley's breeding avifauna has changed dramatically. As noted repeatedly in this book and elsewhere, the Valley's human population has grown almost exponentially, and many habitats have been altered drastically during that time. The major trends have been increases in bird species capable of using agricultural and urban habitats; decreases in forest and wetland birds and those particularly susceptible to brood parasitism by Bronzed Cowbirds; and invasion of the Valley by birds once restricted to areas to the north, south, or west. Table 2 presents those species for which breeding status has changed during the last 125 years.

Several trends can be seen in the lists of disappearing and invading species. Terrestrial species dominate both lists, perhaps because aquatic species have historically tended to have broader distributions and possibly have greater habitat tolerance. There are more "new" species to the Valley than species that have disappeared. Approximately equal numbers of species have invaded the Valley from ranges to the north and south. Most invaders are

Table 2. Bird species whose breeding status has changed in the Lower Rio Grande Valley, 1877–2002. The direction of the species' main breeding range from the Valley is shown. "I" indicates introduced species, not native to North America. "Regular" indicates confirmed breeding in more than one location (city, refuge, etc.) for more than one year. Additional details are given in the species accounts.

North	South
ORIGINALLY BREEDING REGULARLY BUT NOW ABSENT OR EXTREMELY RARE AS BREEDERS	
Common Tern	Rose-throated Becard
Blue-gray Gnatcatcher	Gray-crowned Yellowthroat
Yellow-breasted Chat	White-collared Seedeater
Summer Tanager	
Orchard Oriole	
ORIGINALLY ABSENT BUT NOW REGULAR BREEDERS	
Rock Pigeon (I)	Hook-billed Kite
Black Phoebe (or NW)	Cattle Egret (I)
Western Kingbird	Green Parakeet (I?)
Purple Martin	Red-crowned Parrot (I?)
Cave Swallow (or NW)	Ringed Kingfisher
Barn Swallow	Tropical Kingbird
Loggerhead Shrike	Brown Jay
European Starling (I)	Clay-colored Robin
Lesser Goldfinch	Altamira Oriole
House Sparrow (I)	

species that can forage and nest successfully in urban and/or agricultural habitats, such as Tropical Kingbird, common on golf courses. Lesser Goldfinches are becoming increasingly common in the Valley's suburban "oak forests," while Blue Jays are just getting a toehold here.

Red-crowned Parrots and Green Parakeets take advantage of more diverse and perhaps more predictable urban fruits and nuts, while the Valley's invading swifts, swallows, and martins simply had to use artificial nest sites to become established. Increasing acceptance of urbanization has allowed Loggerhead Shrikes to begin to establish themselves. The least successful invaders in terms of numbers are those that depend on substantial tracts of native habitats, like the Hook-billed Kite and Brown Jay.

Species that have disappeared tend to be birds of mature forest or successional scrub habitats. Some are quite susceptible to cowbird parasitism. Increasing cowbird numbers in the heavily agricultural sections of the Valley may have been too much for the Yellow-breasted Chat, Orchard Oriole, Blue-gray Gnatcatcher, and Summer Tanager. Cowbirds may have helped cause population declines and range contraction in other species, such as Blue Grosbeak and Audubon's Oriole. Habitat loss and deterioration due to lack of flooding have probably also played a major role. For example, Yellow-breasted Chats, Orchard Orioles, and Blue Grosbeaks remain common along the Rio Grande around Eagle Pass and Del Rio, where local rains still cause periodic flooding, supporting a denser layer of shrubs and herbaceous plants, and where the habitat is less fragmented by agricultural development.

For other species, habitat loss or deterioration has probably been the main factor causing declines, such as for species inhabiting marsh edges, like Gray-crowned Yellowthroat and White-collared Seedeater (see later discussion). Although there may be some competition for food, nest sites, or breeding habitat, I am not aware of any cases in which an invading species has "pushed out" a disappearing species. Any possible impact of global warming is hard to see, and discerning such effects would probably require a larger geographic scale or more complete data set.

There is a need for more research on several species whose breeding status is questionable for a variety of reasons. Examples include Red-tailed Hawk, Aplomado Falcon, Eurasian Collared-Dove, Rose-throated Becard, and Yellow-green Vireo, to name just a few. Such cases are examined more fully in the species accounts, and I hope that this book may help stimulate additional research on these and other Valley breeding birds.

CONSERVATION NEEDS OF VALLEY BREEDING BIRDS

In addition to the species that have disappeared as nesters, there are more species that have declined in numbers and range within the Valley in historical times. The Vermilion Flycatcher, Black-throated Sparrow, and Varied Bunting may no longer breed in coastal Cameron County, for example, but still breed in the Valley. The amount of suitable nesting habitat is a prime factor, of course. The species currently in greatest need are those requiring tall riparian forest (such as Red-billed Pigeon and Tropical Parula), those particularly sensitive to cowbird parasitism (such as Audubon's and Hooded orioles), and those needing large tracts of land (such as Hook-billed Kite, Gray Hawk, and other raptors).

Some species can apparently do well in maturing suburban woodlands, especially when a variety of fruiting and flowering trees and shrubs are planted. Plain Chachalaca, Golden-fronted Woodpecker, and Buff-bellied Hummingbird are examples. Nest box programs can continue to help Purple Martins and Black-bellied Whistling-Ducks, while continued growth of trees provides additional nest sites for White-winged Doves, Great Kiskadees, Long-billed Thrashers, and other species. Some birds, like Brown Jay, may always be surprisingly rare, for unknown reasons.

We will never restore the large-scale flooding pattern that typified the Valley before upstream water demands and dams took their toll on river flow. Floods, varying in timing and severity, help to maintain the overall diversity of riverine ecosystems (Bayley 1995). In the Valley, such flooding may have maintained disturbance-dependent plant and bird communities; an example would be the lush herbaceous vegetation developing in drying resacas and supporting White-collared Seedeaters, Gray-crowned Yellowthroats, Yellow-breasted Chats, and other species (Davis 1940; Bayley 1995). Drainage of remaining wetlands has probably drastically reduced the amount of wetland habitat in the Valley, especially in southern Cameron County, with its many resacas.

Flooding of more limited areas and continued wetland maintenance and restoration may help keep selected areas as examples and may attract at least some disturbance-dependent birds (Decamps 1993; Castillo 1997; Molles et al. 1998). Large-scale flooding is no longer feasible, so we will probably never see the habitat needed to support the large numbers of Red-billed Pigeons seen in the 1870s through the 1940s, but we may at least be able to maintain some and restore other appropriate habitat. Finding adequate amounts of fresh water will require a cooperative effort between the United States and Mexico, given rapidly growing Valley and regional populations (Contreras-Balderas and Lozano-Vilano 1994).

Tall thorn forest of Texas ebony, anacua, coma, and other mainly evergreen species may be a partial substitute for tall deciduous forest of Mexican ash, cedar elm, and sugar hackberry. Restoration of the former may be more feasible, given its lower water demands, and it should be encouraged in suitable lowland soils. Such riparian forest, although probably taking considerable time to develop, may help maintain more of our original breeding bird community (Knopf et al. 1988; Naiman et al. 1993). Species that nest in epiphytes, such as Tropical Parula and Northern Beardless-Tyrannulet, will benefit if Spanish moss and ball-moss grow in sufficient quantities in regenerating tall thorn forest, something that will also take time.

Frugivorous birds may help revegetation efforts, especially if the fields to be revegetated are small and fruit sources are nearby (Cardoso Da Silva et al. 1996). A high proportion of Valley woody plants have fruits designed for bird dispersal (Jurado et al. 2001), and many Valley birds are at least part-time frugivores. Northern Mockingbirds are perhaps the most abundant permanent resident frugivore frequenting semi-open habitats, but Great

Kiskadees, Plain Chachalacas, White-eyed Vireos, and other resident species may assist (and benefit from) revegetation efforts. Nonbreeding Cedar Waxwings (*Bombycilla cedrorum*) and American Robins may also consume much fruit and disperse large quantities of seeds in years when bird abundance and fruit abundance match. We need more information on the diet of frugivorous birds and the nutritional quality of fruits (Everitt and Alaniz 1981).

Valley birds may not in general be as dependent on large, contiguous tracts as are birds of temperate deciduous forests, with their forest-interior species. However, given the highly fragmented nature of most of the Valley, efforts at acquiring and revegetating a wildlife corridor should remain a high priority for the national wildlife refuge system. Private land acquisition and land easements will also help greatly, as will continued careful development of ecotourism in and near the Valley. Controlling populations of Bronzed Cowbirds will be a continuing difficulty, given their heavy use of the surrounding agricultural and urban landscape; species like Audubon's Orioles and Summer Tanagers may always depend on more remote, less fragmented landscapes.

We should not, however, assume that only forest and woodland species need our help. Attention is also needed in grasslands and mesquite savannas, where species like Botteri's Sparrow, Cassin's Sparrow, White-tailed Kite, and even Aplomado Falcon may be threatened by creeping invasion of thorn scrub. A balance must be struck between grassland and woodland restoration, ideally based on what is most suitable for a particular soil type and disturbance pattern. The role of fire and limited grazing in maintaining and restoring Valley grasslands and mesquite savanna should be studied further (Vora and Messerly 1990). Differences in soils, moisture regime, management goals, and presence of invasive exotic grasses indicate that careful study would be needed before applying lessons learned in northern sections of South Texas (Scifres and Hamilton 1993).

The current effect of pesticides on birds remains unclear. Some recent studies have shown declines in some pesticides and relatively low levels of others in tissues of wetland and coastal birds (Mora 1996; Mora et al. 1997; Wainwright et al. 2001). However, since pesticide use remains high in Valley farmlands and evidence of contamination has been found in urban resacas, continued research and monitoring are needed (Mora et al. 2001; Wainwright et al. 2001).

Conservation of Valley specialties will require similar efforts in Mexico, since most of these species have such limited U.S. ranges. Habitat conservation and restoration are needed, especially in lowland areas suitable for agriculture and grazing. Continued development of ecotourism will enhance protection efforts in areas such as the El Cielo Man and the Biosphere conservation area near Gómez Farías, in southwestern Tamaulipas. The efforts of private landowners outside officially protected areas need to be encouraged also. A particular problem south of the border is the taking of parrots and several other species—Painted Buntings, Northern Cardinals, Altamira Orioles, and Green Jays—for the national and international pet trade (Contreras-Balderas et al. 2001).

Although we cannot expect to see vast temporary marshes in the lower Valley, or miles of road shaded by tall Mexican ash trees, selected forests and wetlands can and should be maintained for their conservation and educational values. In both habitats, research is needed to determine best management practices for plant and animal species. With more effective water conservation measures, some water can be made available for maintaining biodiversity. Given the growing interest in Valley birds and habitats locally, nationally, and even internationally, we must continue to work creatively to protect declining species.

The warning from other dry-country rivers like the Gila River of Arizona is clear: major habitats can be lost. In Amadeo Rea's 1983 *Once a River: Bird Life and Habitat Changes along the Middle Gila,* University of Arizona ecologist Charles H. Lowe is quoted as noting that "along the formerly great Gila River (the now dry bed of which stretches across the Sonoran Desert of western Arizona) there were extensive marshes, swamps, and floodplains with cattail . . . bulrush . . . giant reed . . . and many trees. The dense vegetation of these well-developed riparian communities often stood 10–15 feet (3–4.5 m) high and supported a tremendous quantity and variety of wildlife."

The lower Rio Grande may be more like the lower Colorado River, where small remnant riparian forests remain in sea of agriculture and disturbed habitats (Rosenberg et al. 1991), than like Rea's middle Gila, but in any case it will take some effort to conserve and enhance what is left. Maintaining the unique temperate-tropical breeding bird life (Gehlbach 1981) of the Valley will help avoid the biotic homogenization occurring all over the world (Lockwood and McKinney 2001) and will sustain the Valley's status as one of North America's special places.

The Valley has no flagship species like the Golden-cheeked Warbler (*Dendroica chrysoparia*) and Black-capped Vireo (*Vireo atricapillus*) of the Texas Hill Country, but we do have flagship biotic communities and biological interactions. The mixed-species nesting associations of kiskadees, kingbirds, orioles, and other birds along a verdant riverbank are in a class of their own. The noise and activity of a healthy marsh with nesting Least Grebes, Least Bitterns, and various herons, egrets, ducks, and rails is another special focus. No one who listens to the dawn chorus in a mosaic of thorn

forest and riparian forest will soon forget the exuberance of the Plain Chachalacas, White-winged Doves, and Olive Sparrows. These associations and
the subtle beauty of a coastal savanna or prairie and salt flat bird community
are all elements our children and future visitors need to be able to experience
and enjoy. Let us help make sure that the lower Rio Grande, *el bajo* Río
Bravo, remains "still a river" to support our diverse breeding bird life.

REFERENCES

Allen, C. R., S. A. Phillips, and M. R. Trostle. 1993. Range expansion by the ecologically disruptive red imported fire ant (Hymenoptera: Formicidae) into the Texas Rio Grande Valley. *Southwestern Entomologist* 18:315–16.

Allen, C. R., R. D. Willey, P. F. Myers, P. M. Horton, and J. Buff. 2000. Impact of red imported fire ant infestation on Northern Bobwhite quail abundance trends in southeastern United States. *Journal of Agricultural and Urban Entomology* 17:43–51.

Amadon, D. 1940. Hosts of the cowbirds. *Auk* 57:257.

Amadon, D., and D. R. Eckleberry. 1955. Observations of Mexican birds. *Condor* 57:65–80.

American Ornithologists' Union. 1998. Check-list of North American Birds, 7th Edition. Washington, D.C.: American Ornithologists' Union.

Amos, E. J. R. 1991. *A Guide to the Birds of Bermuda.* Warwick, Bermuda: Corncrake.

Anderson, J. T., and T. C. Tacha. 1999. Habitat use by Masked Ducks along the Gulf Coast of Texas. *Wilson Bulletin* 111:119–21.

Archer, S. 1989. Have southern Texas savannas been converted to woodlands in recent history? *American Naturalist* 134:545–61.

———. 1990. Development and stability of grassy/woody mosaics in a subtropical savanna parkland, Texas, U.S.A. *J. Biogeography* 17:453–62.

Archer, S., C. Scifres, C. R. Bassham, and R. Maggio. 1988. Autogenic succession in a subtropical savanna: Conversion of grassland to thorn woodland. *Ecological Monographs* 58:111–27.

Arnold, K. A. 1977. County nesting records for caprimulgids in South and Central Texas. *Bulletin of the Texas Ornithological Society* 10:17–18.

———. 1980. Rufous-capped Warbler and White-collared Seedeater from Webb County, Texas. *Bulletin of the Texas Ornithological Society* 13:27.

Arvin, J. C. 2001. *An Annotated Checklist of the Birds of the Gómez Farías Region, Southwestern Tamaulipas, Mexico.* Austin: Texas Parks and Wildlife Department.

Audubon, J. W. 1906. *Audubon's Western Journal: 1849–1850.* Being the MS record of a trip from New York to Texas, and an overland journey through Mexico and Arizona to the gold-fields of California. Cleveland, Ohio: Arthur H. Clark Company.

Baicich, P., and C. J. O. Harrison. 1997. *A Field Guide to the Nests, Eggs, and Nestlings of North American Birds.* San Diego, Calif.: Academic Press.

Baird, S. F. 1859. Birds of the boundary. Pp. 1–32 in *Report on the United States and Mexican Boundary Survey, Made under the Direction of the Secretary of the Interior,* Part II: *Zoology of the Boundary,* ed. W. H. Emory. Austin: Texas State Historical Association (reprint 1987).

Banks, R. C., C. Cicero, J. L. Dunn, A. W. Kratter, P. C. Rasmussen, J. V. Remsen, Jr., J. D. Rising, and D. F. Stotz. 2003. Forty-fourth supplement to the American Ornithologists' Union Check-list of North American Birds. *Auk* 120:923–31.

Banks, R. C., C. Cicero, J. L. Dunn, A. W. Kratter, P. C. Rasmussen, J. V. Remsen, Jr., and D. F. Stotz. 2002. Forty-third supplement to the American Ornithologists' Union Check-list of North American Birds. *Auk* 119:897–906.

———. 2004. Forty-fifth supplement to the American Ornithologists' Union Check-list of North American Birds. *Auk* 121:985–95.

Bartlett, J. R. 1854. *Personal Narrative of Explorations and Incidents in Texas, New Mexico, California, Sonora, and Chihuahua: Connected with the United States and Mexico Boundary Commission, during the Years 1850, '51, '52, and '53.* New York: Appleton.

Bayley, P. 1995. Understanding large river floodplain ecosystems. *BioScience* 45:153–58.

Bedichek, R. 1947. *Adventures with a Texas Naturalist.* Garden City, N.Y.: Doubleday.

Bednarz, J. C. 1987. Pair and group reproductive success, polyandry, and cooperative breeding in Harris' Hawks. *Auk* 104:393–404.

———. 1988. Cooperative hunting in Harris' Hawks (*Parabuteo unicinctus*). *Science* 239:1525–27.

Beebe, William. 1923. *Jungle Days.* Garden City, N.Y.: Garden City Publishers.

Beecher, W. J. 1950. Convergent evolution in the American orioles. *Wilson Bulletin* 62:51–86.

Behrstock, R. A., and T. L. Eubanks. 1997. Additions to the avifauna of Nuevo León, Mexico, with notes on new breeding records and infrequently seen species. *Cotinga* 7:27–30.

Belton, W. 1985. *Birds of Rio Grande do Sul, Brazil.* Part 2: *Formicariidae through Corvidae.* Bulletin of the American Museum of Natural History no. 180.

Bendire, C. 1895. *Life Histories of North American Birds, from the Parrots to the Grackles.* U.S. National Museum Special Bulletin 3.

Benson, K. L. P., and K. A. Arnold. 2001. The Texas Breeding Bird Atlas. Texas A&M University System, College Station and Corpus Christi. http://tbba.cbi.tamucc.edu (July 12, 2001).

Benson, K. L. P., R. H. Benson, and A. Garza de León. 1989. Additions to the avifauna of Coahuila, Mexico. *Bulletin of the Texas Ornithological Society* 22:22–23.

Bent, A. C. 1958. *Life Histories of North American Blackbirds, Orioles, Tanagers, and Allies.* U.S. National Museum Bulletin 211.

Bergstrom, P. W. 1988. Breeding biology of Wilson's Plovers. *Wilson Bulletin* 100:25–35.

Berlandier, Jean Louis. 1826–34. *Journey to Mexico during the years 1826 to 1834.* Trans. Jean M. Ohlendorf. Austin: Texas State Historical Commission.

Berrett, D. G. 1962. The birds of the Mexican State of Tabasco. Ph. D. dissertation, Louisiana State University, Baton Rouge.

Bildstein, K. L. 1993. *White Ibis: Wetland Wanderer.* Washington, D.C.: Smithsonian Institution Press.

Binford, L. C. 1989. *A Distributional Survey of the Birds of the Mexican State of Oaxaca.* Ornithological Monographs 43.

Blair, W. F. 1950. The biotic provinces of Texas. *Texas Journal of Science* 2:93–117.

Blankenship, T. L. and J. T. Anderson. 1993. A large concentration of Masked Ducks (*Oxyura dominica*) on the Welder Wildlife Refuge, San Patricio County, Texas. *Bulletin of the Texas Ornithological Society* 26:19–21.

Boal, C. W., B. D. Bibles, and R. W. Mannan. 1997. Nest defense and mobbing behavior of Elf Owls. *Journal of Raptor Research* 31:286–87.

Bolen, E. G., and M. K. Rylander. 1983. *Whistling-Ducks: Zoogeography, Ecology, Anatomy.* Texas Tech University Museum Special Publication 20:1–67.

Borror, D. J. 1987. Song in the White-eyed Vireo. *Wilson Bulletin* 99:377–97.

Brandt, H. W. 1951. *Arizona and Its Bird Life.* Cleveland, Ohio: Bird Research Foundation.

Brennan, L. A. 1991. How can we reverse the Northern Bobwhite population decline? *Wildlife Society Bulletin* 19:544–55.

Bridges, A. S., M. J. Peterson, N. J. Silvy, F. E. Smeins, and X. B. Wu. 2001. Differential influence of weather on regional quail abundance in Texas. *Journal of Wildlife Management* 65:10–18.

Brown, J. L., A. B. Montoya, E. J. Gott, and M. Carti. 2004. Piracy as an important foraging method of Aplomado Falcons in southern Texas and northern Mexico. *Wilson Bulletin* 115:357–59.

Brush, T. 1983. Cavity use by cavity-nesting birds and response to manipulation. *Condor* 85:461–66.

———. 1993. Great Kiskadee nesting on a Purple Martin box. *Bulletin of the Texas Ornithological Society* 26:21–22.

———. 1995. Habitat use by wintering shorebirds along the Lower Laguna Madre, Texas. *Texas Journal of Science* 47:179–90.

———. 1998a. Recent nesting and current status of Red-billed Pigeon along the lower Rio Grande in Texas. *Bulletin of the Texas Ornithological Society* 31:22–26.

———. 1998b. Olive Sparrow (*Arremonops rufivirgatus*). In *The Birds of North America*, no. 325, ed. A. Poole and F. Gill. Philadelphia: Birds of North America.

———. 1998c. A closer look: Altamira Oriole. *Birding* 30:46–53.

———. 1999a. Current status of Northern Beardless-Tyrannulet and Tropical Parula in Bentsen–Rio Grande Valley State Park and Santa Ana National Wildlife Refuge, southern Texas. *Bulletin of the Texas Ornithological Society* 32:3–12.

———. 1999b. Couch's Kingbird (*Tyrannus couchii*). In *The Birds of North America*, no. 437, ed. A. Poole and F. Gill. Philadelphia: Birds of North America.

———. 2000a. Nesting of Rose-throated Becard *Pachyramphus aglaiae* (Passeriformes: *Incertae sedis*) and Clay-colored Robin *Turdus grayi* (Passeriformes: Turdidae) in Hidalgo County, Texas. *Texas Journal of Science* 52:165–68.

———. 2000b. First nesting record of Blue Jay (*Cyanocitta cristata*) in Hidalgo County, Texas. *Bulletin of the Texas Ornithological Society* 33:35–36.

———. 2000c. Bronzed Cowbirds (*Molothrus aeneus*) still parasitize Hooded Orioles (*Icterus cucullatus*) in the Lower Rio Grande Valley of Texas. *Bulletin of the Texas Ornithological Society* 33:9–11.

———. 2000d. Audubon's Oriole: The shy, beautiful whistler of South Texas. *Texas Birds* 2:4–9.

———. 2001. First nesting records of the Black Phoebe (*Sayornis nigricans*) in southernmost Texas. *Southwestern Naturalist* 46:237–38.

———. 2003. First nesting attempt of Yellow-faced Grassquit (*Tiaris olivacea*) in the United States. *Bulletin of the Texas Ornithological Society* 36:8–9.

Brush, T., and A. Cantu. 1998. Changes in the breeding bird community of subtropical evergreen forest in the Lower Rio Grande Valley of Texas, 1970s–1990s. *Texas Journal of Science* 50:123–32.

Brush, T., B. W. Anderson, and R. D. Ohmart. 1990. Habitat use by cavity-nesting birds of desert riparian woodland. Pp. 191–98 in *Managing Wildlife in the Southwest*, ed. P. R. Krausman and N. S. Smith. Phoenix: Arizona Chapter, Wildlife Society.

Brush, T., and J. C. Eitniear. 2002. Status and recent nesting of Muscovy Duck (*Cairina moschata*) in the Rio Grande Valley, Texas. *Bulletin of the Texas Ornithological Society* 35:12–14.

Brush, T., and J. W. Fitzpatrick. 2002. Great Kiskadee (*Pitangus sulphuratus*). In *The Birds of North America*, no. 622, ed. A. Poole and F. Gill. Philadelphia: Birds of North America.

Burleigh, T. D. 1958. *Georgia Birds.* Norman: University of Oklahoma Press.

Burrows, D. B. 1918. The Audubon Oriole (*Icterus audubonii*). *Oologist* 35:128–31.

Cade, T. J., and C. P. Woods. 1997. Changes in distribution and abundance of the Loggerhead Shrike. *Conservation Biology* 11:21–31.

Cardoso da Silva, J. M., C. Uhl, and G. Murray. 1996. Plant succession, landscape management, and the ecology of frugivorous birds in abandoned Amazonian pasture. *Conservation Biology* 10:491–503.

Carter, M. D. 1986. The parasitic behavior of the Bronzed Cowbird in South Texas. *Condor* 88:11–25.

Cassin, J. 1856. *Illustrations of the Birds of California, Texas, Oregon, British and Russian America.* Philadelphia: J. B. Lippincott (reprint Austin: Texas State Historical Association, 1991).

Castañeda, C. E. 1938. *Our Catholic Heritage in Texas, 1519–1936*, Vol. 3: *The Mission Era: The Missions at Work 1731–1761.* Austin: Von Boeckmann–Jones.

Castillo, C. D. 1997. Effects of artificial flooding on the vegetation and avifauna of riparian woodlands at Santa Ana National Wildlife Refuge, Hidalgo County, Texas. M.S. thesis, University of Texas–Pan American, Edinburg.

Casto, S. D. 1996. Use of dog food by birds in southern Texas. *Bulletin of the Texas Ornithological Society* 29:46–47.

———. 1999. Nest sites of Curve-billed Thrashers at a rural dwelling in southern Texas. *Bulletin of the Texas Ornithological Society* 32:44–46.

———. 2000. H. B. Butcher and the birds of Laredo. *Bulletin of the Texas Ornithological Society* 33:32–35.

Cavazos, I. 1985. *Historia de Nuevo León, con noticias sobre Coahuila, Tamaulipas, Texas y Nuevo Mexico, escrito en el siglo XVII por el Capitan Alonzo de León, Juan Bautista Chapa y el General Fernando Sánchez de Zamora.* Nuevo León, Mexico: Government of Monterrey.

Chance, J. E. (ed.). 1994. *Mexico under Fire. Being the Diary of Samuel Ryan Curtis, 3rd Ohio Regiment, during the American Military Occupation of Northern Mexico 1846–1847.* Fort Worth: Texas Christian University Press.

Chapman, B. R. 1988. History of the White Pelican colonies in South Texas and northern Tamaulipas. *Colonial Waterbirds* 11:275–83.

Chapman, C. A., L. J. Chapman, and L. Lefebvre. 1989. Variability in parrot flock size: Possible functions of communal roosts. *Condor* 91:842–47.

Chavez-Ramirez, F., and A. Moreno-Valdez. 1999. Buff-bellied Hummingbird (*Amazilia yucatanensis*). In *The Birds of North America*, no. 388, ed. A. Poole and F. Gill. Philadelphia: Birds of North America.

Christensen, A. F. 2000. The fifteenth and twentieth century colonization of the Basin of Mexico by the Great-tailed Grackle (*Quiscalus mexicanus*). *Global Ecology and Biogeography* 9:415–20.

Christensen, Z. D., D. B. Pence, and G. Scott. 1978. Notes on the food habits of the Plain Chachalaca from the Lower Rio Grande Valley. *Wilson Bulletin* 90:647–48.

Clark, W. S., and B. K. Wheeler. 1989. Unusual roost site selection and staging behavior of Black-shouldered Kites. *J. Raptor Research* 23:116–17.

Clotfelter, E. D., and T. Brush. 1995. Unusual parasitism by the Bronzed Cowbird. *Condor* 97:814–15.

Clover, E. U. 1937. Vegetational survey of the Lower Rio Grande Valley, Texas. *Madroño* 4:41–66; 77–100.

Coates-Estrada, R., and A. Estrada. 1986. Fruiting and frugivores at a strangler fig in the tropical rain forest of Los Tuxtlas, Mexico. *Journal of Tropical Ecology* 2:349–59.

Coates-Estrada, R., A. Estrada, and D. Meritt, Jr. 1993. Foraging by parrots (*Amazona autumnalis*) on fruits of *Stemmadenia donell-smithii* (Apocynaceae) in the tropical rain forest of Los Tuxtlas, Mexico. *Journal of Tropical Ecology* 9:121–24.

Coldren, M. K., C. L. Coldren, K. G. Smith, and S. S. Lacy. 1998. First neotropic cormorant, *Phalacrocorax brasilianus* (Aves: Phalacrocoracidae), breeding record for Arkansas. *Southwestern Naturalist* 43:496–98.

Collias, N. E., and E. C. Collias. 1984. *Nest Building and Bird Behavior.* Princeton, N.J.: Princeton University Press.

Contreras-Balderas, A. J., J. A. García-Salas, A. Guzmán-Velasco, and J. I. González-Rojas. 2001. Aprovachamiento de las aves cinegeticas, de ornato y canoras de Nuevo León, Mexico. *Ciencia Universidad Autónoma de Nuevo León* 4:462–69.

Contreras-Balderas, A. J., and M. Lourdes Lozano-Vilano. 1994. Water, endangered fishes, and development perspectives in arid lands of Mexico. *Conservation Biology* 8:379–87.

Cooper, A., and D. Penny. 1997. Mass survival of birds across the Cretaceous-Tertiary boundary: Molecular evidence. *Science* 275:1109–13.

Coopwood, B. 1900. Route of Cabeza de Vaca. *Texas State Historical Association Quarterly* 3:229–64.

Dawson, J. W., and R. W. Mannan. 1989. A comparison of two methods of estimating breeding group size in Harris' Hawks. *Auk* 106:480–83.

Davis, L. I. 1940. Breeding bird census: Elm-ash association. *Bird Lore* 42:488–89.

———. 1945a. Rose-throated Becard nesting in Cameron County, Texas. *Auk* 62: 316–17.

———. 1945b. Yellow-green Vireo nesting in Cameron County, Texas. *Auk* 62:146.

———. 1957. Observations on Mexican birds. *Wilson Bulletin* 69:364–67.

———. 1958. Acoustic evidence of relationships in North American crows. *Wilson Bulletin* 70:151–67.

———. 1966. *Birds of the Rio Grande Delta Region: An Annotated Checklist.* Harlingen: Published by the author.

———. 1972. *A Field Guide to the Birds of Mexico and Central America.* Austin: University of Texas Press.

———. 1974. *Birds of the Rio Grande Delta Region: An Annotated Checklist,* rev. ed. Austin: Published by the author.

Decamps, H. 1993. River margins and environmental change. *Ecological Applications* 3:441–45.

Delacour, J., and D. Amadon. 1973. *Curassows and Related Birds.* New York: American Museum of Natural History.

Delnicki, Donald. 1978. Second occurrence and first successful nesting of the Hook-billed Kite in the United States. *Auk* 95:427.

D'Heursel, A., and C. F. B. Haddad. 1999. Unpalatability of *Hyla semilineata* tadpoles (Anura) to captive and free-ranging predators. *Ethology Ecology and Evolution* 4:339–48.

Diamond, D. D. 1998. *An Old-Growth Definition for Southwestern Subtropical Upland Forests.* USDA Forest Service General Technical Report SRS-21.

Dicken, S. N. 1938. Cotton regions of Mexico. *Economic Geography* 14:363–71.

Dickerman, R. W. 1960. Red-eyed Cowbird parasitizes Song Sparrow and Mexican Cacique. *Auk* 77:472–73.

———. 1964. A specimen of Fuertes' Oriole, *Icterus fuertesi,* from Texas. *Auk* 81:433.

———. 1986. Notes on the plumage of the Paramo Seedeater (*Catamenia homochroa*). *Auk* 103:227–30.

Dickey, Donald R., and A. J. Van Rossem. 1938. *The Birds of El Salvador.* Zoological Series 23. Chicago: Field Museum of Natural History.

Dinsmore, J. J., and S. J. Dinsmore. 1993. Range expansion of Great-tailed Grackles in the 1900s. *Journal of the Iowa Academy of Science* 100:54–59.

Dixon, K. L. 1990. Constancy of margins of the hybrid zone in titmice of the *Parus bicolor* complex in coastal Texas. *Auk* 107:429–31.

Drake, K. R., J. E. Thompson, K. L. Drake, and C. Zonick. 2001. Movements, habitat use, and survival of nonbreeding Piping Plovers. *Condor* 103:259–67.

Dresser, H. E. 1865–66. Notes on the birds of southern Texas. *Ibis* 1:312–30; 466–95; 2:23–46.

Dunne, P. 1992. *The Feather Quest: A North American Birder's Year.* New York: Dutton.

Dyrcz, A. 2000. Observations at nests of the Lesser Kiskadee (*Philohydor lictor*) on Barro Colorado Island (Republic of Panama). *Ornitología Neotropical* 11:359–62.

Easterla, D. A., and R. H. Wauer. 1972. Bronzed Cowbird in West Texas and two bill abnormalities. *Southwestern Naturalist* 17:293–312.

Eaton, S. W., and E. P. Edwards. 1947. An unorthodox nest of the Rose-throated Becard. *Auk* 64:466–67.

Edwards, E. P., and R. B. Lea. 1955. Birds of the Monserrate area, Chiapas, Mexico. *Condor* 57:31–54.

Eitniear, J. C. 1997. White-collared Seedeater (*Sporophila torqueola*). In *The Birds of North America,* no. 278, ed. A. Poole and F. Gill. Philadelphia: Academy of Natural Sciences, and Washington, D.C.: American Ornithologists' Union.

———. 1999. Masked Duck (*Nomonyx dominicus*). In *The Birds of North America,* no. 393, ed. A. Poole and F. Gill. Philadelphia: Birds of North America.

Eitniear, J. C., and A. Aragon-Tapia. 1997. Traditional use of limestone cave by nesting Green Parakeets (*Aratinga holochlora*). *Ornitología Neotropical* 8:243–44.

———. 2000. Red-billed Pigeon (*Columba flavirostris*) nest predated by Groove-billed Ani (*Crotophaga sulcirostris*). *Ornitología Neotropical* 11:231–32.

Eitniear, J. C., A. Aragon-Tapia, and J. T. Baccus. 1998. Unusual nesting of the Muscovy Duck *Cairina moschata* in northeastern Mexico. *Texas Journal of Science* 50:173–75.

Eitniear, J. C., and T. Rueckle. 1995. Successful nesting of the White-collared Seedeater in Zapata County, Texas. *Bulletin of the Texas Ornithological Society* 28:20–22.

———. 1996. Noteworthy avian breeding records from Zapata County, Texas. *Bulletin of the Texas Ornithological Society* 29:43–44.

Emory, W. H. 1857–59. *United States and Mexican Boundary Survey Made under the Di-*

rection of the Secretary of the Interior. Intro. by W. H. Goetzmann. Washington, D.C.: C. Wendell (reprint Austin: Texas State Historical Association, 1987).

Enkerlin-Hoeflich, E. C., and K. M. Hogan. 1997. Red-crowned Parrot (*Amazona viridigenalis*). In *The Birds of North America,* no. 292, ed. A. Poole and F. Gill. Philadelphia: Academy of Natural Science, Washington, D.C.: American Ornithologists' Union.

Epps, S. A. 2002. *Parrots of South Florida.* Fort Lauderdale, Fla.: Published by the author.

Eubanks, T. L. 1994. The status and distribution of the Piping Plovers in Texas. *Bulletin of the Texas Ornithological Society* 27:19–25.

Everitt, J. L., and M. A. Alaniz. 1981. Nutrient content of cactus and woody plant fruits eaten by birds and mammals in South Texas, U.S. *Southwestern Naturalist* 26: 301–306.

Everitt, J. L., D. L. Drawe, and R. I. Lonard. 2002. *Trees, Shrubs, and Cacti of South Texas.* Lubbock: Texas Tech University Press.

Fall, B. A. 1973. Noteworthy bird records from South Texas (Kenedy County). *Southwestern Naturalist* 18:244–47.

Farmer, M. 1990. A Herring Gull nest in Texas. *Bulletin of the Texas Ornithological Society* 23:27–28.

Feinsinger, P. 1976. Organization of a tropical guild of nectarivorous birds. *Ecological Monographs* 46:257–91.

Fernandez de Oviedo, G. 1526. *Natural History of the West Indies.* Trans. and ed. S. A. Stoudemire. University of North Carolina Studies in Romance Languages and Literatures no. 32, 1959. Chapel Hill: University of North Carolina Press.

ffrench, R. 1976. *A Guide to the birds of Trinidad and Tobago.* Valley Forge, Penn.: Hardwood.

Ficken, R. W., P. E. Matthiae, and R. Horwich. 1971. Eye marks in vertebrates: aids to vision. *Science* 173:936–38.

Fischer, D. H. 1978. Dew-bathing by Long-billed Thrashers (*Toxostoma longirostre*) and an Olive Sparrow (*Arremonops rufivirgatus*). *Bulletin of the Texas Ornithological Society* 11:49–50.

———. 1980. Breeding biology of Curve-billed Thrashers and Long-billed Thrashers in southern Texas. *Condor* 82:392–97.

———. 1981. Wintering ecology of thrashers in southern Texas. *Condor* 83:340–46.

———. 1983. Growth, development, and food habits of nestling mimids in South Texas. *Wilson Bulletin* 95:97–105.

Fitzpatrick, J. W. 1980. Foraging behavior of neotropical flycatchers. *Condor* 82:43–57.

Fleetwood, R. J., and J. L. Hamilton. 1967. Occurrence and nesting of the Hook-billed Kite (*Chondrohierax uncinatus*) in Texas. *Auk* 84:598–601.

Flood, N. J. 1990. Aspects of the breeding biology of Audubon's Oriole. *Journal of Field Ornithology* 61:290–302.

Forshaw, J. M. 1977. Parrots of the world. Neptune, N.J.: T.F.H. Publishers.

Foster, W. C. (ed.). 1997. *Texas and Northeastern Mexico, 1630–1690, by Juan Bautista Chapa,* trans. N. F. Brierly. Austin: University of Texas Press.

Fraga, R. M. 1988. Nest sites and breeding success of Bay-winged Cowbirds *Molothrus badius. Journal fuer Ornithologie* 129:175–84.

Fulbright, T. E. 2001. Human-induced vegetation changes in the Tamaulipan scrub of La Frontera. Pp. 166–75 in *Changing Plant Life of La Frontera: Observations on Veg-*

etation in the United States/Mexico Borderlands, ed. G. L. Webster and C. J. Bahre. Albuquerque: University of New Mexico Press.

Friedmann, H. 1925. Notes on the birds observed in the Lower Rio Grande Valley of Texas during May, 1924. *Auk* 42:537–54.

———. 1929. *The Cowbirds.* Springfield, Ill.: Charles C. Thomas.

———. 1963. *Host Relations of the Parasitic Cowbirds.* U.S. National Museum Bulletin 233.

Friedmann, H., and L. F. Kiff. 1985. The parasitic cowbirds and their hosts. *Proceedings of the Western Foundation of Vertebrate Zoology* 2:227–302.

Gallegos, T. L. 2001. Patterns of avian productivity indices at Santa Ana National Wildlife Refuge (1995–1999). M.S. thesis, University of Texas–Pan American, Edinburg.

Gamel, C. M. 1997. Habitat selection, population density, and home range of the Elf Owl, *Micrathene whitneyi,* at Santa Ana National Wildlife Refuge, Texas. M.S. thesis, University of Texas–Pan American, Edinburg.

Gamel, C. M., and T. Brush. 2001. Habitat use, population density, and home range of Elf Owls (*Micrathene whitneyi*) at Santa Ana National Wildlife Refuge, Texas. *Journal of Raptor Research* 35:214–20.

Garrett, K. L. 1997. Population status and distribution of naturalized parrots in southern California. *Western Birds* 28:181–95.

Garrett, K. L., K. T. Mabb, C. T. Collins, and L. M. Kares. 1997. Food items of naturalized parrots in southern California. *Western Birds* 28:196–201.

Gawlik, D. E., R. D. Slack, J. A. Thomas, and D. N. Harpole. 1998. Long-term trends in population and community measures of colonial nesting waterbirds in Galveston Bay estuary. *Colonial Waterbirds* 21:143–51.

Gatz, T. A. 1998. White-tailed Kite. Pp. 42–45 in *The Raptors of Arizona,* ed. R. L. Glinski. Tucson: University of Arizona Press and Arizona Game and Fish Department.

Gayou, D. C. 1986. The social system of the Texas U.S. Green Jay *Cyanocorax yncas. Auk* 103:540–47.

———. 1995. Green Jay (*Cyanocorax yncas*). In *The Birds of North America,* no. 187, ed. A. Poole and F. Gill. Philadelphia: Academy of Natural Sciences, and Washington, D.C.: American Ornithologists' Union.

Gehlbach, F. R. 1981. *Mountain Islands and Desert Seas: A Natural History of the U.S.-Mexican Borderlands.* College Station: Texas A&M University Press.

———. 1987. Natural history sketches, densities, and biomass of breeding birds in evergreen forests of the Rio Grande, Texas, and Río Corona, Tamaulipas, Mexico. *Texas Journal of Science* 39:241–51.

Geluso, K. N. 1970. Additional notes on food and fat of Roadrunners in winter. *Bulletin of the Oklahoma Ornithological Society* 3:6.

Gerhard, P. 1982. *The Northern Frontier of New Spain,* rev. ed. Norman: University of Oklahoma Press.

Gibbs, J. P., M. L. Hunter, Jr., and S. M. Melvin. 1993. Snag availability and communities of cavity-nesting birds in tropical versus temperate forests. *Biotropica* 25:236–41.

Glahn, J. F., D. S. Reinhold, and C. A. Sloan. 2000. Recent population trends of Double-crested Cormorants wintering in the delta region of Mississippi: Response to roost dispersal and removal under a recent depredation order. *Waterbirds* 22:333–47.

Glinski, R. L. 1998. Gray Hawk, *Buteo nitidus*. Pp. 82–85 in *The Raptors of Arizona,* ed. R. L. Glinski. Tucson: University of Arizona Press and Arizona Game and Fish Department.

Goldman, E. A. 1951. *Biological Investigations in Mexico.* Washington, D.C.: Smithsonian Institution.

Goldman, L. C. 1951. South Texas region. *Audubon Field Notes* 5:298–300.

———. 1953. South Texas region. *Audubon Field Notes* 7:316–20.

Goodwin, D. 1983. *Pigeons and Doves of the World.* Ithaca, N.Y.: Cornell University Press.

Gorena, R. L. 1995. Feeding and nesting ecology of the Great Kiskadee, *Pitangus sulphuratus texanus* (Passeriformes: Tyrannidae) in the Lower Rio Grande Valley, Texas. M.S. thesis, University of Texas–Pan American, Edinburg.

Gracia-Manzano, C. G. 1988. Ornitofauna de un transecto ecologico en el Municipio de Santiago, Nuevo León, Mexico. Thesis, Universidad Autónoma de Nuevo León, Monterrey, Nuevo León, Mexico.

Greenberg, R., M. S. Foster, and L. Marquez-Valdelamar. 1995. The role of the White-eyed Vireo in the dispersal of *Bursera* fruit on the Yucatan Peninsula. *Journal of Tropical Ecology* 11:619–39.

Greene, E. R. 1966. *A Lifetime with Birds: An Ornithological Logbook.* Ann Arbor, Mich.: Edwards Brothers.

Griscom, L., and M. S. Crosby. 1925–26. Birds of the Brownsville region, southern Texas. *Auk* 42:432–40, 519–37; 43:18–36.

Groschupf, K. D., and C. W. Thompson. 1998. Varied Bunting (*Passerina versicolor*). In *The Birds of North America,* no. 351. ed. A. Poole and F. Gill. Philadelphia: Birds of North America.

Guerra, A. M. 1953. *Mier in History.* Trans. Jose M. Escobar and Edna G. Brown, 1989. Edinburg, Tex.: New Santander Press.

Guthery, F. S., C. L. Land, and B. W. Hall. 2001. Heat loads on reproducing bobwhites in the semiarid subtropics. *Journal of Wildlife Management* 65:111–17.

Halkin, S. L., and S. U. Linville. 1999. Northern Cardinal (*Cardinalis cardinalis*). In *The Birds of North America,* no. 440. ed. A. Poole and F. Gill. Philadelphia: Birds of North America.

Hanson, H. C. 1921. Distribution of the Malvaceae in southern and western Texas. *American Journal of Botany* 8:192–206.

Hatch, S. L., J. L. Schuster, and D. L. Drawe. 1999. *Grasses of the Texas Gulf Prairies and Marshes.* College Station: Texas A&M University Press.

Hathcock, C. R. 2000. Factors affecting reproductive success in hosts of the Bronzed Cowbird (*Molothrus aeneus*) in the Lower Rio Grande Valley, Texas. M.S. thesis, University of Texas–Pan American, Edinburg.

Hathcock, C. R., and T. Brush. 2004. Breeding abundance and nest-site distribution of the Altamira Oriole at Santa Ana National Wildlife Refuge, Texas. *Southwestern Naturalis* 49:33–38.

Hardy, J. W. 1990. The Fish Crow (*Corvus ossifragus*) and its Mexican relatives: Vocal clues to evolutionary relationships. *Florida Field Naturalist* 18:74–80.

Havard, V. 1885. Report on the flora of western and southern Texas. *Proceedings of the U.S. National Museum* 8:449–533.

Haverschmidt, Francois. 1962. Notes on the feeding habits and food of some hawks of Surinam. *Condor* 64:154–58.

Haynie, C. B. 1992. Texas Bird Records Committee Report for 1991. *Bulletin of the Texas Ornithological Society* 25:2–12.

———. 1993. Texas Bird Records Committee Report for 1992. *Bulletin of the Texas Ornithological Society* 26:2–14.

———. 1994. Texas Bird Records Committee report for 1993. *Bulletin of the Texas Ornithological Society* 27:2–15.

———. 1995. Texas Bird Records Committee report for 1994. *Bulletin of the Texas Ornithological Society* 28:32–41.

———. 1998. Texas Bird Record Committee report for 1996. *Bulletin of the Texas Ornithological Society* 31:7–21.

Hayes, F. E. 1992. Intraspecific kleptoparasitism in the Great Kiskadee (*Pitangus sulphuratus*). *Hornero* 13:234–35.

Hayslette, S. E., T. C. Tacha, and G. L. Waggerman. 2000. Factors affecting white-winged, white-tipped, and mourning dove reproduction in the Lower Rio Grande Valley. *Journal of Wildlife Management* 64:286–95.

Hector, D. P. 1985. The diet of the Aplomado Falcon (*Falco femoralis*) in eastern Mexico. *Condor* 87:336–42.

Heinrich, B. 1999. *Mind of the Raven: Investigations and Adventures with Wolf-Birds.* New York: HarperCollins.

Henry, S. G., and F. R. Gehlbach. 1999. Elf Owl (*Micrathene whitneyi*). In *The Birds of North America,* no. 413, ed. A. Poole and F. Gill. Philadelphia: Birds of North America.

Hilbun, N. L., and A. E. Koltermann. 2002. Ranching heritage. Pp. 59–69 in *The Laguna Madre of Texas and Tamaulipas,* ed. J. W. Tunnell, Jr., and F. W. Judd. College Station: Texas A&M University Press.

Hohman, W. L., and S. A. Lee. 2001. Fulvous Whistling-Duck (*Dendrocygna bicolor*). In *The Birds of North America,* no. 562, ed. A. Poole and F. Gill. Philadelphia: Birds of North America.

Honig, R. A. 1992. Western Kingbird (*Tyrannus verticalis*) utilization of electric power substations in Houston (Harris County), Texas, and vicinity. *Bulletin of the Texas Ornithological Society* 25:13–19.

Horgan, P. 1984. *Great River: The Rio Grande in North American History.* Hanover, N.H.: Wesleyan University Press.

Howe, H. F., and G. A. Vande Kerckhove. 1979. Fecundity and seed dispersal of a tropical tree. *Ecology* 60:180–89.

Howell, S. N. G., and S. Webb. 1995. *A Guide to the Birds of Mexico and Northern Central America.* New York: Oxford University Press.

Hubbard, J. P., and D. M. Niles. 1975. Two specimen records of Brown Jay from southern Texas. *Auk* 92:797–98.

Hudon, J., and A. D. Muir. 1996. Characterization of the reflective materials and organelles in the bright irides of North American blackbirds (Icterinae). *Pigment Cell Research* 9:96–104.

Hughes, J. M. 1999. Yellow-billed Cuckoo (*Coccyzus americanus*). In *The Birds of North America,* no. 418. ed. A. Poole and F. Gill. Philadelphia: Birds of North America.

Husak, M. S., and T. C. Maxwell. 2000. A review of 20th century range expansion and population trends of the Golden-fronted Woodpecker (*Melanerpes aurifrons*): Historical and ecological perspectives. *Texas Journal of Science* 52:275–84.

Hutto, R. L. 1989. The effect of habitat alteration on migratory land birds in a West

Mexican tropical deciduous forest: A conservation perspective. *Conservation Biology* 3:138–48.

Ingels, J., Y. Oniki, and E. O. Willis. 1999. Opportunistic adaptations to man-induced habitat change by some South American Caprimulgidae. *Revista Brasileira de Biologia* 59:563–66.

Jackson, J. 1986. *Los Mesteños. Spanish Ranching in Texas, 1721–1821.* College Station: Texas A&M University Press.

Jackson, J. (ed.). 2000. *Texas by Terán: The Diary Kept by General Manuel de Mier y Terán on His 1828 Inspection of Texas.* Austin: University of Texas Press.

Jahrsdoerfer, S. E., and D. M. Leslie. 1988. *Tamaulipan Brushland of the Lower Rio Grande Valley of South Texas: Description, Human Impacts, and Management Options.* Biological Report 88. Washington, D.C.: U.S. Fish and Wildlife Service.

James, J. D., and J. E. Thompson. 2001. Black-bellied Whistling-Duck (*Dendrocygna autumnalis*). In *The Birds of North America*, no. 578, ed. A. Poole and F. Gill. Philadelphia: Birds of North America.

James, P. 1963. Freeze loss in the Least Grebe (*Podiceps dominicus*) in Lower Rio Grande Delta of Texas. *Southwestern Naturalist* 8:45–46.

James, P., and A. Hayse. 1963. Elf Owl rediscovered in Lower Rio Grande Delta of Texas. *Wilson Bulletin* 75:179–92.

Janzen D. H. 1969. Birds and the ant × acacia interaction in Central America, with notes on birds and other myrmecophytes. *Condor* 71:240–56.

———. 1981. *Ficus ovalis* seed predation by an Orange-chinned Parakeet (*Brotogeris jugularis*) in Costa Rica. *Auk* 98:841–44.

Jaramillo, A., and P. Burke. 1999. *New World Blackbirds: The Icterids.* Princeton, N.J.: Princeton University Press.

Jehl, J. R., Jr. 1973. Studies of a declining population of Brown Pelicans in northwestern Baja California. *Condor* 75:69–79.

Jenny, J. P., W. Heinrich, A. B. Montoya, B. Match, C. Sandfort, and W. G. Hunt. 2004. From the field: Progress in restoring the Aplomado Falcon to southern Texas. *Wildlife Society Bulletin* 32:276–85.

Johnsgard, P. A. 2001. *Prairie Birds: Fragile Splendor in the Great Plains.* Lawrence: University Press of Kansas.

Johnsgard, P. A., and M. Carbonnell. 1996. Ruddy Ducks and other stifftails. Norman: University of Oklahoma Press.

Johnson, D. B., and F. S. Guthery. 1988. Loafing coverts used by Northern Bobwhites in subtropical environments. *Journal of Wildlife Management* 52:464–69.

Johnson, D. B., F. S. Guthery, and N. E. Koerth. 1989. Grackle damage to grapefruit in the Lower Rio Grande Valley. *Wildlife Society Bulletin* 17:46–50.

Johnson, K., E. DuVal, M. Kielt, and C. Hughes. 2000. Male mating strategies and the mating system of Great-tailed Grackles. *Behavioral Ecology* 11:132–41.

Johnson, K., and B. D. Peer. 2001. Great-tailed Grackle (*Quiscalus mexicanus*). In *The Birds of North America*, no. 576, ed. A. Poole and F. Gill. Philadelphia: Birds of North America.

Johnson, W. P. 2001. Mottled Duck. In The Texas Breeding Bird Atlas. Texas A&M University System, College Station and Corpus Christi. http://tbba.cbi.tamucc.edu (July 12, 2001).

Johnston, M. C. 1963. Past and present grasslands of southern Texas and northern Mexico. *Ecology* 44:456–66.

Jones, O. L., Jr. 1996. *Los Paisanos: Spanish Settlers on the Northern Frontier of New Spain.* Norman: University of Oklahoma Press.

Judd, F. W., and R. I. Lonard. 2002. Species richness and diversity of brackish and salt marshes in the Rio Grande Delta. *Journal of Coastal Research* 18:751–59.

Jurado, E., E. Estrada, and A. Moles. 2001. Characterizing plant attributes with particular emphasis on seeds in Tamaulipan thornscrub in semi-arid Mexico. *Journal of Arid Environments* 48:309–21.

Keats, J. 1956. *Poetical Works.* Ed. H. W. Garrod. London: Oxford University Press.

Kennedy, C. H. 1950. The relation of American dragonfly-eating birds to their prey. *Ecological Monographs* 20:103–42.

King, K. A., E. L. Flickinger, and H. H. Hildebrand. 1977. The decline of Brown Pelicans on the Louisiana and Texas Gulf Coast. *Southwestern Naturalist* 21:417–31.

Klicka, J. T. 1994. The biological and taxonomic status of the Brownsville Yellowthroat (*Geothlypis trichas insperata*). M.S. thesis, Texas A&I University, Kingsville.

Knopf, F. L., R. R. Johnson, T. Rich, F. B. Samson, and R. C. Szaro. 1988. Conservation of riparian ecosystems in the United States. *Wilson Bulletin* 100:272–84.

Kramer, D. L., and R. L. McLaughlin. 2001. The behavioral ecology of intermittent locomotion. *American Zoologist* 41:137–53.

Kus, B. 1998. Use of restored riparian habitat by the endangered Least Bell's Vireo (*Vireo bellii pusillus*). *Restoration Ecology* 6:75–82.

Lago-Paiva, C. 1996. Cavity nesting by Great Kiskadees (*Pitangus sulphuratus*): adaptation or expression of ancestral behavior? *Auk* 113:953–55.

Lamb, H. H. 1995. *Climate, History and the Modern World,* 2nd ed. New York: Routledge.

Langeland, K. A. 1996. *Hydrilla verticillata* (L.F.) Royle (Hydrocharitaceae), "the perfect aquatic weed." *Castanea* 61:293–304.

Land, C. L. 1999. The thermal environment and reproductive behavior of birds in South Texas. M.S. thesis, Texas A&M University–Kingsville, Kingsville.

Lasley, G. W. 1991. Texas Bird Records Committee Report for 1990. *Bulletin of the Texas Ornithological Society* 24:2–15.

———. 1995. Minutes of the 1995 annual meeting of the Texas Bird Records Committee, September 16, 1995, College Station.

Lasley, G. W., and C. Sexton. 1985. South Texas region. *American Birds* 39:933–36.

———. 1986. South Texas region. *American Birds* 40:1225–28.

———. 1987. South Texas region. *American Birds* 41:458–61.

———. 1988. Texas region. *American Birds* 42:1310–15.

———. 1989. Texas region. *American Birds* 43:502–10.

———. 1990. Texas region. *American Birds* 44:458–65.

———. 1995. Texas region. *National Audubon Society Field Notes* 49:273–78.

Latta, S. C., and C. A. Howell. 1999. Common Pauraque (*Nyctidromus albicollis*). In *The Birds of North America,* no. 429, ed. A. Poole and F. Gill. Philadelphia: Birds of North America.

Lehmann, V. W. 1969. *Forgotten Legions: Sheep in the Rio Grande Plain of Texas.* El Paso: Texas Western Press.

Leisler, B. 1995. Zirkeln bei Webervogeln (Ploceidae): Beziehungen zu Lebensweise und Schnabelbau. *Jurnal fur Ornithologie* 136:267–72.

Leopold, A. S. 1959. *Wildlife of Mexico: The Game Birds and Mammals.* Berkeley: University of California Press.

Lindell, C. 1996. Benefits and costs to Plain-fronted Thornbirds (*Phacellodromus rufifrons*) of interactions with other nest associates. *Auk* 113:565–77.

Linsdale, J. M. 1957. Goldfinches on the Hastings Natural History Reservation. *American Midland Naturalist* 57:1–119.

Llambias, P. E., V. Ferretti, and P. S. Rodriguez. 2001. Kleptoparasitism in the Great Kiskadee. *Wilson Bulletin* 113:116–17.

Lockwood, J. L., and M. L. McKinney (eds.). 2001. *Biotic Homogenization.* New York: Kluwer Academic–Plenum Publishers.

Lockwood, M. W. 1995. A closer look: Varied Bunting. *Birding* 27:110–13.

———. 1999. Texas Bird Records Committee report for 1998. *Bulletin of the Texas Ornithological Society* 32:26–37.

———. 2000. Texas Bird Records Committee report for 1999. *Bulletin of the Texas Ornithological Society* 33:13–22.

———. 2001. Texas Bird Records Committee report for 2000. *Bulletin of the Texas Ornithological Society* 34:1–16.

———. 2002. Texas Bird Records Committee report for 2001. *Bulletin of the Texas Ornithological Society* 35:1–10.

———. 2003. Texas Bird Records Committee report for 2002. *Bulletin of the Texas Ornithological Society* 36: *in press.*

Lonard, R. I., J. H. Everitt, and F. W. Judd. 1991. *Woody Plants of the Lower Rio Grande Valley, Texas.* Texas Memorial Museum Miscellaneous Publication 7.

Lonard, R. I., and F. W. Judd. 1991. Comparison of the effects of the severe freezes of 1983 and 1989 on native woody plants of the Lower Rio Grande Valley, Texas. *Southwestern Naturalist* 36:213–17.

———. 1993. Phytogeography of the woody flora of the Lower Rio Grande Valley, Texas. *Texas Journal of Science* 45:133–47.

———. 2002. Riparian vegetation of the lower Rio Grande. *Southwestern Naturalist* 47:420–32.

Lonard, R. I., F. W. Judd, J. H. Everitt, D. E. Escobar, M. R. Davis, M. M. Crawford, and M. D. Desai. 2000. Evaluation of color-infrared photography for distinguishing annual changes in riparian forest vegetation of the lower Rio Grande in Texas. *Forest Ecology and Management* 128:75–81.

Longoria, A. 1997. *Adios to the Brushlands.* College Station: Texas A&M University Press.

Lorenzana, J. C., and S. G. Sealy. 1998. Adult brood parasites feeding nestlings and fledglings of their own species: A review. *Journal of Field Ornithology* 69:364–75.

Lowery, G. H., Jr., and W. W. Dalquest. 1951. Birds from the state of Veracruz, Mexico. *University of Kansas Publications Museum of Natural History* 3:531–649.

Lowther, P. E., and R. T. Paul. 2002. Reddish Egret (*Egretta rufescens*). In *The Birds of North America*, no. 633, ed. A. Poole and F. Gill. Philadelphia: Birds of North America.

MacArthur, R. H. 1972. *Geographical Ecology: Patterns in the Distributions of Species.* New York: Harper and Row.

Mahler, B., and P. L. Tubaro. 2001. Attenuated outer primaries in pigeons and doves: A comparative test fails to support the flight performance hypothesis. *Condor* 103:449–54.

Marion, W. R. 1976. Plain Chachalaca food habits in South Texas. *Auk* 93:376–79.

————. 1977. Growth and development of the Plain Chachalaca in South Texas. *Wilson Bulletin* 89:47–56.

Markum, D. K., and G. A. Baldassarre. 1989a. Ground-nesting by Black-bellied Whistling-Ducks on islands in Mexico. *Journal of Wildlife Management* 53:707–13.

————. 1989b. Breeding biology of Muscovy Ducks using nest boxes in Mexico. *Wilson Bulletin* 101:621–26.

Martin, R. F. 1974. Syntopic culvert nesting of Cave and Barn Swallows in Texas. *Auk* 91:776–82.

————. 1980. Analysis of hybridization between the hirundinid genera *Hirundo* and *Petrochelidon* in Texas. *Auk* 97:148–59.

Martin, R. F., and S. R. Martin. 1978. Niche and range expansion of Cave Swallows in Texas. *American Birds* 32:941–46.

Mason, C. T., Jr., and P. B. Mason. 1995. *A Handbook of Mexican Roadside Flora*. Tucson: University of Arizona Press.

Matthews, W. K. 1938. A history of irrigation in the Lower Rio Grande Valley. M.A. thesis, University of Texas, Austin.

Maxwell, T. C., and M. S. Husak. 1999. Common Black-Hawk nesting in west-central Texas. *Journal of Raptor Research* 33:270–71.

McCamant, R. E., and E. G. Bolen. 1979. A 17-year study of nest box utilization by Black-bellied Whistling-Ducks (*Dendrocygna autumnalis*). *Journal of Wildlife Management* 43:936–43.

McClintock, W. A. 1931. Journal of a trip through Texas and northern Mexico in 1846–1847. *Southwestern Historical Quarterly* 34:20–37, 141–58, 231–56.

McGregor, R. C. 1899. *Salvia coccinea,* an ornithophilous plant. *American Naturalist* 33:953–55.

McKinney, B. 2002. *Checklist of Lower Rio Grande Valley Birds.* McAllen, Tex.: Valley Nature Center.

McLendon, T. 1991. Preliminary description of the vegetation of South Texas exclusive of coastal saline zones. *Texas Journal of Science* 43:13–32.

McNair, D. B., and W. Post. 2001. Review of the occurrence of vagrant Cave Swallows in the United States and Canada. *Journal of Field Ornithology* 72:485–503.

McShea, W. J., and J. H. Rappole. 1997. Variable song rates in three species of passerines and implications for estimating bird populations. *Journal of Field Ornithology* 68:367–75.

Mellink, E. 1991. Bird communities associated with traditional agroecosystems in the San Luis Potosí Plateau, Mexico. *Agriculture, Ecosystems and Environment* 36:37–50.

Merrill, J. C. 1877. A humming-bird new to the fauna of the United States. *Bulletin of the Nuttall Ornithological Club* 2:26.

————. 1878. Notes on the ornithology of southern Texas, being a list of birds observed in the vicinity of Fort Brown, Texas, from February, 1876, to June, 1878. *Proceedings of the U.S. National Museum* 1:118–73.

Michener, W. K., and R. A. Haueber. 1998. Flooding: Natural and managed disturbances. *BioScience* 48:677–80.

Molles, M. C., Jr., C. S. Crawford, L. M. Ellis, H. M. Valett, and C. N. Dahm. 1998. Managed flooding for riparian ecosystem restoration. *BioScience* 48:749–56.

Monk, S. G. 2003. Breeding distribution and habitat use of Audubon Oriole in the

Lower Rio Grande Valley of Texas. M.S. thesis, University of Texas–Pan American, Edinburg.

Montiel De La Garza, F. G. 1978. Estudios de nidificacion del gavilan blanco *Elanus leucurus majusculus* Bangs y Penard 1920, en Cadereyta Jimenez, Nuevo León, Mexico. Thesis, Universidad Autónoma de Nuevo León, Monterrey, Nuevo León, Mexico.

Montiel de la Garza, F. G., and A. J. Contreras-Balderas. 1990. First Hook-billed Kite specimen from Nuevo León, Mexico. *Southwestern Naturalist* 35:370.

Montoya, A. B., P. J. Swank, and M. Cardenas. 1997. Breeding biology of Aplomado Falcons in desert grasslands of Chihuahua, Mexico. *Journal of Field Ornithology* 68:135–43.

Moore, R. 2004. From dust bowl to estuary: Bahia Grande restoration project set for summer of 2004. *McAllen Monitor,* January 25.

Mora, M. A. 1996. Organochlorines and trace elements in four colonial waterbird species nesting in the lower Laguna Madre, Texas. *Archives of Environmental Contamination and Toxicology* 31:533–37.

Mora, M. A., M. C. Lee, J. P. Jenny, T. W. Schulz, J. L. Sericano, and N. J. Clum. 1997. Potential effects of environmental contaminants on recovery of the Aplomado Falcon in South Texas. *Journal of Wildlife Management* 61:1288–96.

Mora, M. A., D. Papoulias, I. Nava, and D. R. Buckler. 2001. A comparative assessment of contaminants in fish from four resacas of the Texas, U.S.-Tamaulipas, Mexico border region. *Environment International* 27:15–20.

Morton, E. S. 1971. Nest predation affecting the breeding season of the Clay-colored Robin, a tropical song bird. *Science* 181:920–21.

Moulton, D. P., and S. L. Pimm. 1983. The introduced Hawaiian avifauna: Biogeographic evidence for competition. *American Naturalist* 121:669–90.

Mueller, J. M., C. B. Dabbert, S. Demarais, and A. R. Forbes. 1999. Northern Bobwhite chick mortality caused by red imported fire ants. *Journal of Wildlife Management* 63:1291–98.

Naiman, R. J., H. Decamps, and M. Pollock. 1993. The role of riparian corridors in maintaining regional biodiversity. *Ecological Applications* 3:209–12.

Neck, R. W. 1986. Expansion of the Red-crowned Parrot, *Amazona viridigenalis,* into southern Texas and changes in agricultural practices in northern Mexico. *Bulletin of the Texas Ornithological Society* 19:6–12.

Neck, R. W., and D. H. Riskind. 1981. Direct and indirect human impact on Least Tern nesting success at Falcon Reservoir, Zapata County, Texas. *Bulletin of the Texas Ornithological Society* 14:27–29.

Nero, R. W. 1984. *Redwings.* Washington, D.C.: Smithsonian Institution Press.

Oberholser, H. C. 1974. *The Bird Life of Texas,* ed. E. B. Kincaid, Jr. Austin: University of Texas Press.

Oksanen, T., L. Oksanen, and S. D. Fretwell. 1985. Surplus killing in the hunting strategy of small predators. *American Naturalist* 126:328–46.

Oring, L. W. 1964. Notes on the birds of Webb County, Texas. *Auk* 81:440.

Ortiz-Pulido, R. 1997. Actividades frugivoras de *Tyrannus forficatus* en un mosaico de vegetacion durante la migracion. *Ornitología Neotropical* 8:237–39.

Ortiz-Pulido, R., and R. Diaz. 2001. Distribucion de colibries en la zona baja del centro de Veracruz. *Ornitología Neotropical* 12:297–317.

Owen, J. H. 1950. Raven carrying food in foot. *British Birds* 43:55.

Palmer, P. C. 1986. Great Kiskadees observed feeding on reptiles. *Bulletin of the Texas Ornithological Society* 19:31–32.

Parkes, K. C. 1974. The Olive Sparrow of the Yucatan Peninsula. *Auk* 86:293–95.

Paulson, Dennis R. 1983. Flocking in the Hook-billed Kite. *Auk* 100:749–50.

Peer, B. D., and S. G. Sealy. 1999. Laying time of the Bronzed Cowbird. *Wilson Bulletin* 111:137–39.

———. 2000. Responses of Scissor-tailed Flycatchers (*Tyrannus forficatus*) to experimental cowbird parasitism. *Bird Behavior* 13:63–67.

Peer, B. D., and S. G. Sealy. 2004. Fate of grackle (*Quiscalus* spp.) defenses in the absence of brood parasitism: Implications for long-term parasite-host coevolution. *Auk* 121:1172–86.

Pemberton, J. R. 1922. A large tern colony in Texas. *Condor* 24:37–48.

Peña, J. C. 1998. *Quiscalus mexicanus* (Passeriformes: Icteridae) preys upon *Lepidochelys olivacea* (Reptilia: Cheloniidae) neonates [in Spanish]. *Revista de Biologia Tropical* 46:845–46.

Perez, C. J., P. J. Swank, and D. W. Smith. 1996. Survival, movements and habitat use of Aplomado Falcons released in southern Texas. *Journal of Raptor Research* 30:175–82.

Perez, M., S. E. Henke, and A. M. Fedynich. 2001. Detection of aflatoxin-contaminated grain by three granivorous bird species. *Journal of Wildlife Diseases* 37:358–61.

Perrigo, G. H., managing ed. 2002. *Wildlife in Focus: Texas Coastal Bend Wildlife Photo Contest I.* Corpus Christi: Coastal Bend Land Trust.

Peterson, M. J. 2000. Plain Chachalaca (*Ortalis vetula*). In *The Birds of North America*, no. 550, ed. A. Poole and F. Gill. Philadelphia: Birds of North America.

Peterson, R. T., and J. Fisher. 1955. *Wild America: The Record of a 30,000-mile Journey around the Continent by a Distinguished Naturalist and His British Colleague.* Boston: Houghton Mifflin.

Phillips, A. R. 1986. *The Known Birds of North and Middle America,* Vol. 1. Denver: Phillips.

Phillips, A. R., J. Marshall, and G. Monson. 1964. The Birds of Arizona. Tucson: University of Arizona Press.

Phillips, J. C. 1911. A year's collecting in Tamaulipas, Mexico. *Auk* 28 67–89.

Phillips, S. M., and G. E. Einem. 2003. Seaside Sparrows, *Ammodramus maritimus*, breeding in the Rio Grande Delta, southern Texas. *Southwestern Naturalist* 48:465–67.

Picman, J. 1989. Mechanism of increased puncture resistance of eggs of Brown-headed Cowbirds. *Auk* 106:577–83.

Pitelka, F. A. 1948. Notes on the distribution and taxonomy of Mexican game birds. *Condor* 5:113–23.

Pleasants, B. Y. 1981. Aspects of the breeding biology of a sub-tropical oriole, *Icterus gularis*. *Wilson Bulletin* 93:531–37.

Potter, E. F. 1980. Notes on nesting Yellow-billed Cuckoos. *Journal of Field Ornithology* 51:17–29.

Prieto, A. 1873. Historia, geografía, y estadidística del Estado de Tamaulipas. Mexico, D.F.: Tip. Escalerillas.

Proudfoot, G. A., and R. R. Johnson. 2000. Ferruginous Pygmy-Owl (*Glaucidium brasilianum*). In *The Birds of North America,* no. 498, ed. A. Poole and F. Gill. Philadelphia: Birds of North America.

Rappole, J. H., A. R. Tipton, A. H. Kane, R. H. Flores, J. Hobbs, and J. Palacios. 1990. Seasonal effects on control methods for the Great-tailed Grackle. USDA Forest Service General Technical Report RM-171: 120–25.

Rayner, J. M. V., P. W. Viscardi, S. Ward, and J. R. Speakman. 2001. Aerodynamics and energetics of intermittent flight in birds. *American Zoologist* 41:188–204.

Rea, A. M. 1983. *Once a River: Bird Life and Habitat Changes on the Middle Gila.* Tucson: University of Arizona Press.

Richardson, A. 1995. *Plants of Southernmost Texas,* rev. ed. Austin: University of Texas Press.

Richardson, D. S., and G. M. Bolen. 1999. A nesting association between semi-colonial Bullock's Orioles and Yellow-billed Magpies: Evidence for the predator protection hypothesis. *Behavioral Ecology and Sociobiology* 46:373–80.

Ricklefs, R. E. 1980. "Watch-dog" behaviour observed at the nest of a cooperatively breeding bird, the Rufous-margined Flycatcher (*Myiozetetes cayanensis*). *Ibis* 122: 116–18.

Rhoads, S. N. 1892. The birds of southeastern Texas and southern Arizona observed during May, June, and July, 1891. *Proceedings of the Academy of Natural Sciences* 43:98–120, 121–26.

Rhodes, J. F. 1899. The Battle of Gettysburg. *American Historical Review* 4:655–77.

Robertson, B. 1985. *Wild Horse Desert: The Heritage of South Texas.* Edinburg: Hidalgo County Historical Museum.

Robertson, P. B., and A. F. Schnapf. 1987. Pyramiding behavior in the Inca Dove: Adaptive aspects of day-night differences. *Condor* 89:185–87.

Robinson, S. K. 1988. Foraging ecology and host relationships of Giant Cowbirds in southeastern Peru. *Wilson Bulletin* 100:224–35.

———. 1994. Habitat selection and foraging ecology of raptors in Amazonian Peru. *Biotropica* 26:443–58.

———. 1997. Birds of a Peruvian oxbow lake: Populations, resources, predation, and social behavior. *Ornithological Monographs* 48:613–39.

Robinson, W. D., and S. K. Robinson. 1999. Effects of selective logging on forest bird populations in a fragmented landscape. *Conservation Biology* 13:58–66.

Rodriguez-Estrella, R., E. Mata, and L. Rivera. 1992. Ecological notes on the Green Parakeet of Isla Socorro, Mexico. *Condor* 94:523–25.

Rodriguez-Estrella, R., L. R. Rodriguez, and F. Anguiano. 1995. Nest-site characteristics of the Socorro Green Parakeet. *Condor* 97:575–77.

Rohwer, S., C. D. Spaw, and E. Roskaft. 1989. Costs to Northern Orioles of puncture-ejecting parasitic cowbird eggs from their nests. *Auk* 106:734–38.

Romagosa, C. M., and R. F. Labisky. 2000. Establishment and dispersal of the Eurasian Collared-Dove in Florida. *Journal of Field Ornithology* 71:159–66.

Rosenberg, K. V., R. D. Ohmart, W. C. Hunter, and B. W. Anderson. 1991. *Birds of the Lower Colorado River Valley.* Tucson: University of Arizona Press.

Rosenberg, K. V., S. B. Terrill, and G. H. Rosenberg. 1987. Value of suburban habitats to desert riparian birds. *Wilson Bulletin* 99:642–54.

Roth, R. R. 1977. The composition of four bird communities in South Texas brush-grasslands. *Condor* 79:417–25.

Rowley, J. S. 1966. Breeding records of birds of Sierra Madre del Sur, Oaxaca, Mexico. *Proceedings of Western Foundation of Vertebrate Zoology* 1:107–204.

———. 1984. Breeding records of land birds in Oaxaca, Mexico. *Proceedings of the Western Foundation for Vertebrate Zoology* 2:73–224.

Rupert, C. E. 1997. Breeding bird densities and habitat of riparian birds along the lower Rio Grande, Texas. M.S. thesis, University of Texas–Pan American, Edinburg.

Rupert, J. R. 1997. The brood-rearing habitat, brood home range, and fecundity of the Snowy Plover (*Charadrius alexandrinus*) in coastal southern Texas. M.S. thesis, University of Texas–Pan American, Edinburg.

Rupert, J. R., and T. Brush. 1996. Red-breasted Mergansers, *Mergus serrator,* nesting in southern Texas. *Southwestern Naturalist* 41:199–200.

Russell, S. M., and G. Monson. 1998. *The Birds of Sonora.* Tucson: University of Arizona Press.

Sada de Hermosillo, M. L., B. Lopez de Mariscal, and L. Sada de Rosenzweig. 1995. Guía de campo para las aves de Chipinque. Mexico City: Comisión Nacional para el Conocimiento y Uso de la Biodiversidad.

Sanchez, Mario L. (ed.) 1994. *A Shared Experience: The History, Architecture, and Historic Designations of the Lower Rio Grande Heritage Corridor.* Austin: Los Caminos del Rio Heritage Project and Texas Historical Commission.

Sauer, J. R., J. E. Hines, I. Thomas, J. Fallon, and G. Gough. 1999. *The North American Breeding Bird Survey, results and analysis 1966–1998.* Version 98.1. Laurel, Md: USGS Patuxent Wildlife Research Center.

Schaldach, William J., Jr. 1963. The avifauna of Colima and adjacent Jalisco, Mexico. *Proceedings of the Western Foundation for Vertebrate Zoology* 1:1–100.

Schaldach, W. J., Jr., B. P. Escalante P., and K. Winker. 1997. Further notes on the avifauna of Oaxaca, Mexico. *Anales Instituto Biología Universidad Autónoma Mexico,* Series Zoología 68:91–135.

Schmidly, D. J. 2002. *Texas Natural History: A Century of Change.* Lubbock: Texas Tech University Press.

Schneider, J. P., T. C. Tacha, and D. Lobpries. 1993. Breeding distribution of Black-bellied Whistling-Ducks in Texas. *Southwestern Naturalist* 38:383–85.

Scifres, C. J., and W. T. Hamilton. 1993. *Prescribed Burning for Brushland Management: The South Texas Example.* College Station: Texas A&M University Press.

Scifres, C. J., and J. L. Mutz. 1975. Secondary succession following extended inundation of Texas coastal rangeland. *Journal of Range Management* 28:279–82.

Scott, F. J. 1937. *Historical Heritage of the Lower Rio Grande; a Historical Record of Spanish Exploration, Subjugation and Colonization of the Lower Rio Grande Valley and the Activities of José Escandón, Count of Sierra Gorda, together with the Development of Towns and Ranches under Spanish, Mexican and Texas Sovereignties, 1747–1848.* San Antonio, Tex.: Naylor.

Sealy, S. G., and J. C. Lorenzana. 1997. Feeding of nestling and fledgling brood parasites by individuals other than the foster parents. *Canadian Journal of Zoology* 75:1739–52.

Sealy, S. G., J. E. Sanchez, R. Campos R., and M. Marin. 1995. Bronzed Cowbird hosts: New records, trends in host use, and cost of parasitism. *Ornitología Neotropical* 8:175–84.

Selander, R. K. 1959. Polymorphism in the Mexican Brown Jay. *Auk* 76:385–417.

Sennett, G. B. 1878. Notes on the ornithology of the lower Rio Grande of Texas, from observations made during the season of 1877. *Bulletin of the U.S. Geological and Geo-graphical Survey of the Territories* 4:1–66.

———. 1879. Further notes on the ornithology of the lower Rio Grande of Texas, from observations made during the Spring of 1878. *Bulletin of the U.S. Geological and Geographical Survey of the Territories* 5:371–440.

———. 1889. *Micropallas whitneyi*, Elf Owl, taken in Texas. *Auk* 6:276.

Sexton, C. W. 1999. The Vermilion Flycatcher in Texas. *Texas Birds* 1:41–45.

———. 2001. Texas region. *North American Birds* 55:454–58.

Seyffert, K. D. 2001. *Birds of the Texas Panhandle: Their Status, Distribution, and History.* College Station: Texas A&M University Press.

Shanahan, M., S. So, S. G. Compton, and R. Corlett. 2001. Fig-eating by vertebrate frugivores: A global review. *Biological Reviews* 76:529–72.

Sharp, M. S., and R. L. Neill. 1979. Physical deformities in a population of wintering blackbirds. *Condor* 81:427–30.

Shelton, M. L. 2001. Climate of La Frontera. Pp. 39–55 in *Changing Plant Life of La Frontera: Observations on Vegetation in the United States/Mexico Borderlands*, ed. G. L. Webster and C. J. Bahre. Albuquerque: University of New Mexico Press.

Shields, M. 2002. Brown Pelican (*Pelecanus occidentalis*). In *The Birds of North America*, no. 609, ed. A. Poole and F. Gill. Philadelphia: Birds of North America.

Silvius, K. M. 1995. Avian consumers of cardón fruits (*Stenocereus griseus:* Cactaceae) on Margarita Island, Venezuela. *Biotropica* 27:96–105.

Simmons, M. 1992. Tlascalans in the Spanish borderlands. Pp. 107–16 in *The Native American and Spanish Colonial Experience in the Greater Southwest*, Vol. 2: *Introduction to the Research* , ed. D. H. Snow. New York: Garland Publishing.

Skutch, A. F. 1954. *Life Histories of Central American Birds: Families Fringillidae, Thraupidae, Icteridae, Parulidae, and Coerebidae.* Pacific Coast Avifauna 31.

———. 1960. *Life Histories of Central American Birds II. Families Vireonidae, Sylviidae, Turdidae, Troglodytidae, Paridae, Corvidae, Hirundinidae, and Tyrannidae.* Pacific Coast Avifauna 34.

———. 1976. *Parent Birds and Their Young.* Austin: University of Texas Press.

———. 1977. *A Birdwatcher's Adventures in Tropical America.* Austin: University of Texas Press.

———. 1981. *A Naturalist on a Tropical Farm.* Berkeley: University of California Press.

———. 1983. *Nature through Tropical Windows.* Berkeley: University of California Press.

———. 1987. *A Naturalist amid Tropical Splendor.* Iowa City: University of Iowa Press.

———. 1996. *Orioles, Blackbirds, and Their Kin.* Tuscon: University of Arizona Press.

Small, M. F., and C. L. Pruett. 1998. Rhamphothecal hyperkeratosis in a Bronzed Cowbird. *Bulletin of the Texas Ornithological Society* 31:27–29.

Small, M. F., and G. L. Waggerman. 1999. Geographic redistribution of breeding White-winged Doves in the Lower Rio Grande Valley of Texas: 1976–1997. *Texas Journal of Science* 51:15–19.

Smith, A. P. 1910. Miscellaneous bird notes from the lower Rio Grande. *Condor* 12:93–103.

Smith, E. H. 2002. Colonial waterbirds and rookery islands. Pp. 182–97 in *The Laguna Madre of Texas and Tamaulipas,* ed. J. W. Tunnell, Jr., and F. W. Judd. College Station: Texas A&M University Press.

Smith, J. G. 1899. *Grazing Problems in the Southwest and How to Meet Them.* USDA

Div. Agrostatistics Bulletin 16. Washington, D.C.: U.S. Government Printing Office.

Smith, M. H. 1961. The Lower Rio Grande region in Tamaulipas, Mexico. Ph.D. dissertation, University of Texas, Austin.

Smith, P. W. 1987. The Eurasian Collared-Dove arrives in the Americas. *American Birds* 41:1371–79.

Smith, S. M. 1977. Coral-snake pattern recognition and stimulus generalization by naive Great Kiskadees (Aves: Tyrannidae). *Nature* 265:535–36.

———. 1978. Predatory behaviour of young Great Kiskadees (*Pitangus sulphuratus*). *Animal Behaviour* 26:988–95.

Smith, T. B. 1982. Nests and young of two rare raptors from Mexico. *Biotropica* 14: 79–80.

Smith, T. B., and S. M. Temple. 1982. Feeding habits and bill polymorphism in Hook-billed Kites. *Auk* 99:197–207.

Smith, W. J. 1966. Communication and relationships in the genus *Tyrannus*. *Publication of the Nuttall Ornithological Club* 6.

Snow, D. W., and C. M. Perrins. 1998. *The Birds of the Western Palearctic, Concise Edition*. Vol. 1: *Non-Passerines*. Oxford: Oxford University Press.

Snyder, N. F. R., and H. A. Snyder. 1991. *Raptors: North American Birds of Prey*. Stillwater, Minn.: Voyageur Press.

Stone, W. J. 1919. Jacob Post Giraud, Jr., and his works. *Auk* 36:464–72.

Storer, R. W., W. R. Siefroed, and J. Kinaham. 1976. Sunbathing in grebes. *Living Bird* 14:45–56.

Stotz, D. F., J. W. Fitzpatrick, T. A. Parker III, and D. K. Moskovits. 1996. *Neotropical Birds: Ecology and Conservation*. Chicago: University of Chicago Press.

Strong, A. M., R. J. Sawicki, and G. T. Bancroft. 1991. Effects of predator presence on the nesting distribution of White-crowned Pigeons in Florida Bay. *Wilson Bulletin* 103:415–25.

Stutchbury, B. J. M., and E. S. Morton. 2001. *Behavioural Ecology of Tropical Birds*. New York: Academic Press.

Swan, S. L. 1981. Mexico in the Little Ice Age. *Journal of Interdisciplinary History* 11:633–48.

Sutton, G. M. 1949. The Rose-throated Becard, *Platypsaris aglaiae*, in the Lower Rio Grande Valley of Texas. *Auk* 66:365–66.

———. 1951. *Mexican Birds: First Impressions*. Norman: University of Oklahoma Press.

———. 1972. *At a Bend in a Mexican River*. New York: Paul S. Eriksson.

Sutton, G. M., and O. S. Pettingill, Jr. 1942. Birds of the Gomez Farías region, southwestern Tamaulipas. *Auk* 59:1–34.

———. 1943. The Alta Mira Oriole and its nest. *Condor* 45:125–32.

Synatzske, D. R., D. C. Ruthven III, and L. W. Brothers. 1999. Use of deer-proof fence posts by cavity nesting birds in South Texas. *Bulletin of the Texas Ornithological Society* 32:38–41.

Taylor, W. W. 1972. The hunter-gatherer nomads of northern Mexico: a comparison of the archival and archeological records. *World Archeology* 4:167–78.

Telfair, Raymond C., II. 1995. Neotropic Cormorant (*Phalacrocorax brasilianus*) population trends and dynamics in Texas. *Bulletin of the Texas Ornithological Society* 28: 7–16.

Teter, D., and D. L. McNeely. 1995. Abundance and diversity of aquatic birds on two South Texas oxbow lakes. *Texas Journal of Science* 47:62–68.

Texas Game, Fish and Oyster Commission. 1945. *Principal Game Birds and Mammals of Texas: Their Distribution and Management.* Austin: Von Boeckmann–Jones.

Texas Ornithological Society. 1995. *Checklist of the Birds of Texas,* 3rd ed. Austin: Capital Printing.

Thompson, J. 1997. A Wild and Vivid Land: An Illustrated History of the South Texas Border. Austin: Texas State Historical Association.

Thurber, W. A., and A. Villeda. 1984. Notes on parasitism by Bronzed Cowbirds in El Salvador. *Wilson Bulletin* 92:112–13.

Tijerina, A. 1994. *Tejanos and Texas under the Mexican Flag, 1821–1836.* College Station: Texas A&M Unversity Press.

Tipton, A. R., J. H. Rappole, A. H. Kane, R. H. Flores, D. B. Johnson, J. Hobbs, P. Schulz, S. L. Beasom, and J. Palacios. 1990a. Use of monofilament line, reflective tape, beach-balls, and pyrotechnics for controlling grackle damage to citrus. USDA Forest Service General Technical Report RM-171: 126–128.

Tipton, A. R., J. H. Rappole, A. H. Kane, R. H. Flores, J. Hobbs, D. B. Johnson, and S. L. Beasom. 1990b. Use of DRC-1339 and PA-14 to control grackle populations in the Lower Rio Grande Valley. USDA Forest Service General Technical Report RM-171: 133–37.

Traylor, M. A., Jr. 1979. Two sibling species of *Tyrannus* (Tyrannidae). *Auk* 96:221–33.

Tunnell, J. W., Jr., and F. W. Judd (eds.). 2002. *The Laguna Madre of Texas and Tamaulipas.* College Station: Texas A&M University Press.

Tunnell, J. W., Jr., K. Withers, and E. S. Smith. 2002. Conservation issues and recommendations. Pages 275–88 in *The Laguna Madre of Texas and Tamaulipas,* ed. J. W. Tunnell, Jr., and F. W. Judd. College Station: Texas A&M University Press.

Tweit, R. C. 1997. Long-billed Thrasher (*Toxostoma longirostre*). In *The Birds of North America,* no. 317, ed. A. Poole and F. Gill. Philadelphia: Academy of Natural Sciences, and Washington, D.C.: American Ornithologists' Union.

Udvardy, M. F. D. 1983. The role of the feet in behavioral thermoregulation of hummingbirds. *Condor* 82:81–85.

Vaira, M., and G. Coria. 1994. *Leptodactylus ocellatus (Rana criolla). Herpetological Review* 25:118.

Valdes-Perezgasga, F. 1999. Wood Duck *Aix sponsa* breeding in the Nazas River, Durango, Mexico. *Cotinga* 11:13–14.

Van Auken, O. W., and J. K. Bush. 1985. Secondary succession on terraces of the San Antonio River. *Bulletin of the Torrey Botanical Club* 112:158–66.

Van Tyne, J. 1933. Some birds of the Rio Grande delta of Texas. Occasional Papers of the Museum of Zoology, University of Michigan 255:251–5.

Vega, J. H., and J. H. Rappole. 1994. Effects of scrub mechanical treatment on the nongame bird community in the Rio Grande Plain of Texas. *Wildlife Society Bulletin* 22:165–71.

Vehrencamp, S. L., B. S. Bowen, and R. R. Koford. 1986. Breeding roles and pairing patterns within communal groups of Groove-billed Anis *Crotophaga sulcirostris. Animal Behaviour* 34:347–66.

Viele, T. G. 1858. *Following the Drum: A Glimpse of Frontier Life.* Lincoln: University of Nebraska Press.

Vora, R. S. 1990a. Plant phenology in the lower Rio Grande Valley, Texas. *Texas Journal of Science* 42:137–42.

———. 1990b. Plant communities of the Santa Ana National Wildlife Refuge, Texas. *Texas Journal of Science* 42:115–28.

Vora, R. S., and J. F. Messerly. 1990. Changes in native vegetation following different disturbances in the lower Rio Grande Valley, Texas. *Texas Journal of Science* 42:151–58.

Wainwright, S. E., M. A. Mora, J. L. Sericano, and P. Thomas. 2001. Chlorinated hydrocarbons and biomarkers of exposure in wading birds and fish of the Lower Rio Grande Valley, Texas. *Archives of Environmental Contamination and Toxicology* 40:101–11.

Walker, S., and J. Chapman. 1992. Valley of the parrots. *Texas Parks and Wildlife* 1992 (11): 37–41.

Ward, S., J. M. V. Rayner, U. Moeller, D. M. Jackson, W. Nachtigall, and J. R. Speakman. 1999. Heat transfer from starlings *Sturnus vulgaris* in flight. *Journal of Experimental Biology* 202:1589–1602.

Watson, D. M. 1999. Behavioral observations of pine-oak forest birds in southern Mexico. *Cotinga* 12:66–69.

Watt, D. J., and E. J. Willoughby. 1999. Lesser Goldfinch (*Carduelis psaltria*). In *The Birds of North America*, no. 392, ed. A. Poole and F. Gill. Philadelphia: Birds of North America.

Watts, M. D. 1995. Yellow-crowned Night-Heron (*Nyctanassa violacea*). In *The Birds of North America*, no. 161, ed. A. Poole and F. Gill. Philadelphia: Academy of Natural Sciences, and Washington, D.C.: American Ornithologists' Union.

Wauer, R. H. 1996. *Birds of Big Bend National Park and Vicinity,* 2nd ed. Austin: University of Texas Press.

———. 1998. Avian population survey of a Tamaulipan scrub habitat, Tamaulipas, Mexico. *Cotinga* 10:13–19.

Webb, E. A., and C. E. Bock. 1996. Botteri's Sparrow (*Aimophila botterii*). In *The Birds of North America*, no. 216, ed. A. Poole and F. Gill. Philadelphia: Academy of Natural Sciences, and Washington, D.C.: American Ornithologists' Union.

Webster, F., and M. S. Webster. 2001. *The Road to El Cielo.* Austin: University of Texas Press.

Webster, F. S., Jr. 1957. South Texas region. *Audubon Field Notes* 11:416–19.

———. 1958. South Texas region. *Audubon Field Notes* 12:424–28.

———. 1959. South Texas region. *Audubon Field Notes* 13:440–43.

———. 1963. South Texas region. *Audubon Field Notes* 17:469–71.

———. 1964. South Texas region. *Audubon Field Notes* 18:520–23.

———. 1966. South Texas region. *Audubon Field Notes* 20:582–85.

———. 1968a. South Texas region. *Audubon Field Notes* 22:60–69.

———. 1968b. South Texas region. *Audubon Field Notes* 22:623–28.

———. 1970. South Texas region. *Audubon Field Notes* 24:696–99.

———. 1971. South Texas region. *American Birds* 28:75–78.

———. 1972a. South Texas region. *American Birds* 26:84–88.

———. 1972b. South Texas region. *American Birds* 26:875–78.

———. 1973. South Texas region. *American Birds* 27:890–93.

———. 1974. South Texas region. *American Birds* 28:922–25.

———. 1975. South Texas region. *American Birds* 29:1003–1006.

———. 1976. South Texas region. *American Birds* 30:975–78.

————. 1978. South Texas region. *American Birds* 32:1182–85.

Webster, G. L. 2001. Reconnaissance of the flora and vegetation of La Frontera. Pp. 6–38 in *Changing Plant Life of La Frontera. Observations on Vegetation in the United States/Mexico Borderlands,* ed. G. L. Webster and C. J. Bahre. Albuquerque: University of New Mexico Press.

Wermundsen, T. 1997. Seasonal change in the diet of the Pacific Parakeet (*Aratinga strenua*) in Nicaragua. *Ibis* 139:566–68.

————. 1998. Colony breeding of the Pacific Parakeet *Aratinga strenua* Ridgway 1915 in the Volcán Masaya National Park, Nicaragua. *Tropical Zoology* 11:241–48.

Wetmore, A. 1919. Notes on the structure of the palate in the Icteridae. *Auk* 36:190–97.

Wipff, J. K., R. I. Lonard, S. D. Jones, and S. L. Hatch. 1993. The genus *Urochloa* (Poaceae: Paniceae) in Texas, including one previously unreported species for the state. *Sida* 15:405–13.

Withers, K. 2002. Shorebirds and wading birds. Pp. 198–210 in . *The Laguna Madre of Texas and Tamaulipas,* ed. J. W. Tunnell, Jr., and F. W. Judd. College Station: Texas A&M University Press.

Wolf, B. O. 1997. Black Phoebe (*Sayornis nigricans*). In *The Birds of North America,* no. 268, ed. A. Poole and F. Gill. Philadelphia: Academy of Natural Sciences, and Washington, D.C.: American Ornithologists' Union.

Wolfe, L. R. 1968. Varied Bunting. Pp. 132–37 in *Life Histories of North American Cardinals, Grosbeaks, Buntings, Towhees, Finches, Sparrows, and Allies,* ed. A. C. Bent and O. L. Austin, Jr. U.S. National Museum Bulletin 237.

Woodin, M. C., M. K. Skoruppa, G. W. Blacklock, and G. C. Hickman. 1999. Discovery of a second population of white-collared seedeaters, *Sporophila torqueola* (Passeriformes: Emberizidae) along the Rio Grande of Texas. *Southwestern Naturalist* 44:535–38.

Woodin, M., M. K. Skoruppa, and G. C. Hickman. 1998. Breeding bird surveys at the Galvan Ranch, Webb County, Texas. Final report. U.S. Geological Survey and Texas A&M University–Corpus Christi, Corpus Christi.

————. 2000a. Breeding bird surveys and ecotourism potential at Laredo, Webb County, Texas. Final report. U.S. Geological Survey and Texas A&M University–Corpus Christi, Corpus Christi.

————. 2000b. Surveys of night birds along the Rio Grande in Webb County, Texas. Final report. U.S. Geological Survey and Texas A&M University–Corpus Christi, Corpus Christi.

Wright, P. L. 1996. A comparison of secondary successional woody vegetation in two revegetated fields in South Texas and an assessment of habitat use by the Olive Sparrow, *Arremonops rufivirgatris.* M.S. thesis, University of Texas–Pan American, Edinburg.

Wynd, F. L. 1944. The geologic and physiographic background of the soils in the Lower Rio Grande Valley, Texas. *American Midland Naturalist* 32:200–35.

Yosef, R., and F. E. Lohrer. 1995. Loggerhead Shrikes, red fire ants, and red herrings? *Condor* 97:1053–56.

Young, B. E., M. Kaspari, and T. E. Martin. 1990. Species-specific nest site selection by birds in ant-acacia trees. *Biotropica* 22:310–15.

Zink, R. M., and J. T. Klicka. 1990. Genetic variation in the Common Yellowthroat and some allies. *Wilson Bulletin* 102:514–20.

Zonick, C. 1997. Snowy Plover breeding ecology along the Texas Gulf Coast. Report to Texas Parks and Wildlife Department (Resource Protection) and U. S. Fish and Wildlife Service (Ecological Services), Corpus Christi.

Zorrilla, J. F., and M. I. Salinas-Dominguez. 1994. El Noreste: Tamaulipas. Pp. 67–86 in *Vision Historica de la Frontera Norte de Mexico,* D. P. Ramirez, coordinator. Mexicali, Baja California, Mexico: Universidad Autónoma de Baja California Norte.

INDEX

Page numbers shown in *italics* refer to illustration captions.